LEARNING FROM

SCHOOL CHOICE

LEARNING FROM SCHOOL CHOICE

PAUL E. PETERSON

BRYAN C. HASSEL

Editors

BROOKINGS INSTITUTION PRESS
Washington, D.C.

Copyright © 1998 by
The Brookings Institution
1775 Massachusetts Avenue, N.W., Washington, D.C. 20036

Library of Congress Cataloging-in-Publication data

Learning from school choice / Paul E. Peterson and Bryan C. Hassel, editors.
p. cm.
Includes bibliographical references and index.
ISBN 0-8157-7016-2 (cloth). — ISBN 0-8157-7015-4 (pbk.)
1. Educational vouchers—United States—Case studies.
2. School choice—United States—Case studies.
3. Charter schools—United States—Case studies.
I. Peterson, Paul E. II. Hassel, Bryan C.
LB2828.8. L43 1998
379.1′11′0973—ddc21   98-19747
                                    CIP

9 8 7 6 5 4 3 2 1

The paper used in this publication meets the minimum requirements of the American National Standard for Information Sciences—Permanence of Paper for Printed Library Materials, ANSI Z39-48-1984.

Typeset in Times Roman

Composition by Princeton Editorial Associates
Scottsdale, Arizona, and Roosevelt, New Jersey

Printed by R. R. Donnelley and Sons Co.
Harrisonburg, Virginia

Preface

EDUCATION HAS assumed center stage in the national political debate. No issue is more hotly contested than the debate over school choice. Although leaders in both political parties have committed themselves to giving parents a greater say, they disagree on the form that choice should take. Some would limit choice to neighborhood or magnet schools within the district in which families live. Others would extend choice to include schools outside district boundaries. Many support charter schools that offer distinctive alternatives to public schools. Some endorse management of these charter schools by profit-making firms as well as nonprofits. And a growing number of leaders welcome vouchers, scholarships, and tax credits that provide maximum parental discretion in choosing a school, public or private, religious or secular.

The essays in this volume indicate that such educational ferment is welcome. To be sure, the evidence is not so massive and clear-cut that the time is now ripe for an immediate, full-scale redesign of American education. But both the theory underlying choice and the early evidence from school choice practice suggest that the country's educational system could benefit from increased competition and more engagement with parents and families. Certainly, this is no time to suppress current experiments or thwart new possibilities.

Fortunately, we do not need to choose between full-scale restructuring of American education and no innovation at all. Government and politics in the United States is both fragmented and decentralized. Decisions can be taken at the national, state, and local level. Now that choice is on the table, the issue is being addressed not only by Congress and state officials but by thousands of local school boards as well. It is good that such fragmentation precludes wholesale governmental transformation at any one point in time. It is also fortunate that these many points of decision provide multiple openings where experimentation can begin. We hope that what is contained in this volume may prove helpful to those who wish to move forward.

To learn more about school choice developments nationwide, a conference, "Rethinking School Governance," was hosted in June 1997 by Harvard's Program on Education Policy and Governance, located within the Kennedy School of Government's Taubman Center on State and Local Government and the Center for American Political Studies in the Department of Government. Scholars from around the country reported on an array of recent developments. This volume contains revised versions of many of the essays presented at the conference. In addition to the authors of these essays, other conference participants included Jeanne Allen, Tom Carroll, Andrew J. Coulson, Carol D'Amico, Nathan Glazer, Charles Glenn, Christopher Jencks, Helen F. Ladd, Tom Loveless, Susan Mayer, Abigail Thernstrom, Sammis B. White, Alan Wolfe, and Philip Zelikow.

The conference and the preparation of this volume were sponsored by the John F. Kennedy School of Government's research program on Visions of Governance for the Twenty-First Century, the John M. Olin Foundation, and the Alfred Taubman Center on State and Local Government.

Assistance with specific chapters is acknowledged in chapter notes. In addition, the editors wish to thank Joseph Nye, dean of the Kennedy School of Government, and Alan A. Altshuler, director of the Taubman Center on State and Local Government, for supporting this research undertaking; William Howell for his indefatigable research assistance; Rebecca Contreras for her efficient help in organizing the conference; Kristin Jordan Kearns for finding the cover picture; Lugie Jean and Bryant Jean for agreeing to use of their photograph; Ericka McConnell for her photography; Shelley Weiner for cheerful help while assisting with the preparation of this volume; Susan Woollen, who assumed responsibility for the cover design; and Jill Bernstein, who assisted with promotional materials. We are especially grateful to Robert L. Faherty, director of the Brookings Institution Press, and Nancy Davidson, acquisitions editor, for their unfailing commitment to timely, readable, professional books.

Contents

vii

PART THREE PUBLIC SCHOOL CHOICE

PART FOUR VOUCHERS FOR PRIVATE SCHOOLS

PART FIVE   CONSTITUTIONAL ISSUES

Tables

Figures

LEARNING FROM
SCHOOL CHOICE

Part One

INTRODUCTION

ONE

School Choice: A Report Card

Paul E. Peterson

THE PROBLEMS in American education are endemic. For example, compare math and science performance by students in the United States with that in other countries. The Third International Mathematics and Science Study (TIMSS), reporting on tests administered in 1995 to half a million students in forty-one countries, compares the math performance of U.S. students in fourth, eighth, and twelfth grades with that of students abroad. Math tests are thought to be especially good indicators of school effectiveness, because math, unlike reading and language skills, is learned mainly in school. On the math tests, U.S. fourth graders scored passably well.[1] The math test scores of U.S. eighth graders were another matter: the United States ranked below its major industrial peers. By the twelfth grade, the United States was all but last among all the participating countries. The longer U.S. students remain in school, it seems, the further behind they fall.

Even when evaluated on its own terms, public education in the United States seems incapable of self-improvement. The cost of education, when adjusted for inflation, rose by 50 percent, or at an annual rate of more than 2 percent, between 1974 and 1991.[2] Meanwhile, student test score performance remained fairly constant. Between 1970 and 1992, elementary and secondary students achieved, on average, only the slightest of gains in mathematics and reading on the National Assessment of Educational Progress. What is more, these gains were concentrated in the elementary years; high school math scores fell over the two decades. In science, scores fell substantially at all grade levels. Because costs have risen without commensurate gains in benefits, the public school system has become less efficient. Economist Eric A. Hanushek estimates that since the 1970s "productivity in schools has fallen by 2.5 to 3 percent per year."[3] No wonder that, over the past decade, Roper and *Wall Street Journal* polls report that the proportion of Americans who have given public schools a grade of D or F has doubled, rising to 28 percent in 1996.[4]

Facts like these are motivating a political reform movement unlike those of the past. Earlier reformers took for granted the existing governmental arrangements, which consisted of school boards operating according to state legal codes and some federal regulations. As far back as the 1893 report of the Committee of Ten and as recently as the 1982 report of an Education Department commission, it has been assumed that public schools could repair themselves, if given the requisite money, commitment, and top-down supervision.

This old view still has a potent following. President Clinton has persuaded Congress to commit additional public school dollars and has called for new testing standards. But something brand new has turned up in many states and cities: giving parents a choice in order to stir competition among schools. Reformers are calling for within-district choice, interdistrict choice, charter schools, tax credits and deductions, and, most dramatic of all, publicly funded vouchers or scholarships to be used at any recognized school, public or private, religious or secular.

Defenders of the existing system, such as the National Education Association (NEA) and the American Federation of Teachers (AFT), find themselves fighting a rearguard action. As Fordham Foundation president Chester Finn puts it, "The old edifice of public education is large, but it is growing shaky. . . . The teacher unions still wield great clout in many state houses . . . , yet they are starting to find themselves playing more defense than offense. . . . No longer is school choice a fringe notion."[5]

To learn more about developments nationwide, Harvard's Program in Education Policy and Governance (PEPG) hosted a conference in June 1997, at which scholars from around the country reported on an array of recent developments. This volume contains many of the essays presented at the conference. The essays in this book fall into five groups. In part I, the two editors summarize what can be learned about school choice from the essays contained in this book as well as from other sources. In this essay, I consider the overall case for introducing school vouchers into central cities. In the next essay, Bryan C. Hassel considers the case for charter schools.

Part II also uses wide-angle lenses to examine the choice debate. John E. Brandl makes the case for school choice by synthesizing communitarian and competitive market theories, two traditions not always linked together. Jay P. Greene, drawing upon a nationwide study, describes the extent to which democratic values are buttressed and practiced by public and private schools across the country. Finally, Frederick M. Hess, using systematic survey research techniques, provides a telling portrait of reform efforts by central-city school systems.

Part III presents findings from studies of school choice innovations within the public sector. Caroline Minter Hoxby shows that much can be learned by studying the variation in the amount of competition within a public school system, as it has developed over time. David J. Armour and Brett M. Peiser provide highlights from their study of the interdistrict choice experiment in Massachusetts. Gregg Vanourek, Bruce V. Manno, Chester E. Finn Jr., and Louann A. Bierlein summarize the Hudson Institute's national study of charter schools. John E. Chubb reports early test score results from charter and other public schools operated by a profit-making firm. Bryan C. Hassel describes both the politics of charter legislation within state legislatures and the way charter legislation has been implemented.

Part IV is devoted to school voucher and school scholarship experiments. Kenneth Godwin, Frank Kemerer, and Valerie Martinez report key results from the Children's Educational Opportunity program in San Antonio; David J. Weinschrott and Sally G. Kilgore provide an overview of the Golden Rule program in Indianapolis; Jay P. Greene, Jiangtao Du and I describe test scores results from a randomized experiment in Milwaukee; and, finally, Jay P. Greene, William G. Howell and I report on parental satisfaction and test scores of participants in the Cleveland voucher experiment.

The final section of the volume is devoted to constitutional questions. Stephen G. Gilles provides potent constitutional and policy ammunition for the argument that monies given directly to families to be spent at their discretion does not violate the establishment clause of the First Amendment. Joseph P. Viteritti's essay demonstrates the complexities introduced by state constitutional provisions and court interpretations thereof. He shows that the country has no single understanding of either religious "establishment" or the "free exercise of religion."

The Theoretical Case for School Choice

The theoretical stage for the book is well set by Brandl's opening essay, in which he makes the case for school choice by bringing together market theory and communitarianism. In his words: "Government has only ... two powerful . . . self-disciplining instruments— competition and community— for meeting society's objectives."

Drawing on market theory, Brandl argues that a central problem with America's schools is the lack of competition. School choice subjects schools to the same market discipline that other businesses face in a competitive economy: either you satisfy consumers, or you close shop. In the words of the National Governors' Association, "Schools that compete for students, teachers, and dollars will, by virtue of their environment, make those changes that allow them to succeed."[6]

Unlike some market theorists, Brandl finds competition theory quite compatible with communitarianism, because, he says, school choice can provide the sense of commitment best sustained by small, freely chosen communities. He says that parents today find themselves cut off from their children by school bureaucracies. As one former Michigan teacher, now in a choice school, put it, "In my previous public school, we really didn't want parents to be involved. We never said this to anyone, but it was true. The parents knew it."[7] Brandl and other communitarians fear that, with parents excluded, an invitation has been extended to peer groups who harass the rate busters—the more studious of their classmates. In the worst of cases, neighborhood gangs have made public schools so strife-ridden they require metal detectors and armed guards.

Communitarians are also concerned that schools challenge traditions families hold dear, as the controversies over sex education and condom distribution illustrate. They say schools should instead be embedded within the family's religious faith. In the words of Jacques Maritain, the Catholic philosopher, "No teaching deprived of conviction can engender conviction. . . . Those who teach the democratic charter must stake on it their personal convictions, their consciences, and the depths of their moral lives."[8]

Choice critics remain unpersuaded. The market principle, they say, simply does not apply to education. Parents, especially poor parents, do not have enough information to make intelligent choices, and, when given a choice, academic considerations are not paramount. When a major impediment to the achievement of poor children is "their parents' impoverishment, poor education, lax discipline, and scant interest in education," asks commentator Nicholas Lemann, isn't it absurd to think that these same parents will become "tough, savvy, demanding education consumers" once they have the right to choose?[9] Even worse, say the choice critics, is the potential for balkanization, the replacement of the common school with a fragmented patchwork that may serve the well-to-do and the advantaged but leave the poor far behind. "Instead of being distracted by promises to 'save' a handful of students," says the American Federation of Teachers in its critique of the Cleveland scholarship program, "policy-makers could be improving the achievement of all of our youngsters."[10]

Choice Programs

With the introduction of choice programs around the country, these and other claims and counterclaims of school proponents and critics have been put to an empirical test. The most modest applications of the school choice concept have taken place within the public sector. Magnet schools and a variety of other choice schemes have been used for over two decades to promote voluntary racial integration; since 1987 several states, including Arkansas, Minnesota, and Massachusetts, have broadened the concept to allow choice even when racial considerations are not involved.

Charter schools, first authorized by a 1991 Minnesota law, constitute a bigger challenge to the status quo. Expanding slowly at first, they grew from 250 schools in 1995 to an estimated 700 schools in twenty states by the fall of 1997.[11] The charter concept is as follows: an agency of the state gives a group wishing to establish a school a charter and a right to a fixed number of dollars per pupil, free of most governmental and teacher-contract regulation.

With charter schools, the devil is in the details. Alone among the states, Arizona's charter law allows almost any group to charter a school and places no limits on the number of charter schools. Other states, such as Michigan and Massachusetts, do not pose many obstacles to the chartering of a school but limit the number that can be created. Still other states almost eviscerate the concept by giving the authority to charter schools to local school boards. In many of these cases, Bryan Hassel's essay tells us, the only charter schools that are acceptable are those catering to high-risk students whom public schools are happy to hand over.

Two other approaches on the table are more far-reaching than most charter school legislation. The first approach funds choice by means of the tax system. In 1997 Minnesota passed legislation that provides a tax deduction to middle-income taxpayers and tax credits of up to $1,000 a year to low-income families, which may be used for educational expenses at either public or private schools. In Arizona, tax credits are being given to those who donate to private foundations that grant private school scholarships. Although these programs are just beginning, they have already captured the attention of some Washington lawmakers.

The second approach funds choice directly through vouchers or scholarships. In two cities, Milwaukee and Cleveland, state-funded choice programs give eligible families a chance to pick their school. Privately funded scholarship programs serve over 13,000 students in more than thirty cities, including Dayton, Indianapolis, Milwaukee, New York City, San Antonio, and Washington, D. C. The most dramatic program is to begin in San Antonio in fall 1998; all of the students in the Edgewood school district have been offered a scholarship. This program extends the one founded in Albany, where philanthropist Virginia Gilder promised all children attending the city's worst elementary school that she will provide a scholarship of up to $2,000 a year for six years to attend the private school of their choice. In the spring of 1997 parents of one-third (153 of 458) of the children applied for the scholarship.

The choice movement has caught the attention of both political parties. For Republicans, it provides an opportunity to extend their free market principles to educational policy. Dole endorsed choice in his acceptance speech at the 1996 Republican national convention; in 1997 congressional Republicans tried to slip tax breaks for private schools in the budget compromise. For Democrats, embracing school choice poses greater political difficulties, because teachers' organizations, adamantly opposed to choice, provide so many dollars and foot soldiers to Democratic party candidates. Eleven percent of the delegates to the 1992 Democratic convention joined the teachers' unions' caucus; the number of delegates who were NEA members increased from 365 at the 1992 convention to 405 in 1996. The NEA and AFT together have "about $100 million annually" available for political campaign purposes, and only 4 percent of NEA and 2 percent of AFT federal PAC funds were given to Republican candidates.[12] Yet Bill Clinton has endorsed all forms of public school choice as well as charter schools. In what to some was the most interesting moment in the 1996 presidential debate, Clinton even went so far as to say, "If a local school district in Cleveland or any place else wants to have a private school choice plan like Milwaukee did, let them have at it."[13] However, the president vetoed a voucher experiment for the District of Columbia in 1998.

Practical Issues

The choice movement is spreading in good part because its theoretical underpinnings seem more powerful than ever. After the collapse of the

Soviet Union, it takes a brave scholar to deny the greater efficiency and effectiveness of organizations that must stand up to market competition.

The practical case for choice is less clear-cut. Close to 90 percent of all elementary and secondary school children attend schools directly operated by government agencies. Many public schools are beloved by their communities and perform very well indeed. Public schools are justified by powerful ideo-logical slogans—equality of opportunity, separation of church and state—and a compelling symbol, the common school that serves pupils of all races and ability levels.

Caution is recommended before suddenly dismantling a system that has been established over the course of 150 years. The very size of the public school system—over $300 billion a year, or 5.6 percent of GNP—stands as a warning against immediate, wholesale alterations.[14] Even though markets may, in theory, work better than bureaucracies, transforming public or-ganizations into market systems is difficult in practice. To be sure, de-regulation cut the cost of air travel without compromising passenger safety. But before dramatically restructuring American education, school choice reformers need to remember that the first rule is to do no harm. Reforms should be taken gradually, experimentally, focusing on the places of great-est need and urgency.

In any case, reformers have little choice in the matter, because politics in the United States is organized in such a way that change necessarily comes slowly. Points of decision are multiple, giving opponents plenty of oppor-tunities to block action. Politicians love to devise compromises that can be sold as significant change, even though they are barely innovative. Charac-teristically, only marginal reforms survive the legislative labyrinth at either the state or national level.

The biggest danger is not immediate, wholesale transformation, but quite the opposite: reforms so compromised by political negotiations that they are designed to fail. In Milwaukee, for example, school choice reformers had to accept a harsh compromise in 1990 in order to overcome the opposition of state teacher groups. The legislation banned the participation of religious schools and so restricted choice in other ways that 90 percent of all private schools in the city were excluded. Though the program has had a measure of success, it is hardly the ideal scheme choice theorists favor.[15]

What, then, is the appropriate balance to be struck between too much change and too little? Where should reforms be concentrated? How should they be designed? Should choice be limited to schools the state has chartered? Should religious schools play a major role? Where is the probability of gain the greatest, the probability of doing harm the least?

The essays that follow do not point to any one answer to these questions; indeed, though both editors of this volume think more choice is needed, each is inclined to move in a somewhat different direction. Bryan Hassel makes the case for charter schools in the essay that follows this one; in the remainder of this essay, I shall make the case for central-city voucher and scholarship programs.

Central-City School Systems: The Place to Begin

In big cities public school costs are high, the school system has failed miserably, choices are few, and the costs of failure are massive. As Hess demonstrates in his essay, the endless efforts to reform big-city school systems amount to little more than spinning wheels. Or, as columnist William Raspberry put it, "Poor children desperately need better education. Yet the schools they attend—particularly in America's overwhelmingly black and brown inner cities—may be the least successful of all public schools."[16]

In rural and suburban areas, the situation is less desperate. The forces that have undermined urban education—unionization, excessive regulation, ethnic conflict, rising violence—have not penetrated as deeply into most rural communities. And the suburban parts of most metropolitan areas have at least a semblance of school choice. Families consider schools when purchasing a home. When a community's schools excel, property values climb. Daily headlines underline this fact. "Location, Location, Location: Better Schools Mean Higher Property Values," *USA Today* informed its readers in the spring of 1997. Screamed the *San Francisco Examiner* two months later, "High-Ranking Schools Bag Big-Bucks Housing."[17] In suburban communities where schools do not keep pace with these success stories, homeowners have strong incentives to call for corrective action.

Not every metropolitan area offers suburbanites the same range of choice. Those who live in Dade County (Miami), Florida, have only one school district to choose from, while those living in the Boston area have a choice of more than seventy. As Hoxby shows, it makes a difference if suburban families can choose among school districts within a metropolitan area. Hoxby finds that in those metropolitan areas with more school districts, taxpayers paid less, students learned more, students took more academic courses, and school sports programs were deemphasized. (She also finds more grade inflation, implying that schools, when facing competition, try to reassure families that all children are "above average.")

All is not well with suburban schools. But middle-class suburban families are more satisfied with their schools than are families living in central cities. Stanford professor Terry Moe, who recently conducted a nationwide survey of 4,700 respondents, found that school choice that includes private schools, though popular everywhere, commands the greatest support among residents of central cities. While 79 percent of the inner-city poor favor a "voucher plan," just 59 percent of whites living in more advantaged communities do.[18] Given an opportunity to say how strongly they favored the voucher plan, 61 percent of the inner-city poor said they were "strongly" in favor; just 31 percent of the advantaged whites did. Both the inner-city poor and whites living in advantaged areas agreed that school choice would be "especially helpful to low-income kids, because their public schools tend to have the most problems." Eighty-two percent of the inner-city poor and 76 percent of the advantaged whites agreed with this statement.

Moe's findings are confirmed by a 1997 national survey of minority and white Americans conducted by the Joint Center for Political and Economic Studies. Although they asked the question differently, they also found the greatest support for vouchers among minorities: 65 percent of Hispanic respondents and 57 percent of African American respondents supported the idea, compared with 47 percent of white respondents.[19]

It is not difficult to explain the greater support for school choice among minorities living in central cities. Families with greater financial resources use their money either to buy a private education or to purchase homes in small suburban school districts. Significantly, the percentage of all students who go to private schools is much higher in big cities (15.8 percent) than in either suburban (11.7 percent) or rural areas (5.4 percent).[20] Low-income, central-city families lack these resources and often find themselves forced to accept the school to which their child is assigned.

Although it is commonly believed that pupils in most big cities receive an inferior education, the facts are not as well documented as they should be. For all the statistical information available on U. S. public education, one cannot find much reliable, valid information on what is learned in big-city schools, probably because it is not in the interests of big-city school bureaucrats to make this information known. For example, school officials agreed to let the National Assessment of Educational Progress gather statistics on student performances only after it agreed *not* to report results by school district. When big-city school officials release their own test score results, they have enormous flexibility in the way they report these results: special education students may be excluded; students not promoted may be tested for the grade they are in, not the one appropriate for their age; and tests are frequently changed, making comparisons over time difficult.

But the fragmentary evidence that exists is little short of alarming. Cecilia Rouse reports that in Milwaukee student test scores fall as students "progress" through the public schools.[21] Also, when the *New York Times* compared the scores of New York City students with those of students statewide, controlling for the students' racial and income status, it found that the city students scored three percentile points behind the statewide average in third grade, six percentile points behind in sixth grade, and as much as fifteen points behind in high school.[22]

But perhaps big-city schools do poorly simply because they do not have the fiscal resources to do the job. After all, many central cities have lost jobs and people. Falling property values have created fiscal pressures at a time when federal grants-in-aid to cities have been cut.[23] Unfortunately, the facts do not allow the conclusion that the problems of big-city school systems can be solved simply by throwing money at them. Far from suffering fiscal distress, big-city school systems have the fiscal edge. According to a recent Department of Education report, big-city school systems spent over $5,447 per pupil in 1989–90, compared with $5,427 in suburban areas and $4,507 in rural communities. It may be objected that expenses run higher in big cities, but even when adjustments are made for higher central-city costs, per pupil spending by central-city schools, on average, is only 1 percent less than that of their suburban counterparts.[24]

Nor is central-city desegregation the answer, if for no other reason than the absence of enough white students to integrate big-city schools meaningfully. In the fall of 1993, 54 percent of students in central-city schools were minorities, but this figure included many small and medium-sized cities. In the biggest cities, the percentage was much higher, reaching over 85 percent in Chicago, Dallas, Detroit, Houston, Los Angeles, and Washington, D. C. (see table 1-1).

What Happens When Central-City Families Are Given a Choice

Although few are prepared to defend central-city schools as presently operated, many wonder whether giving inner-city children a chance to go to a private school will make any difference. Studies of choice experiments from around the country provide some answers to often-asked questions. A number of charter schools are also serving the inner-city poor. Two studies of charter schools, including the one by Manno and his colleagues in this volume, have found that just about half the students in charter schools come

Table 1-1. *Minority Population in Selected Central-City Public Schools, Fall 1993*
Percent

City	Minority population
Boston	81
Chicago	89
Cleveland	78
Dallas	86
Dayton	65
Denver	69
Detroit	93
Houston	88
Indianapolis	56
Los Angeles	88
Minneapolis	59
Milwaukee	73
New York City	82
Philadelphia	78
Washington	96
All central cities	54

Sources: Thomas D. Snyder and Charlene M. Hoffman, *Digest of Education Statistics, 1995,* NCES 95-029 (U.S. Department of Education, Office of Educational Research and Improvement, 1995), table 91; and Robin R. Henke and others, *Schools and Staffing in the United States: A Statistical Profile, 1994–94,* NCES 96-124 (U.S. Department of Education, Office of Educational Research and Improvement, 1996), p. 19.

from minority backgrounds. Charter schools also seem to be recruiting their fair share of low-income and special education students. Some of the inner-city charter schools seem to be putting together exciting programs. For example, John Chubb's report on charter and other schools operated by the profit-making Edison Project gives, for the first time, some evidence of programmatic success. Initial results may be promising, but most central-city charter schools have only recently been established, limiting the amount of data available on student outcomes.

Six state- or privately funded voucher or scholarship programs that offer low-income, inner-city students a choice of private schools, religious or secular, provide still more information on school choice. Two of the six programs are in Milwaukee; the other four are in Indianapolis, Cleveland, San Antonio, and New York City. Additional large-scale choice programs are under way in Washington and Dayton; data on student outcomes and parental evaluations are currently being collected.

Table 1-2. *Characteristics of Big-City School Choice Programs for Low-Income Families*[a]

City	Sponsor	Religious schools included	Grades	First school year	Initial enrollment	1996–97 enrollment	Number of schools 1996–97	Maximum payment 1997–98 (dollars)	Selection method
Milwaukee	State of Wisconsin	No	preK-12	1990–91	341	1,606	20	3,209	Lottery
Indianapolis	ECCT[b]	Yes		1991–92	746	1,014	70	800	First-come
Milwaukee	PAVE[c]	Yes	K-12	1992–93	2,089	4,465	97	1,000/ele. 1,500/high	First-come
San Antonio	CEO[d]	Yes	1-8	1992–93	930	955	49	One-half tuition	First-come
Cleveland	State of Ohio	Yes	K-3	1996–97	1,996	3,000[f]	55	2,500	Lottery
New York City	SCSF[e]	Yes	1-5	1997–98	1,200	1,200[f]	n.a.	1,400	Lottery

n.a. Not available.

a. Programs having more than 900 students.

b. Educational Choice Charitable Trust.

c. Partners Advancing Values in Education.

d. Children's Educational Opportunity.

e. School Choice Scholarships Foundation.

f. 1997–98 enrollment.

The basic characteristics of the six programs are set forth in table 1-2. The state-funded program in Milwaukee—which has provoked much controversy, in part because in 1990 it became the very first big-city, state-funded choice experiment—has offered in fact the least amount of choice. Though the scholarships are generously funded at a maximum of $4,700, only secular schools may participate, half the student body must be non-choice students, and the family cannot supplement the scholarship. Because of all these restrictions, only twelve schools and some 1,600 students participated in the 1996–97 school year, most of them in elementary schools. To make up the difference, a private group in the city, Partners Advancing Values in Education (PAVE), set up a supplemental program in 1992; it is now providing 4,465 children from low-income families as much as $1,500 to attend any one of ninety-seven religious and secular schools, making it the largest of the six experiments.

The oldest (but least generous) of the privately funded programs, Educational Choice Charitable Trust, was begun in Indianapolis in 1991. Six years later it provided $800 to 1,014 students attending seventy schools, religious and secular. In 1992 the Children's Educational Opportunity (CEO) program was set up in San Antonio; it now gives nearly 1,000 half-tuition scholarships to elementary and middle-school students attending some forty schools. In 1998 this program is scheduled to expand rapidly; scholarships have been offered to all students in one of the city's school districts.

Last year the Cleveland Scholarship Program, serving students in kindergarten through grade three, was begun by the state of Ohio, becoming the first state-funded choice program allowing students a choice that included religious schools. The state scholarship amounts to $2,500 but can be supplemented by families or other sources. In 1997–98, approximately 3,000 students were receiving these scholarships, enabling them to attend one of fifty-five schools.

Finally, in February 1997 the School Choice Scholarships Foundation in New York City announced its scholarship program for 1,300 students in grades one through five. The public response was deafening. Over 20,000 applications for the $1,400 scholarships were received; students attended approximately 250 religious and secular schools. Remaining tuition costs, which in Catholic schools serving low-income neighborhoods run a little over $2,000, are to be paid by the families or other scholarship sources.

Admission to these programs divide into two categories. The privately funded programs in Indianapolis, Milwaukee, and San Antonio have been selecting students on a first-come, first-serve basis, though Indianapolis switched to a lottery in the fall of 1997. In the other three programs, applicants are selected by lottery.

Table 1-3. *Characteristics of Low-Income Pupils Participating in School Choice Programs*
Percent

Program	African American	Latino	Households with two parents	Mothers with some college education	Fathers with some college education
Milwaukee (state)[a]	73	21	31	54	38
Indianapolis	41	4	46	47	36
Milwaukee (PAVE)[b]	51	24	47	26	26[c]
San Antonio	4	82	n.a.	58[d]	58
Cleveland	65	5	37	61	n.a.
New York City	48	45	41[e]	51	36

Sources: John F. Witte, Troy D. Sterr, and Christopher A. Thorn, "Fifth-Year Report, Milwaukee Parental Choice Program," University of Wisconsin, Department of Political Science, December 1995; David J. Weinschrott and Sally B. Kilgore, chapter 12 in this volume; Michael Heise, Kenneth D. Colburn Jr., and Joseph F. Lamberti, "A Preliminary Analysis of Education Vouchers in Indianapolis," Butler University, n.d.; Sammis White, Peter Maier, and Christine Cramer, *Fourth-Year Report of Partners Advancing Values in Education Scholarship Program,* University of Wisconsin–Milwaukee, Urban Research Center, 1996; Kenneth Godwin and others, chapter 11 in this volume; Jay P. Greene, Paul E. Peterson, and William Howell, "Preliminary Report on Cleveland School Scholarship Program," Harvard University, Program in Education Policy and Governance, 1997; and Paul E. Peterson and others, "Initial Findings from the Evaluation of the New York School Choice Scholarships Program," Harvard University, Program on Education Policy and Governance, December 1997, table 2.

n.a. Not available.

a. 1990–94.

b. 1995–96.

c. Estimated. Report says father's education differs slightly from mothers.

d. Percentage of "parents," as reported by Godwin and others, chapter 11.

e. Percentage *not* receiving welfare assistance. Direct measure of family structure not available.

Most students participating in the programs come from disadvantaged families (see table 1-3). A majority come from one-parent families, and in all cities except Indianapolis an overwhelming majority are likely to be either African American or Latino. Most students come from families in which at least one parent says he or she has had some college education, but these self-reports are probably inflated. There are some indications that first-come, first-serve programs are more likely than the lottery programs to have a somewhat more advantaged clientele.

Parental Satisfaction

Participating families love their choice schools. When the winners of the New York lottery were announced last May, winners were ecstatic: "I was crying and crying and crying," smiled Maria Miranda, a permanently disabled single mother living in Brooklyn. "It was the best Mother's Day present I could have asked for."[25] A year into the Cleveland choice program, Pamela Ballard, parent of a new choice school in Cleveland, exclaimed, "After being in the Cleveland public schools, my daughter was listed a behavior problem. She was a 'D' and 'F' student. . . . [Now my daughter's] behavior and grades are wonderful. . . I wish lots of other scholarships . . . were available [because] many cannot afford . . . private schools."[26]

In their enthusiasm, Maria Miranda and Pamela Ballard represent the norm, not the exception. According to four different studies, choice schools are more popular than public schools (see table 1-4). Some studies ask about satisfaction with teachers and instruction, others about the amount learned, discipline, safety, and parental involvement. Three compare the same parents' assessment of public schools upon entry into the choice program with their assessment of the choice schools one or more years later. The Cleveland study uses a different approach: it compares the assessments of parents attending choice schools with the assessments of parents whose children remained in public schools after indicating an interest in the choice program. But the results do not depend much on the specific aspect of the school mentioned in the question or the exact comparisons made. In their answers to almost all questions, parents are more enthusiastic about choice schools, usually by large margins. For example, 44 percent more of the San Antonio choice parents than public school parents said they were satisfied with school discipline. Forty-one percent more were satisfied with the amount their child learned. Of those who moved to choice schools from public schools in Cleveland, the percentage of parents "very satisfied" with the school's academic quality was 34 percent higher than that

Table 1-4. *Differences in Parental Satisfaction with Choice Schools and Public Schools*
Percent

	Subjects of parental gain in satisfaction					
Program	Teacher	Instruction	Discipline	Amount learned	Safety	Parental involvement
Milwaukee (state)[a]	1	16	16	16	n.a.	17
Indianapolis[b]	25	39	40	32	n.a.	n.a.
San Antonio[c]	n.a.	n.a.	44	41	n.a.	n.a.
Cleveland[d]	31[e]	34[f]	22	n.a.	33	35

Sources: John F. Witte and others, "Fourth-Year Report: Milwaukee Parental Choice Program," University of Wisconsin–Madison, Robert La Follette Institute of Public Affairs, December 1994, table A6; Weinschrott and Kilgore, chapter 12; Godwin and others, chapter 11; and Greene, Peterson, and Howell, "Preliminary Report on Cleveland School Scholarship Program."

n.a. Not available.

a. Average gain for the first four years in those very satisfied.

b. Gain after two years in those satisfied and very satisfied.

c. Gain after one year in those very satisfied.

d. Difference between those winning a scholarship and those who applied but were not selected and remained in public schools. Percent "very satisfied."

e. Question asked about satisfaction with "private attention to child."

f. Question asked about satisfaction with "academic quality."

of those who applied but did not enter the program. Thirty-four percent more were satisfied with school safety, 32 percent with school discipline. Similar results were obtained in Milwaukee and Indianapolis. If the only thing that counts is consumer satisfaction, school choice is a clear winner.

Some have argued that consumer preference, especially by low-income-consumers, is not to be trusted. The Carnegie Foundation for the Advancement of Teaching asserted in its 1992 report on school choice, "When parents do select another school, academic concerns often are not central to the decision."[27] However, 85 percent of those in Cleveland public schools who accepted a voucher said they did so because it was "very important" to enhance the academic quality of their child's education; only 37 percent said they were equally motivated by religious considerations.

Impartial observers do not disagree with parents' positive assessment of choice schools. A reporter for *Education Week* reached much the same conclusions Milwaukee parents did: "Classes here are highly structured and yet free of regimentation; there is a sense of order, yet order itself is not the point. The activities are purposeful; the students enthusiastic participants."[28] But it is one seventh grader who, when interviewed, made the most convincing case for her new school: "As soon as I came here it was a big change. Here, teachers care about you. . . . [In public school] the teachers were too busy to help." Worst of all, she said, were the fights: "You really can't avoid it. They'll think you're scared."[29]

Teacher Satisfaction

Teachers' views are consistent with those coming from parents. In San Antonio, for example, public middle school teachers, when asked the same questions as their peers in choice schools, gave dramatically different answers. Fifty-nine percent of the public school teachers said their school environment was *not* conducive to learning, compared with 11 percent of private school teachers. Only a third of the public school teachers claim to assign more than fifteen minutes of homework; over two-thirds of the private school teachers say they make this assignment. Almost exactly the same results are obtained when teachers are asked if they expect half their students to exceed grade level or course objectives that year: about one-third of the public school teachers, compared with over two-thirds of the private school teachers, have such expectations.

Nationwide, private school teachers are much more likely to report that their school is a good place to work. According to a 1994 Department of Education teacher survey, a much higher percentage of private school teachers say that the goals of their school are clear, staff members are recognized for a job well done, teachers participate in making most of the important educational decisions, there is a "great deal" of cooperation among staff, and the administration's behavior is supportive.[30]

Most revealing of all, school teachers are more likely than the average central-city resident to pick a private school for their own children. As one public school administrator told me, "I understand where you are coming from because my kids go to Catholic schools. However, you must understand that, given my job, I cannot help much with your study." The man is hardly unique. Forty percent of the children of Cleveland public school teachers go to private school, compared with 25 percent of all children. In Milwaukee the percentages are 33 versus 23 and in Boston 45 versus 29 percent.[31]

Student Mobility

Choice students are also more likely to stay in the same school from the beginning to the end of the academic year, despite the fact that student retention within any one school is an extraordinary problem in central cities. According to the U. S. Census, low-income, minority populations are highly mobile. For central-city, female-headed households with children between the ages of six and seventeen, the annual residential mobility rate is 30 percent for African Americans and 35 percent for Latinos.[32] Not every change in residence dictates a change in school attendance. But in Milwaukee's public elementary schools, nearly 20 percent leave even before the end of the school year in June.[33] Come the following fall, 35 percent of the students are no longer in attendance at the same public elementary school they were at one year previously.

Schools participating in the state-funded choice plan substantially reduced this migration from one school setting to another. All but 23 percent of the Milwaukee choice students returned to the same elementary school the following fall (compared with 35 percent in Milwaukee's low-income public schools). Within the school year itself, the percentage leaving choice elementary schools was as little as 4 percent in 1993 and just 6 percent in 1994 (much lower than the nearly 20 percent changing from one low-income public elementary school to another).[34] In Milwaukee's privately funded program, turnover rates were similar: 6 percent within the school year, 14 percent from one year to the next. In Cleveland's two new choice schools, 11 percent of the students enrolled at the beginning of the year had left before the end of the year.[35] All in all, it seems that choice schools do a better job at retaining their populations than do public schools serving low-income populations.

Test Scores

These positive results would mean little, perhaps, if students did not learn more in choice schools. Since controversy over this question has raged for more than a quarter of a century, it is best to place recent findings in historical context. The first large-scale study to show that students learn more in private high schools was conducted by a research team headed by the distinguished University of Chicago sociologist, James Coleman.[36] A decade later, an even more comprehensive national study showing similarly positive effects was carried out by John Chubb and Terry Moe at the Brookings Institution. The study was based on surveys of students, teachers, and administrators gathered in 1982 and 1984.[37]

Choice critics attacked both studies for not adequately correcting for "selection effects," an issue that has become central to the current debate. Says former Wisconsin state school superintendent and arch-choice critic

Herbert Grover, "Do private school children outperform children in public schools? It's hard to imagine that they wouldn't, given the initial advantages they enjoy from their parents."[38] Both the Coleman and the Chubb-Moe studies anticipated this argument by taking into account a wide variety of family characteristics, such as education and income. But critics say that no amount of statistical tinkering can ever fully correct for the selection effect: families who pay to send their child to private school are almost certainly more involved in and concerned about their child's education, even after adjusting for demographic characteristics.[39] Even the Coleman research team admitted that the "difference between parents, by its very nature, is not something on which students in public and private schools can be equated" in a statistical analysis.[40]

School choice experiments are providing researchers with new opportunities to circumvent this selection problem. For one thing, they are limited to inner-city children from low-income families. More important, to ensure fairness, scholarship winners are sometimes chosen by lottery, giving these programs the potential of becoming a classic randomized experiment of the kind found in the best medical research.

The advantage of a randomized experiment for researchers derives from its intrinsic simplicity. When a lottery is used to pick scholarship winners, the two groups of students are similar except for the fact that the names of one group were drawn from the hat. When one works with information from a classic randomized experiment, one can in fact reasonably assume that students from public and private schools can be "equated." If children from the winning group do better than the remainder, one can reasonably conclude that it was the school, not the family, that made the difference.

Unfortunately, most school choice experiments conducted thus far have not conformed to a classic randomized experiment. The privately funded programs in Indianapolis, San Antonio, and Milwaukee all admitted students on a first-come, first-serve basis. Such admission procedures have a fairness of their own, and they are easy to administer. It is also the case that test score results from these experiments are mainly positive. For example, the scores of students participating in the school choice program in San Antonio increased between 1991–92 and 1993–94, while those of the public school comparison group fell. But these findings may be contaminated by the selection effect. After all, those families who are quick, clever, and well connected enough to get a first-come, first-serve scholarship are likely to have other attributes that favorably affect their child's educational attainment.

Students also seem to be learning in Cleveland choice schools. My colleagues and I found strong first-year test score gains, especially in math, in two of the schools (which enrolled about 25 percent of the former public school students). If these gains are maintained in future years, this will constitute a substantial achievement. Yet these results are also less than conclusive, because an appropriate control group was not available for comparison purposes.

Only in Milwaukee are data available from a randomized experiment.[41] In 1996 the data became available on the World Wide Web. When Greene, Du, and I examined these data, we found that enrollment in the program had only limited positive effects during the first two years a student was in the program. But, as shown in our essay below, choice students made substantial gains in years three and four. If these gains can be duplicated nationwide, they could reduce by somewhere between one-third and more than one-half the current difference between white and minority test score performance.

That the improved performance does not become substantial until the third and fourth years is quite consistent with a commonsense understanding of the educational process. Choice schools are not magic bullets that transform children overnight. It takes time to adjust to a new teaching and learning environment. The disruption of switching schools and adjusting to new routines and expectations may hinder improvement in test scores in the first year or two of being in a choice school. Educational benefits accumulate and multiply with the passage of time. As Indianapolis choice parent Barbara Lewis explains the process: "I must admit there was a period of transition, culture shock you might call it. He had to get used to the discipline and the homework. . . . But Alphonso began to learn about learning, to respect the kids around him and be respected, to learn about citizenship, discipline, and doing your lessons. . . . My son has blossomed into an honor roll student."[42]

The Milwaukee data we analyzed are the best available, but they are still not definitive. The number of participating schools was small, and valuable data are missing. Higher-quality information may emerge from an evaluation of the experiment now beginning in New York City. The students participating in the program were chosen by lottery from a large pool of over 20,000 applicants, from which a control group is being selected. It remains to be seen whether the payoff is as great as some anticipate.[43]

College Attendance

School choice programs are too recent to provide information on their effects on college attendance, though the PAVE program in Milwaukee reports that 75 percent of those who have graduated from high school have gone on to college.[44] More systematic information on the effects of attendance at a Catholic high school are contained in a recent University of Chicago analysis of the National Longitudinal Survey of Youth conducted by the Department of Education, a survey of over 12,000 young people. Students from all racial and ethnic groups are more likely to go to college if they attended a Catholic school, but the effects are the greatest for urban minorities. The probability of graduating from college rises from 11 to 27 percent if a such a student attends a Catholic high school.[45]

The University of Chicago study confirms results from two other analyses that show positive effects of attendance at Catholic schools on high school completion and college enrollment for low-income and minority students.[46] As one researcher summarized one of these studies, it "indicates a substantial private school advantage in terms of completing high school and enrolling in college, both very important events in predicting future income and well-being. Moreover, . . . the effects were most pronounced for students with achievement test scores in the bottom half of the distribution."[47]

Critiques of School Choice

Despite the evidence that good things happen in private schools for inner-city students and teachers alike, choice critics have raised three important questions: Will choice schools undermine democratic values? Are they constitutional? Will choice schools leave some children behind?

Democratic Values and Balkanization

The purpose of education is to teach more than math and reading; it is also to prepare citizens for a democratic society. According to the harshest critics, school choice will provoke the formation of schools specializing in witchcraft, black nationalism, and the political thought of David Duke. Put more thoughtfully, former *New Republic* editor Michael Kelly has argued that "public money is shared money, and it is to be used for the furtherance of shared values, in the interests of *e pluribus unum.* Charter schools and their like . . . take from the *pluribus* to destroy the *unum.*"[48] Only schools operated by a government agency, it is claimed, can preserve democracy. Princeton theorist Amy Gutmann puts it this way: "Public, not private, schooling is . . . the primary means by which citizens can morally educate future citizens."[49] Or, in the words of Felix Frankfurter, writing the Supreme Court opinion in *Minersville Board of Education* v. *Gobitis,* "We are dealing here with the formative period in the development of citizenship. . . . Public education is one of our most cherished democratic institutions."[50]

Despite the rhetoric and scare tactics, choice critics have failed to offer much evidence that school choice will balkanize America. No reasonable person can believe the American public would routinely turn over school dollars to extremist groups any more than it will allow airlines to fly unregulated or meat to be marketed without inspection. Only the most extreme libertarians think school choice should mean completely unregulated choice. As educational analyst Paul Hill says, "In the long run, schools in a publicly funded choice system will be public because they'll be regulated."[51] But this should not mean that regulated schools are the same as government-operated schools. To make that argument is to claim that government inspection of the meat-processing industry constitutes an establishment of a nationwide system of collective farms.

When one actually looks at what happens in most private schools today, one finds considerable evidence that privatization would lead to less balkanization, not more. Admittedly, choice schools were among the hundreds of strategies invented in the 1950s by southerners seeking to avoid compliance with the *Brown* decision. But the courts struck down any and all attempts to perpetuate racial segregation by means of school choice. Students in private schools today are in fact less racially isolated than their public school peers. As Jay P. Greene shows in his essay, private schools are less racially exclusive than public schools. He also finds that students attending private schools reported greater likelihood of cross-racial friendships, and both teachers and students at private schools reported fewer race-related fights and conflicts.

Nor are private school students social snobs; on the contrary, they are more community-spirited. Greene reports that students at private schools are more likely to think that it is important to help others and volunteer for community causes. They also were more likely to report that they did volunteer in the past two years. Finally, private school students were more likely to say their school expected them to volunteer.

The Church-State Question

Federal constitutional questions do not pose as much of a stumbling block as once seemed, despite some lower court decisions to the contrary. Stephen Gilles argues, in his essay below, that state-provided scholarships do not "establish a religion" as long as parents are free to use these scholarships to send their child to any school, Catholic, Protestant, Jewish, Muslim or secular. The Supreme Court so reasoned in 1983 when it ruled constitutional a Minnesota tax deduction for educational purposes, whether they be used to pay for secular or parochial schooling.[52] The Court reaffirmed this reasoning in *Agostini* v. *Felton* (1997), when it said that public school teachers could provide compensatory educational instruction in parochial schools. Significantly, the Court conditioned its decision on policies that made instruction "available generally without regard to the sectarian-non-sectarian or public-nonpublic nature of the institution benefitted," further justifying its decision on the grounds that no religion was aided except as the result of the "private choices of individuals."[53] Most school choice proposals easily pass such a test.

Constitutional problems loom larger at lower-court levels, because, as is shown in Joseph Viteritti's essay, many state constitutions include restrictions on church-state relationships that are more stringently worded than the federal Constitution. In Ohio and Wisconsin, two lower state courts ruled that choice plans involving religious schools ran contrary to both state and federal constitutions. In both states the issue was being argued before the state supreme court in 1998. The state supreme court in Ohio has allowed religious school involvement in the choice program to continue until it has an opportunity to give the issue full consideration.

Although court interpretations of constitutional requirements are open to many interpretations, courts are often as responsive to public opinion as they are to arcane legal argumentation. And the constitutional case against choice is extraordinarily flimsy, requiring a distinction between secondary and higher education that seems more a function of tradition and practice than any constitutional language. In 1997 President Clinton signed a law passed by an overwhelming majority of Congress that provides tax credits subsidizing a student's education at any college, religious or secular. Families may take the deduction whether their child goes to San Francisco State, Notre Dame, or Concordia College. A similar system of Pell grants for low-income college students has been in place since 1973. No constitutional barrier has ever been erected to prevent the operation of this program. Why should comparable aid to younger children be unconstitutional?

Those Left Behind

But how about those left behind? When all other criticisms fall short, this becomes the argument of last resort. When the anti-choice Carnegie Foundation admitted that for at least one student a choice plan had, in his words, "changed my life around completely," the authors quickly went on to observe that "the picture is far grimmer for the 14,500 students left behind."[54] Echoing these sentiments, AFT President Sandra Feldman says vouchers and scholarships for private schools take "money away from inner city schools so a few selected children can get vouchers to attend private schools, while the majority of equally deserving kids, who remain in the public schools, are ignored."[55]

In making these arguments, choice critics often assume that the more able children from more privileged families will be the first to leave public schools; that children learn mainly from their peers; and that inner-city public schools contain large numbers of middle-class students who are helping to educate their less advantaged peers. Not one of these assumptions is well supported by available data.

WHO GOES TO CHOICE SCHOOLS? First, there is little reason to expect the best and the brightest to flee the public schools to take advantage of inner-city choice programs. For one thing, most big-city school systems have their own programs—magnet schools, gifted classes, and honors tracks—that siphon off the best into specialized educational programs. Also, parents can be expected *not* to change their child's school unless they have doubts about his or her progress. In Milwaukee, for example, parents who signed up for choice schools were more likely to say their previous public school had been in contact with them, probably because their child was having difficulties.[56] Student test score data also indicate that choice applicants are less than the cream of the crop. Among the applicants to New York City's choice program, only 26 percent were performing at grade level in reading and 18 percent in mathematics, far below the 55 percent reported for all New York City elementary students reported by the city school system.[57] However, in the first-come, first-serve programs in Indianapolis and San Antonio, school choice applicants may have been above the norm for the city as a whole.

PEER GROUP EFFECTS. Even so, to claim that "those left behind" suffer as a result depends on the strange assumption that children learn not from teachers but from other children. This idea can be traced back to the famous 1965 school desegregation study, also conducted by James Coleman, in which it was found that most school factors (such as per pupil expenditures, class size, teacher salary, and the number of books in the school library) had little measurable effect on student achievement.[58] However, the socioeconomic background of other children in the school did have a detectable effect on achievement, a tantalizing fact that was overinterpreted to mean that children learned mainly from their peers. But in a comprehensive review of the peer group literature, sociologists Christopher Jencks and Susan Mayer found these effects to be small and inconsistent from one study to the next. They offer an intriguing explanation: peer group effects could be substantial but offsetting. On the one hand, students thrive by picking up facts, ideas, and phrases from their more capable associates. On the other hand, they get discouraged when they cannot keep up. The two factors, working in opposite directions, may have roughly equivalent educational effects.[59]

Jencks and Mayer may be right, but the matter deserves still further consideration. One of James Coleman's first studies, undertaken in the 1950s, well before he undertook either the desegregation or the public-private studies that later captured so much public attention, noticed that in private schools group leaders were academically oriented, while in public schools the popular students were sports stars and cheerleaders.[60] As Cornell professor John Bishop has put it, "Popularity depends first and foremost on being good in sports. Being smart is OK, but being studious . . . increases the chances of being picked on."[61] To explain the difference between public and private schools, Coleman pointed out that in both types of schools the most popular students were those who brought honor to the whole school. In private schools, the whole school benefits from high academic performance, because academic achievement enhances the reputation of the school with potential customers. In public schools, it is often the sports program, more than the academic performance of a few, that brings credit to the school.

If Coleman and Bishop are correct, then peer group effects may in fact help explain the greater learning that takes place in private school. It is not so much that private school students are more capable; it is that the more capable students carry more influence in this setting and "nerds" are subject to less harassment. The problem faced by those "left behind" in the public schools is not the lack of capable peers but the fact that in many inner-city public schools academic achievement has negative cachet.

INNER-CITY SCHOOLS. But even if peer group effects are as strong as choice critics say, their argument carries little weight, because the white, middle-class population has already left the central-city schools for private or suburban ones. Those who are going to be left behind already are. Indeed, the attraction of inner-city school choice is the possibility that a choice-based system could reduce racial isolation within the central city.

Consider the following thought experiment. Suppose a central-city mayor persuaded the state legislature to let the city use all of its school dollars to provide maximum choice for parents. Suppose the mayor distributed the monies by means of vouchers that went to parents for the school of their choice, private or public, secular or parochial. Suppose existing private schools expanded and new private schools formed to take advantage of the increased demand for private education.

Were this to happen, what would be the results? We do not know, but two contrasting scenarios can be constructed. Choice critics envision the best, the brightest, and the most devout fleeing to the private sector. They also expect public schools to fail to respond. As a result, their share of school enrollment will dwindle to a few students whose families do not care about their education. Urban life will continue to segregate along racial and class lines. But Milwaukee's visionary mayor, John Norquist, thinks an alternative scenario is more likely. If choice is provided, he says, "public schools will respond to private-sector competition with an aggressive effort to maintain their clientele, just as United and American airlines did."[62] With opportunities to choose among a variety of schools, young parents with children entering school will forgo the expensive move to the suburb and pick instead a local school suited to their needs. Other families will give up their suburban homes for better schools in the central city and homes closer to their job. Businesses will open up schools so their employees can bring their children with them on their daily commute. The central-city economy picks up, property values rise, racial integration increases, and central-city test scores rise.

It is not certain which scenario is more on target. But the situation today is so dismal, one wonders why the NEA and the AFT are mobilizing all their resources to fight any and all choice experiments. Certainly, if the teacher groups are correct, a few experiments will put the choice idea firmly to rest, freeing the public agenda for other approaches. But perhaps the AFT is afraid that experiments will prove Norquist right. Then, of course, they have good reason to battle on. But those primarily concerned about the educational well-being of poor children living in central cities will find persuasive William Raspberry's urgent recommendation: "It's time for some serious experimentation."[63]

Notes

1. Though the fourth graders trailed students in Japan, Korea, the Netherlands, and the Czech Republic, they did better than students in England, Norway, and New Zealand. "U.S. 4th Graders Score Well in Math and Science Study," *Education Week,* June 18, 1997, p. 22. The U. S. eighth graders clearly outscored only seven countries—

Lithuania, Cyprus, Portugal, Iran, Kuwait, Colombia, and South Africa—none of them usually thought to be U.S. peers. "U.S. Students Rank about Average in 41-Nation Math, Science Study," *Education Week,* November 27, 1996, p. 32. United States National Research Center, "TIMMS High School Results Released," Michigan State University, College of Education, Report 8, April 1998.

2. Helen F. Ladd, "Introduction," in Helen F. Ladd, ed., *Holding Schools Accountable: Performance-Based Reform in Education* (Brookings, 1996), pp. 2–3.

3. Eric A. Hanushek, "The Productivity Collapse in Schools," Working Paper 8 (University of Rochester, W. Allen Wallis Institute of Political Economy, December 1996).

4. Roper Center Review of Public Opinion and Polling, *Public Perspective* (November–December 1993).

5. Chester E. Finn Jr., "Reforming Education: A Whole New World," *First Things* (May 1997), as reprinted in Thomas B. Fordham Foundation, *Selected Readings on School Reform,* vol. 1 (Summer 1997), p. 132.

6. Carnegie Foundation for the Advancement of Teaching, *School Choice: A Special Report* (Princeton, N. J., 1992), p. 47.

7. Bruno V. Manno and others, "How Charter Schools Are Different: Lessons and Implications," *Charter Schools in Action: A Hudson Institute Report,* Final Report, pt. 6, July 1997, p. 6.

8. As quoted in Anthony S. Bryk, Valerie E. Lee, and Peter B. Holland, *Catholic Schools and the Common Good* (Harvard University Press, 1993), p. 39.

9. Nicholas Lemann, "A False Panacea," *Atlantic* (January 1991), p. 104, as quoted in Abigail Thernstrom, *School Choice in Massachusetts* (Boston: Pioneer Institute for Public Policy Research, 1991), p. 40.

10. Dan Murphy, F. Howard Nelson, and Bella Rosenberg, "The Cleveland Voucher Program: Who Chooses? Who Gets Chosen? Who Pays?" (New York: American Federation of Teachers, 1997), p. iv.

11. See chapter 8 in this volume.

12. Myron Lieberman, *The Teacher Unions* (Free Press, 1997), pp. 79, 158.

13. *Weekly Compilation of Presidential Statements,* October 6, 1996, p. 1991.

14. Thomas D. Snyder and Charlene M. Hoffman, *Digest of Education Statistics, 1995,* NCES 95-029 (U. S. Department of Education, Office of Educational Research and Improvement, 1995), table 31.

15. Paul E. Peterson, Jay P. Greene, and Chad Noyes, "School Choice in Milwaukee," *Public Interest* (Fall 1996), pp. 38–56; and Paul E. Peterson and Chad Noyes, "Under Extreme Duress, School Choice Success," in Diane Ravitch and Joseph P. Viteritti, eds., *New Schools for a New Century: The Redesign of Urban Education* (Yale University Press, 1997), pp. 123–46.

16. William Raspberry, "A Reluctant Convert to School Choice," *Washington Post,* May 20, 1997.

17. Carlos A. Bonilla, "Zip Code Segregation in the Public Schools," in Alan Bonsteel and Carlos A. Bonilla, eds., *A Choice for Our Children: Curing the Crisis in America's Schools* (San Francisco: Institute for Contemporary Studies, 1997), p. 79.

18. The question was worded as follows: "According to reformers, the general idea behind a voucher plan is as follows. The parents of each school age child would be eligible for a grant or voucher from the state, representing a certain amount of tax money. They would have the right to send their child to a public school, just as before. Or they could use the voucher to help pay for the child's education at a private or parochial school of their choosing." Information presented by Terry Moe, Department of Government, Stanford University, before the "Rethinking School Governance" Conference, sponsored by the Program on Education Policy and Governance, Kennedy School of Government, Harvard University, June 1997.

19. Joint Center for Political and Economic Studies, *1997 National Opinion Poll,* table 7.

20. Robin R. Henke and others, *Schools and Staffing in the United States: A Statistical Profile, 1994–94,* NCES 96-124 (U. S. Department of Education, Office of Educational Research and Improvement, 1996), p. 17.

21. Cecilia E. Rouse, "Making Sense of the Achievement Effects from the Milwaukee Parental Choice Program" (Cambridge, Mass.: National Bureau of Economic Research, December 1997), fig. 2.

22. Pam Belluck, "Learning Gap Tied to Time in the System: As School Stay Grows, Scores on Tests Worsen," *New York Times,* January 5, 1997, pp. 17, 22.

23. Paul E. Peterson, *The Price of Federalism* (Brookings, 1997), pp. 164–72.

24. Thomas B. Parrish, Christine S. Matsumoto, and William J. Fowler Jr., *Disparities in Public School District Spending, 1989–90,* NCES 95-300R (U. S. Department of Education, Office of Educational Research and Improvement, 1995), table A11.

25. Jacques Steinberg, "Students Chosen for Grants to Attend Private Schools," *New York Times,* May 13, 1997, p. B3.

26. *Improving Educational Opportunities for Low-Income Children,* Hearings before the Senate Committee on Labor and Human Resources, 105 Cong. 1 sess. (Government Printing Office, 1997), p. 10.

27. Carnegie Foundation for the Advancement of Teaching, *School Choice,* p. 13.

28. David Ruenzel, "A Choice in the Matter," *Education Week,* September 27, 1995, p. 28.

29. Carnegie Foundation for the Advancement of Teaching, *School Choice,* p. 69.

30. Henke and others, *Schools and Staffing in the United States,* pp. 106–09.

31. Denis P. Doyle, "Where Connoisseurs Send their Children to School" (Washington: The Center for Education Reform, 1995), as reprinted in Bonsteel and Bonilla, *A Choice for Our Children: Curing the Crisis in America's Schools,* pp. 40–41.

32. Kristin A. Hansen, "Geographical Mobility: March 1991 to March 1992," *Current Population Reports,* series P20–473 (Department of Commerce, 1993).

33. Data on the mobility rates among students in low-income elementary schools in grades two through five are provided in John F. Witte, Andrea B. Bailey, and Christopher A. Thorn, "Second Year Report: Milwaukee Parental Choice Program," University of Wisconsin–Madison, Department of Political Science and the Robert M. La Follette Institute of Public Affairs, December 1992, pp. 19–20.

34. Paul E. Peterson, "A Critique of the Witte Evaluation of Milwaukee's School Choice Program," Occasional Paper 95-2 (Harvard University, Center for American Political Studies, February 1995), pp. 29–36. See also Paul E. Peterson, "The Milwaukee School Choice Plan: Ten Comments on the Witte Reply," Occasional Paper 95-3 (Harvard University, Center for American Political Studies, March 1995).

35. Based on students taking achievement tests at the beginning and end of the year. Since administrators say all enrolled students took both tests, this provides a reasonably good, if probably high, estimate of the turnover rate.

36. James S. Coleman, Thomas Hoffer, and Sally Kilgore, *High School Achievement* (Basic Books, 1982); and James S. Coleman and Thomas Hoffer, *Public and Private Schools: The Impact of Communities* (Basic Books, 1987).

37. John E. Chubb and Terry M. Moe, *Politics, Markets, and America's Schools* (Brookings, 1990).

38. Herbert Grover, "Comments and General Discussion," in Edith Rasell and Richard Rothstein, eds., *School Choice: Examining the Evidence* (Washington: Economic Policy Institute, 1993), p. 250.

39. Arthur S. Goldberger and Glen G. Cain, "The Causal Analysis of Cognitive Outcomes in the Coleman, Hoffer, and Kilgore Report," *Sociology of Education,* vol. 55 (April–July 1982), pp. 103–22; Douglas J. Wilms, "School Effectiveness within the Public and Private Sectors: An Evaluation," *Evaluation Review,* vol. 8 (1984), pp. 113–35; and Douglas J. Wilms, "Catholic School Effects on Academic Achievement: New Evidence from the High School and Beyond Follow-up Study," *Sociology of Education,* vol. 58 (1985), pp. 98–114.

40. Goldberger and Cain, "Causal Analysis of Cognitive Outcomes," p. 110.

41. The initial evaluation of the Milwaukee program was conducted by a Wisconsin research team, which has issued the following reports: John F. Witte, "Achievement Effects of the Milwaukee Voucher Program," paper prepared for the 1997 annual meeting of the American Economics Association; Witte, "First Year Report: Milwaukee Parental Choice Program," University of Wisconsin–Madison, Department of Political Science and Robert M. La Follette Institute of Public Affairs, November 1991; Witte, Bailey, and Thorn, "Second Year Report: Milwaukee Parental Choice Program"; Witte, Bailey, and Thorn, "Third Year Report: Milwaukee Parental Choice Program," University of Wisconsin–Madison, Department of Political Science and Robert M. La Follette Institute of Public Affairs, December 1992; John F. Witte and others, "Fourth Year Report: Milwaukee Parental Choice Program," University of Wisconsin–Madison, Department of Political Science and Robert M. La Follette Institute of Public Affairs, December 1993; and John F. Witte, Troy D. Sterr, and Christopher A. Thorn, "Fifth Year Report: Milwaukee Parental Choice Program," University of Wisconsin–Madison, Department of Political Science and Robert M. La Follette Institute of Public Affairs, December 1994.

For detailed critiques of this study, see Peterson, "A Critique of the Witte Evaluation of Milwaukee's School Choice Program"; and Jay P. Greene, Paul E. Peterson, and Jiangtao Du, with Leesa Berger and Curtis L. Frazier, "The Effectiveness of School Choice in Milwaukee: A Secondary Analysis of Data from the Program's Evaluation," Occasional Paper, Harvard University, Program in Education Policy and Governance, 1996.

42. Barbara Lewis, prepared remarks for testimony before the U. S. Senate Committee on Labor and Human Resources, "Improving Educational Opportunities for Low-Income Children," July 29, 1997.

43. David Myers at Mathematica and I plan to follow both test and control groups for the first four years of the program.

44. Dan McKinley, "Memorandum for the Board of Directors of Partners Advancing Values in Education," Partners Advancing Values in Education, Milwaukee, Wisconsin, August 25, 1997.

45. Derek Neal, "The Effects of Catholic Secondary Schooling on Educational Achievement," University of Chicago, Harris School of Public Policy and National Bureau for Economic Research, 1996, p. 26.

46. William N. Evans and Robert M. Schwab, "Who Benefits from Private Education? Evidence from Quantile Regressions," University of Maryland, Department of Economics, 1993; and David Siglio and Joe Stone, "School Choice and Student Performance: Are Private Schools Really Better?" University of Wisconsin, Institute for Research on Poverty, 1997.

47. John F. Witte, "School Choice and Student Performance," in Ladd, ed., *Holding Schools Accountable,* p. 167.

48. Michael Kelly, "Dangerous Minds," *New Republic,* December 30, 1996.

49. Amy Gutmann, *Democratic Education* (Princeton University Press, 1987), p. 70.

50. *Minersville Board of Education* v. *Gobitis,* 310 U. S. 598 (1940). Frankfurter's reasoning justified a West Virginia regulation forcing Jehovah's Witnesses to salute the school flag, a decision that the Supreme Court reversed in *West Virginia State Board of Education* v. *Barnette,* 319 U.S. 624 (1943) soon after the country had entered the war against Nazi Germany.

51. Paul Hill, *Reinventing Public Education* (University of Chicago Press, 1997), p. 98.

52. *Mueller* v. *Allen,* 463 U. S. 388 (1983).

53. *Agostini* v. *Felton,* 117 S. Ct. (1997). Also, see "Excerpts from Ruling Allowing Aid to Church Schools for Remedial Classes," *New York Times,* June 24, 1997, p. A18.

54. Carnegie Foundation for the Advancement of Teaching, *School Choice,* p. 58.

55. Sandra Feldman, "Let's Tell the Truth," *New York Times,* November 2, 1997, p. 7 (advertisement).

56. Witte, "First Year Report"; and Peterson, "A Critique of the Witte Evaluation."

57. Paul E. Peterson and others, "Initial Findings from the Evaluation of the New York School Choice Scholarships Program," Harvard University, Program on Education Policy and Governance, December 1997, table 1.

58. James S. Coleman and others, *Equality of Educational Opportunity* (U.S. Department of Health, Education and Welfare, Office of Education, 1966).

59. Christopher Jencks and Susan E. Mayer, "The Social Consequences of Growing Up in a Poor Neighborhood," in Laurence E. Lynn Jr. and Michael G. H. McGreary, eds, *Inner City Poverty in the United States* (Washington: National Academy Press, 1990), pp. 111–86; and Susan E. Mayer, "How Much Does a High School's Racial and Socioeconomic Mix Affect Graduation and Teenage Fertility Rates?" in Christopher Jencks and Paul E. Peterson, eds., *The Urban Underclass* (Brookings, 1991), pp. 321–41.

60. James Coleman, *The Adolescent Society* (1961), as summarized in Ronald G. Corwin and Kathryn M. Borman, "School as Workplace: Structural Constraints on Administration," in Norman J. Boyan, ed., *Handbook of Research on Educational Administration* (New York: Longman, 1988), p. 228.

61. "Nerd Harassment," in Susan Mayer and Paul E. Peterson, eds., *When Schools Make a Difference,* forthcoming.

62. Presentation before the Pittsburgh conference on Urban Renewal, July 2, 1997.

63. Raspberry, "A Reluctant Convert to School Choice."

TWO

The Case for Charter Schools

Bryan C. Hassel

SEVERAL AUTHORS of chapters in this volume make the case that the quality
of American education would improve if families had greater choice among
schools and schools were required to compete for students. Paul Peterson's
introductory chapter provides a broad overview of theoretical arguments
and empirical evidence supporting this case. John Brandl's chapter explores
the theoretical rationale in more detail. And several contributions provide
empirical evidence that choice and competition can make a positive difference for the quality of schooling.

Accordingly, in this chapter I do not restate the arguments for choice and
competition. Instead I want to make the case for a particular design of a
system of choice and competition in education: charter schools. Devising
ways to give families more options and break public school monopolies
involves a complex set of policy choices, not a simple yes-or-no decision.
Consequently, it is not enough to agree on the need for more choice or more
competition. The details matter, and we need to engage one another in
debates about the precise designs that we have in mind.

Charter schools, which a Hudson Institute research team and I examine
in detail in subsequent chapters, are often regarded as a compromise between a "true" system of choice, such as the plan advocated in Paul
Peterson's introductory chapter, and the status quo. In this conception
vouchers are not (yet) politically feasible, so those who favor them back
charter schools as a stepping-stone to their desired destination. Defenders
of the status quo recognize the political appeal of choice and seek to defuse

more radical policies by agreeing to allow the establishment of charter schools. No one really wants charter schools, but both sides feel compelled to agree in the hope of improving their prospects in subsequent rounds of political debate.

In this chapter, in contrast, I argue that advocates of greater choice and competition should regard charter schools not just as a temporary compromise to be tolerated, but as the policy we ought to prefer. My argument proceeds in three parts. First I outline the central elements that distinguish charter school policies from voucher systems. Second I make the case that these distinctions make the establishment of charter schools the preferred policy. Third I consider an additional argument against charter schools, the argument that whatever the theoretical appeal of the charter idea, practical and political realities make the establishment of charter schools an unworkable policy.

Differences between Charter and Voucher Plans

To be sure, voucher and charter school policies share a great deal in common. Under both policies families have the opportunity to send their children to schools not operated by the local school district, at least in part at public expense. Under both policies funding follows a child to the school his or her family chooses, creating an incentive for schools to act in ways that families value. Under both policies publicly funded choice schools have more autonomy than conventional public schools to control curricula and instruction and manage their operations.

But there are important differences between charter school programs and voucher plans. One challenge in comparing charter and voucher proposals is that numerous different designs go by the names of charter school programs and voucher plans. To simplify the discussion, I primarily compare the relatively pure charter design proposed by Kolderie with the relatively pure voucher design associated with Chubb and Moe's *Politics, Markets, and America's Schools.*[1] (Actual voucher and charter programs may well differ from these ideal conceptions. For examples of such deviations, see Peterson's introductory chapter in this volume on deviations from the voucher ideal and my other chapter in this volume on deviations from the charter school ideal.) With these two pure designs in mind, it is possible to point out two primary distinctions between charter and voucher plans in terms of the ways they treat access to schools and the ways they treat accountability.

Access to Schools under Charter and Voucher Plans

Two central restrictions govern access to schools under a charter program. First, if oversubscribed, schools must admit students by lottery. They may not select, for example, only those students who perform at high levels on standardized tests, those who exhibit athletic prowess, or those who come highly recommended by their previous schools.[2] In this respect charter schools resemble conventional public schools more than they do private schools: any student has the opportunity to attend any charter school; only bad luck in the lottery can keep a student out. Under a pure voucher plan, in contrast, private schools have the authority to select students on whatever constitutional bases they deem appropriate. Though they cannot discriminate on the basis of race or other suspect bases, they are free to set academic, athletic, or other admissions standards. As a result, some students find that certain schools are not truly options for them because they fall below these standards.[3]

A second restriction on charter schools is that they cannot charge tuition. For each student a charter school enrolls, it receives something like the average per-pupil expenditure in its district or state. It may not ask families to add on to this basic amount any type of required tuition or fee.[4] Accordingly, all charter schools are affordable to all students as a matter of policy. In a voucher system, in contrast, a school may set tuition at whatever level it pleases, even if that level requires families to supplement their vouchers with their own funds. (Chubb and Moe, it should be noted, do not favor allowing families to add on to the public funds earmarked for their children's education.[5]) As a consequence, it is possible for schools that receive voucher funding to be too expensive for some students to attend even with the help of their vouchers.

Accountability under Charter and Voucher Plans

Charter and voucher plans both hold schools accountable by giving families the choice of whether to have their children attend them. By tying funding to enrollment, both policies seek to induce schools to act in ways that families value. Those that fail to please families go out of business or are forced to rely on private tuition to support their operations. Beyond this important similarity, though, charter and voucher plans treat school accountability differently in three respects.

— Authorization. As the name of the policy implies, a charter school must obtain a charter in order to begin educating students at public expense.

Table 2-1. *Summary of the Differences between Charter and Voucher Plans*

Subject	Charter plans	Voucher plans
Access		
Admissions standards	Schools may not impose academic or athletic admissions standards; oversubscribed schools must select students by lot	Schools may impose whatever constitutional admissions standards they see fit
Tuition	Schools may not charge tuition or fees	Schools may charge tuition and fees
Accountability		
Authorization	Schools must obtain charters from public bodies in order to receive public funds	Schools must meet only minimal (procedural) requirements to receive public funds
Performance contracts	Schools that fail to meet contractual performance targets can lose their charters	Schools do not sign performance contracts
Nonreligiosity	Schools may not provide religious instruction or affiliate with religious institutions	Schools may provide religious instruction and/or affiliate with religious institutions

Sources: Basic characteristics of charter plans derived from Ted Kolderie, *Beyond Choice to the New Public Schools: Withdrawing the Exclusive Franchise in Public Education* (Washington, D.C.: Progressive Policy Institute, 1990). Characteristics of voucher plans drawn largely from John E. Chubb and Terry M. Moe, *Politics, Markets, and America's Schools* (Brookings, 1990), pp. 215-26, though the authors do not favor allowing voucher schools to charge tuition in excess of the face value of the voucher (p. 220). Such excess tuition payments, however, are allowed (or even required) under most existing voucher programs, including those profiled in this volume.

Generally this means that it must petition some public body (perhaps the state board of education or the board of a public university) for the right to operate the school. The public body conducts a substantive review of the petition, assessing whether the plan is sound and whether the applicants have the capability to put it into action. Under a voucher program, in contrast, a school has to meet only minimal standards (most of them procedural) in order to open its doors to voucher-holding students, much as a private school does now under most state laws.[6]

— Performance contracts. One essential element of a charter is the specification of performance standards that the school is obligated to meet. If a charter school fails to deliver on its promises (perhaps regarding absolute levels or improvements in student achievement scores, dropout rates, college attendance, and so on), the relevant public authority can revoke its charter. In the current lingo, the school is "accountable for results"—not just to parents, but to the public as well. Private schools receiving voucher funds enter into no such contracts. We might hope that families would abandon poor-performing schools en masse; but if they did not, the substandard schools would continue to be eligible for public funding.[7]

— Nonreligiosity. Both charter schools and private schools under a voucher system receive substantial autonomy to set their own curricula, design their instructional methods, and manage their operations. They are both bound by a minimal set of regulations concerning health and safety, nondiscrimination, disclosure of use of public funds, and other relatively noncontroversial matters. But charter schools face one significant restriction that voucher schools escape: they are not able to offer religious instruction or be affiliated with religious institutions.[8]

Table 2-1 summarizes the critical differences between charter and voucher plans. In the next section I make the case that the charter school arrangements represent the best means of introducing choice and competition into public education.

Why Charter Schools Represent the Right Policy Choice

One element that charter and voucher plans share in common is the continuation of a substantial public investment in children's education. Though some argue for a completely privatized education system in which taxpayers provide no funds for the education of children,[9] most proponents of choice want to redirect the flow of public dollars, not staunch it. My argument in this section is that as long as taxpayers are making such a large investment in K–12 education, it is only reasonable for them to expect to receive something they value in return. The case for charter school programs is that they will deliver greater returns on public investment than will voucher plans.

Let me suggest two sorts of return taxpayers ought to expect from their investment. First, they ought to expect that in the schools where they invest their funds, children are learning. What counts as valuable learning is a matter of some dispute, of course, an important point to which I will return in the final section. But I think most would agree that citizens ought not to be asked, as they have been for so many years, to continue funneling money into schools that are not effective in some sense. Second, taxpayers ought to demand that all students, not just the bright and the well-to-do, have access to publicly funded schools. One of the principal rationales for public funding of education is to ensure that each child can receive an education regardless of his or her family's ability to pay. To the extent that the bright and the well-to-do manage fairly well even under current arrangements, we ought to judge proposed reforms primarily by what they contribute to the learning of those most ill served by the current system, namely the poor and those with low performance levels.

In focusing on these two values, effectiveness and equity, I am setting aside other common rationales for public investment in education. Most notable among these is the idea that the public ought to expect schools to foster certain civic values and virtues, preparing students for their lives as citizens.[10] I am focusing on effectiveness and equity primarily because these are the values that underpin the arguments of choice advocates. The case for choice typically rests in part on the notion that greater competition among schools and choice for families would improve the effectiveness of schools in general and in part on the view that disadvantaged students in particular have a great deal to gain from having access to opportunities beyond those offered by their assigned public schools.[11] This section addresses each of these values, beginning with equity.

Why We Should Guarantee Access to All Students

One of the most common—and most compelling—arguments for greater choice among schools is the notion that the primary beneficiaries of choice would be students who are ill served by the current system. We can think of these students in terms of two broad groups: the economically disadvantaged, who cannot afford to attend private schools or avail themselves of public options that require expensive residential choices, and the educationally disadvantaged, who may or may not have financial resources, but are not well served educationally by the options available to them. We ought to evaluate choice plans in part based on the degree to which they would help these students directly or would help them indirectly by making it possible for them to attend school with more advantaged peers.

Of course opponents of choice plans often argue that choice would increase educational inequities, as well-to-do and well-educated families would be in a better position to take advantage of the choices offered to them.[12] Arguments in support of this proposition range from the straightforward and plausible (that poor and less well-educated families would have relatively less information about school choices) to the complex and questionable (that the "culture" they inhabit may lead poor families to place less value on education, to be afraid of sending their children to school with

Table 2-2. *Types of Schools Eligible for Public Funding under Voucher Plans*

	Admissions	
Tuition	Nonselective	Selective
Does not exceed the amount of the voucher	(1)	(2)
Exceeds the amount of the voucher	(3)	(4)

more advantaged peers, or otherwise to forgo the opportunities presented by choice).

For the sake of argument, let us suppose that these critics are wrong, that information could be readily disseminated about schools and that disadvantaged families would be just as eager (if not more eager) than their more well-to-do peers to find better educational options for their children. If this is the case, the challenge is to design a system of choice in which children currently faring poorly in the educational system would have dramatically improved access to high-quality educational options.

Under a full-blown voucher system, four types of schools would be eligible for public funds, as illustrated in table 2-2. These four types can be postulated by two dimensions discussed in the previous section: admissions standards and tuition. Schools could choose to set admissions standards or not and to charge tuition in excess of the voucher amount or not. So the schools represented by cell 1 would be open to all comers (subject to the constraints of space). The schools represented by cell 2 would be affordable to all, but would exclude students who failed to meet certain standards.[13] The schools represented by cell 3 would be open to all, but only if they could afford the tuition add-on. And the schools represented by cell 4 would exclude students who failed to meet standards or who could not pay the tuition, or both.

In examining the value of making public funds available to these different types of schools, there are two easy cases. First, providing public funds for the schools represented by cell 4 does not strike me as a valuable use of public resources. All, or almost all, of the funds would flow to nondisadvantaged students and subsidize their attendance of schools to which disadvantaged students lacked access.[14] Accordingly, scarce public dollars would do nothing to promote improvement for the students who needed it the most. In contrast, all of the public funds flowing to the schools represented by cell 1 would either pay for the education of disadvantaged students directly or subsidize the attendance by the nondisadvantaged of schools open to the disadvantaged. Most people would probably agree that providing public funds for the schools represented by cell 1 makes sense.

The schools represented by cell 3 are a somewhat more difficult case, but it is hard to develop a convincing public policy rationale for investing scarce public dollars in these schools. Perhaps some would use their excess tuition dollars to provide specialized programs to help low-performing students achieve, a worthy endeavor to be sure. And with public funding middle-class families who would not ordinarily be able to afford such programs would find them within reach. These schools, however, would do little to improve the educational fortunes of the poor.

How to handle the schools represented by cell 2 is the hardest call. These schools would provide the opportunity for high-performing students, including poor students, to attend schools populated by other high performers. The public value of such schools would depend on the complex accounting of peer group effects, which are discussed at some length in Paul Peterson's introductory chapter. If peer group effects were strong, high-performing students would benefit from the chance to be educated with other bright students. But children left behind would lose access to these same students and suffer the consequences. The balance of these positive and negative outcomes has not, to my mind, been sorted out by research to date. On the other hand, if peer group effects were weak, we would be less concerned about the students left behind, as Peterson argues. But the value of the selective schools represented by cell 2 would also be lower, since the students would gain little from the exclusive environments in which they found themselves. All in all, the case for public funding of the schools represented by cell 2 is not strong, though it is certainly stronger than the case for public investment in the schools represented by cells 3 and 4.

The overall value of public investment in schools under a voucher system would depend in part on how students actually sorted themselves into these different groups. In a worst-case scenario, all students who could meet selective enrollment standards would opt for the schools represented by cells 2 and 4, and all those with the ability to pay would choose the schools represented by cells 3 and 4. The schools represented by cell 1 would be attended solely by students disadvantaged in both the economic and the educational senses. The reality would likely fall somewhat short of this extreme case. But it would likely involve the flow of substantial public funds to schools that contributed little to the educational advancement of the most disadvantaged.

Of course a voucher program could be designed to meet these objections. Many actual voucher programs are in fact arranged to do so. Such designs could provide vouchers only to disadvantaged students, provide vouchers that would decline in value as a family's income rose, require participating schools to select students by lottery, limit the amount families could add on to the vouchers, and so on. But to the extent that such designs meet the objections raised, they begin to look more and more like charter school programs.

Charter programs require all schools to fit themselves into cell 1. The early returns from studies suggest that, as a result, charter schools are indeed serving a diverse population of students, including disadvantaged students. Researchers from the Hudson Institute found that in 1996–97, half of charter schools' students were minority group members (compared with one-third in conventional public schools), 40 percent were poor (versus 37 percent in conventional public schools), 13 percent had limited English proficiency, and 13 percent had disabilities.[15] In Hudson's survey of students attending charter schools (reported in chapter 8, this volume), nearly half reported that their performance prior to attending a charter school was "failing," "poor," or "average." Another national study, sponsored by the U.S. Department of Education, came to similar conclusions about the demographics of charter school students.[16]

In sum, if we as taxpayers want to target our investments in ways that will help improve the educational fortunes of the disadvantaged, voucher plans look like a poor choice in comparison with charter school programs. Voucher plans allow a substantial amount of public funds to flow to schools that do little or nothing to help the children most in need of help, the children who provide the most compelling rationale for public investment in education in the first place. Charter plans, in contrast, make public funds available only to schools that are open to these students.

Why We Should Demand Accountability beyond the Marketplace

It is not enough to ensure that the disadvantaged have access to schools funded publicly. Taxpayers should also demand that the schools they fund be effective at educating young people. In any system of choice we might expect parents to hold schools accountable for effectiveness. If students are not learning, parents can exit, choosing other schools. Or they can use their potential to exit to magnify the potency of their voice, pressing schools to improve.

However, when families choose schools, they may care about more than the quality of the education offered. They may care about a school's location, about the backgrounds of the other students who attend the school, about extracurricular activities, about the moral values that school officials espouse, or about any number of other factors that are not directly related to the quality of learning they can expect. Since they have these other factors in mind, it is conceivable that when they weigh them all they will prefer a school that performs poorly in educational terms.

From a variety of sources we have accumulated substantial evidence in support of the contention that families consider a whole range of factors, both academic and nonacademic, when choosing schools for their children. The first source is data from surveys in which parents were asked to select or rank various factors that influenced their choice of schools. To be sure, academic considerations (such as the educational philosophy of the school or the quality of its teachers) tend to come out at the top of lists ranking responses to such surveys. But a whole host of other rationales also emerge, often garnering comparably high numbers of responses. As one might expect, families with options make complex judgments in which they balance the many characteristics of schools against one another to arrive at decisions.[17]

A second source of information is the data on the choices families and students actually make. As Caroline Hoxby points out in this volume, families already exercise various types of "traditional" school choice: choosing between school districts (or attendance areas within school districts) and choosing private schools. And even within schools, especially public high schools, students often have a great deal of choice over the types of coursework they pursue.[18]

When we look at the choices families and students are actually making in these contexts, it becomes clear that factors other than academic quality are in play. In the case of school districts, low-performing school systems continue to fill up the seats in their schools. Presumably many families stay where they are despite poor academic quality because of other factors (related to the schools themselves or, more likely, related to job opportunities, affordability of housing, proximity to family and friends, or other nonschool considerations). Similarly, some families appear willing to send their children to private schools even when their academic quality is questionable. Almost all of the research on differences in achievement between public and private schools has examined differences in mean achievement in the two sectors.[19] This analysis masks the fact that within both sectors there is a broad range of school quality. In other words, there are significant numbers of lousy private schools that still manage to enroll students. Again, families are making decisions based on factors other than academics.

Students' choices among courses in high school provide additional evidence that choosers do not always choose academic quality. The dawn of the "shopping mall high school," in which students can choose from a broad array of course offerings that vary widely in academic rigor, means that students within the same high school may pursue vastly different courses of study. Many students appear to enroll, by choice, in very low-quality academic sequences.[20]

A final source of evidence is outside of K–12 education altogether. For decades the federal government has provided "vouchers" for students to attend postsecondary institutions through programs known as the GI Bill and, more recently, through Title IV funds, which provide for Pell Grants and an array of loan programs. Students have been able to use these subsidies at virtually any accredited postsecondary institution of their choice, including some 5,000 proprietary institutions providing primarily occupation-specific training. Although many of these schools undoubtedly offer high-quality instruction, recent studies by the Department of Education's Inspector General (IG), the General Accounting Office (GAO), and Congress have demonstrated that many proprietary institutions are providing students with little of educational value. The IG determined that in 1990 Title IV funds trained 96,000 students in cosmetology, adding to the 1.8 million licensed cosmetologists eligible for 597,000 jobs in the field nationwide. Using more recent data, the GAO examined proprietary schools in twelve states and found that $273 million in federal dollars was subsidizing 112,000 students to obtain training in occupations that were "oversupplied" in the state; that is, at least two students were receiving training for every predicted job vacancy. The GAO also determined that proprietary students were defaulting on their loans at a rate of 41 percent in 1990, compared with a rate of 22 percent for all postsecondary students.[21]

I am not making the usual paternalistic argument that we need to protect families from their own poor choices. Families and students may have perfectly good reasons for choosing schools that they value on grounds other than their academic reputations. The case I want to make is that whatever the validity of families' judgments, taxpayers should not be expected to subsidize them when they choose schools that contribute little to students' learning. Taxpayers should demand that as a condition for receiving public subsidies, families enroll their children in schools that can demonstrate effectiveness.

Even if the evidence cited is wrong, it is hard to make the case that taxpayers should not set academic standards for the schools they fund. Suppose for the sake of argument that families and students would in fact choose only high-quality academic institutions under a choice plan, subsuming other factors to this one. Under those circumstances a charter school program's requirement that schools meet performance standards should not present a problem to proponents of choice. Underperforming charter schools would be closed, but no one would want to attend them anyway. The charter idea's insistence on performance constrains families' choices only if families want their children to attend low-performing schools.

Charter programs embody performance accountability in two forms, which are described in the previous section: the requirement that schools obtain authorization (charters) in order to begin receiving public funds and the requirement that schools live up to the terms of performance contracts in order to keep receiving these funds. In contrast, voucher plans require only minimal certification (mostly on procedural grounds) and do not impose performance contracts. Accordingly, it is likely that under a voucher plan public funds would flow undisturbed to any number of schools that were not producing educational results valued by the public. This state of affairs sounds a little too much like the status quo for my taste.

One possible variant of the charter school idea would be to hold schools accountable for performance once they were open, but to eliminate the up-front approval process. Just about any school would be given the chance to compete for students, but those that failed to perform would be shut down. This proposal, however, suffers from a serious problem. As analysts have demonstrated in their research on the Milwaukee school choice program, the extent to which students are benefiting from their new schools may take three or four years to become apparent.[22] It would be unfair to close down a school that failed to demonstrate academic quality in its first few years of operation. A few years may not seem like a long time, but it is quite a bit of water under the bridge for the children who attend a poor-quality school while the researchers wait for the data. Charter school programs do not eliminate this waiting period, but they work hard to screen out at least some of the schools that are likely to fail up front.

Charter schools also enforce a third form of accountability: They require all schools receiving public funds to be nonreligious. Of course the prospects of providing public funds for religious schools raises a host of constitutional questions, many of them addressed in contributions to this volume by Paul Peterson, Stephen Gilles, and Joseph Viteritti. But suppose such funding were constitutionally permissible. Would it be good public policy to allow it? Proponents of voucher plans generally say yes; advocates of charter programs generally say no.

To understand the case against including religious schools in a choice plan, it is important to survey the terrain of private education in the United

Table 2-3. *Share of the U.S. Private School Market Held by Religious and Nonreligious Schools, 1993–94*

Type of school	Schools		Students	
	Number	Percentage	Number	Percentage
Religious schools	20,531	78.7	4,202,097	84.5
Catholic schools	8,351	32.0	2,516,028	50.6
Other religious schools	12,180	46.7	1,686,069	33.9
Nonreligious schools	5,563	21.3	768,451	15.5
All private schools	26,094	. . .	4,970,548	. . .

Source: Department of Education, National Center for Education Statistics, *Private Schools in the United States: A Statistical Profile, 1993–94* (Washington, D.C., 1997), tables 1-1 and 1-2.

States today. According to the U.S. Department of Education's 1993–94 survey of private schools, nearly eight in ten of the nation's private schools were religious schools. Since religious schools tend to be larger than non-religious private schools, an even larger share—nearly 85 percent—of private school students attended religious schools.[23] Table 2-3 displays the actual figures.

On the one hand, table 2-3 illustrates that religious schools provide the most obvious ready supply of private schools that would be needed in a shift to a choice-oriented system of schooling. This ready supply is often the principal rationale offered by choice advocates for the inclusion of religious schools in such a system.[24] On the other hand, the current state of the market makes it a strong possibility that the vast majority of schools attended by choice students would be religious schools.[25] Constitutional questions aside, should we ask taxpayers to shift a substantial amount of their investment in education to religious institutions? Should we ask Jewish taxpayers, for example, to subsidize Catholic schools, or vice versa? Perhaps doing so would be no different from asking whole-language supporters to provide funds for phonics instruction or believers in the humanities to back vocational schools. But I am inclined to think such programmatic "beliefs" are less deeply held than the religious beliefs of many citizens, and therefore we ought to think twice before taxing one another to pay for instruction provided by religious schools.

One could imagine a system in which religion-affiliated schools could receive public funding, but they would be required to restrict religious instruction to voluntary sessions, perhaps outside of the regular school day. This may be what Chubb and Moe have in mind when they call for the inclusion of religious schools in a choice program "as long as their sectarian functions can be kept clearly separate from their educational functions."[26] But such a restriction, like the constraints on admissions practices and tuition considered earlier, would blur the distinction between a voucher plan and a charter program, introducing accountability outside of the marketplace into the voucher proposal.

The Political and Practical Feasibility of Charter School Programs

Some readers may find themselves in agreement with the central propositions of this chapter, that taxpayers should expect their investments in schools to support effective schools, especially those that are effective for the most disadvantaged students; and that in contrast to voucher plans, the particular design of charter school programs ensures (in theory at least) that most public dollars end up supporting accessible, high-performing schools. But they may raise an important issue.

For charter school programs to function as described in this chapter, two conditions must be met. First, the public authorities that oversee charter programs must act responsibly. They must wield the considerable power placed in their hands, particularly the power to authorize charter schools and to revoke the contracts of nonperforming schools, with the aim of maximizing the return taxpayers receive on their investment. If one believes the arguments for choice and competition, acting responsibly means allowing many diverse charter schools to open, enough to educate all students who want to attend. And it means extending or revoking contracts purely on the basis of objective measures of school performance.

A second condition that must be met is that it must be possible for a sufficiently large supply of charter schools to emerge to meet families' demand for choice. Charter school laws authorize the creation of charter schools or the conversion of existing public or private schools to charter status. But these laws cannot mandate supply and remain true to the charter ideal of grassroots-initiated institutions. Educational entrepreneurs must rise to the occasion, and the rules must be set so they have a reasonable chance of succeeding. But can we expect these two conditions to hold? Can we expect public officials to behave responsibly and charter school entrepreneurs to appear in sufficient numbers?

In the case of expecting public officials to behave responsibly, we have reason to doubt. The public authorities charged with overseeing charter schools are not autonomous islands in the political system, free from influence from the outside. Indeed, they are not meant to be, since they are called upon to exercise power on behalf of citizens. But since they are not autonomous islands, they are subject to the ebb and flow of political forces, the same ebb and flow that Chubb and Moe argue lies at the root of the problems faced by the current educational system.[27]

Charter school programs, then, are forever subject to having their purposes undermined by those whose interests are challenged. Charter schools' overseers may come under pressure to restrict the granting of charters (either in quantity or in the degree of challenge they pose to conventional districts), to revoke the charters of schools that draw substantial numbers of students and dollars away from existing schools, or to tailor selection criteria and performance measures in ways that channel charter schools down relatively conventional paths, discouraging differentiation. In my own study of charter school programs nationwide, I found ample evidence that political battles over the character of charter school programs continued long after the legislation was passed.[28]

Such pressures are virtually inevitable, since devising a selection process for charter schools and deciding what counts as performance involves making judgments about what types of learning are valuable and the like. If charter schools truly became the primary way we delivered public education in this country, there is every reason to expect that all of the political attention now focused on state and local school policies would be redirected toward shaping the selection processes and performance management systems in charter school programs.

It is this possibility of manipulation that presumably led Chubb and Moe to call for minimal public oversight of the choice system they propose. Their plan, they say, "cannot be construed as an exercise in delegation. As long as authority remains 'available' to higher levels within government, it will eventually be used to control the schools. As far as possible, all higher-level authority must be eliminated," perhaps via constitutional amendment.[29]

For all higher-level authority to be eliminated, however, taxpayers would be required to surrender all but the most procedural judgments about the use of their tax dollars to families and the schools families chose. In light of the arguments I have made in this chapter, I do not think this is acceptable. To the extent possible, advocates of strong charter school programs should press for legislation that, unlike many actual charter laws, would prevent public officials from wielding their authority for ill purposes. But no legislation, not even a constitutional amendment, can remove all discretion from public bodies while still asking them to make important judgments about the value of public investments.[30] And these are judgments, I argue, that we must ask them to make if the interests of taxpayers are to be served.

And what of the supply of charter schools? One source of the appeal of voucher programs is the fact that they bring with them at least the beginning of a supply of schools: the nation's existing private schools. If a large fraction of these could be induced to accept voucher-bearing students, perhaps increasing their capacity to handle the new demand, many choosers would find a slot in a preexisting private school. A charter program, too, might allow private schools to convert, and many do. But participation in a charter program entails accepting a set of rules that many private schools would find unacceptable. Converted private schools would have to drop their selective admissions practices, and they would not be able to charge families tuition or fees. And, most significant, they would have to sever ties with religious institutions. For some private schools (such as the dozens that have already converted to charter status) these restrictions would not present problems. But for others it would make charter status too unappealing to accept. In light of the data presented in table 2-3 on the predominance of religious schools in the private sector, it is reasonable to assume that the vast majority of private schools would remain private under a full-blown charter program.

With most private schools on the sidelines, charter programs have to look to educational entrepreneurs and existing public schools for supply. As I describe in my chapter later in this volume, the challenges facing start-from-scratch schools are severe. Public school conversions face fewer logistical obstacles, but they may confront more severe political hurdles. As charter school entrepreneurs throughout the country are well aware, building a competent supply of charter schools will not be easy.

This prospect, however, does not cast too dark a shadow on the charter school experiment. As daunting as the start-up challenges are, the charter school movement appears to be attracting individuals and organizations capable of overcoming them. In the Hudson Institute's two-year study of charter schools, the first-year report brimmed with stories of start-up difficulties.[31] Although the second-year report also addresses these complications, its main thrust is to suggest that charter schools are successfully tackling these problems. "Based on our observations," the report authors state, "a lot of those problems get solved, or at least eased, as [a] school ages and the people responsible for it gain experience. That doesn't mean the problems solve themselves; it means people devise solutions or find accommodations."[32] The capacity of charter school programs to attract problem solvers to the field of public education is, in the end, one of their most exciting features.

As policymakers seek to introduce greater choice and competition into American public education, they face a complex set of design decisions. Charter school programs represent an approach that seeks to ensure that schools receiving public funds are open to all and are accountable for student learning. Making them work will require political vigilance and practical problem solving, but it is hard to imagine an effective educational reform that would not.

Notes

1. Ted Kolderie, *Beyond Choice to the New Public Schools: Withdrawing the Exclusive Franchise in Public Education* (Washington, D.C.: Progressive Policy Institute, 1990); John E. Chubb and Terry M. Moe, *Politics, Markets, and America's Schools* (Brookings, 1990). Chubb and Moe (pp. 217–18) seek to distance themselves from the voucher label. But the only element that sets their proposal apart from a voucher plan is that no student or family would actually receive something called a voucher. Instead the state would pay schools on behalf of families. But since this funding would follow each child to the school of his family's choice with very few restrictions, there is no functional difference between this system and a system in which families receive vouchers to redeem.

2. In most charter programs charter schools may grant preference to siblings of current students or to children of employees. In at least one state they may grant preference to the children of founders as an incentive for parents to participate in starting charter schools. In practice, some states do not require a lottery in the event of oversubscription, allowing schools to allocate slots instead on a first-come, first-served basis.

3. Chubb and Moe, *Politics, Markets, and America's Schools*, pp. 221–22.

4. In general, charter schools may raise funds from private benefactors to supplement public dollars, so they do not have to be 100 percent publicly funded.

5. Chubb and Moe, *Politics, Markets, and America's Schools*, p. 220.

6. Chubb and Moe, *Politics, Markets, and America's Schools*, p. 219.

7. Chubb and Moe, *Politics, Markets, and America's Schools*, p. 225.

8. In practice, many functioning voucher plans include this same restriction. But the assumption here is that nonreligiosity is a compromise that most voucher advocates (though not all) would prefer not to make.

9. See Andrew J. Coulson, "On the Way to School: History's Verdict on the Great School Reform Debate" (mimeographed).

10. Amy Gutmann, *Democratic Education* (Princeton University Press, 1987).

11. For an effectiveness-based argument see Chubb and Moe, *Politics.* For an access-based argument see Peterson, this volume.

12. See Bruce Fuller, Richard Elmore, and Gary Orfield, eds., *Who Chooses? Who Loses? Culture, Institutions, and the Unequal Effects of School Choice* (New York: Teachers College Press, 1996); Amy Stuart Wells, "The Sociology of School Choice: Why Some Win and Others Lose in the Educational Marketplace," in *School Choice: Examining the Evidence*, Edith Rasell and Richard Rothstein, eds., (Washington, D.C.:

Economic Policy Institute, 1993), pp. 29–48; Peter W. Cookson, Jr., ed., *The Choice Controversy* (Newbury Park, Calif.: Corwin, 1992); Jeffrey Henig, *Rethinking School Choice: Limits of the Market Metaphor* (Princeton University Press, 1994).

13. It is worth noting that many public school districts have schools represented by cell 2 in their systems already, schools such as Boston Latin or any number of selective magnet programs around the country.

14. Of course, such schools could serve the economically disadvantaged by raising private scholarship funds, a practice quite common in current voucher experiments. And the availability of publicly funded vouchers would make these schools more affordable to middle-class families. But the bulk of the most disadvantaged of our students would gain little from these schools.

15. Gregg Vanourek, Bruno V. Manno, Chester E. Finn, Jr., and Louann A. Bierlein, *The Educational Impact of Charter Schools,* Charter Schools in Action Final Report, part 5 (Washington, D.C.: Hudson Institute, 1997).

16. RPP International and the University of Minnesota, *A Study of Charter Schools* (Washington: U.S. Department of Education, 1997).

17. For a review see John Maddaus, "Parental Choice of School: What Parents Think and Do," in Courtney B. Cazden, ed., *Review of Research in Education* (Washington, D.C.: American Educational Research Association, 1990), pp. 267–95.

18. Valerie E. Lee, "Educational Choice: The Stratifying Effects of Selecting Schools and Courses," *Educational Policy* 7, no. 2 (1993), pp. 125–48; A. G. Powell, E. Farrar, and D. K. Cohen, *The Shopping Mall High School* (Boston: Houghton Mifflin, 1985).

19. For a summary see Christopher Jencks, "How Much Do High School Students Learn?" *Sociology of Education* 58 (1985), pp. 128–35.

20. Powell, Farrar, and Cohen, *Shopping Mall High School.*

21. General Accounting Office, *Higher Education: Ensuring Quality Education from Proprietary Institutions* (Washington, 1996); General Accounting Office, *Proprietary Schools: Millions Spent to Train Students for Oversupplied Occupations* (Washington, 1997).

22. Jay P. Greene, Paul E. Peterson, and Jiangtao Du, *Effectiveness of School Choice: The Milwaukee Experiment,* Harvard University Program on Educational Policy and Governance Occasional Paper Series, no. 97–1 (Harvard University Program on Educational Policy and Governance, 1997).

23. U.S. Department of Education, National Center for Education Statistics, *Private Schools in the United States: A Statistical Profile, 1993–94* (Washington, 1997), pp. 57–58.

24. Chubb and Moe, *Politics, Markets, and America's Schools,* p. 219.

25. This outcome is not a foregone conclusion. As Caroline Hoxby illustrates in her contribution to this volume, religious schools have benefited from access to subsidies from their affiliated religious orders. These subsidies may account for the predominance of religious schools in the private school market. Under a choice plan nonreligious private schools would also have access to subsidy funds, leveling the playing field. In addition, it is not clear whether the subsidies currently available to religious schools could be expanded to accommodate the increased enrollment that would likely follow the introduction of a choice plan.

26. Chubb and Moe, *Politics, Markets, and America's Schools,* p. 219.

27. Chubb and Moe, *Politics, Markets, and America's Schools.*

28. Bryan C. Hassel, "Designed to Fail? Charter School Programs and the Politics of Structural Choice" (Ph.D. diss., Harvard University, 1997).

29. Chubb and Moe, *Politics, Markets, and America's Schools,* pp. 218–19.

30. In any case, if advocates of choice lack the political power to keep charter school programs pure, surely they also lack the power to enact constitutional amendments that remove educational decisionmaking from politics forever.

31. Chester E. Finn, Jr., Bruno V. Manno, and Louann Bierlein. *Charter Schools in Action: What Have We Learned?* (Washington, D.C.: Hudson Institute, 1996).

32. Chester E. Finn, Jr., Bruno V. Manno, Louann A. Bierlein, and Gregg Vanourek, *The Birth-Pains and Life-Cycles of Charter Schools,* Charter Schools in Action Final Report, part 2 (Washington, D.C.: Hudson Institute, 1997), p. 1.

Part Two

SCHOOL CHOICE AND SCHOOL REFORM

THREE

Governance and Educational Quality

John E. Brandl

HOW DOES a free people induce private citizens and government employees to act in ways that accomplish public purposes? That is the central challenge of governance, but in our time those making policy for elementary and secondary education have given it scant attention. Legislators have applied huge increases in spending to education. They have promulgated rules. They have funded much research to identify effective educational practices. "Reforms" they have introduced have come and gone. None of these actions has substituted for confronting the governance question. Unacceptably poor education has been the result.

In the first section of this chapter I show that education policymaking has been unsuccessful. In the second section I explain why that is the case. For most of what it does, government's policymaking responsibility is so to orchestrate affairs that when private citizens as well as public employees ordinarily and freely act in ways that accomplish their own objectives, they meet public purposes as well. Arrangements that would do this are not in place in elementary and secondary education. The public schools are now organized in such a way that those working in them are subject to no

This chapter draws upon John E. Brandl, *Money and Good Intentions Are Not Enough, or, Why a Liberal Democrat Thinks States Need Both Competition and Community* (Brookings, 1998).

systematic inducement to accomplish expected results. They do not receive regular rewards or penalties or inspiration that hold them to their task. Of course there are exceptions—the always-generous teacher, the wonder-working principal—but the exceptions illustrate the system's reliance on heroism. The public school system lacks a persistent, day-to-day orientation that would move ordinary individuals to accomplish public purposes. I contend that there are only two ways of supplying that orientation, only two self-disciplining, broadly effective means of carrying out public services in general and education in particular. These are harnessing self-interest through competition and transcending self-interest by encouraging affiliations that inspire other-regarding behavior. I call the latter community. I consider competition in the third section of the chapter and community in the fourth. Successful production of services by government depends on recourse to one or both of these metapolicies. Education has been characterized by neither. The fifth section is a summary of the chapter.

Competition and community do not substitute for policymaking by government. They are the indispensable instruments through which government facilitates the working out of public purposes by a free people. I mean this thesis to apply to government's services in general; throughout this chapter I will continue to draw illustrations of the argument from elementary and secondary education.

The Inefficacy of Education Policymaking in Recent Decades

Americans are becoming accustomed to hearing that their children are ill educated, but the facts still hit harshly. The federal government's National Assessment of Educational Progress (NAEP) regularly gauges the educational achievement of the nation's youth. NAEP finds that most seventeen-year-olds lack "any degree of detailed knowledge across the subdisciplines of science," lack "an overall understanding of specific government structures and their functions," and lack knowledge of some of the most basic historical facts. Fewer than half are familiar with the Declaration of Independence; half are unaware that the Constitution guarantees freedom of religion. Most do not know about the mid–nineteenth century debate on slavery, nor can they tell you about Martin Luther King, Jr., and the Montgomery boycott. Half think that a boat trip from New York to London is as much aided by the Panama Canal as is a voyage from New York to San Francisco. A third of our high school seniors cannot write a persuasive letter, and a third do not know that we have a representative democracy or what separation of powers means. Half of American eleventh graders are studying either pre–high school mathematics or none at all; only half of our seventeen-year-olds can do grade school mathematics—that is, decimals, fractions, percentages, and simple equations. Three in a hundred of our secondary school students study calculus; five times that many do so in Japan, where a higher proportion of young people graduate than do here. And, in general, by the end of their high school years U.S. students rank low in international comparisons of academic achievement.[1]

One rejoinder to this sorry litany is that surely we would do better if only we would increase appropriations to education. But just that has been happening for a long while. Indeed, the budget has been the main instrument of education policy. Real per-student spending a century ago was a thirtieth of today's spending.[2] In barely a generation, the third of a century between 1960 and 1990, per-student spending for elementary and secondary education in the United States rose from $1,621 to $4,960 (in 1990 dollars).[3] That is, three times as many resources (adjusting for inflation) are devoted to the schooling of the average pupil during the 1990s as were spent on each of that child's parents when they were in school a generation earlier. Can it be that children a few decades ago learned a third as much, having had only a third as much money spent on them? Hardly. For most of that period the results of standardized tests dropped before beginning a rise that left average scores in the 1990s about where they were in the 1960s.[4]

It emerges that, on the average and for many years, educational outcomes have been little related to the amount of money spent on schooling. Eric Hanushek assembled 187 studies that investigated whether educational expenditures influence educational outcomes. He concluded not only that there is "no strong evidence that teacher-student ratios, teacher education, or teacher experience have the expected positive effects on student achievement," but that in general "there is no strong or systematic relationship between school expenditures and student performance."[5] The Hanushek finding has been lamented and excoriated, but not persuasively refuted.[6] The grievous fact remains that, on the average, the enormous increases in spending on the schools in recent decades have not yielded corresponding improvements in educational outcomes.

The point of the previous two paragraphs can easily be misunderstood. No one argues that additional expenditures cannot yield better-educated students. There are many schools in which they do. But the sequence of money producing expected results is neither automatic nor even common.

In the 1970s and 1980s a body of research grew up under the name of the Effective Schools Movement. Scholars set out to determine what was different about the more successful schools and found in them strong leadership, an orderly environment, the teaching of basic skills, high expectations of students, the regular assignment and accomplishment of homework, a substantial part of the students' day spent on academic work, systematic monitoring of students' progress, and a sense on the part of students, teachers, and parents of their school as a community.[7]

Researchers have discovered other signs of improved educational outcomes as well. Apparently independently, two sets of researchers have identified a very significant narrowing of the gap in educational achievement between African-American and white students in the United States.[8] However, recently researchers have found that, despite continued increases in education spending on both African-American and white students, poverty levels in both groups have risen and the achievement gap between them may no longer be narrowing.[9]

Ronald Ferguson detected somewhat more useful signs of school resources' yielding increased student achievement in his study of Texas schools. He found that students perform better if their teachers possess strong language skills, many years of experience, or master's degrees, a finding at odds with Hanushek's that is all the more significant since Ferguson determined that disparities in educational achievement later translate into differentials in earnings.[10] In another study Ferguson and Helen Ladd found that in Alabama, teacher quality and class size significantly influence learning achieved by students.[11] However, that finding flies in the face of the research that detects little relationship on the average between spending and results. A plausible reconciliation of the two bodies of research exists: Apparently additional funds applied to a school with a low spending level have a greater effect than funds applied to a school with a high spending level.[12]

One might expect that what has been learned about effective practices would have been applied quickly—that is, for example, that school boards and administrators would be creating more orderly environments and hiring teachers facile with language and that teachers would be assigning homework and holding children to higher standards. Unfortunately, evidence of their effectiveness has not led to widespread adoption of those homely practices. By and large the continually increasing funds being spent on schooling have not been dedicated to uses known to have beneficial effects. The money is mostly being devoted rather to higher teacher salaries and lower class sizes. On occasion these have been helpful for students, but for the country as a whole neither has been strongly related to student achievement.[13]

The education system has grown accustomed to large per-student budget increases, but for a long time to come the states will find it exceedingly difficult even to keep real per-student expenditures constant. The economy is growing more slowly than in the past. The number of students, which dropped in the 1970s and 1980s, is rising. Nearly all of the increase is among Latino and African-American youngsters, who on average are educationally disadvantaged compared to whites.[14] Other demands for spending, starting with health care and prisons, are competing strongly with education. Taxpayers seem disinclined to continue to have a rising fraction of their income go to state and local taxes. And finally, if and as the federal government balances its budget, the prospects for additional aid to education from that quarter diminish. In sum, there is no practical possibility that in the foreseeable future per-student educational spending will rise appreciably. Educational improvement will have to come from some other quarter.

Why Past Education Policy Has Failed

When government goes awry it is usually because people in positions of power advance their own interests at the expense of others in the citizenry. If people are sometimes as tempted to watch out for themselves in their public dealings as they often are when engaged in private endeavors, a government not protected against such impulses will regularly permit some to take advantage of others.

My task in this section is to account for the inadequate record in the American states of both policymaking and policy implementation in education. These activities are largely accomplished, respectively, in legislatures and bureaus. (A bureau is an organization that gets its funding not from customers, but from a sponsor, typically a legislature. Its members are not permitted to keep for themselves any difference between revenues and expenditures; they are subject not directly to material incentives, but to rules stipulating desired behavior. A bureau can receive its funds whether or not the ultimate recipients of its services are satisfied with them.[15] The public schools are bureaus.) The growth and disappointing record of government in the United States in this century can be explained by an emerging new economics of organization. That theory also explains why some of the rationales—the theories—for government action produced by the academy, as well as advice from that quarter on how to structure government, were flawed. They did not recognize the need to protect the public from the self-interested behavior of those with governmental power.

How Faulty Theories Have Contributed to Governmental Inefficiency

Throughout most of the twentieth century the prevailing theories of public finance and bureaucracy in the United States discounted the importance of self-interested behavior on the part of politicians and civil servants. They conveyed a sense that policymakers in government would automatically embody the public interest and that expenditure of funds would mechanically yield commensurate results. The influence of these theories persists, perhaps most of all when it comes to education policy, even in the face of the evidence summarized in the first section of this chapter, which again and again has found that funded policies fall short of reasonable expectations. In this section I examine those formerly dominant theories and consider a quite different emerging explanation of how government operates and why it often fails.

The theory of public finance,[16] a subfield of economics, identified the ways that private markets are liable to failure and proposed remedial actions for government to undertake. The idea was that when private markets fail, government should intervene. Therefore, market failure became an important rationale for government action. However, an implicit assumption of the theory was that government is a single benevolent actor that is inclined to right the market's imperfections and will therefore take the actions suggested by the theory.

In the 1970s and 1980s a more sophisticated "positive theory of public interest regulation"[17] developed, leading to a conclusion that government is in effect an efficiency-inducing political marketplace. The contention was that waste constitutes opportunity. When the inefficiency of market failure occurs it can be in someone's interest to correct the inefficiency if that someone can reap a benefit from doing so. This is a straightforward application to government of the observation that in a competitive private sector opportunities for profit tend to be seized by firms. Therefore, for example, a potential competitor might petition Congress to end another organization's monopoly position (for example, private schools could lobby to receive public finances). Government antitrust action could be beneficial to the prospective competitor and to the society at large. The positive theory of public interest regulation attributes to government decisionmakers a tendency, induced by the lobbying efforts of potential beneficiaries, to move systematically to correct market failures. However, as we shall see, sometimes in government as in private firms any of several types of organizational failure can frustrate the efficiency-encouraging effects of competition.

Of course the test of the positive theory of public interest regulation lies in actual government policies. Although individual instances occur of efficiency-inducing lobbying of government, the message of the first section of this chapter is that great inefficiencies persist. For the society the net benefits of eliminating inefficiencies could be considerable. However, the costs of identifying sources of some inefficiencies and of organizing lobbying efforts to end them evidently exceed the gains for each of the individuals contemplating an effort to change government policy, so large distortions endure. The persistent practice of increasing the budgets of bureaus, starting with the schools, in the face of little improvement in results is prima facie evidence against the positive theory of public interest regulation.[18] The American political system does not automatically whittle away all major inefficiencies.

Neither traditional public finance theory nor the positive theory of public interest regulation accounts for the inefficiencies of government. Indeed, by ignoring ways in which government fails, both have shored up acceptance of current inefficient public policies. As I will show next, a blind spot similar to that in public finance theory occurred in the study of how bureaus carry out government's policies.

For most of this century organization theory in the academy was dominated by Woodrow Wilson's distinction between policy and administration and by Max Weber's image of bureaucracy as rational-legal authority.[19] Wilsonian bureaucrats, fitted by competence to their positions, accepted and carried out tasks not merely obediently, indeed unquestioningly, but adeptly. For Weber a bureau was an organization in which people operate within roles: they are selected, evaluated, and salaried impartially and impersonally on the basis of competence in a role. In his view this made possible what could not be accomplished by other forms of organization— fair and capable administration of the large organizations that were coming to characterize government. Bureaucracy's "purely technical superiority over any other form of organization" is such, Weber wrote, that "the fully developed bureaucratic mechanism compares with other organizations exactly as does the machine with the non-mechanical modes of production."[20] Thus developed the notion of neutral competence, a term of both description and prescription applied for decades by students of public administration to the people who implement government's policies. Politicians make policy and bureaucrats devotedly carry it out, if not eagerly, at least automatically.

Commenting on the Weberian understanding of organizations, the sociologist James Coleman wrote: "The fact that the persons who are employed to fill the positions in the organization are purposive actors as well is overlooked."[21] A story from my time in the Minnesota Senate illustrates. One of the teachers' organizations issued a particularly interesting legislative agenda. Amused legislators noted that among the demands for pay raises and pension improvements there was not even a suggestion that the group's proposals would improve the education of children. The organization issued a revised agenda that included the claim that what it was seeking for its members would benefit Minnesota's youngsters. Wilsonian and Weberian theory diverted attention from the possible interest conflicts between bureaucrats and those for whom they work, and thus from how bureaucracies operate.

Thus, for several decades in the middle of the century influential academic theories in America had it that government consists of legislatures that correct market failures and of executive branch bureaus that assiduously carry out the legislatures' policies. Those theories encouraged the notions that society's problems would be taken up by policymakers, new ideas for improving government would be picked off the shelf and put to use, and appropriated funds would translate into results. If problems still resisted solution, the policy indicated was to apply more funds or do more research on "what works." My own recognition of this jelled sometime after I had been responsible, in the former Department of Health, Education, and Welfare, for designing and overseeing the federal government's research on and evaluation of educational effectiveness. Year after year, for a time under my direction, the federal government has sponsored research that has identified numerous effective experimental schools, teaching techniques, and qualities of successful teachers. Meanwhile, actual practice in the vast majority of the country's schools has not, by and large, reflected those findings. Applying money and making effective practices available do not automatically yield corresponding results. We do not necessarily do what we know, though for years influential theories lulled us into assuming that we do.

The New Economics of Organization

For our purposes the main idea of the new economics of organization is that government suffers from the same failures as does the market. The new economics of organization consists of a not-yet-consolidated collection of theories in the social sciences that have five features in common: (1) The behavior of an organization, governmental or otherwise, is understood as the aggregated actions of the individuals within it. (2) Each of those individuals is ordinarily expected to further his or her own interests. (3) The interests of individuals are commonly expected to be divergent from each other and from the purported purposes of organizations of which they are members. And (4) it is thought to be frequently difficult—that is, expensive—to detect when individuals advance their interests at the expense of others, so it is hard to hold them responsible for such actions. Therefore, (5) organizational failure comes to be construed as the aggregated actions of individuals behaving in ways detrimental to others because they are not systematically constrained from doing so.[22]

At this level of abstraction one could detect the elements of these new theories in the Federalist Papers. They can indeed be thought of as a rebirth of Madisonian thinking, though Madison saw more virtue along with the self-interest in human motivation than do many of his latter-day followers.[23] The several theories from which this understanding is emerging differ in many respects, but this prosaic kernel of what they hold in common promises to revolutionize our understanding of government and our ability to bring about improvements. It is an open question whether a particular instance of market failure will be righted by government, and even whether government action will improve rather than worsen the situation.

If politicians and bureaucrats—I have been both—are able to devote their efforts not to public purposes, but to hanging onto office or to getting bigger budgets for their agencies, some will. Individual and public interests diverge, leaving both private and public organizations subject to faulty performance. This is quite a different picture of government and bureaucracy from the public spiritedness automatically attributed to them by public finance theory, from the efficiency-inducing tendency hoped for by those espousing the positive theory of public interest regulation, and from the Weberian perception of the bureau as a machine. The new academic understanding corroborates the common and disquieting suspicion of the citizenry that people in government are not always doing the public's business.

Schools and other bureaus fail. For that matter, so do private firms. They fall short of productive potential, miss possibilities for innovation, unfairly reallocate resources. Interests conflict. Neither private nor governmental organizations are automatically exposed to external or internal orientation that brings the interests of constituent individuals into congruence with the organizations' purposes or with the welfare of others. Both private and governmental organizations can be flawed, and for the same reasons.

James Madison wrote: "Ambition must be made to counter ambition. . . . This policy of supplying, by opposite and rival interests, the defect of better human motives, might be traced through the whole system of human affairs, private as well as public. . . . The constant aim is to divide and arrange the several offices in such a manner as that each may be a check on the other."[24] However, in contemporary America government organizations are generally less subject to disciplined orientation to operate innovatively and efficiently than are private firms. They are less exposed to the threat of failure. They are more frequently distinguished by monopoly, bureaucracy, and distracted monitoring. They are as apt to cause costly externalities. It is not that private organizations are inherently more efficient than government, but that Americans have permitted their government to be less exposed to the disciplining arrangement—competition—posited as essential by the nation's founders.

As currently arranged, education is prone to failure. Almost all state and local funding for education goes to districts and schools arranged as bureaus that have territorial monopolies on furnishing free education. They do not bear the discipline of having to meet their costs by selling their products to willing customers. Furthermore, information regarding their operation is frequently difficult for outsiders to come by, and the legislatures that create and fund bureaus oversee them only casually. (Until 1997 those lobbying for the public schools in Minnesota were so successful at inhibiting oversight that it was illegal for any test of educational progress that could be used to compare schools or districts to be administered statewide.) This explains the inefficiency and lack of innovativeness of educational bureaus.

Just as firms sometimes are prodded—by competition or by the owners' desire for profit—to operate resourcefully, under certain conditions a bureau such as a school can be enterprising. A school can be efficient, perhaps even innovative, if educators are consistently disposed to work toward their organizations' objectives; if they do not receive fixed wages, but rather face large or complex rewards or penalties to shape their actions; if their interests and those of students do not conflict; if monitoring is easy; if legislators exercise consistent oversight; or if a motivating principal or superintendent impels the organization to act in the public interest. One might pause to ponder how very rarely those conditions are met in our schools. In general, they do not characterize education in our time. Educators have some private interests at odds with the purposes of their schools. Often shirking is undetectable, innovation is not rewarded, careful evaluation is infrequent, and there is little tradition of paying on the basis of performance. The result is little motivation to produce desired outcomes.

No one should get by with dismissing this argument as bureaucrat or teacher bashing. The argument presumes that government employees are similar in their proclivities and talents to everyone else. Indeed, one suspects that the widespread demoralization among teachers is associated with their awareness that because of perverse institutional arrangements, their efforts are often futile. Yet in my experience many public employees, especially teachers, are personally offended when the suggestion is made that it is imprudent to assume that they are regularly public spirited. Many of them seem fully prepared to attribute consistently base motives to politicians and businesspersons while protesting their own altruism. I have had considerable difficulty persuading teachers' groups that the design of government cannot depend on an assumption that, although others should be expected to be self-concerned, one class of employee, teachers, consists of people devoted to the public interest.

The contemporary economics of organization explains the utter inadequacy of elementary and secondary education that I described in the first section of this chapter. Educators might not be inclined to work consistently for the common good, and they are not under persistent external pressure to do so. The society is left with the inefficacious bureaucratic provision of education.

Today there is no serious theory, no plausible argument, that would lead one to expect the schools as currently constituted to meet an acceptable standard. The usual prescriptions of spending more money and urging better management are thoroughly wanting. They emerge from discredited understandings, failed theories, of how government works.

Competition as a Dependable Means of Providing Services

The argument of the first two sections of this chapter—that spending yields unacceptably poor results because people inside and outside government acting in their own interests frustrate public purposes—implies a different understanding of what education policymaking must be. Policymaking must be not appropriating or mandating or exhorting, but designing. It has to be the designing of institutions so that the people in them are inclined to act in such wise as to accomplish the public purposes for which the institutions were created. Where government is not so designed, we should presume that it will not work well; it will not accomplish public purposes. Management, research, funding, mandates, and exhortation have their place, but ordinarily they will not succeed when applied in the kinds of arrangements now characteristic of public education in America. Alignment of individual and group interests is of decisive importance.

Designing Competition into Public Policy

James Madison's insight that a large democratic republic would be possible ranks in importance with Adam Smith's explication of the economic benefits of markets. In their fundamentals the two men's insights were identical.[25] Both recognized the tendency for people to act self-interestedly, especially when dealing with strangers. Both saw the possible ill effects of self-interest if it is permitted to run amok. And both were intrigued with the civilizing influence on free persons of engagement in political and economic give and take. But their central idea was that competition, the institutionalization of countervailing powers, could harness self-interest. If interests were set against interests, largely self-policing systems of politics in the one case and economics in the other could be devised. To this day the possibilities inherent in that idea have not been entirely plumbed.

Somebody should order teachers to buckle down, we say. And somebody should figure out what works in good schools, for then surely other schools would pick up those approaches. Somebody should urge superintendents to be entrepreneurial. Somebody should come up with a larger appropriation for our schools, for then they would accomplish the good deeds that niggardliness is preventing. The blindness inherent in the theories of public finance and of bureaucracy I have discussed persists because no omniscient somebody exists, and even if there were such a person there is no way of guaranteeing that he or she would have public-spirited motives. No more can you, I, or the other recipients of appropriations or exhortations be counted on automatically to respond as hoped. If people are frequently self-interested and pervasive monitoring is neither desirable nor even possible, setting interest against interest becomes an essential recourse both to monitor and to prod. The American political and economic systems depend absolutely on competition, an indispensable harness of self-interest.[26]

The conditions of perfect competition are almost never met in the real world, so in actual competition some diversions are possible; inefficiency happens. But competition's main power comes from inducing innovation. It comes from the fact that consumers and financiers will turn away from an unresponsive or uninnovative organization, public or private, and permit it to go bankrupt and out of existence.

In contemporary debates competition is sometimes confused with privatization, an unhelpful and much narrower concept. Because private activities are liable to many of the same failures as are governmental activitiies, there is no automatic benefit to be gained from the private sector's undertaking a project previously associated with government.[27] In government as well as markets, competition is an essential means by which self-interest is civilized.

Much of public policymaking for education becomes arranging or designing institutions and organizations so that people will tend not to divert resources and will tend to seek out innovations to introduce. Competition remains, as it was for Madison, the foremost institutional arrangement for government's accomplishing, in the public sector as well as the private, the orientation of private interests to broader purposes. Yet currently most public schools and districts in our country are bureaucratic regional monopolies, an arrangement that hardly reflects that vision.

Lately government-designed competitive arrangements for fostering innovation, efficiency, and self-policing in the provision of services have come to be called social markets.[28] Four elements make up their design:

—Citizens' choice of producers from among a variety of potential suppliers of service.

—A purchaser-producer split. A conflict of interest exists when the entity that buys a good or service—especially if it does so with other people's money—also produces and sells it, for then as a buyer it can hardly be expected to search among potential sellers for the best bargain. Besides, as a seller assured of a buyer, it is little apt to hold down costs and seek to improve the quality of the product. Precisely this conflict of interest exists when, as is typical in the United States, a school board buys educational services only from its own employees, who work in schools it owns.

—Debureaucratization. Government organizations that produce services are to be financed not by lump sum transfers from legislatures, but on a contractual basis by people who choose their services.

—Independent monitoring.

In sum, a properly designed social market embodies the features that orient competitive private markets toward efficiency, innovation, and self-policing—numerous sellers vying for the favor of buyers who are at arm's length from them. Sometimes those choosing the services will be public officials; then production should not also be in their hands. A social market includes independent monitoring, and sometimes additional precautions imposed by government.

The Three Kinds of Competition-Inducing Policies

This discussion implies that there are three broad kinds of policies to foster competition where government finances service production: placing

Table 3-1. *The Three Ways of Using Competition in Education Policy*

Policies using competition	Applications in education
Choice by citizen-recipients	
From among government producers	Open enrollment. Families choose any public school in any school district.
From among government or private producers	Vouchers, tax credits. Government funds go not to school boards, but to families that spend them at the schools they choose.
Ensuring a variety of choices	
From among government producers	Charter schools. Schools are owned by government entities other than school boards and operate only as long as they achieve specified results.
	Capitated, site-based funding. Funds go not to school boards, but to schools on the basis of enrollment.
From among government or private producers	Vouchers, tax credits. Families choose their schools, public or private.
Choice by government officials	Government-contracted schools. School boards, perhaps divested of ownership of schools, contract with public or private entities for services.

choice in the hands of citizen-recipients, ensuring a variety of choices of producer, and, when choice by citizens is not feasible, adopting choice by public officials. The first policy vests market demand in citizens; the second protects against monopoly in supply. If either of those two is neglected, competition is undermined. The third policy incorporates a purchaser-producer split when government officials rather than citizens choose. The three policies and their applications to education are shown in table 3-1.

In this volume Paul Peterson reports on the most recent research on the efficacy of such policies of competition in education. He has found that competition has positive effects on parental satisfaction, teacher satisfaction, student mobility, and test scores.[29] Competition corrects much market and government failure.

We have reached a paradoxical conclusion. Because self-interestedness is widespread, competition is an essential civilizer; but social life requires some public-spiritedness, if only because competitive and other arrangements for meeting public purposes need to be designed. Next we will consider the circumstances in which public-spiritedness can be expected to yield satisfactory education and other public services.

Community, the Only Other Dependable Means of Producing Services

Notwithstanding the success of the economic method in explaining much of human behavior, a huge literature dating back thousands of years argues the wrongheadedness of construing society as an aggregation of self-interested individuals. There is much that twentieth-century self-interest theory cannot explain. It cannot explain why people vote. (Some effort is involved, and the effect of a single vote is almost always so tiny that a calculation of one's benefits and costs would lead one to decide not to bother.) It cannot in many circumstances provide an understanding of why any member of a large group would produce public goods without special incentives,[30] since presumably everyone would wait for someone else to do so, then free-ride. Self-interest theory cannot account for why anyone would give anonymous contributions to charity, take back to the owner a wallet found on the street, or leave a tip at a restaurant to which one intends never to return.[31] It does not tell us what to make of courage in battle or faithful spouses or diligent, unmonitored workers. And, to foreshadow a conclusion of this section, self-interest theory is blind to the possibilities of exceptional organizational effectiveness where people are motivated chiefly by love or a sense of responsibility.

The Communitarian Critique

Communitarianism is the conviction that humans are properly understood not as autonomous and self-interested individuals, but as social creatures, whole only in groups and devoted to others in those groups. For our—public policy—purposes, a community is an organization in which membership ordinarily draws people to seek the benefit of others.[32] The question is whether communities can be counted on to accomplish public services.

Communitarianism stands against the liberal idea that underlies the economic vision of society and therefore underlies the new economics of organization discussed in the second section of this chapter. Here *liberalism* takes its definition from its Latin root, *liber,* which means free. Liberalism—in the nineteenth-century understanding of the word, not the colloquial understanding of our time—is the idea that the autonomy or the freedom of the individual takes precedence over any meaning of social welfare, even over any conception of what is good in life. The critique of liberalism by contemporary communitarian philosophers, Alasdair Mac-

Intyre in the lead, is that community is necessary for the good life, but liberalism has given us instead loneliness, greed, and anomie.[33]

Four schools of communitarian thought, espousing four forms of community of varying usefulness for our purposes, can be identified.[34] The ideas of some of them are of little use for public policy, despite their considerable importance for other purposes or their attractiveness in a more utopian world. The first form of community can be termed inclusive; it rests on the notion that the whole country is or should be a community. When, in a celebrated speech at the 1984 Democratic national convention, Mario Cuomo pleaded for all to view the United States as a family, he was invoking inclusive communitarianism. However, the metaphor is fundamentally flawed. The United States is not a family. In large measure we need government because our relationships with others in the polity differ from our ties to family members. Inclusive communitarians wish for but have not found the moral equivalents of war, causes that fire the fervor of all. Devotees will continue to try to generate higher promptings in themselves and others, but inclusive community provides no consistently strong policy instrument. It is not capable of regularly and predictably producing social benefits, and its policy instrument, exhortation, carries nowhere near the power and pervasive influence of competition.

Robert Booth Fowler has rightly called republican community, a second form of community, a contested term.[35] For some it evokes an image of America prior to the drafting of the Constitution, when for a moment this country might have had an opportunity to see and define itself as a collection not of self-seeking individuals, but of pursuers of the common good. They lament an America that emerged from the constitutional era defined by the ideas of individualism, especially the Bill of Rights.[36] America became Lockean, liberal, verging on Hobbesian.[37] Its politics consist very largely of the clashes of interests, not a search for the public interest. It is that search, the devotion to the commonweal, that provides the usual meaning of republican community. We can think of this received understanding of republican community as a version of inclusive community, because its power, such as it is, rests in viewing a whole state or all of America as one cooperative group.

Historian John Patrick Diggins would say that inclusive and republican communitarians lack an "ethic of ultimate convictions."[38] At least for some people, the remaining two forms of community, participatory and mediating, are not subject to that observation. Participatory and mediating community also share another difference from inclusive and republican community: Participatory and mediating communities are not universal, but specific; they involve not the whole of the society, but rather the members of one's own group. It is to the little group that one gives intense, even categorical, loyalties.

Participatory community is a contemporary manifestation of a recurring American phenomenon: the countercultural attempt to create small organizations in which individuals can become lost in the group. As was the case in the past, today's participatory communitarians are inventive, romantic, angry, egalitarian. For them community is created by persons dissatisfied with existing social arrangements large and small, a substitute for traditional forms of family, religion, government, and business.[39] Participation potentially has the power to inspire members to engage consistently in behavior that demonstrates regard for others. To the extent it does so it constitutes a means by which society can dependably carry out public services.

Jane Mansbridge is the country's most astute observer of participatory community. Her observations are sobering. After being an admirer or member of a number of participatory groups (she mentions "free schools, food coops, law communes, women's centers, hot lines, and health clinics"[40]), she spent a decade studying such organizations and comparing them with the adversarial arrangements that characterize politics in the United States. In the end she concluded that participatory community does not present a model for an alternative form of national political life: "Democracies as large as the modern nation-state [must] be primarily adversarial democracies. This is a bitter conclusion. It means rejecting the vision of national unitary democracy where interests coincide naturally, through unselfishness or through the power of an idea."[41]

Mansbridge's moderated support for participatory community amounts to fond apostasy. She no longer sees participatory community as an object of categorical commitment. She now sees it, like the market, as predicated on "equally mixed motives,"[42] thereby, it seems to me, abandoning the argument that participatory community can be a repository of ultimate obligation and a font of consistently other-regarding behavior. Mansbridge effectively allows for no institutions in which devotion to the group is so strong as to become dominant in one's determination of the good.

The fourth form of community might be called mediating community. In 1977 Peter L. Berger and Richard John Neuhaus wrote a gem of a booklet, *To Empower People: The Role of Mediating Structures in Public Policy.*[43] For them mediating structures are those organizations between individuals and the "megastructures, . . . the large economic conglomerates of capitalist enterprise, big labor, and the growing bureaucracies . . . such as in education and the organized professions."[44] Their message is encapsulated in two propositions: "Public policy should protect and foster mediating structures, and wherever possible, public policy should utilize mediating structures for the realization of social purposes."[45]

The category described by Berger and Neuhaus, mediating structure, is broader than my mediating community. Their emphasis is on mediating (that is, on the group as buffer, intervenor); my emphasis here is on community (that is, on the group as the repository of commitment). Therefore, Berger and Neuhaus include neighborhoods and voluntary organizations along with families and religious organizations. In this section the critical question I am addressing is whether the altruistic ties within organizations are strong enough to engender consistently other-regarding behavior. Of course for much of what we do we have mixed motives. Still, the degree to which self-interest influences our actions varies. Even Gary Becker, the University of Chicago economist who has made a career of predicting the behavior of people on the assumption that they act self-interestedly, acknowledges that "altruism dominates family behavior perhaps to the same extent that selfishness dominates market transactions."[46] Berger and Neuhaus implicitly acknowledge that neighborhoods and clubs and even neighborhood schools have less of a hold on people than do families and religions when they emphasize the variety of neighborhoods, including those composed of people who welcome anonymity and lack of affiliation with others. These could hardly be said to demonstrate community.

We are looking for instances of mediating groups in which people are so powerfully and consistently drawn to care for one another as to be better able to provide some services now turned over to government bureaus. My favorite example is Minnesota's Family Subsidy Program. Some years ago while campaigning I met a woman who described to me an experimental program in which her family was participating. She and her husband have a severely retarded son who had been living at government expense in a state hospital. The state had offered to pay them $200 a month (the stipend is now $250) if they wished to have their child live at home. They accepted the offer. They have used the money to fence in their back yard, to buy a helmet to protect their child's fragile head, and even to pay someone to tend the boy while they take an occasional weekend away from their exhausting work. Here is an instance of state government's meeting a responsibility of a decent society, but doing so not through a bureau, but through a form of community, the family. Except perhaps for the public employees who previously attended the child, everyone is better off, including the taxpayers, whose cost has been cut by 90 percent. I successfully sponsored legislation to make the experimental program permanent.

Education and Mediating Communities

James Coleman and Thomas Hoffer have made a case that another kind of mediating community, religious schools, can be similarly more efficacious than government institutions.[47] Coleman and Hoffer have found that compared with public high school pupils—on each of whom society spends, on the average, half again as much money—students in religious schools do strikingly better.[48]

Of course it might be argued that the apparently superior effectiveness of religious schools is due rather to differences in the parents who choose them compared to the parents of public school children. Maybe parents of children in religious schools, who take on added expense and obligations on behalf of their children, also make the effort to provide an enriched home life that explains the relative educational success of their children. Coleman and Hoffer were aware of that possibility. They determined, however, that the differential effects of religious schools persisted even after they matched children as carefully as they could in order to remove the possible effects of selection bias.[49]

Recent research corroborates Coleman and Hoffer's rejection of selection bias as explaining the difference in effectiveness between public and religious schools. A more sophisticated study by William N. Evans and Robert M. Schab of the University of Maryland concluded that "for the typical student, attending a Catholic high school raises the probability of finishing high school or entering a four-year college by 12 percentage points," and that "there was almost no evidence that the . . . estimates [were] subject to selection bias."[50] Economist Derek Neal of the University of Chicago not only did not find positive selection bias, but conjectures that negative selection bias might have been present: "With respect to unobserved traits that enhance academic performance, the best students from upper and middle class homes may not be concentrated in Catholic schools but rather in elite public schools."[51]

The selection bias issue also raises the question of whether religious and other private schools are bringing a new segregation to education as enclaves come together to educate only their kind. In fact, however, middle-class flight from the major cities has left public schools in inner cities highly segregated. In his chapter in this volume, Jay Greene reports that on average private schools are now less segregated and racially more representative of their communities than are public schools. Indeed, private school students report more cross-racial friendships than do public school students.[52]

That the superior effectiveness of religious schools is not attributable to their receiving more easily educated students is not surprising. Evidently there is something in these schools in terms of community that often allows them to provide superior education.[53] Furthermore, one surmises that religious schools sometimes draw from parents as well as teachers increased attentiveness to children's educational progress. Community brings forth altruism.

There are organizations in which societal responsibilities are carried out better or less expensively than in bureaus or firms because, for whatever reason, people in them are drawn to help one another. For most people perhaps only family ties and religious ties (which represent "by far the most common associational membership among Americans"[54]) constitute community, but when other groups generate consistent other-regarding behavior, that is fine. Community becomes a possible instrument of policy, because community ordinarily causes people to act in ways that are beneficial to others; they need less inducement, compensation, supervision, and monitoring.

Using Community to Produce Services

The case for community provision of government-financed services is less straightforward than is the case for competition, because community does not embody a mechanism akin to that long recognized in the operation of competitive markets. Nevertheless, the American tradition of and penchant for individual choice, the bankruptcy of bureaucratic production, and the empirical evidence of the efficacy of community all point to the appropriateness of a large-scale shift by the states from bureaus to communities for the production of a variety of services. Four elements make up a policy of using community:

—Indirect government finance. Government funds go to individuals, who then choose a community from which to obtain their services. Of course, sometimes when recipient choice is infeasible government will contract directly with a community—for example, for education of orphans or persons who are mentally impaired.

—Nondistribution constraint. Unlike in private firms, members of the community cannot keep any profits that are generated. The value of a constraint on distribution of profits lies in its encouraging probity on the part of, and therefore trust in, any group subject to such a constraint. The more difficult it is to measure service quality and the less observable the processes of service provision, the more appropriate is the nondistribution constraint.

—Underfunding. Producing groups will object, but a policy of resorting to community entails providing less government funding than might be necessary to purchase services from a private firm. This is not in order to punish or even mainly to prod groups to be efficient, but rather to ensure that producers are in fact motivated by a sense of community, with members so inspired as to be willing to work for less than those situated in for-profit organizations.

—Independent monitoring.

The Complementarity of Competition and Community

What strikes one most when studying the policies of competition and community is their complementarity. America does not decide between competition and community, individuality and associativeness, but embraces both. Noticing the complementarity of choice and community helps one to identify a mistake sometimes made by persons attempting to describe how a policy of using community works. "All choice plans," writes Thomas J. Kane, "rely upon exit, or the threat of exit, as the primary means of sending the message to schools to improve."[55] Not necessarily. In this chapter I have illustrated the possibility of choosing community—that is, choosing to be a beneficiary of and a practitioner of altruism. Choice can foster loyalty and industry. It is not at all clear that the primary means by which schools improve when they are chosen is responding to the threat of exit.

Referring once again to table 3-1 yields an important observation. All of the policies in the first two categories, those that place choice in the hands of citizens and those that ensure a variety of choices, are consistent with a policy of community. That is, when government resorts to subsidizing individuals to enter competitive markets for education and other services, the possibility exists for both competitive pressures and community inspiration to work toward innovation and efficiency.

It can now be seen that table 3-1 amalgamates both competition and community. An agenda of competition and community for the provision of education calls for the establishment of three main policies: authorization for citizens to choose their schools, ensuring that they have choices, and, if citizen choice is infeasible, having government officials choose. Several precautions protect against bureaucratization and against schools' falsely presenting themselves as communities: indirect funding, nondistribution of profits, underfunding, a purchaser-producer split, and independent monitoring.

Summary

To this day elementary and secondary education in America has been carried out largely by government-owned monopoly bureaus. There is no theory, no explanation, of why satisfactory results should be expected from such an arrangement. Satisfactory education depends on incorporating into education policymaking what we know about governance—that is, it depends on adopting an agenda of competition and community. Using competition and community would entail the following:

—Directing more state money from government to individuals, less to school boards.

—Requiring arm's–length competitive arrangements between school boards and those from whom they buy services.

—Submitting public as well as private schools to competition.

—Educating children not necessarily in government-owned schools but in communities.

—In general, constituting government as arranger, funder, and monitor— but not necessarily as producer—of schooling.

The governance lessons for education are that government has major responsibilities, that when government owns and operates monopoly schools it frequently fails, and that two alternatives to bureaucratic public schools—competition and community—offer promise of better fulfilling those responsibilities.

Notes

1. The National Assessment of Educational Progress (NAEP), *Accelerating Academic Achievement: A Summary of Findings from 20 Years of NAEP* (Washington: U.S. Department of Education, 1990), p. 21; NAEP, *The Civics Report Card* (Washington: U.S. Department of Education, 1990), p. 8; NAEP, *Accelerating*, p. 22; NAEP, *The U.S. History Report Card* (Washington: U.S. Department of Education, 1990), p. 109; NAEP, *Accelerating*, p. 26; NAEP, *History*, p. 109; NAEP, *History*, p. 109.; NAEP, *Accelerating*, p. 26; NAEP, *Accelerating*, pp. 17–18; NAEP, *Civics*, p. 109; NAEP, *Civics*, p. 109; NAEP, *Accelerating*, p. 62; NAEP, *Accelerating*, p. 20; International Association for the Evaluation of Education Achievement, *The Underachieving Curriculum: Assessing U.S. School Mathematics from an International Perspective* (Urbana-Champaign: College of Education, University of Illinois, 1987), pp. vi, vii; David P. Baker, "Compared to Japan, the U.S. is a Low Achiever . . . Really: New

Evidence and Comment on Westbury," *Educational Researcher,* April 1993, p. 19; Linda Darling-Hammond, "Achieving Our Goals: Superficial or Structural Reforms?" *Phi Delta Kappan,* December 1990, p. 288; U.S. Department of Education, *Digest of Education Statistics* (Washington, 1991), pp. 383–85.

2. Gary Burtless, "Introduction," in Burtless, ed., *Does Money Matter?: The Effect of School Resources on Student Achievement and Adult Success* (Brookings, 1996), p. 21.

3. Allan Odden has compiled the state-by-state changes in real education spending for 1960–1990 in "Linkages Among School Reform, School Organization and School Finance," The Finance Center of The Consortium for Policy Research in Education, University of Southern California, Los Angeles, February 18, 1993.

4. Bureau of the Census, *Statistical Abstract of the United States 1995* (Washington: U.S. Department of Commerce), p. 175.

5. Eric Hanushek, "The Impact of Differential Expenditures on School Performance," *Educational Researcher,* May 1989, p. 47. The United States Department of Education has also found "no correlation between . . . input measures and student achievement." See "Measuring Educational Results," *State Policy Report* (Alexandria, Va.: State Policy Research, July 1989), p. 3.

6. See Larry V. Hedges, Richard D. Laine, and Rob Greenwald, "Does Money Matter? A Meta-analysis of Studies of the Effects of Differential School Inputs on Student Outcomes," *Educational Researcher,* vol. 23 (April 1994), pp. 5–14. See also an exchange between Hedges and others and Hanushek in *Educational Researcher,* vol. 23 (May 1994), pp. 5–8, 9–10.

7. See Stewart C. Purkey and Marshall S. Smith, "Effective Schools: A Review," *Elementary School Journal,* March 1983; W. E. Bickel, "Effective Schools: Knowledge, Dissemination, Inquiry," *Educational Researcher,* vol. 83, 12 (4), pp. 427–52, 1983; Herbert J. Walberg, "Educational Strategies That Work," *New Perspectives,* vol. 17 (Winter 1985), pp. 23–26; U.S. Department of Education, *What Works: Research About Teaching And Learning,* 2nd edition (Washington, 1987); and U.S. Department of Education, *Accelerating.*

8. See Marshall S. Smith and Jennifer O'Day, reported in Consortium for Policy Research in Education, "Equality in Education: Progress, Problems and Possibilities," *Policy Brief* (New Brunswick, N.J.: Rutgers University, undated); David W. Grissmer, Sheila Nataraj Kirby, Mark Berends, and Stephanie Williamson, *Student Achievement and the Changing American Family* (Santa Monica, Calif.: Rand, 1994), chapters 5 and 6. The Rand researchers surmise that perhaps federal programs that have targeted minority youth have had beneficial results, a hypothesis that deserves testing.

9. Smith and O'Day, "Equality,"p. 8.

10. Ronald Ferguson, "Racial Patterns in How School and Teacher Quality Affect Achievement and Earnings," (unpublished manuscript, John F. Kennedy School of Government, Harvard University, December 1990).

11. Ronald F. Ferguson and Helen F. Ladd, "How and Why Money Matters: An Analysis of Alabama Schools," in Ladd, ed., *Holding Schools Accountable* (Brookings, 1996), pp. 265–98.

12. Burtless, *Does Money Matter?,* p. 20, attributes this conjecture to Stephen Childs and Charol Shakeshaft.

13. U.S. Department of Education, *Digest of Education Statistics,* pp. 72, 88; and Hanushek.

14. Bureau of the Census, "Populations Projections of the U.S., By Age, Sex, Race, and Hispanic Origin: 1992 to 2050," (Washington, U.S. Department of Commerce, 1992), pp. vii, viii, 12, 28, 28, 29; *Statistical Abstract,* p. 151.

15. For definitions of a bureau see William A. Niskanen, *Bureaucracy and Representative Government* (Chicago: Aldine-Atherton, 1971), p. 15; John D. Donahue, *The Privatization Decision* (New York: Basic Books, 1989), p. 131; and Janet Rothenberg Pack, "The Opportunities and Constraints of Privatization," in William T. Gormley, Jr., ed., *Privatization and Its Alternatives* (Madison: University of Wisconsin Press, 1991), p. 292.

16. I refer here to what economists call neoclassical welfare economics, a term with little meaning for those not versed in the discipline.

17. For an expanded description of the positive theory of public interest regulation see Roger G. Noll, "Economic Perspectives on the Politics of Regulation," chapter 22 in Richard Schmalensee and Robert D. Willig, eds., *Handbook of Industrial Organization* (New York: North Holland, 1989). The argument of the positive theory of public interest regulation—that is, "a presumption of efficiency in political practices and public sector arrangements," has been termed the (University of) "Chicago Twist" by A. Breton in "Toward a Presumption of Efficiency in Politics," *Public Choice,* September 1993. pp. 53–65.

18. See P. Dasgupta and J. E. Stiglitz, "Potential Competition, Actual Competition and Economic Welfare," *European Economic Review,* Vol. 32, March 1988, pp. 569–77.

19. See Woodrow Wilson, "The Study of Administration," *Political Science Quarterly,* Vol. 56, December 1941, pp. 481–506 (originally published in 1887) and Max Weber, *The Theory of Social and Economic Organization* (New York: Free Press, 1964).

20. Max Weber, "Bureaucracy," in H. H. Gerth and C. Wright Mills, eds., *Max Weber: Essays in Sociology* (New York: Oxford University Press, 1958), p. 214.

21. James Coleman, *Foundations of Social Theory* (Harvard University Press, 1990), p. 423.

22. Terry Moe seems to have invented the term *the new economics of organization.* See Moe's "The New Economics of Organization," *American Journal of Political Science,* Vol. 28, November 1984, pp. 739–77. The theories referred to encompass several subdisciplines, including rational choice theory as it is applied to both public and private sectors (that is, both public choice theory and property rights theory), agency theory, and transaction cost analysis. In all of those theories people are understood as "rent seeking." A rent is a payment for a resource in excess of opportunity cost—that is, over and above the highest valued use to which the resource could be put. Therefore, rent seeking is effort devoted to getting from someone else more for a resource than it is worth. The term is usually applied to efforts to get benefits from government—that is, from persons who make payments from other people's funds, not their own.

23. See Bernard Grofman and Donald Wittman, eds., *The Federalist Papers and the New Institutionalism* (New York: Agathon Press, 1989).

24. See Alexander Hamilton, James Madison, and John Jay, *The Federalist Papers* (New York: New American Library, 1961), no. 51, p. 322.

25. See Jerry Z. Muller, *Adam Smith in His Time and Ours: Designing the Decent Society* (New York: Macmillan, 1993).

26. Recently several large sectors of the U.S. economy experienced increased competition after the federal government took deregulatory actions. Empirical estimates of the efficiency savings for the economy find little or no savings in the cable television and brokerage industries, but very large savings in the airline, railroad, and trucking industries. See Clifford Winston, "Economic Deregulation: Days of Reckoning for Microeconomists," *Journal of Economic Literature,* September 1993, vol. 31, p. 1284 (inclusion pages and 1263–89). Winston describes deregulation as "one of the most important experiments in economic policy of our time" (p. 1263) and concludes that "the evidence clearly shows that microeconomists' predictions that

deregulation would produce substantial benefits for Americans have been generally accurate" (p. 1287).

27. Some economists argue that there is an inherent tendency toward improved efficiency in privatization. See, for example, Maxim Boycko, Andrei Shleifer, and Robert W. Vishny, "A Theory of Privatization," *The Economic Journal,* Vol. 106, March 1996, pp. 309–19. They write: "Privatization of public enterprises can raise the cost to politicians of influencing them, since subsidies to private firms necessary to force them to remain inefficient are politically harder to sustain than wasted profits of the state firms. In this way privatization leads to efficient restructuring of firms" (p. 309).

28. See Howard Davies, *Fighting Leviathan: Building Social Markets That Work* (London: Social Market Foundation, 1992).

29. See Paul E. Peterson's introductory chapter in this volume.

30. A public good is one that if consumed or enjoyed by one person, remains entirely available to others. For example, under some circumstances any of the following can be a public good: police protection, the services of a lighthouse, language, the products of research, a concert, generosity. In *Collective Action: Theory and Applications* (Ann Arbor: University of Michigan Press, 1992), p. 196, Todd Sandler summarizes the conditions under which members of a large group might agree to produce a public good. He writes: "Successful instances of collective action appear to have one or more of the following features: (a) private or excludable joint products, (b) a pattern of payoffs favorable to dominate players, (c) an exclusion mechanism coupled with a toll scheme, or (d) repeated interactions among players." All of his examples, distilled from the literature of recent decades on the economics of collective action, assume self-interested behavior, so they all entail situations in which individuals are able to reap benefits for themselves in excess of the costs they incur (otherwise, under the logic of contemporary economics, they would not undertake the actions).

Economists sometimes try to subsume altruism into their calculus by assuming that altruists gain satisfaction from benefiting others. In *A Treatise on the Family* (Harvard University Press, 1981), p. 174, Gary Becker writes: "Since an altruist maximizes his own utility . . . he might be called selfish, not altruistic." Such a construction is circular, unhelpful. In this chapter we are seeking situations in which persons, motivated by love or duty, undertake actions benefiting others. In those cases the costs to themselves might exceed the benefits to themselves. See Samuel P. Oliner and Pearl M. Oliner, *The Altruistic Personality: Rescuers of Jews in Nazi Europe* (New York: The Free Press, 1988) for numerous examples. The Oliners are concerned with people who risk life and livelihood to help others, taking actions that can be explained by invoking altruism. Daniel M. Hausman and Michael S. McPherson, in a review of the relationship between economics and ethics—an essay that is generally sympathetic with the views of neoclassical economics—conclude that "the view of rationality economists endorse—utility theory—may not even be compatible with moral behavior, and it does not provide a rich enough picture of individual choice to permit one to discuss the character, causes, and consequences of moral behavior" (in "Taking Ethics Seriously: Economics and Contemporary Moral Philosophy," *The Journal of Economic Literature,* Vol. 31, June 1993), p. 688.

31. Robert H. Frank seems to delight in listing such everyday behavior, which economics is at a loss to explain. See, for example, his "Melding Sociology and Economics: James Coleman's *Foundations of Social Theory,*" *Journal of Economic Literature,* March 1992, p. 153.

32. The customary definition of a community is an organization whose members perceive their ends as common. See Allen E. Buchanan, "Assessing the Communitarian Critique of Liberalism," *Ethics,* Vol. 99, July 1989, pp. 852–82, and references there. I prefer the definition given earlier in the text, because I wish to emphasize the possibility

of government's using communities to bring benefits to some persons by encouraging the community membership of others.

33. See Alasdair MacIntyre, *After Virtue: A Study in Moral Theory* (Notre Dame, Ind.: University of Notre Dame Press, 1981), pp. 204–205. More recently MacIntyre has written, "In spite of rumors to the contrary, I am not and never have been a communitarian." See "I'm Not a Communitarian, but . . . ," *The Responsive Community: Rights and Responsibilities,* Summer 1991, p. 91. Despite his declaration, I term him a communitarian and for two reasons: His is a communitarian critique of liberalism, and he wishes for a more communitarian society (but believes that to be most unlikely). He fears that communitarian efforts could backfire into totalitarianism. The reason he rejects being called a communitarian is that current conditions in America and the West are so wretchedly libertarian as to "exclude the possibility of realizing any of the worthwhile types of political community which at various times in the past have been achieved" (p. 91).

34. The following owes much to Robert Booth Fowler's classification and discussion of communitarian thought, though some of my categories are different from his, and readers will detect differences in our understandings of republican community. See Fowler's *The Dance with Community: The Contemporary Debate in American Political Thought* (Lawrence: University Press of Kansas, 1991).

35. Fowler, *Dance with Community,* p. 64.

36. See Gordon S. Wood, *The Creation of the American Republic 1776–1787* (New York: Norton, 1972); Robert N. Bellah, Richard Madsen, William M. Sullivan, Ann Swidler, and Steven M. Tipton, *Habits of the Heart: Individualism and Commitments in American Life* (Berkeley: University of California Press, 1985); and J. G. A. Pocock, *The Machiavellian Moment: Florentine Political Thought and the Atlantic Republican Tradition* (Princeton University Press, 1975).

37. Locke himself was no celebrator of unbridled self-interest. He "condemn[ed] the unregulated pursuit of self-interest that Hobbes considered natural" (James T. Kloppenberg, "The Virtues of Liberalism: Christianity, Republicanism, and Ethics in Early American Political Discourse," *The Journal of American History,* June 1987, p. 16). Locke wrote: "He that has not a mastery over his inclinations . . . he that knows not how to resist the importunity of present pleasure, or pain, for the sake of what reason tells him, is fit to be donne, wants the true principle of Vertue, and industry; and is in danger never to be good for anything" (quoted in Kloppenberg, "The Virtues," p. 16). Kloppenberg sees religion, classical republicanism, and liberalism all as having influenced the founders of the American republic. All require individuals to be subject to constraints on self-interest. Indeed, Kloppenberg writes (p. 29) that "laissez faire liberalism was not present at the creation of the American republic but emerged over the course of the nation's first hundred years."

38. Diggins, *The Lost Soul of American Politics: Virtue, Self-Interest, and the Foundation of Liberalism* (University of Chicago Press, 1984), p. 296. Cited in Fowler, *The Dance,* p. 131.

39. See especially Roberto M. Unger, *Politics: A Work in Constructive Social Theory* (Cambridge University Press, 1987).

40. Mansbridge, *Beyond Adversary Democracy* (New York: Basic Books, 1980), p. vii.

41. Mansbridge, *Beyond Adversary Democracy,* p. 293.

42. Mansbridge, *Beyond Self-Interest* (University of Chicago Press, 1990), p. xiii.

43. Washington, D.C.: American Enterprise Institute for Public Policy Research.

44. Berger and Neuhaus, *To Empower People,* p. 2.

45. Berger and Neuhaus, *To Empower People,* p. 6.

46. Becker, *A Treatise,* p. 195.

47. James S. Coleman and Thomas Hoffer, *Public and Private High Schools: The Impact of Communities* (New York: Basic Books, 1987). As will be seen a bit later, Coleman and Hoffer find differences in the efficacy of public and Catholic schools. These differences, they conclude, are not due to Catholicism in particular, but to the community found in some religious schools.

48. Coleman and Hoffer, *Public and Private High Schools,* p. 213.

49. Coleman and Hoffer, *Public and Private High Schools,* pp. 33, 212, 213, 219.

50. William N. Evans and Robert M. Schab, "Finishing High School and Starting College: Do Catholic Schools Make a Difference?" (unpublished manuscript, Department of Economics, University of Maryland, College Park, November 1993), p. i.

51. Neal, "The Effect of Catholic Secondary Schooling on Educational Attainment," Working Paper 5353 (Cambridge, Mass.: National Bureau of Economic Research, November 1995), p. 25.

52. See Jay P. Greene's chapter in this volume.

53. Others have also discerned efficacy in community. See Anthony S. Bryk, Valerie E. Lee, and Peter B. Holland, *Catholic Schools and the Common Good* (Harvard University Press, 1993); Nathan Glazer, "American Public Education, The Relevance of Choice," *Phi Delta Kappan,* Vol. 74, April 1993, pp. 647–50; and Paul Hill, Gail E. Foster, and Tamar Gendler, "High Schools With Character," Rand Report R-3944-RC (Santa Monica, Calif.: The Rand Corporation, 1990).

54. Robert Putnam, "Bowling Alone, Revisited," *The Responsive Community,* Spring 1995, p. 22.

55. Kane, "Comments on Chapters Five and Six," in Ladd, ed., *Holding Schools Accountable,* p. 209.

FOUR

Civic Values in Public and Private Schools

Jay P. Greene

PUBLIC AND PRIVATE SCHOOLS evoke certain images in most people's minds. We tend to imagine private schools as elite, predominantly white, institutions for the affluent. Whatever their academic merits, private schools are not thought to provide experience or instruction that promote integration, tolerance, or public spiritedness, values we desire in citizens of a democratic country. Private schools are said to be separate institutions, serving families with separate values. Public schools, on the other hand, are imagined to be "the common school" envisioned by Horace Mann more than a century ago, mixing people of all races, classes, and origins. According to this vision, public schools take people from all backgrounds and make Americans of them, teaching tolerance and a commitment to the public good.

Although these perceptions of public and private schools are difficult to shake, the evidence is becoming clear that public and private schools are not what we imagine them to be. An analysis of data from the National Education Longitudinal Study (NELS) suggests that private schools are

Research assistance was provided by Brett Kleitz, Jongho Lee, and Nicole Mellow. Support for this project was provided by grants from the Program on Education Policy and Governance at Harvard University, the Public Policy Clinic in the Department of Government at the University of Texas, the University of Houston, the Bradley Foundation, and Larry Bernstein.

83

doing a better job than public schools of integrating students of different races, teaching them tolerance, and imparting a sense of public spiritedness. These analyses confirm and improve upon earlier work based on the High School and Beyond data set. The picture that is emerging from these data is that private schools are at least as capable as public schools of producing good citizens. Providing parents with public funds they can use to send their children to private schools is unlikely to harm our democratic values—and it may, in fact, strengthen them.

The Theory

A system of universal, publicly operated schools was developed in the nineteenth century, in large part to ensure the dissemination of desired values to new generations of citizens. The debate in the eighteenth and nineteenth centuries, however, was primarily about whether education should be publicly financed and universally required, not whether schools should be government operated. With the notable exceptions of Thomas Paine and John Stuart Mill, who argued that the government should pay for education but allow families to choose who should provide it, most writers on the topic assumed that the government would run schools.[1] Thomas Jefferson, Alexis de Toqueville, Horace Mann, and John Dewey all emphasized the importance of universal education in promoting the civic values necessary for a successful democracy.[2] Motivated by the powerful arguments these thinkers advanced, and motivated in part by concerns about the civic values possessed by waves of primarily Catholic immigrants, universal public education became policy throughout the United States by the start of the twentieth century.[3]

Universal education has clearly produced benefits for U.S. democracy and productivity. The question is whether those benefits depend on government operation of schools to be achieved. Upon any investigation to answer this question, one quickly encounters a strong, emotional attachment to public education. People commonly report that they believe in public education, regardless of whether they actually send their children to public school (examples include President Bill Clinton, Vice President Al Gore, and many members of Congress).[4] People do not similarly say that they believe in the county hospital, even if they believe in universal access to health care. The government operation of schools has achieved its place in our secular faith in much the same way that the Constitution and the flag have.

To question the importance of government operation of schools in producing desired democratic values, therefore, verges on secular blasphemy. If *secular blasphemy* seems too strong, consider these comments from leading political theorist Benjamin Barber: "In attacking not just education, but *public* education, critics are attacking the very foundation of our democratic civic culture. Public schools are not merely schools *for* the public, but schools of publicness: institutions where we learn what it means to *be* a public and start down the road towards common national and civic identity. As forges of our citizenship, they are the bedrock of our democracy."[5] These sentiments were echoed recently by Secretary of Education Richard Riley in his response to school choice proposals:

> Quality public schools are the foundation of a democracy and a free enterprise economic system. Therein lies the power of the American system of education—it is truly public. The "common school"—the concept upon which our public school system was built—teaches children important lessons about both the commonality and diversity of American culture. These lessons are conveyed not only through what is taught in the classroom, but by the very experience of attending school with a diverse mix of students. The common school has made quality public education and hard work the open door to American success and good citizenship and the American way to achievement and freedom.[6]

As can be seen, the level of emotional attachment to publicly operated schools is very high.

To pound the table and beat one's chest proclaiming that public schools benefit democracy, however, does not make it so. This claim requires empirical support. Do public schools actually produce students who are more publicly spirited than private schools? Are public schools really closer to the ideal of the common schools, with superior integration to that found in private schools? As we shall see later in this chapter, these claims are not supported by the evidence.

Democratic Values Are a Process, Not an Outcome

There are, however, strong theoretical arguments for the importance of publicly operated schools in promoting democratic values. In her influential book *Democratic Education,* Amy Gutmann argues that one cannot determine the desirability of school choice in promoting democratic values based on the extent to which students in public and private schools possess desired values, or, as she puts it, "on consequentialist grounds."[7] She even concedes the empirical observation that private schools are better at teaching what most of us would recognize as democratic values: "The evidence is scanty, but it suggests that private schools may on average do better than public schools in bringing all their students up to a relatively high level of learning, in teaching American history and civics in an intellectually challenging manner, and even in racially integrating classrooms."[8]

The difficulty with granting individual parents control over educational choices, Gutmann argues, is that we cannot know what democratic values we would like to see taught in schools until we have engaged in democratic deliberations about what those values are. "The problem with voucher plans," she writes, "is not that they leave too much room for parental choice but that they leave too little room for democratic deliberation."[9] The only way to ensure "our collective interests in the moral education of future citizens" is to leave the determination of education policy under public control instead of granting control to individual parents.[10]

In essence, Gutmann's argument seems to be that democratic values are whatever democratic processes decide—that is, unless they decide the wrong thing. To be fair, Gutmann is willing to allow a local school board to choose policies that are foolish "as long as the school board institutes nonrepressive and nondiscriminatory policies."[11] The trouble is that virtually all important school policies run the risk of being claimed to be either repressive or discriminatory. Does teaching a given set of values repress those students who do not share those values? Does failing to teach those values discriminate against the students who would want them taught? Any local school board decision of any importance to the democratic education of future citizens is going to raise questions about discrimination and repression.

If the democratic deliberations and processes of the local school board can be trumped when discrimination or repression occurs, who in Gutmann's opinion should review the actions of the local governing majority? The appeals process appears to go up and down. Above the local school board, national majorities and ultimately national judges monitor the repressive and discriminatory potential of local decisions. Below the school board, teaching professionals and their unions act as guardians of "nonrepression" and "nondiscrimination."[12]

Since almost all decisions made by local school boards related to civic values raise questions of repression or discrimination and since the ultimate arbitrators of the validity of local decisions are unelected federal judges and unelected teaching professionals and their unions, the primacy that Gutmann at first gives to the outcomes of local democratic deliberation quickly shifts to the primacy of unelected elites judging the expected consequences of local policies. Taken to its logical conclusion, Gutmann's view is rather undemocratic and relies heavily on consequentialist arguments. Her rejection of school choice because it involves too little democratic deliberation appears inconsistent with the frequency and ease with which the important decisions of local democratic deliberation could be overturned by unelected elites according to her idea.

In case the role of unelected elites seems exaggerated in my retelling of Gutmann's argument, notice that almost half of *Democratic Education* consists of arguments about the policies that local majorities either must adopt or cannot adopt. Local majorities cannot ban books, even to promote desired civic values. They can make decisions about adopting books for libraries and classrooms, but deciding whether books have been excluded because of legitimate limits on space or because of discriminatory or repressive reasons is a responsibility that ultimately belongs to unelected federal judges and teaching professionals.[13] Local majorities cannot decide to teach creationism, even if the decision is the product of democratic deliberation, because creationism represents a repressive imposition of religion on others. (Apparently this argument is stronger in Gutmann's estimation than concerns about the repression of excluding creationism from being taught to religious minorities who prefer this approach.)[14]

Local majorities, Gutmann argues, are obligated to take active steps to eradicate sexism by attempting to hire additional women administrators and by altering the content of their curricula.[15] They are also required to ensure equality of opportunity, meaning that they must "use education to raise the life chances of the least advantaged (as far as possible) up to those of the most advantaged."[16] Local majorities are also constrained in their democratic deliberations to promote racial integration in schools.[17] And, to ensure that these local majorities have the resources to meet all of these requirements, school funding should increasingly come from state and federal sources.[18]

What Gutmann advocates is not simply a process of democratic deliberation void of concerns about outcomes. In fact, it is clear that she really begins with outcomes, namely "nonrepression" and "nondiscrimination," and then allows for local democratic deliberation on whatever is left over. If the requirements of nonrepression and nondiscrimination are as constraining on local deliberation as they appear to be, the loss of some democratic deliberation in allowing school choice should hardly be worrisome as long as the goals of nonrepression and nondiscrimination are being met. In other words, it would be fair to assess school choice based on its consequences relative to these two goals and not reject it simply for removing one layer of democratic deliberation. The choices of parents and the activities of schools could still be regulated in a school choice system by democratic majorities who would choose their regulations in a deliberative way to ensure nonrepression and nondiscrimination. In this way school choice could be allowed while still permitting democratic deliberation and some public control to achieve the goals of nonrepression and nondiscrimination.

Public Schools Encourage Political Participation

A related concern is that public governance of schools teaches parents and other concerned adults about how to participate in a democratic process. The public school is the democratic institution in which more adults are likely to participate in some way than in any other institution of government. Giving parents vouchers with which they can alter education policies more easily by exiting a school than by participating in a democratic process to alter policies with voice might deprive parents of this important lesson in political participation. (*Exit* and *voice* are terms developed by Albert O. Hirschman.)[19] As one critic of school choice put it: "It is precisely because a public school system limits 'shopping' that it encourages parents to think like citizens. Since they are 'stuck' in a particular school district, they have very strong incentives to exercise their political skills to make it better. And, because it is a *public* school, they are guaranteed the right to exercise those skills."[20]

This is a somewhat peculiar notion of how to develop good citizens. Following this logic, it might be desirable to have the government produce a steady stream of frustrating policies to help citizens develop their skills in participating in altering those policies. Of course it is also possible that a steady stream of frustrating policies might alienate citizens, discouraging them from participating politically. Similarly, frustrating public school policies may alienate more than they cultivate political participation.

It should also be remembered that exit is an important way in which many citizens, especially advantaged ones, change their public school opportunities. Many people, especially those with sufficient resources, choose where they live based on the desirability of public school policies and outcomes. If those education policies turn out to be undesirable, those with means can move to other public school districts. In this sense some people are not stuck in public schools that force them to participate to improve the schools. Conversely, it should be remembered that many privately operated schools experience high levels of participation in the formulation and implementation of school policies. Simply because people can exit private schools does not mean that voice is not available to them or even encouraged by the schools. In fact, many people may choose private schools precisely because they are more receptive to participation.

These are empirical issues. Do public schools actually solicit more participation from parents than private schools? Does any democratic benefit for parents come at the expense of the democratic values taught to students? Theory alone cannot determine the effects of public and private schooling on participation. Mark Schneider and colleagues have recently found that giving parents a choice about their children's education actually increases participation and enhances social capital.[21]

Choice Makes Consumers, Not Citizens

A third argument against the democratic effects of school choice is that choice makes consumers, not citizens. Giving parents the ability to choose a school only encourages them to focus on self-interest at the expense of concern for the common good. As Jonathan Kozol put it: "[Choice] will fragmentize ambition, so that the individual parent will be forced to claw and scramble for the good of her kid and her kid only, at whatever cost to everybody else."[22] Public schools apparently restrain our self-interest and cultivate public spiritedness.

Like the other theoretical arguments, these claims ultimately depend on empirical support. One can know whether it is true that private schooling encourages selfishness while public schooling encourages altruism only by examining the evidence. None exists to support this claim. Even the logic of this argument is puzzling. Must there be a trade-off between being a consumer, or even being self-interested, and being a good citizen? The credit card balances of millions of Americans suggests that it is possible to be both.

Besides, many government benefits in other areas are provided by means of vouchers, with recipients acting as consumers. Medicare, for example, is essentially a voucher system for health care. The government will pay for a patient's triple bypass surgery, but the patient gets to choose the doctor, the hospital (public or private, religious or secular), and even to some extent the procedure to be used. Food stamps and rent subsidies are issued by similar voucher programs. The government pays for some housing and food, and the recipient chooses (within limits) what housing to take and what food to buy. Do we believe that medicare, food stamps, and rent subsidies encourage selfishness or undermine the common good by allowing recipients to be consumers? Would it be preferable on democratic grounds to require that seniors receive health care in government hospitals from appointed doctors or that poor citizens be required to live in government-owned housing and eat in government-run soup kitchens? These scenarios seem absurd, but it is not clear how their democratic implications differ from requiring children to attend geographically zoned government-operated schools if they want to receive government-paid education.

A Theory of the Civic Value Benefits of School Choice

There are no well-developed theoretical arguments as to why either school choice or privately operated schools should be desirable on democratic grounds. In part this is because school choice advocates have generally ceded this ground to their opponents. They either suggest that school choice raises democratic concerns, but these are outweighed by expected achievement gains, or they deny any public stake in the values taught by schools, arguing that school choice is purely a matter of parental rights. However, there are theoretical reasons for believing that private schools should be associated with more desirable civic values than public schools. There is not space to develop a full argument along these lines, but the following illustrates the tack that such an argument might take.

First, one might expect private schools to do a better job of teaching democratic values because they simply do a better job of teaching. Whatever qualities may make private schools better able to teach math and reading may also make them better able to teach the lessons of civics. By providing access to higher-quality private education, school choice may also provide access to higher-quality democratic education.

Second, privately operated schools may help develop important civic values, such as tolerance, by creating the strong identity and self-esteem that are frequently associated with greater tolerance. Private schooling and school choice allow parents more easily to raise their children with their preferred identities and values. Some critics point to this as evidence of the "Balkanization" that they fear private schooling could encourage. Curiously, authors sometimes express the advantage of public education in forging a "common national and civic identity" while at the same time stressing that "respect for our differences . . . is the secret to our strength as a nation, and is the key to democratic education."[23] Clearly it is desirable to enhance both national and particular identities. Enhancing national identity is not at odds with enhancing particular identity; in fact, considerable research on tolerance suggests that stronger self-esteem produced by a strong identity can be associated with greater tolerance for others.[24] If one is comfortable with who one is, one is more likely to allow others to be who they are.

Private education and school choice is more likely than public education and lack of choice to contribute to stronger self-identities and self-esteem. Being able to choose a Catholic education makes it easier to have a strong Catholic identity. Access to a Jewish education is likely to contribute to a stronger Jewish identity. Blacks who seek an Afrocentric curriculum may develop stronger identities as African Americans. Not everyone is likely to choose schools that reinforce particular ethnic or religious identities. Many will choose schools that emphasize particular subject areas or that teach using certain techniques. Schools that emphasize the arts, for example, may reinforce people's identities as artists, and schools that emphasize Montessori methods of teaching may allow people to more strongly identify with other believers in Montessori approaches. The difficulty with some public education is that it is provided using a one-size-fits-none approach. Choosing a private education can allow families more closely to match needs, values, and identities with the offerings of various schools. By allowing students to feel better about themselves by giving them a clearer picture of who they are, private schools may produce students who are more likely to tolerate others than are public school students.

But when can students learn to be American? This is the wrong question for a number of reasons. First, it implies that there is a tension between being a good American and being a strong Catholic, Jew, African American, artist, or fan of Montessori approaches. This question bears a striking resemblance to the questions posed to John Kennedy about whether he could really be a good Catholic and a good president at the same time. Second, it implies that the development of a person's religious, ethnic, or other identity is something that should be done in one's spare time. It implies that at school students should learn neutral abilities or develop general identities as Americans. In the rest of their time (which is remarkably short relative to school) they can learn about their religious, ethnic, or other identities. Those matters are thought to be private and superfluous, like hobbies that people may indulge when otherwise not occupied. If we really believe in respecting our diversity, we have to allow people to develop their particular identities more than we would allow them to develop a devotion to fishing. If skeptics fear that there would then be nothing left to hold us together as a country, they need only look at the incredibly powerful homogenizing influences in our society, from fashion to entertainment to shared electoral institutions.

A third theoretical benefit of providing parents with the resources to choose a private education in terms of democratic values is that private schooling can transcend segregation in housing. Public schools draw their students from within politically shaped boundaries. Some of these boundaries were drawn to segregate people of different races and backgrounds,[25] but others, once drawn, encourage people to segregate themselves for fear of being on the "wrong" side of the line.[26] By attaching people's single largest asset, a house, to where their children go to school, public schools have made people even more cautious about mixing with other groups. People are afraid to buy a home in an area that would send their children to public schools with students of different backgrounds because the consequences of failure in their effort at integration extend beyond problems with education to a loss of value in their highly leveraged, single largest asset.

Private schools may help reduce this cautiousness about mixing by reducing the consequences of failure. If parents dislike the effects of integration they suffer only the inconvenience of finding a different school, not the financial blow of lower property values. Private schools may also provide overarching categories of association that may bridge racial and ethnic differences. Catholic schools may more easily mix students of different racial and ethnic backgrounds because they may share a common identity as Catholics. A private school devoted to emphasizing a certain subject or approach may similarly allow people of different racial and ethnic backgrounds to mix more easily because families can share their common devotion to that subject or approach. By basing the student mix on voluntary association rather than housing, private schools may make people more comfortable with integration. With better integration in private schools may come other civic values, such as tolerance.

Whether providing parents with public funds to choose private schools detracts from or promotes democratic values is not something that can be determined theoretically. The theoretical arguments against private schooling are not logically compelling and are even less persuasive given their lack of supporting evidence. And although the arguments in favor of the positive democratic effects of private education are plausible, they also require supporting evidence. Are private schools and their students actually characterized by higher levels of integration, greater degrees of tolerance, and a stronger commitment to the common good? These are the questions addressed in the next section.

The Evidence

The evidence presented here focuses on four issues: racial integration in public and private schools, race relations and tolerance, volunteering and commitment to community, and general self-assessments of effectiveness in teaching civic values. The data are taken from the National Education Longitudinal Study (NELS). This study was sponsored by the Department of Education and surveyed a representative national sample of twelfth graders in 1992. In addition, surveys were administered to the students' parents, teachers, and school administrators. NELS was not designed primarily to assess the values taught in public and private schools, but within the vast amount of information that was collected are a number of items that shed light on these issues. NELS has information on the racial composition of schools, some questions related to racial tolerance, and some items on volunteering activity and general public spiritedness. Some of the survey items measure the quality of civic education indirectly and imperfectly, but from all of the data it is possible to obtain a general picture of the democratic values taught in public and private schools.

Earlier Research on Integration in Public and Private Schools

Evidence began replacing imagination of the nature of public and private schools with the collection and analysis of the High School and Beyond data set in the 1980s. Little information that directly measured students' tolerance or public spiritedness was obtained, but considerable data were collected on the integration of racial groups in public and private schools. Coleman and colleagues reported, based on the High School and Beyond data, that private schools, on average, educate a smaller percentage of minority students than public schools do on average. But they also found that the distribution of minority students in the private sector was less segregated than the distribution in public schools.[27] Greeley and Bryk and associates similarly reported lower average percentages of minority students in Catholic schools, which constitute the majority of all private schools, but better integration of those fewer minorities within the Catholic school system than in public schools.[28] Coleman and colleagues, Greeley, and Bryk and associates also observed better educational outcomes for minorities in private schools than for their public school counterparts. Coleman and colleagues further estimated that the racial and class integration within private schools would improve if economic barriers to private school attendance were reduced via vouchers or tuition tax credits.[29] More recently Chubb and Moe examined data from NELS, which was the successor to High School and Beyond.[30] They found that private schools engage in less tracking and ability grouping, which improves the diversity of students within private schools and may improve educational outcomes for minority students.

These findings have been subjected to a variety of critiques. Braddock and Taeubur and James, for example, objected to the distinction that Coleman and colleagues made between segregation within public and private schools and segregation across public and private school sectors.[31] They argued that the fact that minorities within the private school sector are more evenly distributed than minorities in the public schools is more than outweighed by the fact that the average percentage of minority students educated by private schools is lower than in public schools. In aggregate, they argued, private schools contribute to segregation by acting as a haven for whites fleeing racially integrated public schools. Taeuber and James suggested that "segregation should be examined within specific administrative and geographic settings" rather than separately within public and private school sectors, taking the proportion of minorities in each as a given.[32]

The claims of Coleman and colleagues, Greeley, Bryk and associates, and Chubb and Moe that educational outcomes are better for minorities in private schools have been subjected to the same type of criticism as the more general claim that private schools produce better outcomes for comparable students than do public schools. Murnane, Goldberger and Cain, Willms, Alexander and Pallas, and Smith and Meier, among others, have argued that the apparent superiority of private school outcomes may be largely attributable to the selection of academically advantaged students for admission to private schools.[33] Attempts to control for known differences between the characteristics of students who attend public and private schools have been plagued by the possibility that unknown differences may have been producing the better outcomes in private schools. Recent evidence from the random assignment to public and private schools in the school choice experiment in Milwaukee, however, lends strength to the conclusion that the superior performance of students in private schools is not simply a function of the type of students in private schools.[34] Since the Milwaukee analyses involved only black and Hispanic students, these studies specifically supported the claim that minority academic achievement is better in private schools.

New Evidence from NELS on Integration in Public and Private Schools

The debate on racial segregation in public and private schools during the 1980s stalled over a disagreement about the appropriate question to ask: Is it more important to focus on the distribution of racial and ethnic groups within the public and private school sectors or on the distribution across those sectors? Those who concentrated on the distribution within the public and private systems found private schools to be a positive force for racial integration. Those who focused on the distribution of racial and ethnic groups across the public and private sectors found private schools to be a hindrance to racial integration because of the shortage of minorities in those schools.

I have developed a measure of integration that avoids this dispute between within-sector and across-sector integration by rephrasing the question altogether. The more relevant question for measuring integration is this: Are private school students in classrooms that are more likely to be representative of the proportion of minorities in the nation than are public school students? If, on average, private school students have classes that more closely reflect the ethnic composition of the nation than do public schools, we can say that private schools are more integrated. Comparing the racial mix students experience in their classrooms to the mix nationally should identify any "white flight" across sectors while at the same time incorporating the important segregating effect of distribution within sectors.

Two variables addressed in NELS help measure the integration in public and private schools.[35] In 1992 teachers were asked to identify the number of minority students (black, Hispanic, or Asian) and the total number of students in their classes. Dividing the former by the latter gives the percentage of minority students in each class. This "classmix" variable is nice, because it measures the racial percentages of students in classrooms, not in schools. If, as Chubb and Moe (1996) argued, tracking students in public schools may segregate students within schools, measuring the racial composition at the school level may not accurately describe the more important experience of sharing classes with students of other races and ethnicities.

According to NELS, the national average percentage of minority students in twelfth-grade classrooms in 1992 was 25.6 percent. The average percentage of minority students in public schools was 26.2 percent, whereas the average proportion in private schools was 20.7 percent. From these numbers one might (falsely) conclude that public school students were in classes that had racial mixes that were more representative of the national average than were private school students. But by looking at the distribution

Table 4-1. *Distribution of Public and Private School*
Students in Classes with Different Percentages of
Minority Students, 1992[a]

Percentage minority students in class	Public school students	Private school students
0–5	32.2	26.0
5–10	13.9	12.4
10–15	8.8	9.6
15–20	7.9	16.5
20–25	4.5	5.8
25–30	2.9	11.1
30–35	3.0	3.2
35–40	2.5	3.3
40–45	1.7	2.3
45–50	2.8	1.4
50–55	1.0	0.4
55–60	1.4	0.4
60–65	1.1	0.8
65–70	1.3	0.8
70–75	1.7	0.3
75–80	2.1	2.3
80–85	1.1	0.2
85–90	1.8	0.6
90–95	2.3	0.1
95–100	6.1	2.6

Source: Author's analysis of data from U.S. Department of Education, National
Center for Education Statistics, *National Education Longitudinal Study,* 1992.

a. The national average of the percentage of minority students in classrooms is
25.6 percent. All analyses were performed using a sample weighted by the NELS
variable F2CXTWT to ensure its representativeness.

of the percentage of minority students in public and private classrooms, it
becomes clear that in 1992 private school students were more likely to be in
integrated classrooms.[36]

As can be seen in table 4-1, 36.6 percent of private school students were
in classrooms that were within roughly 10 percent of the national average
percentage of minority enrollment. That is, more than a third of private
school students were in classes in which between 15 percent and 35 percent
of the students were of minority backgrounds. In public schools only 18.3
percent of the students were in classes in which between 15 percent and 35
percent of the enrollees were minority students. Private school students
were twice as likely to be in these well-integrated classrooms as public

school students. And private school students were much less likely to be in highly segregated classrooms. More than half (54.5 percent) of public school students were in classes with fewer than 10 percent minority students or more than 90 percent minority students. Fewer private school students, 41.1 percent, were in these highly segregated classes.

It is possible to calculate the better integration in private schools more precisely. Taking the absolute value of the difference between the percentage of minority students in each student's classroom and the national average of the percentage of minority students, one can determine exactly how far the average public and private school student's classroom percentage of minorities was from the national percentage. The average public school student was in a classroom that was 25.1 percentage points away from the average national percentage of minority students, compared to 17.8 percentage points for the average private school student. That is, the percentage of minority students in private school classes tended to be 7.3 percentage points closer to the national average than the percentage in public school classes. The differences in integration between public and private schools in 1992 were large and statistically significant.

But perhaps this comparison is distorted by the fact that private schools are not evenly distributed across the country. Given that private schools are concentrated in urban areas, where there are more minorities, while private schools are scarce in rural areas, where there are fewer minorities, the distribution of private schools may skew the results. Public schools in rural areas should not be punished for the lack of minority students in their classes if there are few minority students in their areas. Nor should private schools be overly rewarded for attracting minority students in urban areas where many minority students are present.

As can be seen in table 4-2, however, even when the integration rates in public and private schools are compared in different areas of the country, private schools are still clearly better racially integrated. In northeastern urban areas, for example, the proportion of minority students in private school classes in 1992 was 13.9 percentage points closer to the average national percentage of minorities than the percentage of minority students in northeastern urban public school classes.[37] This significantly greater "representativeness" of private school classes is also seen when comparisons are made within northeastern suburbs, northeastern rural areas, midwestern cities, midwestern rural areas, western cities, western suburbs, and southern cities. In midwestern suburbs, western rural areas, and southern suburbs private schools were better integrated than public schools in those areas, but the differences are not statistically significant. Only in

Table 4-2. *Amount by Which the Percentage of Minority Students in Private School Classrooms Was More Representative of the National Average, by Area of the Country, 1992[a]*

Area of country	Amount by which the percentage of minority students in private school classrooms is closer to the national average than the percentage in public school classrooms	Significance $p <$
Nationwide	7.3	0.01
Northeastern urban	13.9	0.01
Northeastern suburban	7.2	0.01
Northeastern rural	13.5	0.01
Midwestern urban	18.6	0.01
Midwestern suburban	0.2	0.13
Midwestern rural	13.8	0.01
Western urban	18.1	0.01
Western suburban	11.6	0.01
Western rural	0.5	0.56
Southern urban	15.2	0.01
Southern suburban	1.5	0.53
Southern rural	−19.5	0.01

Source: Author's analysis of data from U.S. Department of Education, National Center for Education Statistics, *National Education Longitudinal Study,* 1992.

a. All analyses were performed using a sample weighted by the NELS variable F2CXTWT to ensure its representativeness.

the rural South were private schools less well integrated than public schools. The white flight to private schools in the rural South that has been used by many to suggest that private schools undermine integration appears to have been the exception, not the rule. Even in the rural South private schools are less well integrated because they have concentrations of too many minority students, not too few. Throughout the rest of the country private schools are better able to produce a racial mix in classrooms that is closer to the national percentage of minority students than are the public schools in their areas.

Racial Tolerance in Public and Private Schools

We might all hope that schools not only mix people of different backgrounds, but also improve the tenor of relations between groups. NELS asked a series of questions of students, teachers, and school administrators that addressed this issue. Students were asked whether students at their schools made friends with students of other racial and ethnic groups.

Table 4-3. *Racial Tolerance in Public and Private Schools, 1992*[a]
Percent

Variable	Private (actual)	Public (actual)	Private (adjusted)	Public (adjusted)
Students who strongly agree that students make friends with students of other racial and ethnic backgrounds	31.2	17.6	29.2	18.0
Students who strongly disagree that fights often occur between racial or ethnic groups	64.3	28.6	60.6	27.1
Teachers who report that racial conflicts among students are not a problem	64.6	39.5	64.2	40.2
Administrators who report that racial conflicts among students are not a problem	73.0	54.9	71.1	55.5

Source: Author's analysis of data from U.S. Department of Education, National Center for Education Statistics, *National Education Longitudinal Study,* 1992.

a. All differences between public and private school results are significant at p <.01. The adjusted results are derived from a logit regression that controls for students' socioeconomic status and the racial composition of the class. The coefficients for these models are available from the author upon request. All analyses were performed using a sample weighted by the NELS variable F2CXTWT to ensure representativeness.

Students, teachers, and school administrators were also asked about the extent of racial conflicts in their school. The results show a dramatically greater degree of racial tolerance in private schools.[38] Almost a third (31.2 percent) of private school students strongly agreed that students made friends with students of other racial and ethnic groups in their schools, compared to 17.6 percent of public school students (see table 4-3). Controlling for the socioeconomic status of the students and the racial composition of the classes did not alter these results.

With regard to the extent of racial conflicts, the differences between public and private schools were even more striking. Almost two-thirds of private school students (64.3 percent) strongly disagreed that "fights often [occurred] between racial or ethnic groups," while only 28.6 percent of public school students strongly disagreed with this statement. Teachers were also asked to rate how serious a problem "racial/ethnic conflict among students" was. Among private school teachers, 64.6 percent reported that racial conflict was not a problem versus 39.5 percent of public school teachers. When school administrators were asked the same question, 73.0 percent of those at private schools reported that racial conflict was not a problem compared to 54.9 percent of public school administrators. None of these results are altered by introducing controls for socioeconomic status and racial composition, and all of the differences are statistically significant. Private schools not only do a better job of racial integration, but appear to be doing a better job of achieving the racial tolerance that we hope comes with integration. In 1992 students, teachers, and administrators consistently reported that private schools were better able to form cross-racial friendships and avoid racial conflicts than public schools.

Volunteering and a Commitment to Community

We have seen that private schools are better integrated and characterized by greater racial tolerance, qualities that describe the inner workings of the schools, but how well do they relate to the communities in which they reside? Are they insular havens of an elite, or are they committed to working for the public good? Based on the responses students gave in NELS on questions about volunteering, it seems that private schools are characterized by strong public spiritedness.

Students were asked whether they had engaged in any "unpaid volunteer or community service work" in the past two years. Almost two-thirds (63.2 percent) of private school students had, compared to fewer than half (45.6 percent) of public school students (see table 4-4). Even after controlling for socioeconomic status, the gap between public school and private school volunteering remains unchanged. Private school students not only reported that they were more likely to volunteer, but they were more likely to volunteer more often. More than a third (34.3 percent) of private school students said that they volunteered at least once a week, whereas about a tenth (10.2 percent) of public school students said that they volunteered that often.

These differences are not produced by socioeconomic status. There is something about private schools that is associated with more volunteering. It is possible that more private school students volunteer because they are required to do so by their schools. Although it is true that 15.5 percent of the private school students and 13.4 percent of public school students who volunteered reported that they did so because it was required, this difference is small, even if statistically significant. On the other hand, the results do not tell how many students were required to volunteer by their schools; they tell only how many said that their volunteering was caused by a requirement. Perhaps private school students have internalized the lesson and believe that they would volunteer even if it were not required. It is also

Table 4-4. *Volunteering and Commitment to Community in Public and Private Schools, 1992*[a]
Percent

Variable	Private (actual)	Public (actual)	Private (adjusted)	Public (adjusted)
Students who have volunteered in the last two years	63.2	45.6	61.7	41.4
Students who volunteer at least once a week	34.3	10.2	31.3	9.6
Students who report that they volunteer because it is required	15.5	13.4	17.3	13.7
Students who say that it is very important to help others in the community	36.2	32.6	36.7	31.7
Students who say that it is very important to volunteer	47.2	34.8	47.1	34.7

Source: Author's analysis of data from U.S. Department of Education, National Center for Education Statistics, *National Education Longitudinal Study,* 1992.

a. All differences between public and private school results are significant at p <.01. The adjusted results are derived from a logit regression that controls for students' socioeconomic status and race and the racial composition of the class. The coefficients for these models are available from the author upon request. All analyses were performed using a sample weighted by the NELS variable F2CXTWT to ensure representativeness.

possible that volunteering is taught at private schools by example rather than by requirement. If this is so, initiatives to require community service in public schools, like the one recently adopted in Chicago, may fail to achieve their goals if not implemented in the proper context.

The greater degree of volunteering in private schools also seems to be yielding a greater commitment to community and to helping others. When asked to rate how important it is to help others in the community, 36.2 percent of private school students said that it is very important, compared to 32.6 percent of public school students. On the importance of volunteering, 47.2 percent of private school students said that it is very important versus 34.8 percent of public school students. These differences are statistically significant and persist even after controlling for students' race, their socioeconomic status, and the racial composition of the school. It appears as if the reinforcement of particular identities that characterizes many private schools does not come at the expense of commitment to others. Private school students are more likely to volunteer, more likely to volunteer often, and more likely to believe that volunteering and helping others are very important things.

General Self-Assessments on Teaching Democratic Values

In addition to information on integration, racial tolerance, and volunteering, NELS asked school administrators to rate how well their schools promote certain goals compared to other schools. In particular, administrators were asked how well their schools promote practice in citizenship, how well they promote awareness of contemporary social issues, and how well they teach values and morals compared to other schools. On promoting citizenship, 29.3 percent of private school administrators gave their schools "outstanding" ratings versus 17.3 percent of the public school administrators (see table 4-5). The results were similar when administrators were asked how well their schools promote awareness of social and contemporary issues. Private school administrators gave their schools an outstanding rating 25.6 percent of the time, whereas public school administrators rated their schools outstanding 17.0 percent of the time. The most striking difference between public and private school self-assessments can be seen in how well the administrators said their schools teach values and morals. Nearly three-quarters (71.8 percent) of private school administrators rated their schools outstanding in teaching values and morals compared to only

Table 4-5. *Administrators' Self-Assessments of Schools' General Effectiveness in Teaching Civic Values, 1992*[a]
Percent

Variable	Private (actual)	Public (actual)	Private (adjusted)	Public (adjusted)
Administrators who rate their schools as outstanding in promoting citizenship	29.3	17.3	30.1	17.5
Administrators who rate their schools as outstanding in promoting awareness of contemporary and social issues	25.6	17.0	28.6	17.0
Administrators who rate their schools as outstanding in promoting teaching of values and morals	71.8	11.1	73.6	10.9

Source: Author's analysis of data from U.S. Department of Education, National Center for Education Statistics, *National Education Longitudinal Study*, 1992.

a. All differences between public and private school results are significant at p <.01. The adjusted results are derived from a logit regression that controls for students' socioeconomic status and the racial composition of the class. The coefficients for these models are available from the author upon request. All analyses were performed using a sample weighted by the NELS variable F2CXTWT to ensure representativeness.

11.1 percent of public school administrators. Although many political theorists are convinced that public schools do a better job of providing civic education, the public school administrators seem not to be so confident. According to the people who actually run the schools, private schools offer a superior democratic education to that offered in public schools.

Conclusion

Having some evidence is a considerable improvement over speculating or making assumptions about the implications of public and private education for civic values. But the evidence from NELS does not necessarily address all of the questions we would like answered, and even the ones that are answered may not be answered in the way we would prefer. NELS did not provide information on the long-term political effects of public and private education on civic values, because the subjects have only recently graduated high school. NELS did not ask the commonly accepted questions developed by political scientists to measure tolerance, trust in government, and social capital. The questions that NELS did ask often relied on self-assessments that may have been biased.

Is it possible that the results presented here are simply the product of systematic differences in how public and private school respondents answer questions? On the issue of racial integration, the information is not subject to a self-assessment bias. The proportions of minority students in public and private classes were what they were. On the reporting of cross-racial friendships, racial conflicts, volunteering behavior, and general effectivess in teaching democratic values, bias is a greater concern. But there is no reason to believe that private school respondents consistently overrated activities in their schools or that public school respondents underrated them.

In fact, it appears as if public school administrators may have misrepresented their schools more than private school administrators. On the questions related to racial conflicts, for example, the responses given by private school students, teachers, and administrators were very consistent with each other, but public school students, teachers, and administrators were not consistent with each other (see table 4-3). Private school students strongly disagreed that racial fights occurred often 64.3 percent of the time. Similarly, two-thirds of private school teachers reported that racial conflict among students was not a problem. Although private school administrators saw even fewer racial conflicts, with 73.0 percent saying that they were not a problem, the differences between the responses from students, teachers, and administrators in private schools were small.

In public schools students, teachers, and administrators told very different stories about the extent of their racial conflicts. Only 28.6 percent of public school students strongly disagreed that racial fights often occurred in their schools. Public school teachers, however, saw fewer racial problems than their students, with 39.5 percent reporting that racial conflicts were not a problem. Public school administrators saw even fewer racial problems than the teachers did, with 54.9 percent reporting that racial conflicts were not a problem in their schools. It seems reasonable to infer from the inconsistency of the results from public school respondents and the consistency of results from private school respondents that public school administrators are either more out of touch with what is happening in their schools or more likely to underreport their problems than private school administrators.

It is therefore plausible that the higher ratings private school administrators gave their schools for teaching citizenship, awareness of contemporary issues, and moral values may actually understate the superiority of the democratic education in private schools. The credibility of the high rating that private school administrators gave their schools for teaching moral values is further enhanced by the similarity of this result to the high ratings that parents in Cleveland gave to their private choice schools (see the chapter by Greene, Howell, and Peterson in this volume). The consistency of all of these results suggests that we should take seriously the self-assessments which show that better civic education is provided in private schools.

But it is still reasonable to worry about whether the stronger democratic values associated with private schools will translate into stronger democratic values for students who would choose private schools under a voucher system. Perhaps the superiority of the values in private schools is a function of the students who are in private schools, not the education actually provided by the schools. However, the fact that controlling for socioeconomic status and racial composition of the schools makes little difference in the results suggests that the better values in private schools are not simply a product of the students who are in those schools. Besides, the idea that students select a private education because they have superior democratic values contradicts the standard indictment of private school families as elitist, separatist, or extremist. The best way to determine more definitively whether private schools produce more democratic students or simply attract more democratic students is to conduct randomized experiments in which identical populations are assigned to public and private schools and their values are measured over time. Happily, randomized school choice experiments are underway in Dayton, New York, and Washington, D.C., that should permit precisely this type of study.

The evidence from NELS suggests that there is no reason to fear that school choice programs will undermine democratic education by allowing more students to choose private schools. There is even good reason to believe that school choice programs may improve democratic education as well as educational achievement.

Notes

1. Thomas Paine from *The Rights of Man* as quoted in David W. Kirkpatrick, *Choice in Schooling: a case for tuition vouchers* (Loyola University Press, 1990) p. 33. John Stuart Mill, *On Liberty* (NY: W. W. Norton and Co., 1975), p. 98.

2. Arthur J. Newman, *In Defense of the American Public School* (Berkeley: Mc-Cutchan Publishing 1978).

3. Paul E. Peterson, *The Politics of School Reform 1970–1940* (University of Chicago Press, 1985).

4. Nina H. Shokraii, "How Members of Congress Practice School Choice," The Heritage Foundation, F.Y.I. No. 147, September 9, 1997.

5. Benjamin R. Barber, "Education for Democracy," *The Good Society* 7 (Spring 1997), pp. 1–7 (quote on p. 1).

6. Richard W. Riley, "What Really Matters in American Education," U.S. Department of Education, published on the Web at http://www.ed.gov/Speeches/09-1997/index.html (September 23, 1997).

7. Amy Gutmann, *Democratic Education* (Princeton University Press, 1987), p. 67.

8. Gutmann, *Democratic Education,* p. 65.

9. Gutmann, *Democratic Education,* p. 70.

10. Gutmann, *Democratic Education,* p. 69.

11. Gutmann, *Democratic Education,* p. 72.

12. Gutmann, *Democratic Education,* pp. 71–88.

13. Gutmann, *Democratic Education,* pp. 97–101.

14. Gutmann, *Democratic Education,* pp. 101–04.

15. Gutmann, *Democratic Education,* pp. 111–14.

16. Gutmann, *Democratic Education,* p. 131.

17. Gutmann, *Democratic Education,* pp. 160–71.

18. Gutmann, *Democratic Education,* pp. 139–48.

19. Albert O. Hirschman, *Exit Voice, and Loyalty* (Harvard University Press, 1987).

20. Marc Landy, "Public Policy and Citizenship," in H. Ingram and S. R. Smith, eds., *Public Policy for Democracy* (Brookings, 1993), p. 98.

21. Mark Schneider, Paul Teske, Melissa Marschall, Michael Mintrom, and Christine Roch, "Institutional Arrangements and the Creation of Social Capital: The Effects of Public School Choice," *American Political Science Review* 91(1997), pp. 82–93.

22. Jonathan Kozol, "I Dislike the Idea of Choice, and I Want to Tell You Why," *Educational Leadership* 50 (1992), p. 92.

23. Barber, "Education for Democracy," pp. 1, 6.

24. John L. Sullivan, James Pierson, and George E. Marcus, *Political Tolerance and American Democracy* (University of Chicago Press, 1982).

25. Gary Orfield and Susan E. Eaton, *Dismantling Desegregation* (New York: New Press, 1996).

26. Gregory Weiher, *The Fractured Metropolis* (SUNY Press, 1991).

27. James Coleman, Thomas Hoffer, and Sally Kilgore, "Questions and Answers: Our Response," *Harvard Educational Review* 51 (November 1981), pp. 526–45; Coleman, Hoffer, and Kilgore, "Achievement and Segregation in Secondary Schools: A Further Look at Public and Private School Differences," *Sociology of Education* 55 (April/July 1982), pp. 162–83.

28. Andrew M. Greeley, *Catholic High School and Minority Students* (New Brunswick, N.J.: Transaction Books, 1982); Anthony S. Bryk, Valerie E. Lee, and Peter B. Holland, *Catholic Schools and the Common Good* (Harvard University Press, 1993).

29. James S. Coleman, Kathryn S. Schiller, and Barbara Schneider, "Parent Choice and Inequality," in Barbara Schneider and James S. Coleman, eds., *Parents, Their Children, and Schools* (Boulder: Westview Press, 1993).

30. John E. Chubb and Terry M. Moe, "Politics, Markets, and Equality in Schools," in Michael R. Darby, ed., *Reducing Poverty in America* (Thousand Oaks, Calif., Sage Publications, 1996).

31. Jomills Henry Braddock II, "The Issue Is Still Equality of Educational Opportunity," *Harvard Educational Review* 51 (November 1981), pp. 490–96; Karl E. Taeuber and David R. James, "Racial Segregation among Public and Private Schools," *Sociology of Education* 55 (April/July 1982), pp. 133–43.

32. Taeuber and James, "Racial," p. 133.

33. Richard J. Murnane, "Evidence, Analysis, and Unanswered Questions," *Harvard Educational Review* 51 (November 1981), pp. 483–89; Arthur S. Goldberger and Glen C. Cain, "The Causal Analysis of Cognitive Outcomes in the Coleman, Hoffer, and Kilgore Report," *Sociology of Education* 55 (April/July 1982), pp. 103–22; Douglas J. Willms, "Catholic School Effects on Academic Achievement: New Evidence from the High School and Beyond Follow-up Study," *Sociology of Education* 58 (April 1985), pp. 98–114; Karl L. Alexander and Aaron M. Pallas, "School Sector and Cognitive Performance: When Is a Little a Little?" *Sociology of Education* 58 (April 1985), pp. 115–27; Kevin B. Smith and Kenneth J. Meier, *The Case Against School Choice* (Armonk, N.Y.: M. E. Sharpe, 1995).

34. Jay P. Greene, Paul E. Peterson, and Jiangtao Du, "Effectiveness of School Choice: The Milwaukee Experiment," *Program on Education Policy and Governance Occasional Paper 97–1* (March 1997), Harvard University; Cecilia Elena Rouse, "Private Vouchers and Student Achievement: An Evaluation of the Milwaukee Parental Choice Program," *Quarterly Journal of Economics* (forthcoming).

35. U.S. Dept. of Education, National Center for Education Statistics, *National Education Longitudinal Study,* 1992.

36. U.S. Dept. of Education, *NELS.*

37. U.S. Dept. of Education, *NELS.*

38. U.S. Dept. of Education, *NELS.*

FIVE

Policy Churn and the Plight of Urban School Reform

Frederick M. Hess

We had the bad news [superintendent] for . . . 51 weeks. He had a reputation as a boy wonder. Anybody in [this district] will tell you how he wrecked a good organization. . . . The superintendent poisoned the relationship with the teachers and the administration. His first thing was, "I'm not going to change anything." That lasted 10 days. For the next 50 days, and I counted this, a major change was made every day. I'm not kidding. . . . As bright and as quick as he was, he was so impulsive it was unbelievable. He didn't think about culture or what people do. He just came in and knocked around. . . . He's now superintendent of [another district]. . . . He's got the ability to get a job, but not to keep a job.

—A senior school administrator interviewed in 1995

CRITIQUES OF URBAN SCHOOLING invariably start with the presumption that urban public school systems are in a state of crisis, and end with clarion calls for more change and new "solutions." The disagreements begin when the critics start to debate which remedies are most likely to improve urban school performance. Perhaps the predominant dispute in contemporary education policy is the one between the advocates of choice-based remedies and those who oppose choice-based approaches. Like other disputes about

This chapter draws upon Frederick M. Hess, *Spinning Wheels: The Politics of Urban School Reform* (Brookings, 1998).

how to improve urban schooling, this debate has in many ways been characterized by imprecise explanations of just why it is that urban school systems fare so poorly and how it is that choice-based solutions will affect those problems. Both advocates and opponents of choice tend to rely on traditional market metaphors, ignoring the particular institutional context that shapes education governance. Before designing remedies, whether choice-based or otherwise, it is crucial that we develop a fuller understanding of the problems that cripple urban schooling.

The Need to Address the Real Problems in Urban Schools

Current efforts to improve urban education are based on a flawed understanding of the institutional constraints that bind urban school systems. Much of the education debate overlooks a simple but crucial point—that the leaders of urban school systems currently have little incentive to focus on long-term school productivity. A prerequisite to improving urban schooling is that school leaders have incentives to focus on improving student performance. The implications of this analysis for school governance are discussed at the end of the chapter.

Critiques of urban schooling have dominated the education discourse in the United States for much of the past twenty or thirty years. An ensuing flurry of reform proposals has produced a great deal of activity, but little real change in urban schooling. What explains this frustrating state of affairs? Reform advocates believe existing pedagogy to be inappropriate or inadequate and school systems to be paralyzed or immobile. They contend that extensive reforms are necessary to address these continuing problems.[1] The Institute for Educational Leadership summarized three major reports published in 1992 and 1993 by noting, "All of them are strong testimonials to the need for change."[2] Observers report a similar faith in reform among educational administrators, particularly superintendents and principals.[3]

However, the contention that insufficient energy has been devoted to reform is refuted by the record.[4] Only one year after the 1983 publication of *A Nation at Risk,* a high-profile report deploring the condition of the nation's public schools, there were 275 state-level task forces evaluating education and recommending new policies, and that number had increased by 1990. In 1995 there were at least a dozen major networks promoting school reform, ranging from the New American Schools Development Corporation to the Coalition for Essential Schools.[5] A 1995 press release by the California Department of Education bragged that 1,883 schools in

California alone were engaged in reform as part of the Goals 2000 national reform effort. These extensive efforts have produced few substantive results, prompting the Rand Corporation's 1995 report *Reinventing Public Education* to begin with the question, "Why has a decade of work on school reform produced so little?" Education scholars have agreed that reform efforts intended to address unsatisfactory school performance have produced few results and little real change."[6]

Given frustration with the status quo and the resources devoted to reform, the inability of ambitious reform efforts to produce significant change is puzzling. Traditional explanations of this state of affairs emphasize the inertia of public school bureaucracies and/or the poor planning and design of reforms. Although these analyses have merit, they do not explain why planning has been poor and why organizational leaders have not found ways to reshape the core behavior of school organizations. These problems are not the root causes of reform's ineffectualness, but are symptomatic of structural pressures in urban schooling.

Quite simply, urban school reform is not really about improving education. Reform represents a district's continuous response to political necessity—not a district's dramatic break with the status quo. In fact, a state of perpetual reform *is* the status quo. This surfeit of reform is responsible for many of the problems that reforms are then expected to solve. The cruel paradox is that the same impulses that drive reform also ensure that reform will be pursued under conditions that make large-scale success highly unlikely. The most significant reason education reform has not produced results is that reform is not primarily *about* producing results. Instead, reforms are intended to rally community support without imposing the costs required by significant and sustained efforts at improvement.[7]

Emphasis on the politically attractive aspects of reform has resulted in inattention to the details of implementing reform. For example, Pauly has observed, "A clear and consistent finding of education policy research is that policies and reforms often fall apart when they encounter the realities of daily life in the classrooms."[8] Meaningful change requires time to focus on selected reforms and then to nurture those efforts at the school sites. However, superintendents feel compelled to launch a barrage of change and to maintain a proactive stance, producing a successive stream of new initiatives. Schools and teachers are given little time to become acclimated to one initiative before the next is launched.[9]

This churning of policy is inimical to long-term improvement. In fact, hyperactive reform agendas may hinder performance by distracting schools from the core functions of teaching and learning. Evidence on the performance of parochial schools and high-performing schools suggests that the best schools are characterized by focus and that they develop expertise in specific approaches.[10] Elmore has summarized this argument: "Really good schools—schools that represent the very best examples of teaching and learning—often aren't very innovative; indeed, their main strength often seems to be that they persist in, and develop increasingly deep understandings of, well-developed theories of teaching and learning."[11] All too often the cumulative effect of successive generations of reform is instability, wasted resources, and faculty alienation. As one ineffectively implemented wave of reform gives way to another, a residue of reform fragments settles over cynical and resentful teachers. This cycle disrupts school performance and makes it more difficult for subsequent reformers to convince teachers that their initiatives will be sustained.

The institutional incentives in urban school districts encourage policymakers to treat reform as a political tool.[12] Urban school systems are plagued by poor measures of real performance, by a loose connection between those nominally responsible for system productivity and the system's actual productivity, and by insistent demands that the schools demonstrate rapid and visible improvement. The unmanageability of urban systems discourages incremental efforts at improvement in favor of more visible measures intended for public consumption.

An urban school system is governed by amateur board members who are accountable for the mediocre performance of urban schools, but have little power to generate short-term solutions. These board members rely on the superintendent to provide the district with forward direction. Putting the superintendent out front increases the pressure on the superintendent to produce visible and impressive results. In this high-stakes situation, if things go poorly the board is able to help the system get off to a fresh start by replacing a disappointing superintendent with one who inspires community confidence. As Johnson has noted, "The dismissal of an ineffective superintendent is thought to mark the end of bad times; the appointment of a new superintendent is heralded as the beginning of a new age."[13] Board members who fail to use the superintendent in this fashion court political risk and risk being replaced by impatient community members who want evidence that things will improve quickly.

The Temptation to Be a Reformist Superintendent

Superintendents, in turn, feel a need to act quickly and visibly. The difficulties in accurately assessing urban district outcomes[14] mean that evaluations of district policymakers are influenced only modestly by their actual impact. The most widely used proxies for school system performance, such as changes in test scores, only minimally reflect the impact an urban superintendent can have within the three- to four-year tenure of most superintendents.[15] As a consequence, leaders are primarily judged by their input—by how likely it appears that they will be able to improve the schools.[16] Additionally, the problems of controlling core performance in an urban system make it much easier for superintendents to appear effective by initiating new proposals than by focusing on implementation.[17] Active administrators who appear to embody competence and promise are lauded as leaders.[18]

The lack of accountability in school system performance means that superintendents have to be judged by proxy. Since superintendents can rarely be judged on the actual improvement they produce, they are instead judged on input—how hard they appear to be working to produce improvement, how innovative they are, and how promising a future they project.[19] Superintendents benefit from being judged on input.[20] Since it is immensely difficult for urban policymakers to produce short-term change in the teaching and learning core, it increases their control over their fate.

Reform initiatives are amenable to administrative control, tend to be viewed as "win-win" measures, rarely produce identifiable losers, and project a widely appealing facade of progress. Consequently, policymakers have an incentive to milk reform, and they use it to project a hopeful image of forthcoming improvements. One Pittsburgh respondent in a study I conducted of fifty-seven urban school districts (as reported later in this chapter) observed: "The administrators make all kinds of flowery statements about their success [with reform], but are never pushed by the media to prove where it is happening."

The incentives encouraging superintendents to be proactive are not malicious. Effective leadership requires that a superintendent retain his or her position, enjoy public confidence, and rally fiscal and volunteer support from the local community—all of which are aided by a superintendent's reputation for competence, innovation, and active problem solving.[21]

Superintendents are aware that their expected tenure is no more than three or four years.[22] Faced with a short "shelf life," a superintendent needs to rapidly establish a reputation as an effective leader.[23] This emphasis comes at the expense of careful program design, oversight, and implementation.[24] Emphasizing follow-through is often professionally self-defeating in the high-turnover urban superintendency, because professional status accrues to those policymakers who initiate or design programs.[25] Implementing a predecessor's program is a caretaker role that inhibits a superintendent's ability to establish a strong professional reputation.

The urban superintendent faces a dilemma. Focusing on selected initiatives enhances the likelihood of producing significant change, but attracts relatively little notice and makes it unlikely that the superintendent will be able to finish the job he or she set out to do. On the other hand, by initiating a great deal of activity and leaving his or her successors to worry about results, the superintendent can set a district on the right path and can trust others to finish the job. The proactive superintendent is positioned to take credit for apparent successes, whereas the managerial successor is often seen as a mere technician. Whether or not the schools are viewed as improving, professional and political realities reward those superintendents who are seen as proactive.

There is another, highly ironic, motivation that is encouraging proactivity. Community support is crucial to any urban district's ability to improve its schools. District policymakers have a much better chance of producing substantial improvement if they enjoy business support, parental cooperation, the active participation of community organizations, and the backing of municipal officials. The surest way to earn this kind of support is to cultivate a community reputation as a promising innovator. A superintendent who initiates reforms is feted in the local media, praised by the mayor and local business community, and offered a honeymoon in which to reshape a troubled school system. Superintendents are propelled into proactivity—if only as a tactic to rally resources and support. Superintendents who focus on the long term and fail to propose quick fixes will be handicapped by a lack of support and resources. Superintendents who proceed in a controlled, deliberate, incremental fashion will find their effectiveness hobbled by a lack of community prestige. In short, current arrangements create a situation in which pursuing significant change in a responsible manner undermines a district's ability to secure the resources and community trust necessary to enact significant change.

Evidence I collected on the nature of urban school reform in fifty-seven urban districts during 1992–95 is consistent with a political understanding of reform. Data were collected through structured interviews with six fixed-position education observers in each district. An immense amount of reform has been proposed, with new measures launched almost every year. Almost all reform initiatives are enacted, and local district observers consider the routine generation of new reform proposals to be the status quo. Finally, the high rates of activity are reported to have serious effects on the implementation and success of reforms.

The Extent of Policy Churn

The lack of large-scale research on school reform has meant that most discussion proceeds without an empirical foundation. I undertook my study after realizing that what was needed first was to determine how much reform was actually being accomplished. I was able to make a first-cut estimate by compiling the composite number of reforms proposed in each of the fifty-seven sample districts. Data were collected on five different types of school reform: modifications in the school day and school calendar, curricular reform, evaluation reform, teacher development reform, and site-based management (SBM).[26] (For more information of the methodology I used, see the appendix to this chapter.) Each of the five reform areas studied has been promoted by reformers as a major initiative demanding significant time and energy, which would imply that districts will be selective in initiating these reforms. On the other hand, a political understanding of reform would suggest that districts might pursue activity without regard to practical problems.

There was a great deal of reform activity during 1992–95. The mean district proposed significant reform in 3.35 of the five reform areas during this period. Over two-thirds of districts proposed reforms in at least three of the five policy areas, and every district attempted reform in at least two areas. Because only five kinds of reform were examined, it is unclear how many other kinds of policy initiatives districts may have also undertaken.

Given the design of this study, these data actually understate the number of initiatives. Respondents were asked whether a significant reform had been proposed in each of the five reform areas studied. Each respondent who reported that a significant reform measure had been proposed in an area was then asked to briefly describe the most significant proposal. Within the same district, different respondents frequently reported different proposals as the most significant for a given type of reform. The composite totals above lump together those various proposals within each of the five categories of reform. Table 5-1 presents an example of how many different kinds of "most significant" proposals were reported in two districts.

Table 5-1. *The Most Significant Reform Proposals Reported in Two School Districts, 1992–95[a]*

District	Most significant curriculum proposals cited by respondents	Most significant evaluation proposals cited by respondents
Fullerton Elementary School District	Restructure framework	Use portfolios
	Change system's mechanics	Use more tests and evaluation
	Increase hands-on/student orientation	Revise tests
	Increase critical thinking in curriculum	Increase school-site role
Milwaukee Public Schools	Increase graduation requirements	Use portfolios
	Increase multiculturalism	Use graduation test
	Increase critical thinking in curriculum	Modify promotion policies
	Overhaul books	
	Modify values (sex) education	

Source: Author's research, conducted in 1995.

a. Each policy area can encompass several reform initiatives.

Table 5-1 indicates that Milwaukee Public Schools respondents cited three different "most significant" proposals for evaluation reform and five for curriculum reform. Variation equal to that in Milwaukee also showed up in smaller districts, such as the 10,470-student Fullerton Elementary School District in California. The number of diverse proposals in these districts highlights the fact that districts are initiating much more reform activity than is suggested by the summary figures. The full extent of reform can be depicted more clearly by totaling the number of reform initiatives cited by respondents in each district.[27] Of the five types of reform studied, the mean district reported 11.4 significant proposals between 1992 and 1995.

This tidal wave of reform may be proceeding in one of two ways. Districts may be enacting multiple reforms in a burst of coordinated activity, or they may be continually initiating sequential initiatives. Ambiguities in the data make it impossible to definitively say which is the case, but the summary results suggest that activity is continuous. Respondents in thirty-five of the fifty-seven sample districts reported that a significant reform was proposed each year of 1992–95. Respondents in nine other districts reported that a significant measure was proposed every year of

1991–94. In sum, more than 75 percent of the sample districts reported the proposal of significant measures each of at least four consecutive years during 1991–95. This behavior was evident both in the more active and in the less active districts. Too much should not be made of these findings, because respondents were often imprecise about dates. However, the data appear to rule out the notion that activity is primarily launched in coordinated bursts of reform.

Districts almost always enact proposed reforms. About 90 percent of proposed "third wave" reforms were reportedly enacted.[28] The superintendent and the board seek to avoid reforms which will ignite an adverse local reaction. Measures are cleared with the union leadership and written within the parameters of the union contract in order to minimize the likelihood of active union opposition.

School systems operate very differently from state or national governments, where dozens of measures are proposed for each bill that passes. Board members and superintendents seek broadly appealing reforms in order to help smooth over the conflict implicit in managing urban school districts on a day-to-day basis. A board member in one district explained why the board had taken a while to enact evaluation reform: "The board was unified behind the [evaluation reform] policy [that was eventually adopted]. We probably just gave up on it for a while because it was so controversial. I think sometimes we tend to give up just so we don't get into an area where we can't get along with one another, and then we try to enact them in different ways."

Board members prefer to let the system administration generate policy and to not act on reforms until near unanimity is ensured. This kind of unanimity emerges from informal back-room discussion, whether or not that kind of discussion is technically legal under open meeting laws. A union president explained: "It's hard to say who dominates policy, because [district X] is a mish-mash where we all work on each other and out of that comes policy. . . . By law [the school board] has to do all of [their business] in open meetings. In reality, I think that board members talk to each other. They discuss things in ones and twos, because more than two cannot meet in the same room to discuss anything dealing with board policy. Do they talk on the telephone? Sure. . . . I know they talk to each other in ones and twos. I talk to them, so I know they talk to each other."

Another way to assess the nature of school reform is to ask why it is that reform is not accomplished. Instead of measuring activity, it is possible to examine the nature of inactivity. When respondents in my study indicated that districts had not pursued reform, what was the reason given? Presumably, if reform is a measured response to educational needs, respondents would suggest that the absence of reform meant that reform was unnecessary or had previously been attempted.

When districts did not make a proposal in a policy area, respondents only rarely said that district inaction was due to a satisfactory state of affairs or the fact that the policy had already been changed. Just 11 percent of respondents, barely more than one in ten, said an untried reform was not needed or had not been considered.[29] In the vast majority of cases, respondents indicated that reforms that had not been attempted were in the works or had been hung up in some fashion. This was the case even though urban districts have been reforming avidly for decades, and so have frequently reworked these policy areas several times in recent years. Considering, proposing, and enacting reforms is the norm. Reforms are not enacted to solve particular problems; they are proposed, enacted, and then reproposed in a continuous process.

As the foregoing discussion would suggest, third wave reforms have not fulfilled their promise. Respondents did not consider the reforms to have been particularly successful. One open-ended question asked of respondents was, "What has been the greatest success in [the district]'s school system during the past three years, and how was it achieved?"[30] Fewer than 20 percent of respondents cited structural or pedagogical reforms as their district's greatest recent success, even though reform efforts are explicitly designed to improve school performance. The 18 percent of respondents who cited these reforms when discussing district success barely outnumbered the 14 percent who could name no significant success or who said that the district's greatest success was surviving.

Policy Churn as an Impediment to Implementation of Reform

Decades of effort have failed to improve school performance on a systemwide scale.[31] Miller has noted that "the problem of 'scaling up'—of translating the successful practices of a few exemplary models into the widespread adoption of those practices—has never been solved."[32] Much of the ineffectiveness of school reform has been traced to failures in implementation.[33]

Implementation is immensely difficult to study, largely because it is the act of attempting to make policies function as designed. We are forced to judge implementation by observing the difference between intended and actual consequences, an immensely difficult task. In order to ameliorate these difficulties, most studies look intensively at a handful of schools or school districts, hoping to more precisely measure intended and actual consequences.

In my study a very different approach was used to assess the validity of the obvious, but generally unheeded, proposition that districts that do more will do it less well. Much more complex models of implementation are useful and appropriate,[34] but the testing of more refined hypotheses must await the collection of more finely grained data on district-level reform. Because direct measures of implementation are not available and because an in-depth examination of numerous reforms in numerous districts was not feasible in my study, respondent evaluations of implementation and reform success were used to compare reform performance across districts. This approach is obviously imperfect, particularly because respondents used imperfect information to summarize complex phenomena in a simple manner. Nonetheless, because it enables us to consider the nature of multiple reform efforts in a large number of districts, this approach is a reasonable complement to more precise studies of smaller samples.

Despite its failings, several satisfactory elements made this methodology useful and valid. First, respondents were selected for their relationship to local education, and the mean respondent reported following local education for more than seventeen years. The respondents had a wealth of knowledge about their local school systems. Second, questions did not focus on the personal feelings of respondents. Instead, respondents were primarily asked to evaluate a particular quantity: the implementation and success of specified reforms. Third, any biases should have been equally distributed across school districts, since the same types of respondents were used across the sample districts. Fourth, respondents were asked to evaluate phenomena in which most had a limited personal stake. Finally, because the evaluations are being used to assess not the absolute performance of any reform, but only the relative performance of the five reforms, it was not a problem if respondents systematically rated reform too high or too low.

More than anything else, effective school reform requires that a school system focus on making the desired changes work.[35] That requires time, costs, energy, stability, and experience. In a review of the effective school literature, Purkey and Smith noted, "Most schools will need additional time, money, and information if their staffs are to break old habits . . . and to acquire new attitudes and expectations."[36] As long as school personnel believe that an initiative is only a short-term intrusion, they have little incentive to take it seriously. Faculty members are more likely to commit to reform if an initiative is expected to be in place for the long haul and is supported by sufficient resources. Faculty support, in turn, is crucial if proposals are to impact the classroom core.

Reformers have shown a particular inattention to the monetary costs of reform.[37] The tendency to underestimate the resources required by new reforms causes districts to provide woefully inadequate levels of training and staff support, even though training and faculty commitment are key to efforts to determine whether a given reform is effective.[38] The more appealing questions of getting reform launched have overshadowed crucial but mundane issues of resources and training.

Effective reform requires a district to make a long-term commitment to a specific initiative. This permits faculty members to refine the necessary skills and fosters organizational learning and coordination.[39] Districts that have successfully empowered professionals and decentralized operations have usually taken at least five years to do so.[40] The long-term time commitment needs to be complemented by stable leadership, consistent and clear direction, and attention to follow-through.[41]

The Relative Performance of Reform

If policy churn is partially responsible for the unimpressive results of reform, districts that attempt to pursue more initiatives are likely to have less success with reform. The fate of reforms in these districts that proposed more than 3.5 kinds of reform was compared to the fate of reforms in less active districts.[42] Respondents evaluated the performance of reforms by rating, on a scale of zero to ten, the degree of implementation and the success of each measure that they reported to have been enacted. A zero meant that a measure had not been implemented or was, thus far, unsuccessful, and a ten indicated complete implementation or complete success. In order to focus clearly on the effect of local policy churn, initiatives that respondents indicated had been state mandates are omitted.[43]

The mean district reported 3.35 reform proposals on the composite scale of zero to five, but the median was slightly higher than that. To examine the effect of high levels of reform activity, the fate of reforms in districts that attempted 3.5 or fewer reform proposals was compared to the fate of reforms in districts attempting more than 3.5 proposals. The extent to which reforms were implemented was measured by asking respondents who reported that a proposal had been enacted, "How thoroughly has this reform been implemented at the school level?" Respondents answered on a scale of zero to ten, where a zero indicated that the policy was not at all implemented and a ten meant that it was completely in place. The reported success of policies was compared using composite responses to the question, "Thus far, how successfully has the policy achieved its stated goals?" Respondents answered on a scale of zero to ten, where a zero meant that the policy had been not at all successful and a ten meant that it had been very successful.[44] District composites for each type of reform were used in this analysis.

Districts that attempted less reform were reported to have implemented the measures they did attempt more thoroughly. For the fifty-eight reforms reported by a majority of local respondents to have been locally initiated and proposed after the beginning of 1992, districts attempting less reform were rated 25 percent more successful in implementing the reforms they proposed. The advantage enjoyed by low-activity districts was equally pronounced for the reported success of reforms. Low-activity districts were reported to have been more successful with every one of the five types of reform. Overall, reforms were reported to have been 25 percent more successful in low-activity districts.

One traditional explanation of the failure of urban school reform is that insuperable obstacles are presented by urban environments. Although these problems are central to the dynamic driving the school reform treadmill, they do not explain the relatively inferior performance of high-activity districts. The environmental critique implies that the implementation of reform should be primarily a function of urban difficulties, and the evidence does show that wealthier districts fare better with reform. However, low-activity districts outperform high-activity districts, even among urban districts in similar economic situations. The thirty-seven locally initiated reforms proposed after 1992 in districts with median household incomes below the sample mean ($27,806 in 1989) were reportedly implemented 36 percent more thoroughly in low-activity districts than in high-activity districts. The measures were also reportedly 24 percent more successful in low-activity low-income districts ($n = 35$). Similarly, reforms were reportedly implemented 3 percent more thoroughly and were 27 percent more successful in low-activity high-income districts ($n = 21$). Reduced reform activity appears to improve implementation much more strongly in low-income districts than in wealthy ones. Since poorer districts have more extreme problems and fewer resources with which to solve them, it is reasonable that poor districts reap greater benefits from focused efforts. If anything, the political problems of school reform appear to aggravate inequities between the haves and the have-nots.

It is unclear whether districts are primarily hampered by trying to do too much at once or by a failure to stick with selected reforms. One way to get an insight into this issue is by comparing the performance of reform in districts with more stable leadership to districts with less stable leadership. Districts in which superintendents turn over more frequently have more difficulty sustaining commitment to specific reforms. However, districts with long-serving superintendents also propose reform at a reduced rate. In order to separate the consequence of inadequate follow-through from the problem of hyperactivity, it is necessary to look at the effect of superintendent turnover in districts with similar levels of reform activity. One potential problem with this analysis is that reforms launched by veteran superintendents are likely to be more thoroughly implemented simply because these superintendents have been in place a long time. Consequently, in this analysis it is significant that all reforms not launched during 1992–95 are excluded.

Using the same universe of post-1992 reforms as before, the fate of measures launched in high-activity districts with superintendents who had been in place for four or more years was compared to that of those launched in districts where the superintendents had been in place three years or less. The twenty-three reforms were reported to have been 40 percent more thoroughly implemented and 48 percent more successful in districts with long-term superintendents. Although the number of observations is small, the data imply that the failure to stick with initiatives is a problem distinct from the problem of reform overload. The evidence suggests that leadership turnover (implying the sequential launching of measures) has a negative impact separate from the total amount of reform launched. Even when only recent measures are included and when only districts that are highly active in reform are considered, districts with stable leadership enjoyed superior implementation and outcomes.

The previous discussion compares the fate of reforms in districts above and below a relatively high threshold of activity. This discussion is unable to examine the impact of extremely low levels of activity or to fairly address the argument that the few districts that launch everything at once might be pushing comprehensive and focused reform agendas that will outperform piecemeal reform efforts. The effects of policy churn can be more clearly illustrated by comparing the outcomes of reform in extremely low-activity districts with those in high-activity and extremely high-activity districts.

There were thirty-two reforms reported by a majority of local respondents to have been locally initiated and proposed after the beginning of 1992 in districts that proposed 2.5 or fewer reforms or more than 3.5 reforms (see table 5-2). The results in table 5-2 should be interpreted cautiously due to the limited sample size.

Table 5-2. *Impact of Activity Level on Reform Performance*

Total number of reforms proposed in the district	Average number of successful reforms	Number of observations
4.0 or more	6.5	5
More than 3.5 but fewer than 4.0	4.9	20
2.5 or fewer	7.9	7

Source: Author's research, conducted in 1995.

Reforms in extremely low-activity districts (2.5 or fewer proposals) were reported to be 61 percent more successful than reforms in standard high-activity districts (more than 3.5 but fewer than 4.0 proposals). Districts that did much less reform did it much, much better. Interestingly, the few reforms attempted in extremely high-activity districts (4.0 or more proposals) fared 33 percent better than those in standard high-activity districts. This provides some evidence of the proposition that districts benefit from pursuing comprehensive reforms that tackle everything in an integrated fashion. However, measures in the extreme low-activity districts still fared 21 percent better than those in extremely high-activity districts. The evidence strongly suggests that more active districts implement reform less thoroughly and that their reforms fare relatively poorly.

Conclusions

Reform, rather than being the remedy to what ails urban schools, has generally been a distraction and a hindrance. Reform is an expensive endeavor that requires time, money, and energy and imposes significant opportunity costs on urban school systems. A series of partial reform efforts can undermine the school-level stability, focus, consistency, enthusiasm, trust, and commitment that are the keys to effective schooling. The irony of school reform is that the sheer amount of activity—the fact that reform is the status quo—impedes the ability of any particular reform to have a lasting effect. An immense amount of reform was accomplished during 1992–95, and the extent of those efforts impeded the implementation and effectiveness of individual initiatives.[45]

To say that school reform has been a disappointment does not imply that every reform will fail. However, the churning of policy distracts administrators, teachers, and community members from fostering faculty commitment and expertise—the real keys to school improvement. Dramatic top-down reforms, which tend to be hobbled by vague conceptions of how teaching and learning will improve, rarely foster this commitment. Rapid leadership turnover and the constant search for new solutions cause commitments to the initiatives of former superintendents to dry up and programs to be abandoned. The result is that faculty members and administrators become disillusioned and increasingly resist further change. The problem has not been that nothing ever changes, but that everything changes.

In effect, policy churn punishes teachers who throw themselves into reform efforts. The disinterested and unmotivated teachers who are the targets of most reform activity safely ride out the successive waves of reform behind the closed doors of their classrooms. Those teachers who invest their energy, disrupt their classrooms, and sacrifice their time find their efforts wasted if reforms dissipate. Veteran teachers quickly learn to close their classroom doors and simply wait for each reform push to recede, ensuring that each subsequent wave of reform is largely manned by newer teachers who lack institutional memory.

The problem of policy churn is an institutional one that requires attention to school governance rather than to traditional educational remedies. Do choice-based remedies—explicitly intended to reconfigure governance incentives present a promising response to the problems of policy churn? Answering that question requires the consideration of at least three easily overlooked points. First, policy churn can be only partially traced to the public sector. It is also due in large part to unique challenges of providing a comprehensive, long-term education to a heterogeneous population. These challenges are particularly severe in urban areas that lack clear accountability measures, that are extremely resistant to leadership control, and that are troubled by vast environmental problems. Second, policy churn is aggravated by problems—such as the sprawling size of urban districts and the lack of accountability mechanisms—that can be remedied through solutions other than choice-based ones. Third, choice remedies are likely to address the problems of policy churn with varying degrees of efficacy, depending on how they are structured.

Carefully constructed choice-based plans could help to discourage policy churn. Choice-based solutions are based on the notion that emphasis on school outcomes will increase—using consumer demand to focus school leaders on performance rather than visible activity. Choice plans can break up the massive urban systems into smaller entities that are controlled by administrators closer to the classroom faculty members. Smaller systems, whether they be made up of a handful of schools or a single school, could enhance accountability by making it easier for local observers to judge system output and to hold leaders accountable for outcomes. Smaller systems also make it easier for the leadership to control the quality of schooling. Leaders responsible for fewer schools and fewer classrooms will have an easier time fostering positive school cultures, supporting the faculty, facilitating classroom instruction, and increasing teacher accountability. Choice plans that increase the system leadership's leverage over school performance will make it relatively more attractive for the system leadership to concentrate on efforts to improve core performance.

Finally, choice plans that permit students to sort themselves by interest and ambition make it easier for parents and community members to evaluate system performance. More homogeneous student bodies reduce the number of competing expectations and make it relatively easier to benchmark system performance against clear sets of desired outcomes.

Many of these ways in which choice-based remedies might reduce policy churn can be traced to changes in organizational configuration, not simply to the magic of the marketplace. Similarly, choice schools that concentrate on producing and measuring outcomes will increase the focus on core performance and reduce the temptation to engage in symbolic activity. However, there is no guarantee that the competitive dynamic in a choice system will compel school leaders to concentrate on outcomes. It is possible that consumers, lacking effective performance measures, will be forced to rely on the same kinds of input proxies that currently trouble urban systems. This could encourage schools to compete on the basis of input measures. A school's need to differentiate itself in a competitive marketplace and to have some "sizzle" to offer potential customers could conceivably increase the rate of policy churn. In fact, reform efforts could become selling points under choice arrangements. If families lack clear and compatible outcome proxies with which to judge schools, they will be encouraged to rely on the same sort of input proxies that currently encourage symbolic leadership.

Choice can help to reduce policy churn by making outcomes more transparent or by offering school leaders more control over the core, both of which will probably happen if individual schools become independent entities under choice. However, it is useful to remember that it is possible to produce smaller, more focused, more easily observed, more effectively assessed, and less publicly visible schools through means other than choice. One other approach is the construction of a standard accountability system—along the lines of the Japanese or western European school systems—which would make outcome data more accessible, interpretable, and reliable. At this point it is too early to say which specific remedies hold the most promise for addressing the problems of policy churn.

Appendix: Methodology

The data presented in this chapter measure reform efforts during 1992–95 in a stratified random sample of fifty-seven urban school districts in places with populations of 50,000 or more. The data were obtained through 325 structured interviews the author conducted with similarly positioned observers in each district during a nine-month period in 1995. The 325 interviews represented a 95 percent success rate, as the study called for interviews with 342 targeted respondents, six in each of the fifty-seven districts. The extraordinarily high success rate was largely due to the use of a twelve-callback rule, in which the author made twelve attempts to contact each respondent before "no response" was recorded.

Respondents were used as privileged observers, meaning that they were asked to report on what had transpired in local school affairs and were selected because they would be able to offer a comprehensive view of system activity.[46] The multiple interviews conducted in each district were averaged into a composite for the district. This averaging was done because the unit of analysis in this study was the district, not the individual. The individual responses were gathered as a means of understanding the process of urban school reform.

The six types of individuals interviewed in each district were selected both because they were likely to be highly informed observers of the local education scene and with an eye toward ensuring that a variety of perspectives on school affairs would be obtained. The first interviewee in each district was the education reporter for the major local daily newspaper. From the reporter were obtained the names of the head of the teachers' union, the "most knowledgeable" senior school administrator, the head of the local chamber of commerce or the most influential local business group, the head of the most influential local minority organization, and the "most knowledgeable" school board member. If the journalist could not supply a name or if a targeted individual was unavailable, I used a structured format to obtain the appropriate informant. The interviews included both closed-ended and open-ended questions, permitting both quantitative analysis of the results and narrative discussion of the findings. I personally scheduled and conducted all interviews.

The key variable used in this chapter is the measure of the extent of reform activity in each district. To measure the amount of activity, respondents were asked whether a significant reform was proposed in each area. The five yes or no responses provided by each respondent were compiled into a districtwide composite by using *the percentage of respondents who reported a proposal made* as the composite measure of reform activity. If every respondent in a district reported that a professional development proposal was made, the district's composite professional development proposal score would be 1.00. A district with four yes and two no responses regarding curriculum proposals of reform would have an issue composite of 0.67. This approach effectively weighted the amount and the visibility of reform along a continuum of zero to one using the variance implicit in local responses. A composite measure of total district activity was generated by summing the zero to one composite scores for each of the five reform areas. For example, a district in which every respondent said that every reform had been proposed would score a 5.00, whereas a district where every respondent reported that no proposal had been made in any area would score a 0.00.

Notes

1. Barth notes that one proreform argument is that "urban schools are seen as so helpless, so hopeless, so broken that it seems there's little to lose by giving them a good hard kick. To use a dated metaphor it's like kicking a broken radio. Perhaps the tube filaments will align by chance in a different way, and the radio will work. In any case, since it's already broken, what is there to lose?" Roland S. Barth, "Restructuring Schools: Some Questions for Teachers and Principals," *Phi Delta Kappan* 73 (October 1991), pp. 123–28 (quote on p. 124).

2. Jacqueline Danzberger, Michael Kirst, and Michael Usdan, *Governing Public Schools: New Times New Requirements* (Washington, D.C.: Institute for Educational Leadership, 1992).

3. Gene Gallegos, "Transforming America's Schools," *Thrust for Educational Leadership Review* (1996), pp. 26–27.

4. Murphy has termed the 1980s "the most widespread, intense, public, comprehensive, and sustained [reform] effort in our history." In the mid-1980s Doyle and Hartle (1985:1) observed that the United States was involved in the "greatest and most concentrated surge of educational reform in the nation's history." Joseph Murphy, *Restructuring Schools: Capturing and Assessing the Phenomena* (New York: Teachers College Press, 1991), p. viii; Denis Doyle and Terry Hartle, *Excellence in Education: The States Take Charge* (Washington, D.C.: American Enterprise Institute for Public Policy Research, 1985), p. 1.

5. Diana Tittle, Welcome to Heights High: *The Crippling Politics of Restructuring America's Public Schools* (Columbus: Ohio State University Press, 1995).

6. Paul Hill, *Reinventing Public Education* (Santa Monica: Rand Corporation Institute on Education and Training, 1995), p. ix. See also Larry Cuban, "Hedgehogs and Foxes among Educational Researchers," *The Journal of Educational Research Review*

89 (1995), pp. 6–12; Richard F. Elmore, "Getting to Scale with Good Educational Practice," *Harvard Educational Review* 66 (1996), pp. 1–26; William Firestone, Susan Fuhrman, and Michael Kirst, "State Educational Reform Since 1983: Appraisal and the Future," *Educational Policy Review* 5 (1991), pp. 233–50; Michael Fullan, *The New Meaning of Educational Change* (New York: Teachers College Press, 1991); Eduard Miller, "Idealists and Cynics: The Micropolitics of Systemic School Reform," *The Harvard Education Letter* 3 (1996); Theodore Sizer, *Horace's Hope: What Works for the American High School* (Boston: Houghton Mifflin, 1996); David Tyack and Larry Cuban, *Tinkering toward Utopia: A Century of Public School Reform* (Harvard University Press, 1995).

7. This is not as radical an argument as it may sound. For instance, Pincus has noted, "For the schools' purposes, verbal adoption of innovations may be entirely sufficient." John Pincus, "Incentives for Innovation in Public Schools," *Review of Educational Research* 44 (1974), p. 125. Fullan, *New Meaning,* p. 28, has agreed, writing, "The incentives system of public schools . . . makes it more profitable politically and bureaucratically to 'innovate' without risking the costs of real change."

8. Edward Pauly, *The Classroom Crucible: What Really Works, What Doesn't, and Why* (New York: Basic Books, 1991), p. 115.

9. In a study of Milwaukee's experience with school reform over time, Mitchell observed, "In some cases, the ink is barely dry on one project before the next is begun." Susan Mitchell, *Why MPS Doesn't Work: Barriers to Reform in the Milwaukee Public Schools* (Milwaukee Policy Research Institute, 1994), p. 14.

10. Anthony Bryk, Valerie Lee, and Peter Holland, *Catholic Schools and the Common Good* (Harvard University Press, 1994); Sara L. Lightfoot, *The Good High School: Portraits of Character and Culture* (New York: Basic Books, 1983); Stewart Purkey and Marshall Smith, "School Reform: The District Policy Implications of the Effective Schools Literature," *The Elementary School Journal* 85 (1985), pp. 353–89.

11. Richard F. Elmore, "Innovation in Education Policy," paper prepared for the Conference on Fundamental Questions of Innovation, Duke University, 1991.

12. For a discussion of the superintendent's central role see Gene Carter and William Cunningham, *The American School Superintendent: Leading in an Age of Pressure* (San Francisco: Jossey-Bass, 1997); Susan M. Johnson, *Leading to Change: The Challenge of the New Superintendency* (San Francisco: Jossey-Bass, 1996); Theodore Kowalski, *Keepers of the Flame: Contemporary Urban Superintendents* (Thousand Oaks, Calif.: Corwin Press, 1995); L. Harmon Zeigler, Ellen Kehoe, and Jane Reisman, *City Managers and School Superintendents: Response to Community Conflict* (New York: Praeger Publishers, 1985).

13. Johnson, *Leading to Change,* p. xi.

14. For a discussion of the difficulties with assessing the performance of school systems see Chester Finn, *We Must Take Charge: Our Schools and Our Future* (New York: Free Press, 1991); Myron Lieberman, *Public Education: An Autopsy* (Harvard University Press, 1993); Gary Orfield and Carol Ashkinaze, *The Closing Door: Conservative Policy and Black Opportunity* (University of Chicago Press, 1991); Sizer, *Horace's Hope.*

15. Tony Wagner, *How Schools Change: Lessons from Three Communities* (Boston: Beacon Press, 1994).

16. Stone has argued that, due to political pressures, "policymakers often create the illusion of control where there is none. People have a deep desire to believe that things are under control, that someone is responsible, and that we are not the victims of fate." Deborah Stone, *Policy Paradox and Political Reason* (Harper Collins, 1988), p. 115.

17. Larry Cuban, *How Teachers Taught: Constancy and Change in American Classrooms 1890–1980* (Albany: State University of New York Press, 1984); Seymour

Sarason, *The Predictable Failure of Educational Reform: Can We Change Course Before It's Too Late?* (San Francisco: Jossey-Bass, 1991); Karl Weick, "Educational Organizations As Loosely Coupled Systems," *Administrative Science Quarterly* 21 (1976), pp. 1–19.

18. The symbolic politics literature strongly suggests that it is much better to attempt reasonable actions, even if the actions are wrong, than to appear inactive or indecisive. George Gallup commented in 1962, "I would say that any sharp drop in popularity is likely to come from the President's inaction in the face of an important event. Inaction hurts a President more than anything else. A President can take some action, even a wrong one, and not lose his popularity." In Murray Edelman, *The Symbolic Uses of Politics* (Urbana: University of Illinois Press, 1972), p. 78.

19. Reviewing the history of school reform, Tyack and Cuban, *Tinkering toward Utopia,* p. 10, write, "Superintendents who wanted to keep their jobs needed to convince their school boards and policy elites that they were ready to adapt improvements." Carter and Cunningham, *American School Superintendent,* p. 99, contend that for superintendents "it is safer to do too much than it is to do too little. Although most boards can forgive a superintendent for trying too hard, very few accept halfhearted effort."

20. Like professionals of all stripes, superintendents are also inclined to attempt new things in order to utilize their training and skills. James Q. Wilson, *Bureaucracy: What Government Agencies Do and Why They Do It* (New York: Basic Books, 1989).

21. This point is similar to Mayhew's observation that a member of Congress must first be reelected in order to pursue any other goal, however ennobling that larger goal may be. David Mayhew, *Congress: The Electoral Connection* (Yale University Press, 1974).

22. Council of Great City Schools, *Superintendent Characteristics* (Washington, D.C., 1992).

23. Carter and Cunningham, *American School Superintendent,* p. 76, have noted, "School districts are not allowed the luxury of taking a long term perspective. They are forced to make quick fixes. . . . Educators are expected to turn things around quickly, and turning things around . . . includes showy, highly visible improvements that gain local, state, or national prominence."

24. The notion that organization leaders focus more on activity that advances their professional positions than on more mundane responsibilities is not unique to education. Wilson, *Bureaucracy,* p. 217, has written, about organizational management generally, that "executives rarely put those energies into administrative matters because they tend to be judged not by whether their agency is well-run but by whether the policies with which they are identified seem to succeed or fail."

25. Hugh Heclo, "Issue Networks and the Executive Establishment," in Anthony King, ed., *The New American Political System* (Washington, D.C.: American Enterprise Institute, 1978).

26. The five issues were the programmatic elements of a eight-part series *Education Week,* the education community's newspaper of record, ran on school reforms in early 1993. The five issues were the policy core of "third wave" school reforms in the 1990s. The timing of the features (spring of 1993) indicated that these issues were in mainstream circulation during the period studied.

27. The total number of measures proposed is only approximate, because respondents named only the most significant initiative (even if there were more) and because respondents described the initiatives with varying degrees of specificity (making it difficult to clearly understand the initiative a respondent was explaining). The total number of reform proposals was calculated by putting all respondent descriptions of each type of reform into categories. The total number of proposals in a district was

calculated by summing the different initiatives within each type of reform, then adding the totals from all five types of reform.

28. These extremely high passage rates contrast with the adversarial model evident in more professional legislatures, where most proposed measures never pass. It is possible that the rates are partially a function of question wording, but this is unlikely for several reasons. First, the respondents were generally veteran observers of school affairs, which makes it likely that they would have heard of major proposals, enacted or not. Second, rejected measures might very well attract more notoriety than enacted ones, meaning that respondents could easily be biased toward citing rejected proposals. Finally, a good deal of evidence in this study suggests that reform policymaking in school districts is much more tranquil than is commonly thought.

29. This reflects Wagner's finding that school community members unquestioningly assume that reform is necessary: "One of the most startling and unexpected findings . . . was that while most adults shared a commitment to educational change, they had never discussed why we need fundamental educational reform." (*How Schools Change,* p. 251.)

30. Each respondent had one response coded. For those respondents who offered more than one success, the first one they mentioned was coded unless they specified that they considered a subsequently mentioned success to be the greatest success.

31. Paul Berman and Milbrey McLaughlin, Federal Programs Supporting Educational Change, vol. 7: Factors Affecting Implementation and Continuation (Santa Monica: Rand Corporation, 1977); Elmore, "Getting to Scale with Good Educational Practice."

32. Miller, "Idealists and Cynics," p. 1.

33. Fullan, *New Meaning;* Purkey and Smith, "School Reform."

34. For instance, see Paul A. Sabatier and Daniel A. Mazamanian, "The Implementation of Public Policy: A Framework of Analysis," in Mazamanian and Sabatier, eds., *Effective Policy Implementation* (Lexington, Mass.: D. C. Heath, 1981).

35. Richard F. Elmore, Penelope Peterson, and Sarah McCarthy, *Restructuring in the Classroom: Teaching, Learning, and School Organization* (San Francisco: Jossey-Bass, 1996); Fullan, *New Meaning;* Johnson, *Leading to Change;* Wagner, *How Schools Change.*

36. Purkey and Smith, "School Reform," p. 384.

37. Rick Ginsberg and Robert Wimpelberg, "Educational Change by Commission: Attempting Trickle-down Reform," *Educational Evaluation and Policy Analysis Review* 9 (1987), pp. 344–60.

38. Jane David, *Restructuring in Process: Lessons from Pioneering Districts* (Washington, D.C.: National Governors' Association, 1989); Milbrey McLaughlin, "The Rand Change Agent Study: Ten Years Later," in Allan Odden, ed., *Educational Policy Implementation* (Albany: State University of New York Press, 1991); Pauly, *Classroom Crucible.*

39. John Clarke and Russell Agne, *Interdisciplinary High School Teaching: Strategies for Integrated Learning* (Boston: Allyn and Bacon, 1997).

40. David, *Restructuring in Process;* Murphy, *Restructuring Schools.*

41. Elmore, Peterson, and McCarthy, *Restructuring in the Classroom.*

42. Only reforms reported to have been proposed after the beginning of 1992 were included. The post-1992 specification is necessary because, even though respondents were interviewed in 1995 and were specifically asked for reforms proposed in "the last three years," a number of respondents cited measures proposed in 1991 or earlier. The problem with including these measures is that, by dint of being in place for five or seven years, these measures enjoy an inflated score for implementation and success. The year in which a type of reform was enacted was estimated by averaging the dates of enactment reported by all local respondents who indicated that a measure was proposed.

43. A proposal was deemed to be required by the state if a majority of respondents reporting a proposal said, in response to a question inquiring about whether the state required action, that the measure had been required by the state.

44. There is a problem here in that respondents are evaluating reforms only in terms of their goals rather than on some kind of universal scale. However, comparing the success of reforms in any more abstract fashion would require information beyond what it was feasible to acquire in my study.

45. This argument will not come as a shock to students of school reform, as it employs insights developed by such earlier scholars as Chubb and Moe, Cuban, Elmore, and Sarason. See John E. Chubb and Terry M. Moe, *Politics, Markets, and America's Schools* (Brookings, 1990); Larry Cuban, *Urban School Chiefs under Fire* (University of Chicago Press, 1976); Richard F. Elmore, "Teaching, Learning, and Organization: School Restructuring and the Recurring Dilemmas of Reform," paper presented at the annual meeting of the American Educational Research Association, Chicago, 1991; Sarason, *Predictable Failure.*

46. The extent of knowledge and experience possessed by local observers of politics and policy is often not appreciated. For instance, when asked, "How long have you been following local educational affairs?" the mean respondent estimated that he or she had been observing local education for seventeen years.

Part Three

PUBLIC SCHOOL CHOICE

Analyzing School Choice Reforms That Use America's Traditional Forms of Parental Choice

Caroline M. Hoxby

THE MAJORITY OF THE STATES in the United States are currently considering or have recently passed reforms that increase the ease with which parents may choose schools for their children.[1] At first view these reforms seem to take elementary and secondary education into wholly unknown territory. Yet this view neglects the fact that choices made by American parents have traditionally been an important force in determining the education their children receive. Parents' ability to choose among fiscally independent public school districts (through residential decisions) and to choose private schools (by paying tuition) are such an established feature of American education that they are almost taken for granted. Yet through these choices American parents exercise more control over their children's schooling than do many of their European counterparts.[2] However, American parents are not all equally able to exercise choice. High-income parents routinely exercise more choice than low-income parents because high-income

The author gratefully acknowledges helpful comments from Nathan Glazer, Bryan Hassel, Paul Hill, Lawrence Katz, and Paul Peterson. Ilyana Kuziemko provided very able research assistance for this chapter. All errors are the author's own.

parents have more school districts and private schools within their choice set. Moreover, there is significant variation in the degree of choice across different areas of the country. Some metropolitan areas, for instance, have many independent school districts and/or a number of private schools.[3] Other metropolitan areas are completely monopolized by one school district or have almost no private schooling.

In this chapter I attempt to answer three related questions. First and foremost, what general facts can we learn by examining the traditional forms of school choice in the United States? In particular we need to understand the relationships between school choice and student achievement, student segregation (along lines of ability, income, and taste for education as well as race and ethnicity),[4] school efficiency, teachers' salaries and teacher unionism, and the degree to which parents are involved in and influence their children's schools. Second, how do the general facts that we garner from traditional school choice carry over to analyses of reforms such as charter schools, vouchers for private schools, and open enrollment programs? Third, what information do we still need if we are to accurately predict the effects of reforms? And what empirical strategies might we use to get such information? For evidence I draw upon previous empirical work included in several studies.[5] Although I briefly sketch the empirical strategy of each study, I do not attempt to present the results or methodology in detail. Rather, my goal in this chapter is to summarize the results and discuss their implications for school choice reforms.

How Analysis of Traditional Choice Informs the Debate over School Reform

Analysis of school choice reforms should begin with the two basic, traditional forms of school choice in the United States, choice among public school districts and choice between public and private schools. These two traditional forms of choice already give some parents a substantial degree of choice, and the effects of their choices are useful for predicting the effects of reforms. Moreover, empirical evidence on how traditional choice affects students is the *only* way we can learn about the general equilibrium and long-term effects of school choice. For instance, there are a few recent or ongoing studies (including one I am conducting) that evaluate charter and voucher schools using randomized "treatment" and "control" groups of students. The studies by Greene, Peterson, and Du and Greene, Howell, and

Peterson are excellent examples.[6] Studies like these can inform us about the effects of voucher or charter schools on the students who actually use the schools. Unfortunately, such studies can tell us nothing about the effects that a widespread voucher or charter school policy would have on who attends public schools or how public schools respond to competition. Analysis of the two traditional forms of choice does inform us about these crucial issues. Furthermore, school choice reforms are always layered on top of traditional choice, and households will make different traditional choices as reforms are added.

Traditional Choice Among Public School Districts: Background and Predictions

In this section I describe choice among public school districts. Later I briefly discuss *intra*district choice, a scheme that has only some of the characteristics of choice among districts. A household chooses among public school districts by choosing a residence. The degree to which households can exercise this form of choice depends heavily on the number, size, and residence patterns of the school districts in the area centered around the jobs of the adults in these households. There are some metropolitan areas in the United States that have many small school districts with reasonably comparable characteristics. Boston, for instance, has seventy school districts within a thirty-minute commute of the downtown area and many more within a forty-five-minute commute. Miami, on the other hand, has only one school district (Dade County) that covers the entire metropolitan area. People with jobs in rural areas typically have only one district or a few school districts among which to choose.

Choice among public school districts—as a form of choice—has several important properties. The first is that districts that are good, efficient providers of schooling tend to be rewarded with larger budgets. This fiscal reward process works because conventional American school finance makes each district's budget depend somewhat on local property taxes, which in turn depend on house prices within the district, which in turn depend on how marginal home buyers value the local schools. Rewards for good, efficient provision of schooling can be obtained so long as districts have a significant amount of fiscal autonomy (especially over marginal revenues and expenditures).[7] The fiscal reward process tends to be sustainable over the long term because it depends on decentralized choices. This is in contrast to centralized reward systems—for example, financial or other "merit" awards for successful school districts that are distributed by the state. These tend to be unsustainable because states cannot, after the fact, credibly adhere to processes that reduce (in relative terms) the amount of money going to failing school districts.[8]

The second important property of traditional choice among public school districts is that parents who prefer different amounts of school spending and different types of schools sort themselves into different districts. As a result, each district is more homogeneous than the metropolitan area is in general, and the residents of each district tend to vote for taxes and support schools that approximately fulfill their spending and curricular desires. This means that districts offer differentiated schooling that follows local parents' preferences to a certain degree.

In consequence, choice among public school districts creates residential patterns that mirror households' desired levels of school spending. This is in contrast to residential patterns that purely reflect households' incomes or housing desires. Of course desired school spending depends partly on income, but it also depends on how much a household prefers to spend money on schooling relative to other goods or investments. Low-income or minority households are the most likely to be prevented from making reasonably optimal investments in their children's schooling, because their ability to choose residences in more than one district may be severely constrained by their budgets or discrimination.

Another consequence of choice among public school districts is that parents' preferences have some sway over what local schools do. Any given school district's budget is, for instance, allocated more according to parents' preferences (than, say, according to the preferences of school staff members or the state department of education) when parents have more choice among districts. This is simply because, when parents have more choices, school budgets are more elastic with respect to parents' preferences, and therefore policy is more responsive to their preferences.

Evidence of what happens when an area has more choice among public school districts is useful mainly for analyzing charter school reforms and open enrollment reforms. A charter school is a school that receives a charter to educate public school students, receives a "tuition" payment (from public revenues) for each pupil it enrolls, and admits students nonselectively or at random. Although charter schools are "public" schools, they are supposed to have a high degree of administrative autonomy and as much fiscal autonomy as a stable tuition payment per pupil can give them.[9] Opening a charter school thus has some but not all of the features of creating an additional public school district to compete with the initial district.

An open enrollment program allows students to attend schools in districts outside their districts of residence. Whether an open enrollment program closely resembles an expansion of choice among public school districts depends largely on the financial transfers that accompany transferring students. If an open enrollment program has financial transfers that closely simulate the fiscal pressures of choice among public school districts, the program is a means of intensifying traditional choice among public school districts by reducing mobility costs and allowing many more households to be on the margin between districts. Most actual open enrollment programs, however, do not have financial arrangements that simulate the fiscal pressures of choice among districts. The financial transfer is usually small compared to the receiving district's own average expenditure per pupil. A financial transfer that is only a small fraction of a district's per-pupil expenditure guarantees that the movement of students from one district to another must remain tiny relative to the size of the receiving district—even in the long run. A somewhat perverse financial arrangement that sometimes occurs in an open enrollment plan is that the money that accompanies the transferring student comes wholly or partly from the state rather than from the sending district.

In summary, studying traditional choice among public school districts is helpful for analyzing charter school and open enrollment reforms because all three types of choice give us a general sense of on what bases parents choose among schools, how public schools differentiate themselves given that they are all subject to public scrutiny and public constraints, whether public providers react to competition for students by improving their programs, how the degree of choice among public providers affects parents' willingness to pay for private school alternatives, and how students self-segregate among schools when they can choose, but receiving schools cannot discriminate among them.[10] Traditional choice among public school districts is less helpful for understanding charter school and open enrollment reforms to the extent that (1) the financial arrangements of the reforms have quite different properties than traditional choice, and (2) charter schools and open enrollment programs depend on the sufferance or cooperation of local school districts, making them less sustainable than traditional choice.

Choice Between Public and Private Schools: Background and Predictions

The second way in which parents have traditionally been able to exercise choice in the United States is by enrolling their children in private schools.

Figure 6-1. *Percentage of K–12 Students Enrolled in Private Schools, 1960–90*

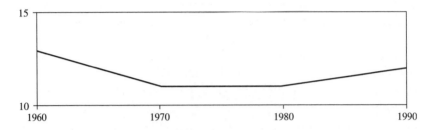

Source: Author's calculations based on data from the U.S. Census of Population 1960, 1970, 1980, 1990.

Private school tuition in America is not subsidized by public monies (as it is in some European countries), so parents can afford private schools only if they can pay tuition and also pay taxes to support local public schools.[11] Partly as a result, private schools tend to enroll fewer than 15 percent of American elementary and secondary students. This percentage reached a peak of just under 15 percent in the early 1960s, declined to 10 percent by 1980, and has since rebounded to 12 percent. Figure 6-1 depicts the percentage of K–12 students enrolled in private schools between 1960 and 1990.

There is tremendous variation in the schooling offered and the tuition charged by private schools in the United States. Approximately 90 percent of private school students attend schools that are affiliated with religious groups, but these include a variety of Christian and non-Christian groups and have tuitions that range from token amounts ("$100 or what parents can pay") to over $10,000. The remaining 10 percent of private school students attend schools with no religious affiliation; these include many of the independent college preparatory schools that charge tuitions of $5,000 or more. More than 65 percent of American private school students attend schools affiliated with the Catholic Church; these vary from modest parochial schools with token tuitions to elite college preparatory schools that compete with the independents for students. The modal private school student in the United States attends a Catholic school that is parochial or diocesan and charges a tuition of about $1,000 (for elementary school) or $2,200 (for secondary school).

A key feature of American private schools is that they typically subsidize tuition with monies from donations or (less often) income from endowments. The share of schooling costs that is covered by subsidies is larger in schools that serve low-income students, but even relatively expensive private schools charge subsidized tuitions. For instance, Catholic elementary schools, on average, cover 50 percent of their costs with donations from local households, donations channeled through the local diocese, and teachers' and parents' contributed services and goods. (Teachers who are members of religious orders also implicitly subsidize the schools, because their salaries are minimal.) Catholic secondary schools are less subsidized: On average, tuition payments to Catholic secondary schools cover about 75 percent of the actual costs of schooling. Even the most expensive religiously affiliated private schools in the United States—those affiliated with the Friends (Quakers)—charge tuitions that average only 80 percent of their costs.[12] Note that schools that serve low-income households and charge highly subsidized tuitions are frequently oversubscribed and must ration school places through waiting lists.

Some cities and areas of the United States have significantly larger shares of students in private schools than others. Metropolitan areas, for instance, range from highs of 33 percent of students in private schools to lows of approximately 0 percent of students in private schools. This variation is created by historical accident, the donations available for subsidizing private schools in an area, and the quality of public schools. I return to these sources of variation a bit later.

Choice between private and public schools has several important properties. First, private schools that efficiently offer high-quality education tend to be rewarded by gaining more applicants. At the very least, the larger applicant pool allows a private school to be more selective. More often, a larger applicant pool allows a private school to expand. Symmetrically, public schools that do not offer quality education efficiently are likely to lose students to private schools. The students who are drawn away are, for any given public school, those with the greatest taste for the type of education offered by private schools. A second property of choice between private and public schools is that private schools are likely to have an ambiguous impact on the finances of local public schools. On one hand, an increased supply of private schools tends to draw into the private school sector parents who, had their children remained in public schools, might have supported generous public school spending. This phenomenon tends to decrease voter support for public school spending. On the other hand, an increased supply of private schools draws into the private school sector students who would otherwise have had to be educated at public expense. This phenomenon tends to increase public school spending *per pupil*.

Increased private school availability should change patterns of residential segregation because private school parents who would want to live in districts with expensive public schools if private schools did not exist will be willing to live in less expensive districts. Such changes in residential segregation, however, are limited by the fact that private school parents prefer to live with neighbors who have similar professions, educations, and preferences for other local public goods. For instance, private school parents are unlikely to live with low-income neighbors just to avoid paying taxes to support moderately expensive public schools. Finally, private schools put mild pressure on public schools to pay the same input costs that private schools pay. In particular, private schools are less likely to be unionized and to accept supply contracts for political reasons. If they do not pay union wage premiums and pay competitive prices for supplies, their lower costs indirectly put a little pressure on public schools to be cost efficient. The pressure is small, though, because the fact that private school parents continue to pay taxes to support public schools drives a considerable price wedge between private and public schools with comparable costs.

Evidence of the effects of traditional private school choice is most useful for predicting the effects of vouchers. Some properties of vouchers would be quite similar to those of traditional private school choice: Successful private schools would be rewarded with larger pools of applicants, and the least efficient public schools would most likely lose students. The fiscal impact vouchers would have on public schools is ambiguous, but possibly less positive than the fiscal impact of private school competition on public schools. The difference is that vouchers typically would be funded with monies from the local public schools. Some students who would attend private schools even in the absence of a voucher program would use vouchers: This would have a negative impact on per-pupil spending in the sending districts. However, this effect would be offset by the positive impact on per-pupil spending that would occur whenever a student used a voucher who would have, in the absence of a voucher program, attended the public schools. This positive impact would occur because all voucher amounts proposed thus far have been significantly smaller than per-pupil spending in the sending public school districts. Some of the indirect fiscal impacts of vouchers on per-pupil public school spending would be positive as well. For instance, some parents with a taste for quality education would be likely to remain in districts that they would abandon for suburban districts if vouchers were not available. Keeping parents like these has a positive effect on a district's property prices, and therefore on the tax base that supports public schools.

Interactions between the Two Traditional Forms of School Choice

We expect that the two traditional forms of school choice will substitute for one another to some degree. Parents who are able to choose districts that offer schooling and per-pupil costs closer to their desires will have less incentive to send their children to private schools. Of course, public and private school choice are unlikely to be complete substitutes for one another, because the two sectors function under somewhat different constraints. For instance, parents with strong preferences for religious education cannot satisfy these in the public sector; parents with strong preferences for public schooling cannot satisfy these in private schools.

Similarly, we expect some interaction among the reforms. Availability of charter schools is likely to reduce the use of private school vouchers or open enrollment programs. Logically, the more one reform offers a needed type of choice, the less the alternative reforms will be desired or used. For instance, the less autonomy charter schools have, the more parents will want to use private school vouchers. Also, areas that already have substantial amounts of choice among public school districts or choice of private schools are unlikely to make heavy use of charter school programs or open enrollment programs (unless the latter have perverse fiscal arrangements). Besides, areas with substantial amounts of choice among public school districts are less likely to make heavy use of vouchers. The same cannot be said of areas that already have substantial amounts of choice of private schools. Since vouchers would give an opportunity to transfer to parents already using private schools, vouchers would be highly utilized in areas with high private school shares. The means testing in most proposed voucher programs will attempt to reduce transfers by parents already using private schools.

Evidence on the Effects of Competition among Public School Districts

To determine the effects of competition among public schools, we might compare metropolitan areas that have had long-term differences in parents' ease of choice among districts.[13] Ease of choice depends both on the number of districts in the area and on the evenness with which enrollment is spread over those districts. Choice is easier in a metropolitan area where parents choose among twenty districts of equal size than in an area where three quarters of enrollment falls into one of twenty districts, which in turn is easier than in an area with only one school district. A Herfindahl index based on districts' enrollment shares is a good measure of the ease of choice because it incorporates both these facts—the number of districts and the evenness of districts' enrollment shares.[14]

Table 6-1 shows the how much metropolitan areas differ in the degree of choice available among public school districts. The differences are largely a result of historical accident and geography. However, we might worry that districts' enrollments can reflect their success: A highly successful and efficient district might attract a disproportionate share of its metropolitan area's enrollment. It might even attract smaller districts to consolidate with it. These phenomena would tend to make simple comparisons of metropolitan areas with public school enrollments concentrated in a few districts versus metropolitan areas with enrollments spread evenly over many districts biased against finding positive effects of competition among districts. Formally, the observed degree of choice available among public school districts is possibly related to the school quality experienced by the typical student.

To obtain unbiased estimates we need to identify geographic or historical factors that increase a metropolitan area's tendency to have many small independent school districts. We need instrumental variables related to the demand for independent school districts, but unrelated to contemporary public school quality. I use the fact that metropolitan areas with more streams had more natural barriers and boundaries that, because they increased students' travel time to school, caused the initial school district lines to be drawn up so there were smaller districts.[15]

This estimation strategy allows me to control for a wide range of background variables that might also influence schools or students. For instance, I control for the effect of household income, parents' educational attainment, family size, family composition (single-parent households), race, region, metropolitan area size, and the local population's income, racial composition, poverty, educational attainment, and urbanness. Because I have good measures of self-segregation by school and school district (for racial, ethnic, and income segregation), I can differentiate the effects of choice on self-segregation from the effects on student achievement and school efficiency.[16]

My best estimates of the effects of competition among public school districts, displayed in table 6-2, are gauged in terms of an increase in the Herfindahl index of one standard deviation. This corresponds to a substan-

Table 6-1. *Degree of Choice among Public School Districts of Illustrative Metropolitan Areas*

Metropolitan areas with the most choice among public school districts		Metropolitan areas with the least choice among public school districts	
Metropolitan area	*Herfindahl index[a]*	*Metropolitan area*	*Herfindahl index[a]*
Albany, N.Y.	0.0333	Honolulu, Hawaii[b]	1
Bergen-Passaic, N.J.	0.0346	Miami, Fla.	1
Boston, Mass.	0.0352	Las Vegas, N.V.	1
Middlesex-Somerset-Hunterdon, N.J.	0.0366	Fort Lauderdale, Fla.	1
Pittsburgh, Pa.	0.0368	Daytona Beach, Fla.	1
Riverside-San Bernardino, Calif.[c]	0.0370	Fort Myers, Fla.	1
Monmouth-Ocean, N.J.	0.0377	Albuquerque, N.M.	1
Minneapolis, Minn.	0.0416	Hagerstown, Md.	1
Atlantic City, N.J.	0.0490	Jacksonville, N.C.	1
San Francisco, Calif.[c]	0.0531	Sarasota, Fla.	1
Binghamton, N.Y.	0.0563	Odessa, Tex.	1
York, Pa.	0.0568	Cheyenne, Wyo.	1
Scranton, Pa.	0.0572	Lakeland/Winter Haven, Fla.	1
Johnstown, Pa.	0.0573	Reno, N.V.	1
San Jose, Calif.	0.0576	Boca Raton, Fla.	1
Dayton, Ohio	0.0578	Wilmington, N.C.	1
Allentown, Pa.	0.0598	Ocala, Fla.	1
Anaheim-Santa Ana, Calif.[c]	0.0616	Melbourne/Palm Bay, Fla.	1
Seattle, Wash.	0.0631	Lompoc, Calif.[c]	1
Rochester, N.Y.	0.0638	Panama City, Fla.	1
Phoenix, Ark.	0.0642	Bradenton, Fla.	1

Source: Author's calculation based on U.S. Department of Education, National Center for Education Statistics, *School District Data Book,* 1990.

a. An alternative measure of choice among school districts is the raw number of districts in a metropolitan area. However, this measure favors larger metropolitan areas for any degree of choice. The metropolitan areas with the largest numbers of districts are Greater New York City, 286; Chicago, Ill., 209; Philadelphia, Pa., 166; Detroit, Mich., 117; Boston, Mass., 114; Bergen-Passaic, N.J., 94; Los Angeles, Calif., 82; Monmouth-Ocean, N.J., 78; Pittsburgh, Pa., 74; Minneapolis, Minn., 68; Middlesex-Somerset-Hunterdon, N.J., 68; Tulsa, Okla., 65; Portland, Ore., 62; Oklahoma City, Okla., 59; Dallas, Tex., 59; Phoenix, Ariz., 56; Cincinnati, Ohio, 56; Riverside-San Bernardino, Calif., 55; Cleveland, Ohio, 54; Albany, N.Y., 54; and St. Louis, Mo., 53.

Another measure of choice among school districts is the number of districts per 10,000 school-age persons. This measure favors metropolitan areas that have large land areas for their populations. The metropolitan areas with the largest numbers of districts per 10,000 school-age persons are Bismark, N.D., 11.76; Redding, Calif., 10.02; Burlington, Vt., 9.40; Dover, N.H., 9.08; Glens Falls, N.Y., 8.84; Enid, Okla., 8.16; Atlantic City, N.J., 8.14; Great Falls, Mont., 7.98; Salem, Ore., 7.70; Billings, Mont., 7.63; Pittsfield, Mass., 7.60; Texarkana, Ark., 7.48; Denison-Sherman, Tex., 7.29; Peoria-Pekin, Ill., 7.24; Tulare, Calif., 6.84; Yuba City, Calif., 6.62; and Grand Forks, N.D., 6.56.

b. Hawaii is one school district fiscally, so the school district is larger than the metropolitan area of Honolulu. Obviously there is no school district in the state of Hawaii.

c. California has school districts that have almost no fiscal independence, so it is also virtually one fiscal school district. Therefore, it is somewhat deceptive to describe metropolitan areas such as Riverside-San Bernardino, San Francisco, San Jose, and Anaheim-Santa Ana as having significant choice among school districts.

Table 6-2. *Effects of Competition among Public School Districts*[a]

Variable	Effect
Effect on per-pupil spending	17 percent decrease
Effect on student achievement as measured by test scores	3 percentile point improvement
Effect on student achievement as measured by wages	4 percent increase
Effect on student achievement as measured by educational attainment	0.4 additional years of education
Effect on parents' involvement in students' school careers	30 percent increase in probability that parents visit school annually

Sources: Caroline Hoxby, "Does Competition among Public Schools Benefit Students and Taxpayers?" 1997 revision of Working Paper 1979, Cambridge, Mass.: National Bureau of Economic Research (NBER), 1994; and Caroline Hoxby (1998) "When Parents Can Choose, What Do They Choose? The Effects of School Choice on Curriculum and Atmosphere," in Susan Mayer and Paul E. Peterson, eds., *When Schools Make a Difference*, forthcoming.

a. Consider an increase of one standard deviation in the number of school districts in a metropolitan or a decrease of one standard deviation in the concentration of enrollment among school districts in a metropolitan area. Note that smaller effects are found for metropolitan areas in which school districts do not have financial autonomy (most revenue is state determined).

tial increase in the degree of choice among districts; for instance, it is the difference between having 3 and 13 equal-sized districts or the difference between having 4 and a very large number (100, say) equal-sized districts. An increase of one standard deviation in the degree of choice among districts causes a small (and statistically significant) improvement in student achievement.[17] Students' reading and math scores improve by about 2 percentile points, for instance. However, an increase of one standard deviation in choice among districts causes a large improvement in schools' efficiency. This is because the small improvement in student achievement takes place even though schools lower their per-pupil costs by 17 percent when they face an increase in choice of a standard deviation. What is striking is the opposite sign of these effects: An increase in choice improves student achievement even while accomplishing substantial cost savings. The implications for schools' productivity (the ratio of student achievement to dollars spent) are powerful.

What about the effects of competition among districts on the segregation of students? These turn out to be insignificant for a reason that may not occur to us at first glance. The degree of racial, ethnic, and income segregation that a student experiences is related to the degree of choice among *schools* in a metropolitan area, but not to the degree of choice among *districts.* (In fact, the point estimates have the wrong sign for the latter relationship.) In other words, students are just as segregated in schools in metropolitan areas that have few districts as they are in metropolitan areas that have many districts. Households sort themselves into neighborhoods inside districts; neighborhoods and schools are small enough relative to districts that district boundaries have little effect on segregation. This result demonstrates how important it is to compare realistic alternatives. The realistic alternative to a metropolitan area with a high degree of choice among districts is not a metropolitan area in which all schools are perfectly desegregated and every student is exposed to similar peers. The realistic alternative is a metropolitan area with a low degree of choice among districts and a substantial degree of segregation among schools.

Choice among public school districts has several other effects worth noting. First, choice among districts and choice between public and private schools are substitutes for one another. An increase of a standard deviation in the degree of choice among districts lowers the share of children who attend private schools by about 1 percentage point (on a base of about 12 percentage points, recall). When parents have more choice within the public sector, they are more likely to be satisfied by their public options and are less likely to choose private options.

A second effect is that when parents have more choice among districts they tend to be more involved in their children's schooling.[18] For instance, an increase of one standard deviation in the degree of choice causes one out of every three parents to visit the school in the course of a year and causes school administrators to say that parents have a more significant influence on school policy.[19] Furthermore, parents appear to induce schools to actually pursue the policies that parents, on average, say in surveys that they want to be pursued: more challenging curricula, stricter academic requirements, and more structured and discipline-oriented environments. For instance, a standard deviation in the degree of choice in a metropolitan area raises the probability by 8 percent that a school's regular mathematics sequence ends in a twelfth-grade course that contains at least some calculus.[20]

Finally, the beneficial effects of choice among districts on schools' productivity depend on districts' having a significant degree of fiscal independence. In states such as California where districts depend almost entirely on state per-student allocations for their budgets, the positive effects of choice on student achievement and cost savings are reduced by more than half. This is probably because successful schools are not rewarded through the property tax or budget process for improving achievement or reducing costs. This result has implications for analyses of reforms, which do not always give participating schools sufficient fiscal independence to allow them to benefit financially from their own success.

Evidence of the Effects of Private School Competition

To determine the effects of private school competition on public schools and public school students, we might compare areas with and without substantial private school enrollment.[21] Table 6-3 shows the U.S. metropolitan areas with the highest and lowest percentages of students enrolled in private schools. There is substantial variation in private school attendance, even within states. However, low-quality public schools raise the demand for private schools as substitutes for public schools. Therefore, simple comparisons among metropolitan areas would confound the effect of greater private school competitiveness with the increased demand for

Table 6-3. *Percentages of Students in Private Schools in Illustrative Metropolitan Areas*

Metropolitan areas with the highest percentages of students in private school		Metropolitan areas with the lowest percentages of students in private school	
Metropolitan area	*Percentage of students in private schools*	*Metropolitan area*	*Percentage of students in private schools*
Dubuque, Iowa	33.95	Edinburg-McAllen-	3.38
New Orleans, La.	28.50	Mission-Pharr, Tex.	
Honolulu, Hawaii	27.55	Las Cruces, N.M.	4.37
Philadelphia, Pa.	26.74	Brownsville, Tex.	4.56
St. Louis, Mo.	25.67	Lawton, Okla.	4.59
Jersey City, N.J.	24.67	Texarkana, Ark.	4.62
Stamford, Conn.	24.20	Peterville, Calif.	4.88
San Francisco, Calif.	23.81	Orem-Provo, Utah	4.90
New York, N.Y.	23.24	Killeen-Temple, Tex.	5.00
Cleveland, Ohio	22.43	San Angelo, Tex.	5.02
Trenton, N.J.	22.32	Hickory, N.C.	5.05
Wilmington, Del.	22.23	Pine Bluff, Ark.	5.14
Bergen-Passaic, N.J.	21.97	Casper, Wyo.	5.14
Erie, Pa.	21.95	Odessa, Tex.	5.22
Cincinatti, Ohio	21.67	Pueblo, Colo.	5.26
Milwaukee, Wisc.	21.18	Fresno, Calif.	5.27
Baton Rouge, La.	20.96	Fayetteville, N.C.	5.82
Chicago, Ill.	20.58	Sherman-Denison, Tex.	5.88
Green Bay, Wisc.	20.55	Merced, Calif.	5.89
Salem-Gloucester, Mass.	19.89	Yuba City, Calif.	5.91

Sources: Hoxby, "Does Competition among Public Schools Benefit Students and Taxpayers?"; and Hoxby "When Parents Can Choose, What Do They Choose?"

private schools where public schools are poor in quality. Formally, private school enrollment is likely to be endogenous to (partly caused by) public school quality, and this endogeneity would lead simple estimates to be biased toward finding negative effects of private school competition on public schools.

To obtain unbiased estimates, we need to identify factors that increase the supply of private schools in an area and that are unrelated to public school quality. Formally, we need instrumental variables that shift the supply of private schools and are unrelated to the demand for private schools that is generated by low-quality public schools. I use the fact that a denomination's private schools have more resources with which to provide tuition subsidies in areas that are densely populated by that denomination. Since religious composition of an area is largely a matter of historical accident, it is not likely to have an independent effect on public school quality. Areas with higher Catholic population shares, for instance, have larger shares of teaching services donated by members of religious orders (worth 30 to 35 percent of costs) and provide larger shares of Catholic school income through offerings (25 to 50 percent of costs). Therefore, denominations' population shares fulfil the conditions for a good instrument: They are positively correlated with the supply of private schools, but are likely to be uncorrelated with the part of the demand for private schools that is generated by public school quality. Catholic population shares provide the best instrumental variables not only because school subsidies are a relatively high-priority use of Catholic Church funds, but also because Roman Catholicism is spread across the entire United States (it is not all concentrated in one state or one region) and is associated with many ethnic groups (unlike some other denominations, which are associated with only one or two ethnic groups).

Note that this estimation strategy allows me to control for a variety of background factors that might be correlated both with the demand for private schools and with public school quality (or public school students' performance). For instance, I control for the effect of a household's belonging to a denomination. If being Catholic, say, affects a household's demand for public school spending or the achievement of its children, this effect is controlled for (and not confounded with the effect of more or less private school competition). I also control for the effect of certain ethnic group concentrations in an area, for the effect of racial and ethnic homogeneity in an area, for the effect of religious homogeneity in an area, and for the effect of religiosity of an area. Numerous other background factors are controlled for: family income, the share of households in poverty, parents' educational

Table 6-4. *Effects of Competition for Public Schools from Private Schools*[a]

Variable	Effect
Effect on public schools' per-pupil spending	Approximately 0
Effect on achievement of public school students as measured by test scores	8 percentile point improvement
Effect on achievement of public school students as measured by wages	12 percent increase
Effect on achievement of public school students as measured by educational attainment	12 percent increase in the probability of college graduation

Source: Caroline Hoxby, "Do Private Schools Provide Competition for Public Schools?" Working Paper 4978, NBER, 1994.

a. Consider an increase in exogenous tuition subsidies of $1,000 or an increase in exogenous private school enrollment of 10 percent.

attainment, family size, family composition (single-parent households), urbanness, population density, and region of the country.[22]

My best estimates of the effect of more competition from private schools, shown in table 6-4, suggest that if private schools in an area receive sufficient resources to subsidize each student's tuition by $1,000, the achievement of *public* school students rises. This is true whether the measure of achievement is test scores, ultimate educational attainment, or wages. The effect on mathematics and reading scores is an improvement of 8 percentile points. The effect on educational attainment is an 8 percent increase in the probability of graduating from high school and a 12 percent increase in the probability of getting a baccalaureate degree. The effect on wages (for those who work, later in life at ages 29–37) is a 12 percent increase.

Interestingly enough, the estimates indicate that competition from private schools does not have a significant effect on public school spending per pupil. This is probably because the two forces described earlier offset one another. On the one hand, an increased supply of private schools tends to draw into the private school sector parents who, had their children remained in public schools, might have supported generous public school spending. This phenomenon tends to decrease voter support for public school spending. On the other hand, an increased supply of private schools draws students into the private school sector who would otherwise have had to be educated at public expense. This phenomenon tends to increase public school spending *per pupil.*

What about the effects of private school competition on the self-segregation of students among schools? I will not dwell on these estimates, because their ability to predict the effects of private school voucher programs is limited. This is because the estimates are based on private schools that have religious affiliations, mainly Catholic schools. In contrast, proposed voucher programs often exclude private schools with religious affiliations and always constrain private schools that accept vouchers to either accept all voucher applicants or accept some random sample of them.

The one thing about the estimates that is noteworthy because it has general applicability is that all the self-segregation effects are very small. This is for two reasons. First, public schools are already quite segregated along lines of race, ethnicity, parents' income, and students' performance. When people attempt to imagine the effect of increasing private school availability, they sometimes conjure up a notional public school that is perfectly desegregated. Possibly the effects of private school competition on such a notional public school would be dramatic. However, even if we could estimate such effects, they would be irrelevant, since actual public schools do not correspond closely to this ideal. The actual self-segregation effects of traditional private school competition are small simply because a large increase in self-segregation cannot be obtained by sorting out an already segregated public school. The second reason that self-segregation effects are small is that an increase in private school competition typically allows self-segregation in public schools to increase slightly while self-segregation in private schools decreases slightly. These effects tend to offset one another.

My best estimates suggest that, if private schools in an area receive enough resources to subsidize tuition by $1,000, segregation along lines of race, ethnicity, income, and students' performance decreases at private schools by small but statistically significant amounts and changes at public schools by amounts that have positive point estimates, but are statistically not different from zero.[23]

Finally, note that both private school competition and competition among public schools tend to hold down input costs. Specifically, both types of competition constrain the salary increases that teachers' unions gain for their members (the union wage premium of 12 percent is reduced by about one-third for a standard deviation increase in competition among districts and by about one-half for a $1,000 subsidy for private schools).[24] This result parallels a standard result from private industry: Increased competition in the market for a product (in this case, the market offering schooling to students) tends to decrease the wage premiums earned by unionized workers and other inputs that are supplied by suppliers with market power.

Intradistrict Choice Programs

Intradistrict choice has been used by a number of large school districts for some time. The least dramatic forms of intradistrict choice are magnet or alternative schools to which students typically apply based on their preference for alternative curricula or schooling environments. In the more dramatic forms of intradistrict choice (Manhattan's District 4 or Cambridge, Massachusetts), every student must actively express a preference for a school. Intradistrict choice shares some features of the two traditional forms of school choice discussed above. In particular, the fact that parents and students make an active choice is likely to make them more committed and involved in schooling. However, intradistrict choice programs rarely give schools a degree of fiscal or curricular autonomy similar to that they enjoy in independent school districts or private schools. It is important to recognize that a district that gives fiscal or curricular autonomy to a school in a given year has not given the school long-term autonomy unless the district can bind itself not to revoke that autonomy. Such binding often proves to be politically impossible. For instance, intradistrict choice programs sometimes exhibit long-term fiscal incentives that are perverse because the district cannot, after the fact, resist taking money from successful schools and giving it to unsuccessful schools.

The gathering of evidence on intradistrict choice is in an exploratory phase. My own work demonstrates only that simple estimates (comparing districts that have intradistrict choice to districts that do not) are badly biased.[25] The bias is caused by the fact that districts do not randomly enact intradistrict choice programs. Such programs are usually associated with the hiring of superintendents who are given a free hand to "turn around" districts that have recently experienced sharp decreases in student achievement. It is difficult to create a control group of schools that form a good comparison for this type of school. Even before and after studies do not enable us to disentangle the effects of intradistrict choice from the effects of getting a new superintendent who is paid more and given greater latitude than previous administrators.[26]

Lessons for Reform and What We Still Need to Know

The evidence on the effects of traditional school choice teaches us several lessons that are helpful for analyzing reforms. They are as follows.

First, public schools can and do react to competition by improving the schooling they offer and by reducing costs. They are not passive organizations that allow their students and budgets to be withdrawn without responding. Realistic increases in the competition they face produce significant improvements in students' test scores, educational attainment, and wages. Second, public schools' responses do not depend just on whether they lose students; their responses also depend on the fiscal rewards and penalties attached to gaining or losing students. When competition has little fiscal implication, a public school is less likely to react. When cost competition is weakened by a large price wedge (such as that between public and private schools), public schools reduce costs less than they do when cost competition is on a more level playing field (like that between two similar public school districts).

Third, the segregation effects of increasing school choice via reforms are likely to be small, because schools in the United States (not merely districts) are already quite segregated. To accurately predict the effects of reforms on segregation, one must consider a realistic alternative, not an idealized public school with perfect desegregation. Fourth, parents who have greater choice are more involved in their children's schooling. Parents' influence on school policy, which is greater when choice is greater, will reflect, on average, their stated preferences for tougher curricula and stricter school atmospheres. Note, however, that greater choice is also likely to make schools more diverse through parents' influence—because like-minded parents will be better able to group together in sending their children to the same schools. (I have no evidence on this last point.) Finally, different types of school choice substitute for one another to a limited degree.

Given these lessons, what other pieces of information do we need in order to analyze school choice reforms? Three information deficiencies stand out. Since we know that the fiscal impact of choice is an important determinant of its effects on schools, the financial arrangements of charter school programs, open enrollment programs, and voucher programs will be key determinants of such effects. These financial arrangements often receive little thought, and they are chosen more for convenience and political reasons than because they generate good financial incentives. States that want to avoid perverse financial incentives should consider financial arrangements that purposely mimic the fiscal impacts of the two traditional forms of school choice. In order to estimate the effects of more dramatic fiscal incentives, we will need to observe actual choice reforms made under a variety of financial arrangements.

The second information deficiency pertains to the long-term sustainability of reforms. All three of the reforms discussed create schools or programs that have less long-term autonomy than the schools that compete in the two traditional forms of school choice. Public school districts have indefinite lifetimes and will not have difficulty raising tax revenues as long as parents want to send their children to the schools. Private schools have similarly indefinite lifetimes and can raise tuition revenues as long as they attract parents. Although some charter school laws are written to give a high degree of fiscal autonomy to charter schools, all charter schools must get their charters renewed by the state (at least) and depend on other organizations to decide their per-pupil payments. It remains to be seen whether charters and per-pupil payments are politically maintainable when and if charter schools become successful competitors for the revenues and students of public school districts. Most open enrollment programs have even less inherent political sustainability. These programs, at least as written thus far, require the ongoing cooperation of local public school districts (the receiving districts almost always must voluntarily cooperate, though involuntary cooperation is sometimes exacted from the sending districts). The voucher programs passed thus far depend on the sufferance of the sending districts, but some proposed programs have made the vouchers less dependent on those districts. Careful analyses of district-level and state-level politics will be necessary for predicting the long-term sustainability of all three reforms.

Finally, traditional school choice gives us only limited information about the supply response we can expect from private schools under a voucher program or from charter schools. Supply responses are estimated in the analyses of choice among public schools and choice between public and private schools. (For instance, giving private schools additional resources that are equivalent to a $1,000 tuition subsidy creates a 4.1 percent increase in Catholic school enrollment—on a base of about 10 percent.) However, proposed charter school programs and voucher programs sometimes take us beyond the range where extrapolation from traditional school choice results is reasonable. Making a voucher of $3,500 available to all poor students, for instance, would produce a long-term supply response that would be difficult to predict, since the availability and long-term horizon would exceed those of current voucher programs (like Milwaukee's) and the voucher amount would exceed that of most current private school subsidies.

Notes

1. For useful surveys of the reforms, see A. Tucker and W. Lauber, *School Choice Programs: What's Happening in the States* (Washington, D.C.: Heritage Foundation Press, 1995).

2. Americans are more residentially mobile than Europeans, but the typical European family can also effectively choose a school for early grades by choosing a residence. The most important reasons that Americans have more choice are the fiscal independence and autonomous curricular control that typical American school districts enjoy. Much of the fiscal independence of American school districts has been eroded since 1950. In 1950 the median America school district raised almost 70 percent of its revenue from a local tax base. By 1990 the median raised only 35 percent of its revenue from local sources. Also note that Europeans may find it easier to make informed school choices because all students take certain national examinations and schools' scores are publicized. American students take a wide variety of standardized tests (if any); there is heavy self-selection of the Scholastic Aptitude Test (SAT) and American College Test (ACT) tests; and letter grading standards differ substantially among schools. For discussion of the effect of external examinations on the incentives that schools face, see John Bishop, "Signalling, Incentives, and School Organization," Working Paper 94-25, Cornell University, 1994.

3. These points are elaborated later with references to tables 6-1 and 6-3.

4. The word *segregation* is often exclusively associated with racial segregation. I describe segregation along a number of lines, such as ability and income. Segregation can also be described as *student sorting,* a term that encompasses a variety of phenomena such as "cream skimming" or "cherry picking."

5. Caroline Hoxby, "Does Competition among Public Schools Benefit Students and Taxpayers?" 1997 revision of Working Paper 1979, Cambridge, Mass.: National Bureau of Economic Research (NBER), 1994; Caroline Hoxby, "Do Private Schools Provide Competition for Public Schools?" Working Paper 4978, NBER, 1994; Caroline Hoxby, "The Effects of Private School Vouchers on Schools and Students," in Helen F. Ladd, ed., *Holding Schools Accountable: Performance-Based Reform in Education* (Brookings, 1996), pp. 177–208; Caroline Hoxby, "How Teachers Unions Affect Education Production" *Quarterly Journal of Economics* CXI, no. 3, (1996), pp. 671–718; Caroline Hoxby, "Are Efficiency and Equity in School Finance Substitutes or Complements?" *Journal of Economic Perspectives* 10, no. 4, (1996), pp. 51–72; Caroline Hoxby "When Parents Can Choose, What Do They Choose?" in Susan Mayer and Paul E. Peterson, eds., *When Schools Make a Difference,* forthcoming. Copies of unpublished papers can be obtained from my web site (through www.harvard.edu) or by sending me mail or electronic mail.

6. See chapters 13 and 14 in this volume.

7. Note that the fiscal reward process works through the residential decisions of marginal home buyers. If marginal home buyers choose to locate in other districts because district X is a poor or inefficient provider of schooling, all house prices in district X fall in consequence. There is no need for all households to relocate for all houses' prices to affect the districts' fiscal rewards.

8. See Charles T. Clotfelter and Helen F. Ladd, "Recognizing and Rewarding Success in Public Schools," in Ladd, ed., *Holding Schools Accountable*, pp. 23–64.

9. In practice, however, states' charter school laws vary greatly in the degree of administrative and fiscal autonomy that they give to charter schools. Arizona, for instance, probably has the most autonomous charter schools. They report directly to a state board (not the local districts that might suffer from their success), they are allowed

to expand to meet demand, and they earn increasing credibility with (and decreasing scrutiny from) the state board if they perform well. In other states charter schools may have little administrative autonomy because they are automatically subject to all clauses of the local teachers' union collective bargaining agreement. In some states charter schools have little fiscal autonomy because their tuition payments depend directly on the per-pupil spending of the local school districts (so that a successful charter school in a failing district is automatically penalized when homeowners dislike the local public schools). The least fiscally autonomous charter schools are those that must annually renegotiate their tuition payments with their local districts.

10. Public schools must admit all students in their attendance areas. Charter schools and open enrollment schools must admit a random sample from the group of eligible students who are interested in attending.

11. There are and have been some public subsidies for private school expenses, including small tuition tax deductions and credits. Minnesota currently has a tax credit for nontuition private schooling expenses. Some states also require local public districts to provide certain textbooks and bus transportation to private school students.

12. Although tuition understates the true costs of private schooling, private school-ing does cost significantly less than public schooling on average. Over the entire period from 1976 to the present, per-pupil costs in private schools have always been between 50 and 60 percent of contemporary per-pupil costs in public schools.

13. For this section, see Hoxby, "Does Competition among Public Schools Benefit Students and Taxpayers?" (1997 rev.).

14. The notes to table 6-1 show two alternative measures of choice among public school districts and explain why the alternative measures are less useful than Herfindahl indexes. A Herfindahl index based on enrollment shares is as follows. Suppose a metropolitan area has J school districts, which we index by $j = 1, \ldots, J$. Suppose each school district has a share, s_j, of total metropolitan area enrollment. Then the Herfindahl index is

$$\sum_{j=1}^{J} s_j^2$$

When there is no choice in a metropolitan area because there is only one public school district, the index is equal to 1. As more districts are added and as enrollment is spread more evenly over those districts, the index gets closer to 0.

15. This typically took place about the time of Anglo-American settlement, which varies with the area of the country. Many of the original petitions for district boundaries cite streams as a reason for not extending the district lines further. Streams are by far the most common natural boundaries for school districts. Note, however, that many of the streams that are preserved in boundaries are small and have never had industrial importance. Today many of the boundary streams are of negligible importance in travel.

16. The estimation equations can be summarized as follows. The main equation is of the form

$$y_{ik} = \alpha H_k + X_{ik}\beta + X_k\delta + \varepsilon_k + \varepsilon_{ik},$$

where y is an outcome such as a student's test score or a school's per-pupil spending, i indexes students or schools (depending on the outcome), k indexes the metropolitan area, H is the Herfindahl index that measures the degree of choice among public school districts, X_{ik} is a vector of background variables that describe the student or school (for instance, the race and gender of the student or the homogeneity of household incomes of students who attend the school), and X_k is a vector of background variables that describe the metropolitan area (for instance, its racial composition and size). The two-tiered error structure adjusts the standard errors for the fact that the degree of choice varies only at the level of the metropolitan area.

There is also an implied first-stage equation that estimates the effect of streams on the concentration of public school districts in the metropolitan area. This equation is

$$H_k = S_k \gamma + \overline{X}_{ik} \kappa + X_k \lambda + \upsilon_{ik},$$

where H_k, X_{ik}, and X_k are as above (except that X_{ik} is effectively averaged for the area) and S_k is a vector of variables that measure the prevalence of large and small streams in the metropolitan area.

I multiply the Herfindahl index by -1 so that it is a measure of choice rather than a measure of concentration (the lack of choice).

17. I use the term *statistically significant* to refer to estimates that are statistically significantly different from zero using an asymptotic 5 percent level.

18. For this paragraph, see Hoxby, "When Parents Can Choose."

19. Specifically, the measure of parental influence over school policy rises by two-thirds of a standard deviation.

19. Interestingly, an increase in the degree of choice encourages grade inflation, which I measure by comparing students' course grades to their performance on national standardized exams in the same subjects. This suggests that although parents want their children to be exposed to harder "real" curricula, parents are loath to set higher nominal standards for their children—perhaps because local grade deflation might be misinterpreted by colleges in the admissions process.

21. For this section, see Hoxby, "Do Private Schools Provide Competition for Public Schools?" and Hoxby, "The Effects of Private School Vouchers."

22. The estimation equations can be summarized as follows. The main equation is of the form

$$y_{ik} = \mu V_k + X_{ik} \nu + X_k \pi + \iota_k + \iota_{ik}$$

where y is an outcome such as a student's wage or a school's per-pupil spending, i indexes students or schools (depending on the outcome), k indexes the area (metropolitan areas and counties, depending on their urbanness), V is the average tuition subsidy offered by private schools in area k, X_{ik} is a vector of background variables that describe the student or school (for instance, the student's own religion or the racial homogeneity of the school), and X_k is a vector of background variables that describe the area (for instance, its income composition or religiosity). The two-tiered error structure adjusts the standard errors for the fact that average tuition subsidies vary only at the level of the area.

There is also an implied first-stage equation that estimates the effect of denominations' population shares on the tuition subsidies private schools offer. This equation is

$$V_k = D_k \rho + \overline{X}_{ik} \theta + X_k \tau + \omega_{ik},$$

where V_k, X_{ik}, and X_k are as above (except that X_{ik} is effectively averaged for the area) and D_k is a vector of population shares of denominations $m = 1, \ldots, M$ in area k.

23. Income segregation is measured using students' eligibility for free lunches.

24. Hoxby, "How Teachers' Unions Affect Education Production."

25. Hoxby, "When Parents Can Choose."

26. In addition, before and after studies suffer from bias produced by a phenomenon sometimes called Ashenfelter's dip. The bias results from the fact that treatment (intradistrict choice) is assigned to school districts that have recently experienced a negative departure from their own history. Since districts typically display mean reversion (return to their historic paths) anyway, simple before and after studies exaggerate the effect of intra district choice programs.

SEVEN

Interdistrict Choice in Massachusetts

David J. Armor and Brett M. Peiser

THERE IS no better illustration of the demand for school reform today than is seen in the rapid rise of school choice in myriad forms, as illustrated by many of the chapters in this volume. The establishment of magnet schools, private school voucher experiments, statewide open enrollment policies, and the fast-growing charter school movement reveal deep interest in program innovation, alternative governance structures, and especially expansion of access. There are many forces behind the expanding school choice movement, but none is more important than the belief that public school systems—especially larger urban systems—will benefit from application of free market principles. Although other chapters in this volume undertake more comprehensive theoretical analyses of the free market concept, it is appropriate to summarize those portions being tested in this chapter.

According to proponents of school choice, low-quality public education stems from a combination of entrenched bureaucracies (including unions), populations with high levels of poverty, and a captive consumer base that provide little incentive to improve quality. The way to improve quality is to free the captive audience, eliminate local monopolies, remove restrictions

This chapter is based on a study sponsored by the Pioneer Institute, 85 Devonshire Street, Boston, Massachusetts, which also published a full report by the same authors, *Competition in Education: A Case Study in Interdistrict Choice,* 1997.

on public school funds, and provide unrestricted choice among all public and nonpublic schools. The resulting free market conditions, so the argument goes, will improve educational quality at both individual and systemic levels. First, assuming that higher-quality public or private schools exist in an area, families who seek better programs will be able to transfer their children to these higher-quality schools and thereby improve the educational outcomes for their children. Second, the resulting competitive process will ultimately force lower-quality systems to improve their programs or face continuing losses and deterioration. This systemic impact is perhaps the more important of the two, since it is only by this second process that education will be improved for all students, not just for those choosing to leave a low-quality system.

Most critics of school choice contend that free market principles do not apply to public education. They advance an elitist argument instead, stating that choice will mainly benefit more affluent families who have the least need for better schools. They argue that public education will be harmed because better students will leave poorer school districts in search of programs in more affluent communities, leaving behind hard-to-teach students from poor families in increasingly disadvantaged school systems. Many will leave simply because of social or racial prejudice, not because of low-quality programs. Struggling urban school systems cannot respond to the competitive challenge because of a combination of inadequate funding, government regulations, and demographic conditions over which they have no control. Moreover, low-income and minority families are less likely to be aware of better schools than middle-class families, thereby making lower levels of participation by such families inevitable. The result is that weak school systems become weaker while strong ones become stronger, and benefits accrue to middle-class rather than poor families.

To this point the bulk of research on the benefits of school choice has focused on individual outcomes under the first scenario, in which students attending higher-quality private or suburban public schools are compared to those in lower-quality urban public schools.[1] There is still considerable debate about the academic benefits of school choice for individual students, and it is probably too early to determine whether the benefits outweigh the costs because school choice programs are still evolving and are serving a relatively small fraction of the population.

With the notable exception of a series of studies by Caroline Hoxby, there has been less research on the systemic effects of school choice, especially whether market competition can enhance school quality for everyone, including schools and school districts that lose students as a result of competitive forces.[2] Hoxby has used national data to conduct econometric analyses of the relationships among public and private school competition, school resources, and student outcomes. In the case of public school competition, she has found that increased choice due to greater numbers of separate school districts in a metropolitan area is associated with slightly improved student performance (test scores, educational attainment, and future wages) and significantly lower costs per pupil. In the case of private versus public school competition, she has found that increased private school enrollment in counties improves student performance in public schools (educational attainment and future wages).

The main limitation of Hoxby's studies has been her operational definition of school choice, which is simply the number of private schools or the number of public school districts within a geographic area. Therefore, in her studies she has evaluated the effects of what she calls the "traditional" choices that families make when deciding where to live or whether to use public or private schools. Since Hoxby's analyses have not included assessments of the impact of specific school choice policies on changes in the behavior of families or public school systems, her findings are not directly transferable to the types of choice policies being implemented or tested at the present time. Therefore, in these econometric studies Hoxby has not directly evaluated the various arguments about the social, racial, and systemic effects of open enrollment or voucher policies as implemented to date.

The study reported in this chapter was designed to test the market competition thesis using data from the statewide open enrollment (interdistrict public school choice) program in Massachusetts. The Massachusetts choice policy is especially well suited to testing the effects of competition because of some unique characteristics. First, unlike most states with significant minority populations that offer open enrollment, Massachusetts places no controls on racial impacts. Racial controls allow school districts to deny transfers that have adverse racial impacts, thereby constraining market competition. The absence of racial controls allows for a better test of the social and racial impacts of choice, which have been major points of contention between proponents and critics of choice. Second, Massachusetts requires sending districts to pay substantial tuition fees (capped at $5,000 per choice student) to receiving districts out of their state aid receipts rather than simply having state money follow students. This means that the financial consequences of choice losses for a net losing district in Massachusetts are much greater than, say, in Minnesota, where the average cost is about $3,000 per student for losing districts.

The study addressed three primary questions: First, what are the social, racial, and financial consequences of interdistrict choice—and, in particular, does the absence of racial controls in Massachusetts have adverse impacts on districts with high levels of minority enrollments? Second, does interdistrict competition for students improve the quality of education by impelling net losing districts to undertake program improvements to mitigate or recover their losses? Third, are the motivations of families who opt for school choice more consistent with the competition thesis (they are seeking academic quality) or with the elitist argument (they are avoiding poor or minority students)?

Data and Methods

Legislation requiring interdistrict choice in Massachusetts was signed into law by Governor William F. Weld in March 1991 as part of a fiscal recovery act. By the 1995–96 school year nearly 6,800 students were using interdistrict choice, and, of the 331 districts statewide, 89 were receiving districts and 206 were sending districts. Districts cannot restrict choice transfers out, but they can vote to prevent choice transfers in. Therefore, about two-thirds of Massachusetts school districts are affected by interdistrict choice in some way.

When the choice program began, a sending district had to pay full tuition costs (defined as per-pupil operating costs) to a receiving district out of its own state aid funds. In 1993 the state legislature set tuition at 75 percent of per-pupil expenditures, with a cap of $5,000, and made some other changes as part of an Education Reform Act. The state defined a minimum "foundation" budget needed to provide a quality education, and school districts that were below the foundation level would get extra state aid to bring them to foundation levels over a seven-year period. Other changes provided for 100 percent reimbursement of tuition losses due to choice for below-foundation districts during their first year of loss and 100 percent of any increases in tuition losses thereafter. Above-foundation districts were to receive 50 percent reimbursement of tuition payments in the first year of choice losses and 25 percent thereafter. Transportation subsidies were also made available to low-income (free lunch) choice students through the receiving district.

The data for the study came from a variety of sources, including standardized school data maintained by the state Department of Education and data collected specifically for this study. Most of the latter data came from

20 school districts selected for case studies. We selected a nonrandom sample of 10 pairs of school districts; one district in each pair was a net receiving district with more than 100 transfers in, and the other district was the net sending district with the largest number of transfers to that receiver (all but one of these senders also had 100 or more transfers out).[3] The sample used in this case study represents more than half of the largest senders and receivers in the state. One of the state data files is a profile of all school districts in the state, which includes the demographic characteristics of school districts, total school enrollment by race, school expenditures, school socioeconomic status (SES) such as percent of students eligible for free or reduced-price lunches, and a series of academic characteristics such as average attendance, percentage of students dropping out or planning college, and average achievement test scores.

In order to assess racial and financial effects, we relied on state data on all individual choice students in the 1994–95 school year, including race and the amount of tuition paid for each student. The existence of data on individual choice students allowed us to compute a district's racial composition with and without interdistrict choice students as well as net tuition gains or losses for each district. Our analysis of the social and academic characteristics of choice students also relied on surveys of choice parents and students from the 10 selected receiving districts, as well as state data on achievement test scores for tenth graders in 1995–96.

Although this study concentrated on the interdistrict choice policy, there was some limited analysis of data from two other choice programs in Massachusetts for the purpose of evaluating racial impacts. One was the rapidly growing charter school program, which enrolled about 5,500 students at 22 schools in 1996–97; the other was the long-standing METCO program, which enrolls about 3,200 minority students from Boston and Springfield in 37 surrounding suburban districts for the purpose of voluntary desegregation. Because of the large number of METCO transfers, most of these suburban districts have voted not to accept any interdistrict choice students.

To test the market competition thesis we relied on both case study information and state data. Case study data were obtained from school district site visits and staff interviews to determine the effects of choice losses or gains on district resources, programs, and policies. In most districts we interviewed 3 or 4 school staff members, typically the superintendent, a school committee member, and 1 or 2 principals; occasionally we interviewed an assistant superintendent or a business manager. Altogether we interviewed 69 staff or school committee members in 19 districts, including 18 superintendents, 14 school committee members, 13 high school principals, 8 middle or junior high school principals, and 7 elementary school principals.[4] The staff interviews covered the specific impact of choice gains or losses on school programs and policies, staff perceptions of the reasons for choice transfers in or out of their district, and staff views of the choice law.

In order to validate interview findings and to assess the effects of programmatic changes on choice enrollment and finances, we also used official state reports of enrollment, tuition, and expenditure data for the 20 districts we studied. These reports provided data on longitudinal enrollment trends, tuition payments, and per-pupil expenditures for four years, from 1992–93 to 1995–96. Beyond our case study sample, there were only nine other net sending districts in Massachusetts that had 100 or more transfers out as of 1994–95. We examined trends in choice enrollment between 1992–93 and 1995–96 in these additional sending districts to test the robustness of our findings from the 10 sending districts used in the case study.

Data we used in assessing the views and motivations of choice parents and students were taken from surveys of choice families drawn from our case study districts. We randomly selected between 40 and 50 choice families from each of the 10 receiving districts in the case study sample. After obtaining appropriate informed consent, we conducted structured telephone interviews with parents to determine their reasons for changing school districts and other views about the choice law. We interviewed a total of 309 parents from the 10 receiving districts for an average of 31 per school during the first six months of 1996. For all but two districts we interviewed 25 or more parents. Students from consenting choice families who were in eighth grade and higher were given a brief written questionnaire in a group setting during our site visits. A total of 213 students completed the questionnaire, for an average of 21 students per school. Our parent and student response rate was approximately 70 percent of families sampled.

Finally, we used data from a statewide citizen survey sponsored by the Pioneer Institute as part of a separate study of school choice. A total of 700 adult residents of Massachusetts were interviewed during July 1996, which included an oversampling of 200 parents in the 10 largest cities and 100 minority parents in Boston. We relied on the portions of that survey that assessed support of or opposition to specific choice policies broken down by race or ethnicity.[5]

Socioeconomic and Academic Comparisons

Comparing all sending districts to all receiving districts using the statewide profile of school districts for the 1994–95 school year, we found only very small differences in average SES or academic characteristics. The average percentage of adults with B.A. degrees in the communities and average attendance rates were identical; most of the other differences were very small and not significant. The average percentage of minority (black or Hispanic) students was only 7 percent among all senders and 5 percent among all receivers. Finally, receivers scored slightly higher than senders on tenth-grade reading and math tests (4 and 3 points, respectively), but the differences are not statistically significant.[6] There were larger SES differences between sending and receiving districts in districts where choice students constituted more than 2 percent of total enrollment, which we will call high-impact senders or receivers. High-impact senders were 5 percentage points lower in terms of adults with B.A. degrees, 6 points higher in poverty rate, 4 points higher in minority enrollment, and 11 to 13 points higher in tenth-grade test scores. Because of the smaller number of districts in these categories, however, none of these differences are statistically significant.

Table 7-1 shows the SES and academic differences for the 20 receivers and the largest senders in our case study sample. The differences were generally larger for the districts in our sample than for all high-impact senders and receivers. The table also has a third column that shows several SES and academic characteristics for our sample of choice students who have transferred from the 10 sending districts to the 10 receiving districts.

Considering community SES characteristics, these large receivers were more affluent than their corresponding senders, with family incomes averaging about $13,000 higher, and the percentage of adults who were college graduates was nearly twice as high (33 versus 19 percent). These receiving districts also had much lower poverty rates than sending districts (7 versus 32 percent) and lower percentages of minority students among their school populations (3 versus 22 percent). With regard to academic characteristics, our case study receivers had about half the dropout rate, a higher percentage of seniors planning to attend four-year colleges, and test scores that were about 100 points higher on average than those of senders.

Table 7-1 also compares the average characteristics of choice families with children attending these large receiving districts with the average characteristics of sending and receiving school populations. Choice family incomes were somewhat lower on average than the average incomes of

Table 7-1. *Characteristics of Districts and Students in Case Study, 1994–95*

Characteristic	Sending districts	Receiving districts	Choice families[a]
Community SES			
Mean income (dollars)	41,862	55,139	53,000
Percent parents with B.A. degrees	19	33	48
School SES			
Percent poverty students	32	7	...
Percent minority students[b]	22	3	6
Percent black students	9	2	4
Academic data			
Percent dropouts	16	7	...
Percent students planning four-year college	53	69	79
Tenth-grade reading scores	1,286	1,386	1,380
Tenth-grade math scores	1,273	1,377	1,374
Number of districts	10	10	...
Number of parents/students			309/213

a. Income and percent B.A. degrees from parent survey (N = 309); race and college plans from student survey (N = 213); test scores from 1996 state administration (N = 216).

b. Black and Hispanic.

families in receiving districts but much higher than those in the sending districts, and the college graduation rate among choice parents was 15 percentage points higher than the averages in the receiving districts. Consistent with these results, the percentage of choice students planning to attend four-year college was also 10 points higher than that of students in receiving districts. Finally, the average tenth-grade test scores of choice students were much higher than those of students in large sending districts and about the same as those of their peers in receiving districts.

The information in table 7-1 indicates that Massachusetts choice families are more likely to be white and have higher SES than the nonchoice families remaining in their sending districts. In fact, choice families even exceed receiving district families in terms of both parents' education and students' college aspirations, but they are slightly lower in family income and about the same in terms of students' test scores. This particular pattern suggests that children in choice families are achieving at a much higher rate than the average students in sending schools and also have a much stronger interest in higher education—even stronger than that of the average receiver students—but may not necessarily have the resources to afford private school tuition at either the secondary or the college level.

When we compared individual receiving districts to their corresponding largest senders, we found that not all receivers had significantly higher reading scores than their respective senders; the differences for the Pentucket-Haverhill, Avon-Brockton, and Uxbridge-Northbridge pairs were small, and in the case of Holliston-Hopkinton the sender had higher reading scores than the receiver. Further, when we compared choice students to the populations of their respective sending districts, the data also revealed that choice students are not always the academic "cream" of their sending districts; three comparisons showed that choice students had lower reading scores than their peers in their sending districts, and one comparison showed almost no difference. Therefore, only four of the ten pairs (Acton-Maynard, Harvard-Leominster, Pentucket-Haverhill, and Lunenberg-Fitchburg) have a pattern that coincides with the position of critics who argue that low-achieving senders lose high-achieving students to high-achieving receivers.

It seems clear from these results that the social and academic impacts of choice are more complex than is portrayed by either critics or proponents of choice policies. On the one hand, the data support the critics' views that choice students on average tend to be more affluent and academically talented than the students in the average sending district and that they migrate from lower-SES, lower-achieving districts to more affluent and higher-achieving districts. On the other hand, this "average" depiction masks a much more complex picture in which individual districts do not fit the average profile, particularly with respect to academic ability.

Racial Representation and Impact

Having shown that, on average, large sending districts tend to have higher minority enrollments than large receivers, we focused our assessment of racial impacts on two questions. First, how representative are various choice populations with respect to statewide enrollment?[7] Second, what is the impact of interdistrict choice on the racial makeup of sending and receiving districts; that is, is it having segregative effects as some critics allege?

Table 7-2 compares the statewide racial composition (with and without Boston) with the racial composition of interdistrict choice, METCO, and charter school student populations. Although the interdistrict choice population is disproportionately white compared to the state enrollment, it is much less so when Boston is excluded. Even so, interdistrict choice stu-

Table 7-2. *Racial-Ethnic Composition of Choice Populations Compared with State Public School Enrollment, 1995–96*[a]
Percent unless otherwise indicated

Racial-ethnic group	Interdistrict choice[b]	METCO	Charter schools	All choice students	State	State less Boston
White	92	0	52	58	79	84
Black	2	86	23	27	8	5
Hispanic	2	8	18	9	9	8
Asian	1	2	2	2	4	3
Actual numbers	6,219	3,194	5,465	14,878	895,881	834,392

a. Excluding "Other" and "Unknown" categories; columns do not add to 100 percent.
b. 1994–95 school year.

dents are about 4.5 percent black and Hispanic compared to a statewide school population (less Boston) that is about 13 percent black and Hispanic. On the other hand, the METCO program has a very high African-American enrollment, whereas the charter school program overrepresents both black and Hispanic students compared to statewide figures.

Considering all programs, the total choice population in Massachusetts is reasonably representative of Hispanic, Asian, and other minority groups, and it overrepresents African-American students compared to the statewide enrollment. Although this analysis is not intended to downplay the under-representation of minority students in the interdistrict choice program, it is important to stress that, from the standpoint of state policy, minority students are fully represented in the three choice programs created by the state.

Aside from the representativeness of various choice populations, what about the impact of choice on the racial makeup of school districts? Our most important yardstick of racial impact is a comparison of racial composition of districts with and without interdistrict choice students. We computed this impact by first counting the number of choice students who transferred into or out of each school district by race, then adding or subtracting these numbers from total enrollment by race; this yielded the total enrollment by race without choice transfers.[8] We then estimated the effect of choice on racial composition by subtracting the percentage of white or minority students without choice from the actual percentage of white or minority students. Basically, this would be the change in racial composition if all choice students returned to their sending school districts. We also tabulated these changes according to the size of the

Figure 7-1. *Effect of Choice on Racial Composition of Senders: Change in Percentage of White, Black, and Hispanic Students*

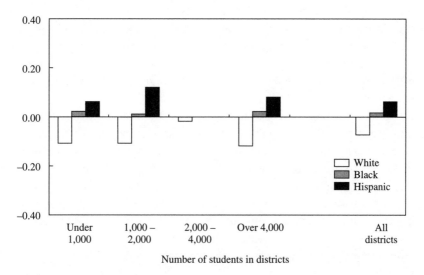

Number of students in districts

school districts, because larger sending districts also tended to have higher minority enrollments.

Figure 7-1 shows that the overall effect of choice losses for all sending districts combined has been to reduce the percentage of white students by less than a tenth of a percentage point (–0.08 percent), to raise the percentage of black students by only a hundredth of a point (0.01 percent), and to raise the percentage of Hispanic students by less than a tenth of a point (0.06 percent). Considering sending districts with more than 4,000 in total enrollment, which also have the highest minority concentrations, the effect of choice lowers the percentage of white students by just over a tenth of a point (–0.12 percent) and raises the percentage of Hispanic students by just 0.08%.

The racial and ethnic effects differ for receiving districts in that racial balance generally improves relative to state averages, although the changes are generally less than 1 percentage point. The reason for this seemingly paradoxical result is that, although the choice population in our case study was less minority than that of the typical sending district, at the same time it was more minority than the typical receiving district (see table 7-1). Therefore, our study indicated that the effect of choice is to increase slightly the minority composition of both sending and receiving districts.

We can perhaps better illustrate the racial impacts of choice if we examine the magnitude and direction of these effects for individual sending and receiving districts. To make this analysis most relevant to policy, we calculated the impact of choice on the racial composition of 35 districts with more than 100 choice transfers in or out.[9] These districts accounted for nearly half of the total open enrollment population, and with the exception of Boston they included the districts with the highest minority enrollments in the state.

Table 7-3 makes it clear that the impacts of choice on racial composition are generally very small. It is true that sending districts with the largest choice losses include many with high minority concentrations, while receiving districts with the largest choice gains all have low minority enrollments. But it is also true that some of the largest senders have very low minority enrollments. The largest sender, Springfield, has the highest minority enrollment, whereas the second-largest sender, Triton, has the lowest minority enrollment. There are clearly factors other than high minority enrollments that lead to large losses of choice students.

The most important information in the table is in the last column, which shows negligible effects on the racial composition of all sending districts, including those with the highest minority enrollments. Among the largest senders, the greatest racial impact was on Springfield, but the effect on its racial composition was only seven-tenths of a percentage point; that is, in spite of 256 transfers out, most of whom were white, the effect was to increase the percentage of minority students in Springfield from 66.5 to 67.2 percent. The reason for this small effect was that Springfield's total enrollment was very large (about 24,000) compared to the transfers out, so the transfers had a very small effect on the racial makeup of the remaining population.

The largest racial effect for receiving districts was Avon, which showed an increase of 1.2 percent in the minority student population due to choice. This was because the students choosing Avon, most of whom were from Brockton, had a higher proportion of minority students than the Avon population. Note that the effect of choice on Brockton's racial composition was negligible. This result demonstrates that choice can actually improve the racial composition of receiving districts even though the statewide choice population is predominantly white. All of the remaining receivers in our study showed negligible or no effects of choice on racial composition, the absolute values of which were less than or equal to three-tenths of 1 percent.

Table 7-3. *Racial and Ethnic Impact of Choice for Largest Senders and Receivers, 1994–95*

District	Number of transfers	Actual percent minority students[a]	Percent minority without choice	Change in percent of minority students
Sender with more than 100 transfers out				
Springfield	253	67.2	66.5	0.7
Triton	219	1.3	1.3	0.0
Fitchburg	185	30.4	29.8	0.6
Brockton	175	43.3	43.0	0.3
Leominster	164	18.4	18.2	0.2
Lynn	154	34.5	34.2	0.3
Haverhill	153	16.4	16.1	0.3
Lowell	152	24.9	24.7	0.2
Gloucester	145	1.8	1.7	0.1
Amesbury	142	1.3	1.4	−0.1
Maynard	130	5.9	5.5	0.4
Milford	118	8.4	8.3	0.1
Pittsfield	110	9.4	9.3	0.1
Northbridge	105	2.4	2.6	−0.2
Salem	104	25.7	25.3	0.4
Ayer	103	23.0	22.6	0.4
Worcester	103	34.1	33.9	0.2
Receivers with more than 100 transfers				
Holliston	306	2.0	2.0	0.0
Acton-Boxborough	284	2.4	2.6	−0.2
Avon	213	9.9	8.7	1.2
Pentucket	198	1.1	0.8	0.3
Nashoba	191	4.4	4.1	0.3
Harvard	183	2.1	2.0	0.1
Newburyport	176	1.3	1.3	0.0
Hamilton-Wenham	174	1.2	1.1	0.1
Berkshire Hills	147	3.5	3.8	−0.3
Marblehead	140	4.0	4.0	0.0
Manchester	138	0.6	0.6	0.0
Uxbridge	136	0.6	0.6	0.0
Lunenberg	133	2.2	2.0	0.2
Hampden-Wilbrahm	130	3.1	3.0	0.1
Masconomet	116	1.9	2.0	−0.1
Southwick-Tolland	106	2.5	2.6	−0.1
Milford	103	8.4	8.3	0.1
Triton	103	1.3	1.3	0.0

a. *Minority* defined as African-American or Hispanic.

Financial Impacts

In our study we explored the financial impact of choice for the sending and receiving districts with the largest choice losses or gains, which are the same as those listed in table 7-3, by calculating absolute tuition payments or receipts and expressing net gains or losses as percentages of total expenditures for 1994–95. Considering sending districts first, the absolute values of tuition payments for choice students are indeed large, ranging from a low of about $350,000 for Ayer to a high of about $955,000 for Springfield. But many of these districts also have very large enrollments and budgets, particularly those with higher poverty and minority enrollment levels, so the relative effect of choice as a percentage of expenditures is quite small in these cases.

The highest tuition payments are made by Springfield, which also has the highest poverty level and the highest percentage of minority students, and yet these tuition payments represent less than 1 percent of Springfield's total expenditures. The situation is similar for Brockton and Lynn, which both have high poverty and minority levels, but the financial impact of choice losses is only about 1 percent of total expenditures. It should be noted that these figures do not reflect tuition reimbursements for below-foundation districts, which further reduce the financial impact of choice losses.

Significantly, the largest financial losses in terms of percentages have been experienced by Triton (–3.1 percent), Gloucester (–3.2 percent), and Maynard (–5.5 percent), all of which have relatively low poverty levels and low to very low minority enrollments (see table 7-3). The reason for these large relative effects is that these districts are quite small, with enrollments of less than 4,000, and therefore the loss of 100 or more students has a much larger impact relative to their total expenditures. In other words, the most adverse financial effects are not borne by the school districts with the highest minority and poor populations, but rather by small districts that are predominantly white.

The financial effects of choice for receiving districts with the largest choice enrollments are much greater, relative to expenditures, than for sending districts. Not only are the absolute values of tuition receipts large— two districts, Holliston and Acton-Boxborough, receive more than $1 million in tuition payments—but the relative impact on percentage gains is also great. Avon, Harvard, and Manchester have realized gains of more than 10 percent of their total expenditures as a result of choice (Avon is highest at 20 percent), and many others have gains in the 5 to 9 percent range.

Again, the reason for these large relative gains is that the typical receiving district is smaller than the typical sending district.

It appears from these data, then, that choice does not lead to significant negative effects on poorer sending districts with high percentages of minority students, mainly because their enrollments—and corresponding budgets—are among the largest in the state. Indeed, negative financial effects are greatest in smaller sending districts that tend to have low proportions of minority and poor students.

Testing the Competition Thesis

Our test of the competition thesis in an interdistrict choice plan began with an operational definition of the thesis in the context of public school systems. When faced with new or increased competition in the marketplace, an enterprise can respond in several ways. First, if the competition does not lead to any significant losses or adverse effects for a given enterprise and it is satisfied with its market share, there is no reason for management to make any changes to its product or its way of doing business (response 1). Second, if new competition leads to serious losses in market share because people prefer the new product over the old, the management of the losing enterprise can institute corrective actions, such as heeding consumer views and improving its product, thereby recovering some or all of its losses (response 2).[10] Or it can fail to take corrective actions for whatever reason or make the wrong corrections (such as improving its advertising instead of the product) and continue to lose market share (response 3).

Applying this model to public schools, a district that loses choice students can respond in these ways as well. A district may not experience any adverse effects from choice losses, and therefore has no reason to change (response 1); we will label such a district a "no effect" district. If a district experiences adverse effects and changes its policies and programs in order to restore or prevent future losses (response 2), we will call it a "change" district. Finally, as in the business sector, we would expect some adversely affected school districts to fail to change for a variety of reasons (response 3), such as unwillingness to change or ineffective changes; we will label these "no change" districts. If the market competition thesis applies to public school districts, many more sending districts should fall into response categories 1 and 2 than into category 3.

What pattern of responses should we expect if the competition thesis does not apply to public school districts? First, most districts that lose a significant number of choice students should experience adverse effects, especially if they have high concentrations of poor and minority students. Therefore, few districts with large choice losses should be "no effect" districts, especially if they have high percentages of poverty and minority students. Second, those districts that are adversely affected should not be able to make effective changes to recover their losses, which means that most districts with large losses should fall into response category 3. If we believe the strongest critics of choice, no school district should fall into response category 2 (that is, be a "change" district).

Classification of Sending District Responses

Each sending district in our case studies was classified as one of the three types of districts based on in-depth interviews with staff members, as summarized in table 7-4. Three sending districts were classified as "no effect" districts, three as "change" districts, and three as "no change" districts. One sending district did not participate in the site visit interviews, but analyses of objective data strongly suggest that it would be a "no effect" district.

The staff members of the "no effect" districts perceived few adverse effects on programs and resources resulting from the loss of choice students. Although they were not happy about the loss of students, they indicated that there had been no negative effect on programs, such as laying off teachers, dropping or changing courses or activities, or reducing operational expenses (although some mentioned adverse effects on desegregation). Indeed, most of these staff members saw no problems with the quality of their programs; they believed the real reasons for choice losses were related either to misperceptions about the quality of their academic programs or, especially, to racial motivations. The 11 staff members interviewed in these three districts reported no major changes in policies or programs designed to stop or slow down the losses. Two of these districts

Table 7-4. *Responses to Competition by Sending Districts in Case Study*

Response[a]	Number of districts	Size	Percent minority
No effect	3	All large	All high
Change	3	All small	All low
No change	3	Medium	1 low, 2 high

a. Based on interviews with district staff members.

had voted against becoming receiving districts as of the 1995–96 school year, which is the simplest policy change that allows recovery of some revenue losses, and the third did not become a receiver until 1995–96.

The majority of the 12 staff members interviewed in the three "change" districts stated that the loss of choice students had serious, if not devastating, effects on the quality of their school programs and resources. They said, further, that after recovering from the initial shock, their school systems and communities had responded aggressively to this negative impact by making significant changes in school programs, policies, and local funding levels. Staff members in more than one district described the choice losses as a "wake-up call." In some cases the improvements simply restored lost resources, and in other cases the improvements actually increased resources beyond their levels before implementation of the choice policy, resulting in increased numbers of teachers, new technology, and new construction. Unexpectedly, because the ultimate result of choice was significant improvement in their programs, the "change" district staffs' view of the choice law was both positive and supportive in spite of initial adverse effects. All three of these districts were receiving districts by 1992–93, near the beginning of implementation of the choice law.

In the three "no change" districts the staff interviews revealed less consensus about adverse effects due to choice losses, although, in contrast to what had been said by the "no effect" group, at least one staff member in each "no change" district cited adverse effects on programs and resources. In contrast to the "change" districts, the "no change" districts made few attempts to change programs or policies in response to choice losses, although at least one staff member in each of two districts mentioned that the districts had improved their public relations efforts, since they believed choice losses were caused by misperceptions of district programs. Some of the staff members in these districts also cited racial motivations as reasons for choice losses. Two of the "no change" districts had been receiving districts since 1994–95, and one district indicated that choice losses had led it to accept choice transfers starting in 1996–97. Our overall impression from the interviews was not that staff thought reform was impossible, but rather that staff disagreed about the impact of the losses and were ambivalent about the need for reforms.

There was very little variation among the staff members at net receiving districts about the impact of the choice law, with large majorities reporting positive effects in a number of specific program and resource areas. Only one receiving district failed to see significant benefits as a result of its gains; this district felt the choice program was harming a neighboring sending district, and it voted to discontinue its receiving status as of 1996. From the viewpoint of market competition, it is significant that a number of the net receiving districts were having problems sustaining their academic programs before choice, mainly due to small (and shrinking) enrollments. In these cases the choice law actually strengthened their programs and made them more competitive.

The interview data provide considerable evidence that school districts have responded to choice losses in ways consistent with the market competition thesis. In particular, only three sending districts fall into a pattern that should predominate if public school systems were harmed by and could not benefit from competition. But the ultimate test of whether competition is beneficial is whether the program improvements undertaken in the "change" districts were effective in actually reversing the trends in choice enrollment, either by reducing transfers out or by increasing transfers in. We would not expect such reversals in the "no change" and "no effect" groups, since they have not attempted to improve their programs in response to choice. We would also expect that both the "change" and the "no change" groups would experience greater initial adverse effects from enrollment and tuition losses than the "no effect" group.

Validation of Response Types

Analysis of objective enrollment data not only validates these expectations, but demonstrates the significant benefits of competition for the "change" group. Figure 7-2 shows the trends in actual choice enrollment as a percentage of total enrollment for the three response categories between fiscal year 1993 and fiscal year 1996. The three districts in the "change" group demonstrate substantial relative choice losses in the early years, more than twice as many as "no change" districts and five times as many as the "no effect" districts. Most important, the "change" districts actually reversed their relative losses starting in 1994–95, and by 1995–96 their relative losses were fewer than those of the "no change" districts. The district with the greatest degree of success actually changed from a net sending district in 1994 to a net receiving district in 1996. The other two districts in the "change" group also demonstrate positive trends, one with a 49 percent reduction and one with a 40 percent reduction in net relative losses. These reductions were caused by a combination of reduced transfers out and increased transfers in.

The "no change" districts demonstrate early loss rates about twice the magnitude of those of the "no effect" districts, but, unlike the "change"

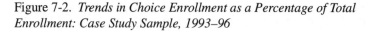

Figure 7-2. *Trends in Choice Enrollment as a Percentage of Total Enrollment: Case Study Sample, 1993–96*

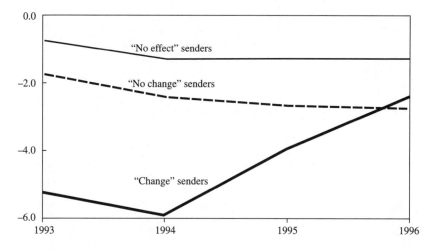

districts, they experienced an increase in relative losses during the same period that the "change" group was reducing its relative losses. The "no change" group includes one district with no reductions in net losses and two districts with reductions in net losses of only 11 percent each. For one of these districts the reduction was the result of a decision to become a receiving school, which by definition means the choice law was the causal agent. In any event, neither of these reductions approach the magnitude documented for the "change" districts. The "no effect" districts demonstrate very small relative losses of about 1 percent throughout the period. One district in the "no effect" group demonstrates no reduction in net choice losses, one district shows an insignificant reduction of 5 percent, and one district shows a reduction of 25 percent, nearly all of which came from a decision to become a receiver in 1995–96.

Since the support for the market thesis found in our case study is based on a small sample of sending districts, we must be cautious about generalizing from these results. To test the robustness of these findings we examined enrollment trends in the remaining large net sending districts with 100 or more choice transfers out as of the 1994–95 school year.[11] Our analysis of the districts in the case study found a relationship between choice losses as a percentage of total enrollment (relative losses) and perception of serious adverse effects. All of the "change" districts, which reported the most severe impacts, experienced relative choice losses of more than 4 percent of their total enrollments in their worst year, whereas all of the "no effect"

Figure 7-3. *Trends in Choice Enrollment as a Percentage of Total Enrollment:*
Other Senders with More Than 100 Students Transferring Out, 1993–96

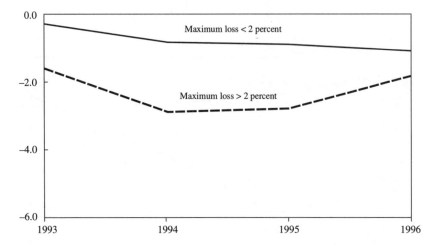

districts experienced worst-year losses of less than 2 percent of their total
enrollments. The "no change" districts had worst-year relative losses of
between 2 and 3 percent, and each of these districts had at least one staff
member who perceived adverse effects of choice. There appears to be a
threshold of around 2 percent for the perception of serious adverse effects
of choice losses.

A summary of the relative losses in five districts with net losses of more
than 2 percent and four districts with net losses of less than 2 percent is
shown in figure 7-3. The low-impact districts demonstrate a trend of increasing losses relative to their total enrollments, whereas the high-impact
districts reached a maximum negative impact in 1994, but reduced that
impact by about a third by 1996. Moreover, three of the four low-impact
districts were not receivers as of 1995–96, whereas four of the five high-impact districts were receivers by at least the 1993–94 school year. These data
offer further support for the findings of the case study, that market forces
appear to be at work in school districts as a result of the choice law.

Impact of Choice on Expenditures

We have discussed the effects of choice on financial gains or losses from
tuition payments, but to this point we have not looked at the impact of
choice on total district expenditures. Even though the tuition losses have
been large for some of the sending districts, these losses must be evaluated

Figure 7-4. *Trends in per Capita Expenditures*

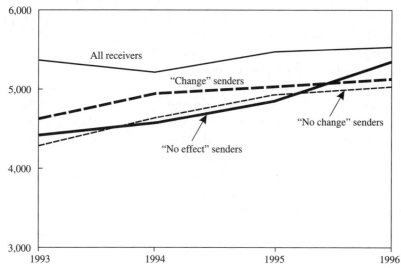

Average expenditures per pupil (dollars)

in the context of the Massachusetts program to provide aid to districts with funding below the foundation level needed to provide quality education. This program has funneled large supplemental payments to poor districts, many of which have also had large choice losses.

Figure 7-4 shows the financial effects of choice in the districts in our case study by showing the trends in per capita expenditures for receivers and the three sending groups between 1993 and 1996. Although the receiving districts had higher per capita funding than the sending districts, they demonstrated only modest increases in per-pupil expenditures during this period in spite of substantial gains in choice tuition income, perhaps no more than the effects of inflation. Since most receivers were above the foundation level, they were not receiving any special increases in state aid; therefore, it appears as if their choice tuition receipts have simply been absorbed by the increased number of choice students they have had to educate.

More important, however, is the fact that both "no effect" and "no change" districts demonstrated substantial gains in per-pupil expenditures in spite of substantial choice losses, due primarily to foundation aid. In fact, the "no effect" districts, all of which were below the foundation levels, demonstrated the most striking gains in per capita expenditures, reducing the gap between them and receiving districts from $1,000 in 1993 to about $200 in 1996 in spite of large choice losses. Likewise, the "no change" districts, two of which were below the foundation levels, also demonstrated increased funding, and by 1996 they had drawn almost even with the "change" districts. The "change" districts, only one of which has been below the foundation level, have also experienced increased per-pupil expenditures, but at a lower rate than the other two groups of senders. All sending districts, regardless of their response to choice losses, have closed the per-pupil expenditure gap with receiving districts to within $500 or less.

In other words, the large tuition payments made by these below-foundation sending districts have been more than replaced by foundation aid, which has clearly reduced the incentive to make any changes to reduce choice losses. The two sending groups that did not change their programs have realized as much financial gain as the sending districts that did change in response to choice losses. Of course, since two of these "change" districts were above the foundation levels, they could not rely on foundation aid to make up their reduced revenue from choice losses.

Summary of Market Competition Effects

The bulk of the evidence presented here supports the applicability of free market concepts to public schools. With respect to the systemic effects of competition, there are several ways in which our specific findings are consistent with the market thesis and inconsistent with the arguments of critics who reject the application of market competition to public schools.

The behavior of three of the nine sending districts we studied conforms to a classic market response: They lost a substantial fraction of their enrollment, their leadership correctly perceived an adverse impact due to the loss of students, they responded by changing their policies and programs, and, most important, they demonstrated the effectiveness of the improvements by significantly reducing their net choice losses, in one case by actually becoming a net receiver.

The behavior of three additional sending districts conforms to another expected market response: They lost a small fraction of their enrollment, they did not perceive or actually experience significant adverse effects on their resources and programs, and consequently they had no reason to change their programs in order to stop the losses. All of these "no effect" districts were below the foundation levels, so increased state aid may have reduced their incentives to implement reforms to reduce choice losses. The behavior of a fourth sending district not visited fits the "no effect" profile according to the enrollment and financial data.

Of the remaining nine Massachusetts sending districts with large choice losses, the five high-impact districts also reversed their choice losses;

therefore, their behavior corresponds to the patterns observed in the districts in the "change" category. The four low-impact senders demonstrated slightly increasing choice losses, so their behavior corresponds to that of the districts in the "no effect" category. Therefore, 16 of 19 sending districts with 100 or more choice losses in 1994–95 appear to have demonstrated the responses expected under the market thesis.

The three districts that experienced adverse effects but did not improve their programs ("no change") also represent a response expected according to market dynamics. For a variety of reasons, including indecisive leadership and poor decisionmaking, not all enterprises will succeed in a market environment. If free market forces work properly, however, only a small fraction of enterprises should fall into the "no change" category at any one time, which appears to have been the case in our study.

The "no change" districts also fail to correspond to a response scenario depicted by critics of the market thesis, which is that losing districts are powerless to prevent or reverse those effects because they are the poorest districts with inadequate resources that are further impaired by choice losses. The staff interviews in the "no change" districts indicated more indecisiveness than powerlessness, and in fact the staffs did not agree on whether choice losses had had serious adverse effects on their programs. Indeed, the per-pupil expenditure data in figure 7-4 show that the "no change" districts experienced larger increases than the "change" districts (because of foundation aid), which may be the reason for a lack of consensus about adverse effects. There is no indication here, either from staff interviews or from objective resource data, that the "no change" districts had inadequate resources to address those program deficiencies that contributed to choice losses.

One finding that is consistent with critics of choice is that most of the staff members in "no effect" districts and some in the "no change" districts cited racial motivations as reasons for choice losses. This result, if substantiated, is inconsistent with the competition thesis, because racial composition is a demographic factor over which districts have little control. For this reason it is important that we evaluate additional evidence about the motivations of families who opted for choice.

Reasons for Participating in Choice

Figure 7-5 shows the major reasons cited by choice families for transferring students to their current schools. Taken from parent and student surveys conducted for this study, the results make it clear that the vast majority

Figure 7-5. *Family Reasons for Choosing Schools*

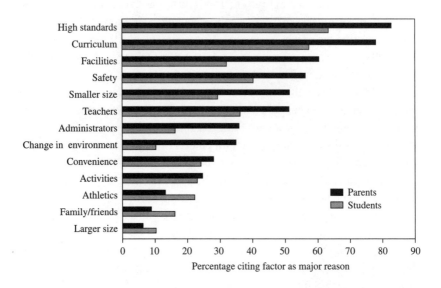

Percentage citing factor as major reason

of choice parents and students say that they chose schools because of perceptions of academic quality, with the dominant reason being higher academic standards. The second most important reason, for both parents and students, was the availability of specific courses. Most of the non-academic reasons, such as convenience, activities, athletics, and friends, were the least important reasons for transfers.

Although none of the closed-end questions referred specifically to racial motivations, one of the more important reasons cited, safety, might be seen by some as a surrogate for racial concerns; safety was the fourth most important reason for parents and the third most important for students. We also asked an open-end question about reasons for transfers, and we noted that terms such as "crime," "violence," "gangs," or "drugs" were frequently used to illustrate safety concerns (no racial reasons were noted in the open-end responses). Given national studies of urban schools that show a correlation between school violence and higher concentrations of poverty and minorities, it is possible that the districts in our sample with more violence and safety problems might also have larger minority enrollments. The question, then, is this: Was the motivation for leaving a district really racial, or were these families acting on a legitimate concern about safety in schools with higher rates of crime and violence?

Given the number of staff members in the "no effect" and "no change" districts who believe that choice transfers are racially motivated, we should not necessarily accept parent and student concerns about safety at face value. On the other hand, the beliefs of the administrators may also be self-serving, supporting their own belief in the status quo: Their programs are good; choice students leave because of race and not programs, and nothing should be done to bring these families back.

To gain further insight into these issues, we considered the reasons for transfer cited by other groupings of families and staff members. For example, the ranking of reasons for various subgroups of parents and students—nonwhite persons, single parents, renters, and persons with lower income—is virtually identical to that for the total sample, with higher standards and curriculum the top two reasons for all groups. We note that safety was the number four reason for nonwhite parents and the number three reason for nonwhite students, as for the total sample. Further, very few staff members from the ten receiver districts and the three "change" senders cited race as the motivation for choice families; the dominant reason for these staff members was also academic quality, especially higher standards and better curriculum. We are led to conclude, based on the consistency of these groups of parents, students, receiver district staff members, and "change" district staff members, that academic considerations, not race or class, are the dominant motivations for choice families who change school districts.

Given the lower minority representation in the interdistrict choice population, it would also be helpful to know the reasons families, especially minority families, give for not using the interdistrict choice option. Since we do not have such data, we rely instead on a general survey of Massachusetts citizens regarding their views on different choice options. Generally large majorities of African-American adults believe, more than do white adults, that choice will improve the education of poor and minority students and will create more cost-effective schools, although a slight majority (53 percent) also believe that choice will increase economic and racial segregation. Most important, a greater majority of black adults than white adults support interdistrict choice (75 to 59 percent), and the same is true for charter schools (76 to 65 percent). It would appear, then, that the underrepresentation of minority families in opting for interdistrict choice is not due to lack of support of interdistrict choice, a conclusion also supported by the large number of minority participants in both METCO and charter schools. Rather, it is more likely that minority families are not aware of interdistrict choice options or are unaware of the availability of subsidized transportation for families below the poverty line.

Conclusions

In our study we found that, for the most part, school districts with large choice gains or losses and the families who transfer between them are behaving consistent with market principles. Nearly all school districts with large gains support the choice policy and have used the funds to make improvements in their programs. The school districts with the largest relative choice losses have responded by changing their programs, which in turn has helped them recover some or all of their losses. The experience of turning adversity into advantage led the leadership of these districts to become supporters of the choice law to even a greater degree than receiving district staff members. Our surveys of parents and students and our interviews with school staff members have strongly suggested that the motivation for changing districts has been predominantly academic, with the most important reason being higher academic standards and better curriculum. Aside from being consistent with the market thesis, this finding also challenges a major argument of choice critics, which is that choice families who leave school districts with high minority concentrations are motivated primarily by social or racial concerns rather than by academics.

This brings us to one important finding that supports an argument against choice and market competition. Massachusetts interdistrict choice families and students tend to be whiter, have higher SES, and score higher on achievement tests than the nonchoice population in their sending districts. Also, choice students tend to leave districts that are poorer, more minority, and with lower academic profiles in favor of districts that are more affluent, less minority, and with higher academic profiles. We stress that this statement applies to the average choice student and family, and that there are some sending-receiving relationships in which either the schools are very similar or the choice students are less advantaged than those in the sending district as a whole.

In our study we did not find, however, that choice has had serious adverse effects on racial balance or on the financial status of sending districts with more minority families. Although interdistrict choice students underrepresent minority populations in sending districts, the number of choice students is generally small in comparison to the total enrollments of sending districts with more minority families. Therefore, the loss of choice students has no appreciable impact on either the racial composition of sending districts with more minority families or their overall financial status. We also found that the representation problem has been confined to the interdistrict choice program. If we consider all choice students who have left their resident school districts, including METCO and charter school students, we find that the total choice population is representative of the statewide Hispanic population and actually overrepresents the statewide African-American population.

The strong interest in school choice demonstrated by minority student participation in METCO and charter schools and the strong expression of support for school choice on the part of minority parents in the citizen survey have convinced us that the minority representation issue is an important problem, but not fatal to interdistrict choice. Since minority families are just as interested as white families in using choice to increase the educational opportunities of their children, as indicated by the resident survey and their participation in other school choice programs, the most likely explanations of their underrepresentation in the interdistrict choice program are lack of awareness of choice options or inadequate mechanisms for providing transportation for low-income families.

Overall, the data from the Massachusetts interdistrict choice program are generally supportive of the desirability of statewide open enrollment policies. The evidence in favor of such policies includes the facts that many thousands of families are using the interdistrict choice program, they are very happy with it, and it has led to significant program improvements in some of the most impacted sending districts. The choice law is also supported by a majority of school staff members of the school districts in our case study. Moreover, there is no reason to impose racial restrictions on choice transfers. Although the Massachusetts interdistrict choice population underrepresents poor and minority families at this time, a condition that should be addressed, choice is having no significant adverse impact on racial balance, and indeed in some cases choice has actually improved it.

Based on our findings, there are some policy lessons to be learned from the Massachusetts experience that might enhance the benefits and limit the potential harms of open enrollment programs, either in Massachusetts or in other states. Several policy areas might be addressed, including representation, access, and program efficacy.

If the rate of minority participation is low in some programs, states may need to assess awareness of and interest in choice options among minority and low-income families, possibly by conducting surveys among parent populations. Other than low levels of awareness themselves, there may be deficiencies in transportation subsidies, which may be necessary to increase the participation rates of low-income families.

If there is low awareness of choice options and transportation subsidies among low-income or minority families, states must ensure that choice options and transportation subsidies are well advertised among school populations. In particular, if advertising of choice openings is simply left to the discretion of local school district staff members, districts with lower-quality programs will have no incentive to advertise choice openings in neighboring districts with better-quality programs. Likewise, there may be little incentive for receiving districts to advertise transportation subsidies for low-income students if they are receiving enough middle-class transfers.

To improve access for low-income and minority parents and to maximize the benefits of choice for all families and school systems in a state, participation should be universal for all school districts that have space available. That is, school districts should not be allowed to prevent transfers to them if space is available. School boards should retain control over the determination of physical capacity, but capacity should not be manipulated to keep out students from other districts. Universal participation should in no way limit local control over curricula, academic standards, and staffing decisions.

Tuition transfer payments should be allowed to reflect real market forces, with the possible exception of reimbursements for a short transition period to prevent catastrophic tuition losses and to give districts some time to fix their programs. In Massachusetts there is little question that the foundation aid program has reduced incentives for reform in some of the large sending districts. Although we are not criticizing foundation aid here, there is no need to offer special reimbursements for below-foundation districts as foundation goals are realized over the next several years. For market competition to have its full effect, there need to be clear financial rewards and penalties for districts that gain or lose market share.

Finally, there are widespread misperceptions about the financial harms and benefits of the choice program in Massachusetts. Educators in growing districts are the first to claim that educating an additional 100 students requires more money; this is usually computed as average per-pupil costs, which are clearly higher than the marginal costs of educating the additional students. But educators in shrinking districts are the last to acknowledge that losing 100 students means some cost savings, which are at least equal to the marginal costs of educating 100 students! A shrinking market share in a public school system means reducing teaching staff members, which most school administrators are loath to admit (or execute). Other than teaching basic economics in schools of education, states with open enrollment policies (or that are planning to adopt them) would be wise to set or adjust tuition payments according to some rational analysis of true costs for receiving districts and true savings for sending districts.

None of these suggestions should diminish the fact that the current Massachusetts open enrollment law is a beneficial policy overall and could be made better by improving racial representation and by fine-tuning the funding formulas. If these recommendations are adopted, it is likely that the Massachusetts open enrollment program will continue to grow. Growth in interdistrict choice will mean that more families will benefit from greater educational choices, and more school districts will benefit either by being net receivers or by experiencing "wake-up calls" to improve their programs for all students.

Notes

1. See, for example, James S. Coleman and Sally Kilgore, *High School Achievement* (Basic Books, 1982); John E. Chubb and Terry M. Moe, *Politics, Markets, and America's Schools* (Brookings, 1990); John F. Witte and others, "Fourth Year Report: Milwaukee Parental Choice Program," University of Wisconsin–Madison, Department of Political Science and Robert M. La Follette Institute of Public Affairs, December 1993; Paul E. Peterson, Jay P. Greene, and Chad Noyes, "School Choice in Milwaukee," *The Public Interest,* no. 125 (Fall 1996), pp. 38–56.

2. Caroline Hoxby, "Does Competition among Public Schools Benefit Students and Taxpayers?" 1997 revision of Working Paper 1979, Cambridge, Mass.: National Bureau of Economic Research (NBER), 1994; Caroline Hoxby, "Do Private Schools Provide Competition for Public Schools?" Working Paper 4978, NBER, 1994, and Chapter 6 in this volume.

3. The districts used in the case study were as follows: Receivers: Acton-Boxborough, Avon, Hampden-Wilbraham, Harvard, Holliston, Lunenberg, Manchester, Marblehead, Uxbridge, Pentucket; senders: Brockton, Gloucester, Fitchburg, Haverhill, Hopkinton, Leominster, Lynn, Maynard, Northbridge, Springfield.

4. One sending district declined to participate in the study.

5. See *Massachusetts Attitudes Concerning School Choice* (Boston: Pioneer Institute for Public Policy Research, August 1996).

6. The district-level standard deviation is approximately 78 for each test.

7. One complication in making a comparison between the interdistrict choice population and the statewide population is that Boston comprises nearly half of the statewide African-American enrollment and a sizable portion of the state Hispanic population, yet almost none of the Boston suburban districts within reasonable commuting distance participates in interdistrict choice. Therefore, in order to assess the racial equability of choice in Massachusetts, we compared the statewide racial composition to the compositions of all choice populations, including open enrollment, METCO, and charter school populations.

8. This resident enrollment is somewhat hypothetical, since if there were no choice law some of these students would return to private or parochial schools. The inclusion of all students in our calculation is conservative, however, because it tends to inflate the racial impact on senders.

9. We dropped two vocational districts, Minuteman and Greater Lawrence, which have 188 transfers in and 133 transfers out, respectively, because these districts already draw from large areas composed of many separate school districts. There is a significant

drop of 4 percent in the white student population (and a corresponding increase in the Hispanic student population) due to choice transfers out of Greater Lawrence.

10. In some markets an enterprise may have a good product, but consumers are not aware of it; we doubt this applies to public school systems that are losing resident students, because the local families should be quite familiar with the product.

11. These nine districts were Amesbury, Ayer, Clinton, Lowell, Milford, Pittsfield, Salem, Triton, and Worcester.

EIGHT

Charter Schools as Seen by Students, Teachers, and Parents

Gregg Vanourek, Bruno V. Manno,
Chester E. Finn, Jr., and Louann A. Bierlein

GIVEN TODAY'S APPETITE for education reform among American citizens and the explosive growth of charter schools nationally, scores of analysts and agencies are scrambling to learn about their enrollment patterns, demographics, and educational characteristics. Yet nobody, to our knowledge, has engaged in a systematic nationwide effort to ask the clients and teachers of charter schools what they think of these new educational providers. So we did. During the 1996–97 school year, the Hudson Institute's Charter Schools in Action Project gathered four sets of quantitative data that yield a revealing portrait of fifty charter schools enrolling some 16,000 students in ten states. The primary things we looked at were satisfaction levels among the schools' essential constituents, comparisons between charter schools and schools that students would otherwise be attending (or had previously attended), reasons for choosing charter schools, and basic demographics.

What is offered here, then, is not just an echo of others' work—such as the excellent Department of Education charter school study, various state-level reports, the two essays on charter schools by Bryan Hassel in this volume, or even our own report from last year[1]—but a new and distinctive body of information intended to supply policymakers, educators, journalists, and fellow analysts with early feedback from the "constituents" of charter schools. We begin with their foremost constituents: the students.

How Students Grade Their Charter Schools

Nearly 5,000 charter school students in grade five and above completed survey forms. They were asked what they liked (fifteen options were provided) and disliked (17 options) about their charter schools and encouraged to check all that applied. On average, they noted 4.6 likes and 2.7 dislikes (see table 8-1).

When students were asked, "What do you like about this school?" their most frequent answers were "good teachers" (58.6 percent), "they teach it until I learn it" (51.3 percent), and "they don't let me fall behind" (38.5 percent). We found it interesting that the top three answers had to do with instruction. The next most frequent answer—"computers and technology" (35.7 percent)—was somewhat surprising, since our site visits yielded many complaints about a lack of technology due to budget constraints. Some charter schools, however, have developed sophisticated technology programs.

The next cluster of answers—"nice people running the school" (34.9 percent), "teacher's attention" (33.9 percent), "class size" (33.9 percent),

Table 8-1. *Students' Likes and Dislikes about Charter Schools*[a]
Percent

Students' likes		Students' dislikes	
Good teachers	58.6	Poor sports program	29.4
Teach it until I learn it	51.3	Not enough other activities	29.4
Don't let me fall behind	38.5	Food	28.6
Computers and technology	35.7	Too much homework	28.5
Nice people running the school	34.9	Boring	23.4
Teacher's attention	33.9	Not enough computers/	
Class size	33.9	technology	21.8
Curriculum	33.3	Too strict	19.7
Safety	27.5	Difficult commute	14.5
School size	25.4	Poor facilities	12.1
Other out-of-school activities	19.8	I could be learning more	11.7
A lot is expected of me	19.7	Bad teachers	9.1
Opportunities for parent		School too big or too small	7.5
participation	15.9	Not enough homework	6.9
Sports program	15.8	Classes too big or too small	6.7
Food	12.0	Too tough academically	6.7
		Not safe enough	6.3
		Not strict enough	6.0

a. Sample A student survey respondents from thirty-nine charter schools across ten states; $n = 4,954$ (February 1997); percentages may not add to 100 percent due to invalid responses and nonresponses.

Table 8-2. *Students' Comparisons of Charter Schools with Previous Schools*[a]
Percent

Students	Teachers			Interest in schoolwork		
	Better	About the same	Worse	Better	About the same	Worse
All students	60.7	27.0	4.8	49.9	35.4	7.7
Prior public school students	65.2	24.7	5.5	52.4	34.4	8.4
Prior private school students	48.5	37.1	6.6	42.1	43.7	9.6
Other[b]	51.1	32.3	1.9	46.5	37.2	4.4
White	64.9	25.0	4.0	52.9	34.9	7.4
Black	56.1	26.3	7.4	50.5	31.4	8.1
Hispanic	60.3	25.0	5.5	49.8	33.7	8.5
Asian	62.0	29.3	4.0	50.0	40.7	5.3
Native American	44.2	47.7	3.8	37.6	50.0	7.8

a. Sample A student survey respondents from thirty-nine character schools across ten states; $n = 4,954$ (February 1997); percentages may not add to 100 percent due to invalid responses and nonresponses.

b. Children who were home schooled, who attended other charter schools before these, or who did not attend school last year.

and "curriculum" (33.3 percent)—mostly had to do with educational practices. Overall, among the eight most frequent answers, six concern teaching and learning. In contrast, when students were asked, "What do you dislike about this school?" three of the four most common responses concerned nonacademic matters: "poor sports program" (29.4 percent), "not enough other activities" (29.4 percent), "food" (28.6 percent), and "too much homework" (28.5 percent). Although these dislikes were noted by only a quarter to a third of students, they do send a message to charter school leaders about what they will need to work on in the future to keep their constituents happy.

Charter Schools versus Schools Previously Attended

In two questions students were asked to rate features of their charter schools against those of their previous schools. In students' responses to both questions, charter schools rate significantly higher (see table 8-2).

Three students out of five (60.7 percent) said that their charter school teachers were better than the teachers at their previous schools. And half (49.9 percent) said that they were more interested in their schoolwork. Just one in twenty reported worse teachers and one in thirteen reported less interest in schoolwork. Bear in mind that surveys were given only to

Table 8-3. *Students' Ratings of Their Performance, by Race or Ethnicity*[a]
Percent

Students	School	Excellent	Good	Average	Poor	Failing
All students	Previous school	16.0	26.7	26.3	13.3	10.3
	Charter school	20.9	41.2	24.4	5.3	1.8
	Change	4.9	14.5	−1.9	−8.0	−8.5
White students	Previous school	19.0	27.6	24.8	12.7	10.0
	Charter school	23.4	43.2	22.2	4.6	1.4
	Change	4.4	15.6	−2.6	−8.1	−8.6
African-American students	Previous school	12.5	22.7	28.0	14.9	10.2
	Charter school	20.2	38.4	24.0	5.7	2.5
	Change	7.7	15.7	−4.0	−9.2	−7.7
Hispanic students	Previous school	12.2	25.3	27.1	14.1	12.8
	Charter school	18.6	40.7	26.2	7.0	1.8
	Change	6.4	15.4	−0.9	−7.1	−11.0
Asian students	Previous school	13.3	28.7	26.7	12.7	15.3
	Charter school	18.0	40.0	29.3	6.0	2.0
	Change	4.7	11.3	2.6	−6.7	−13.3
Native American students	Previous school	14.6	29.5	36.6	10.9	5.3
	Charter school	15.4	39.9	35.1	5.3	1.0
	Change	0.8	10.4	−1.5	−5.6	−4.3

a. Sample A student survey respondents from thirty-nine charter schools across ten states; $n = 4,954$ (February 1997); percentages may not add to 100 percent due to invalid responses and nonresponses.

youngsters in the middle and high school grades, a pupil population often considered hard for schools to please. From table 8-2 we can deduce that there is particular satisfaction among students who have left traditional public schools and that student satisfaction crosses racial and ethnic lines.[2]

Comparative Academic Performance

Charter school students report that they are doing better, on average, at their charter schools than at their previous schools (see table 8-3).

The percentages of students doing excellent or good work rose by 4.9 percent and 14.5 percent, respectively. Those doing average work declined a little. The percentage doing poorly fell by 8.0 percent and that failing by 8.5 percent. Clearly the numbers are moving in the right direction. Dramatic improvement occurred in many cases. Among students who reported that they had done poorly at their previous schools, 16.9 percent were now doing excellent work and 43.3 percent were doing good work. Of those failing at their previous schools, 19.8 percent were doing excellent work and 36.5 percent were doing good work (see table 8-4).

Table 8-4. *Students' Performance*

Students' performance improvement (as noted by students)[a]	Performance	Percent
Students performing poorly at previous schools who are now:	Excellent	16.9
	Good	43.3
	Average	30.7
	Poor	5.9
	Failing	1.1
Students failing at previous schools who are now:	Excellent	19.8
	Good	36.5
	Average	29.6
	Poor	6.5
	Failing	3.5
Students' performance improvement (as noted by parents)[b]		
Students performing below average at previous schools who are now:	Excellent	8.2
	Above average	23.8
	Average	55.1
	Below average	11.7
	Poor	1.2
Students performing poorly at previous schools who are now:	Excellent	18.9
	Above average	25.6
	Average	36.5
	Below average	16.0
	Poor	3.2

a. Sample A student survey respondents from thirty-nine charter schools across ten states; n = 4,954 (February 1997); percentages may not add to 100 percent due to invalid responses and nonresponses.

b. Sample B parent survey respondents from thirty charter schools across nine states; n = 2,978 (February 1997); percentages may not add to 100 percent due to invalid responses and nonresponses.

Charter school parents also appraised the academic performance of their children at their previous schools and (as of February 1997) at their charter schools (see table 8-4). Among parents who reported that their children had done below average work at their previous schools, 8.2 percent indicated that their sons and daughters were doing excellent work at their charter schools, and 23.8 percent said their children were doing above average work. Of those whose children did poorly at their previous schools, 18.9

Table 8-5. *Parents' Ratings of Their Children's Overall Performance*[a]

Percent

Type of student	Performance	Previous school	Charter school	Change
Total students	Excellent	14.0	24.5	10.5
	Above average	20.0	32.2	12.2
	Average	27.0	30.3	3.3
	Below average	12.0	4.0	–8.0
	Poor	5.3	0.6	–4.7
Special education students[b]	Excellent	5.9	11.0	5.1
	Above average	10.6	26.8	16.2
	Average	36.8	48.6	11.8
	Below average	32.2	11.8	–20.4
	Poor	14.5	1.8	–12.7
Gifted students[c]	Excellent	26.9	37.4	10.5
	Above average	33.3	40.7	7.4
	Average	26.5	19.0	–7.5
	Below average	8.4	2.3	–6.1
	Poor	4.9	0.6	–4.3
Students with limited English proficiency	Excellent	22.7	27.6	4.9
	Above average	20.5	35.3	14.8
	Average	39.8	28.4	–11.4
	Below average	10.2	7.8	–2.4
	Poor	6.8	0.9	–5.9

a. Sample B parent survey respondents from thirty charter schools across nine states; $n = 2,978$ (February 1997); percentages may not add to 100 percent due to invalid responses and nonresponses.

b. Identified by their parents as "not learning quickly, needing extra help," having a "physical disability," having "behavior problems," and/or having a "learning disability."

c. Identified as being a "fast learner, often bored."

percent reported excellent work and 25.6 percent reported above-average work by their children. Again, the numbers are moving in the right direction.

In our sample alone, 814 children moved out of the poor or failing category by changing to charter schools. That is 70 percent of all the children who said they were in that performance category in their previous schools—a remarkable achievement. According to table 8-5, more students were doing excellent or above-average work in their charter schools than in their previous schools (as reported by parents). Indeed, the number of their children doing excellent or above-average work increased by 22.7 percent, whereas the number doing below-average or poor work decreased by

12.7 percent. What is striking is that these trends also hold true for special education students, gifted students, and students with limited English proficiency.

Levels of Satisfaction among Parents

When parents were asked, "How satisfied are you with specific features of this school?" a clear trend emerged: most of the top answers ("class size," "curriculum," "school size," "individual attention by teachers," "academic standards for students") were education related, whereas most of the lower-ranked answers concerned such noninstructional matters as facilities, extracurricular activities, transportation, food, and sports. Note, though, that even the "bottom" answers were very positive. If converted to letter grade equivalents, all of the "grades" would be As or Bs. Overall, parents seemed remarkably pleased with most aspects of their child's charter school (see table 8-6).

When parents were asked to rate their children's charter schools against their other options ("Please compare this charter school with the school your child would otherwise be attending this year"), they ranked the charter schools higher on every single indicator—but especially on individual attention and class or school size, and also on curriculum and teaching. The school facilities received the worst rating from charter school parents—a grade that is unsurprising to us after forty-five site visits to charter schools, many of them housed in very meager quarters. Yet 42 percent of parents said that the charter school facilities were better, whereas only 15 percent said they were worse than their previous school facilities (see table 8-7).

Parent satisfaction levels are also high for parents of children with special needs (special education students, gifted children, and students with limited English proficiency). About two-thirds of parents with children in these categories think the charter schools are better than the schools their children would otherwise attend with regard to curriculum, quality of teaching, providing extra help when needed, and parental involvement (see table 8-8).[3] The surveys revealed strong satisfaction and a high degree of conviction among parents that the charter schools were better for their youngsters than other available options in a wide array of areas. Several state-level evaluations of charter schools have drawn similar conclusions.[4]

Table 8-6. *Overall Parental Satisfaction with Charter Schools*[a]
Percent

Indicator	Very satisfied	Somewhat satisfied	Uncertain	Not too satisfied	Quite dissatisfied
Opportunities for parent participation	75.9	17.7	5.1	1.1	0.3
Class size	75.2	19.2	3.0	2.3	0.3
Curriculum	71.6	22.9	3.4	1.9	0.2
School size	74.5	18.6	4.5	1.9	0.6
Individual attention by teachers	70.8	21.5	5.2	2.0	0.5
Academic standards for students	67.8	22.4	6.7	2.5	0.6
Accessibility and openness	66.1	23.6	7.3	2.2	0.8
How much school expects of parents	66.0	23.2	7.8	2.2	0.8
People running the school	62.2	26.4	7.7	2.7	1.0
Quality of teaching	56.6	32.4	8.1	2.2	0.8
Technology	55.8	24.6	11.3	5.9	2.3
School facilities	44.8	34.1	9.6	8.5	3.0
Extracurricular activities	43.1	28.9	20.0	5.7	2.2
Transportation to/from school	49.8	22.9	10.5	10.0	6.9
Food	42.3	27.4	14.3	9.3	6.7
Sports program	23.0	37.0	10.3	22.8	6.8

a. Sample B parent survey respondents from thirty charter schools across nine states; $n = 2,978$ (February 1997); percentages may not add to 100 percent due to invalid responses and nonresponses.

These satisfaction levels for charter schools stand out at a time when there is growing dissatisfaction with traditional public schools. According to recent surveys by Public Agenda, 61 percent of Americans complained about public school standards being too low, and 60 percent said that schools do not place enough emphasis on "the basics."[5] Almost half (47 percent) of Americans said that they did not believe that a high school degree is a guarantee that a student has learned the basics.[6] In a 1995 report Public Agenda described popular support for America's public schools as "fragile" and "porous" and warned of a "public poised for flight" unless schools begin to deliver what the public considers to be the essential elements of education (which it listed as safety, higher standards, order, and smaller classes).[7]

Table 8-7. *Overall Parent Rating of Charter School versus School Child Would Otherwise Attend*[a]
Percent

Indicator	Better	About the same	Worse
Class size	69.3	16.3	2.5
Individual attention by teachers	69.9	16.7	2.7
School size	68.6	13.1	4.4
Quality of teaching	65.7	19.7	2.0
Parent involvement	64.0	21.3	2.2
Curriculum	65.0	20.8	3.1
Extra help for students	64.3	19.7	3.3
Academic standards	63.0	22.2	3.0
Accessibility and openness	60.5	23.0	2.5
Discipline	60.2	23.6	3.6
Basic skills	58.8	25.7	2.4
Safety	59.5	24.5	3.5
School facilities	42.0	27.1	15.1

a. Sample B parent survey respondents from thirty charter schools across nine states; $n = 2,978$ (February 1997); percentages may not add to 100 percent due to invalid responses and nonresponses.

Table 8-8. *Parents' Rating of Charter Schools versus School Their Children Would Otherwise Attend (Students with Special Needs)*[a]
Percent

Indicator		Special education[b]	Gifted[c]	Limited English proficiency
Curriculum	Better	64.5	69.6	75.4
	About the same	21.8	18.3	15.4
	Worse	4.9	3.0	0.8
Quality of teaching	Better	67.1	67.6	61.5
	About the same	20.6	19.5	22.3
	Worse	2.4	2.4	0.0
Extra help	Better	68.1	65.9	64.6
	About the same	17.6	20.6	18.5
	Worse	4.3	3.2	0.8
Parent involvement	Better	65.0	68.3	52.3
	About the same	23.6	19.2	27.7
	Worse	1.8	2.4	0.8

a. Sample B parent survey respondents from thirty charter schools across nine states; $n = 2,978$ (February 1997); percentages may not add to 100 percent due to invalid responses and nonresponses.

b. Identified by their parents as "not learning quickly, needing extra help," having a "physical disability," having "behavior problems," and/or having a "learning disability."

c. Noted as being a "fast learner, often bored."

How Teachers Grade Their Charter Schools

When teachers were asked, "How satisfied are you with specific features of this school and your experience in it?" the answers indicated a high degree of satisfaction with key aspects of the schools (see table 8-9).

Combining the "very satisfied" and "somewhat satisfied" columns, we can see that 93.2 percent of charter school teachers were satisfied with their schools' educational philosophies, 94.4 percent were satisfied with their fellow teachers, 90.9 percent were satisfied with the schools' sizes, 85.4 percent were satisfied with the schools' administrators, 91.3 percent were satisfied with the students, and 84 percent were satisfied with the challenge of starting a new school. These are impressive numbers, especially given the newness of the schools.

Table 8-9. *Teachers' Satisfaction with Their Charter Schools*[a]
Percent

Indicator	Very satisfied	Somewhat satisfied	Uncertain	Not too satisfied	Quite dissatisfied
Fellow teachers	61.2	33.2	3.3	2.1	0.2
Educational philosophy	61.6	31.6	4.3	1.9	0.6
School size	59.1	31.8	5.6	3.1	0.4
Students	50.9	40.4	5.4	2.9	0.4
Challenge of starting a new school	50.5	33.5	13.7	2.0	0.4
Administrators	53.6	31.8	7.1	5.3	2.2
Teacher decisionmaking	46.6	31.9	11.6	7.4	2.5
Governing board	38.4	32.2	22.7	4.1	2.5
Staff development	34.2	38.9	12.5	11.9	2.5
Instructional materials	35.7	37.3	8.2	15.3	3.5
Relations with community	21.3	46.6	23.5	7.0	1.6
Parental involvement	26.8	42.1	9.7	16.9	4.5
Salary level	25.5	43.7	9.2	17.5	4.1
Nonteaching responsibilities	23.8	36.0	21.0	14.7	4.5
Fringe benefits	24.6	34.5	19.4	14.9	6.7
Physical facilities	23.0	37.0	10.3	22.8	6.8
Relations with school district	12.1	26.0	40.7	15.7	5.5
Relations with teacher union	9.7	6.8	69.3	8.0	6.2

a. Sample C teacher survey respondents from thirty-six charter schools across ten states; n = 521 (February 1997); percentages may not equal 100 percent due to invalid responses and nonresponses.

Table 8-10. *Teachers' Views on Charter Schools' Success*[a]
Percent

Indicator	Much success	Some success	Little or no success
Providing for safety	66.3	31.0	2.7
Providing excellent educational alternative	62.4	35.1	2.5
Positive influence on education in community	61.1	36.4	2.5
Maintaining discipline	60.2	34.6	5.3
Building a high-quality staff	55.9	40.6	3.5
Involving teachers in decisionmaking	56.9	37.1	6.0
Raising student achievement	48.0	49.6	2.3
Setting/maintaining high academic standards	46.6	48.7	4.7
Strong curriculum, powerful methods	45.9	49.4	4.7
Attracting the kinds of students it hoped to have	42.4	53.8	3.7
Educating hard-to-educate students	40.1	57.0	2.9
Keeping students in school	43.0	50.9	6.0
Suitably assessing pupil performance	37.7	57.4	4.9
Providing necessary teacher training	40.6	50.7	8.7
Obtaining necessary resources	39.1	52.9	7.9
Providing necessary instructional materials	42.2	46.5	11.2
Running smoothly	33.7	59.3	7.0
Involving parents	36.0	54.7	9.3
Integrating technology with the curriculum	37.9	47.0	15.0
Giving teachers adequate preparation time	31.7	43.6	24.7

a. Sample C teacher survey respondents from thirty-six charter school across ten states; $n = 521$ (February 1997); percentages may not equal 100 percent due to invalid responses and nonresponses.

When teachers were asked to evaluate their schools' success so far in certain areas, the results were again positive (see table 8-10).

The percentages of teachers who reported that their schools had experienced much success or some success in specific areas broke down as follows: 97.6 percent reported that their schools had been successful in raising student achievement, 97.5 percent in providing an excellent educational alternative, 97.3 percent in providing safety, and 97.1 percent in educating hard-to-educate children. Teachers reporting that their schools had experienced little success or no success in specific areas broke down as follows: 24.7 percent reported that their schools had been unsuccessful in giving teachers adequate preparation time, 15 percent in integrating technology with the curriculum, and 11.2 percent in giving teachers sufficient instructional supplies. In every single area covered in the survey, at least three-fourths of the teachers surveyed reported that their charter schools were having much success or some success. That is one reason why our 1997 survey showed that 82 percent of these teachers planned to return to their charter schools the next year and fewer than 3 percent said they hoped to be elsewhere.

Why Do Families Choose Charter Schools?

Policymakers and analysts project onto the charter school movement various theories about why people might opt for these schools. Asking why real families actually choose charter schools is an important reality check. Our surveys probed why parents made their choices, whether they are pleased with the change, and whether they expect to stick with it (see table 8-11).

Most of the leading answers ("higher standards," "educational phil-osophy," "better teachers") had to do with educational matters. Nor is it surprising that parents would be drawn to the small sizes of most charter schools and their welcoming view of parental involvement. (According to the new federal study, the average enrollment of U.S. charter schools is only 275 students, and 61.9 percent of charter schools have enrollments of fewer than 200 students.[8])

Some of the reasons parents gave (or did not give) for choosing charter schools were more surprising: Only a few (16.9 percent) cited "child was doing badly" as their reason for electing the charter school, and just a fifth (20.1 percent) cited safety concerns. It is interesting to note that the number of parents who said they chose the charter school because their "child was doing badly in regular school" (16.9 percent) closely mirrors the percentage (17.3 percent) who, in response to another question, described the child's previous academic performance as below average or poor. Still, even the responses on the low end in table 8-11 were actually given by a lot of parents. For instance, one in five parents reported that their "child's special needs were not being met" by his or her previous school.

Why Do Teachers Choose Charter Schools?

Teachers were asked, "How big a factor were the following in your decision to teach in this school?" (see table 8-12). Their leading choices

Table 8-11. *Reasons Parents Chose Charter Schools*[a]
Percent

Reason	Lower-income parents (<$30,000)[b]	Middle-income parents ($30,000–59,000)	Upper-income parents (>$60,000)	Total
Small size of charter school	52.5	54.2	57.6	53.0
Higher standards at charter school	44.2	47.9	50.6	45.9
Program closer to my educational philosophy	37.2	48.2	59.7	44.0
Greater opportunity for parent involvement	45.5	45.7	37.9	43.0
Better teachers at charter school	45.3	39.3	40.3	41.9
Unhappy with curriculum/ teachers at previous school	29.8	39.2	42.2	34.5
My child wanted to come here	34.9	27.3	25.2	30.3
Location of charter school more convenient	41.9	20.6	13.4	29.5
Charter school offers before-/after-school programs	33.2	18.9	13.3	24.3
People told me this is a better school	27.5	19.0	11.7	21.8
Previous school was unsafe	25.9	18.5	10.8	20.1
My child's special needs were not met at previous school	20.3	22.4	17.8	19.9
Prefer private school but could not afford	21.5	17.9	15.2	18.7
My child was doing badly in regular school	20.4	16.6	9.5	16.9
Other	7.1	14.4	15.2	11.0

a. Sample B parent survey respondents from thirty charter schools across nine states; $n = 2,978$ (February 1997); percentages may not equal 100 percent due to invalid responses and nonresponses.

b. $30,000 was our lower income threshold because it captured all families (with four or fewer children) who were eligible for the federal free and reduced-price lunch programs.

were "school's educational philosophy" (76.8 percent), "wanted a new school" (64.8 percent), "like-minded colleagues" (62.9 percent), "good administrators" (54.6 percent), and "class size" (54.2 percent). Least commonly cited as a big factor were "convenient location" (28.2 percent), "school less influenced by union" (23.9 percent), "safety" (15.1 percent),

Table 8-12. *Key Factors in Teachers' Decisions to Teach in Charter School*[a]
Percent

Factor	Big factor	Somewhat of a factor	Not a factor
School's educational philosophy	76.8	18.0	5.2
Wanted a new school	64.8	25.1	10.1
Like-minded colleagues	62.9	26.4	10.6
Good administrators	54.6	30.0	15.4
Class size	54.2	25.0	20.9
Teachers have more authority	41.9	33.7	24.4
Committed parents	38.3	37.9	23.8
Less bureaucracy	40.2	34.4	25.4
School size	35.7	35.3	28.9
Eager/good students	31.1	38.6	30.3
Convenient location	28.2	36.9	34.8
Less influenced by union	23.9	24.5	51.5
Safety	15.1	29.2	55.7
Attractive compensation	10.2	33.1	56.6
Difficulty finding another position	8.7	16.6	74.8

a. Sample C teacher survey respondents from thirty-six charter schools across ten states; $n = 521$ (February 1997); percentages may not equal 100 percent due to invalid responses and nonresponses.

"attractive compensation" (10.2 percent), and "difficulty finding other employment" (8.7 percent). Table 8-12 suggests that charter school teachers appear more interested in educational quality and professional/entrepreneurial opportunities than salary and convenience.

When asked, "What would you likely be doing this year if you weren't teaching in this school?" only 36.7 percent said "teaching in another public school." Some 13.1 percent said "teaching in another charter school," 8.6 percent said "teaching in a private school," and a whopping 27.1 percent answered "other." Apparently charter school teachers are an unconventional bunch. Over a quarter say that they'd be doing something other than teaching if they weren't teaching in a charter school. This suggests that charter schools are tapping into sources of instructional horsepower not attracted to more conventional schools.

Who Teaches in Charter Schools?

The average charter school teacher comes in with 5.6 years of public school teaching experience, 1.7 years of private school teaching experience, 1.4 years of experience teaching in a university or elsewhere, and 0.6 years of experience home schooling (see table 8-13).

Table 8-13. *Teacher Demographics*[a]

Characteristic	Response	Percentage (unless otherwise indicated)
Previous years of teaching experience	Public school	5.6 years
	Private school	1.7 years
	University/elsewhere	1.4 years
	Home schooling	0.6 years
Certification	Certified in this state	71.6
	Certified but not in this state	3.7
	Working on state certification	17.0
	Not certified/not working on it	7.7
Current membership in teachers' union	Yes	23.6
	No	75.6
	No response	0.8
Previous membership in teachers' union	Yes	40.9
	No	57.4
	No response	1.7
Salary level (compared with other job options)	Significantly higher here	16.1
	Slightly higher here	18.7
	About the same	27.5
	Slightly lower here	20.3
	Significantly lower here	17.3
Likely to be doing this year if not teaching in this charter school	Teaching in another charter school	13.1
	Teaching in a regular public school	36.7
	Teaching in a private school	8.6
	Other	27.1
	No/multiple responses	14.6

a. Sample C teacher survey respondents from thirty-six charter schools across ten states; $n = 521$ (February 1997); percentages may not equal 100 percent due to invalid responses and nonresponses.

Almost three quarters (72 percent) of charter school teachers are certified, while 17 percent more are working on certification. That means that nine out of ten are or probably soon will be certified in the states in which they are teaching, notwithstanding the otherwise unconventional cast of much of the charter teaching force. About a quarter (23.6 percent) of charter school teachers are currently members of teachers' unions (compared to 40.9 percent who used to be). Fewer than a quarter (22.9 percent) of charter school teachers taught in regular public schools the year immediately prior to the survey, whereas 13.6 percent were recent college graduates, 4.2

Table 8-14. *Where Do Charter School*
Teachers Come From?[a]

Previous employment (or educational program) during 1995–96 school year	Percent
This charter school	49.4
Another charter school	0.8
Regular public school	22.9
Private school	7.9
Home school	3.1
Recent graduate	13.6
Not teaching (but had taught before)	4.2
Had never taught	4.8

a. Sample D school survey respondents from forty-nine charter schools across nine states; $n = 1,005$ teachers (October 1996); percentages may not equal 100 percent due to invalid responses and nonresponses.

percent were returning to the profession after an absence, and 4.8 percent were coming from another field altogether. Almost half (49.4 percent) had taught in the same charter school the previous year (see table 8-14.)

In comparing salary levels, 34.8 percent of charter school teachers reported that they made more money in the charter school than they would in another school, compared to 27.5 percent who said they made about the same and 37.6 percent who said they made less. During our site visits we learned that charter schools offer a great deal to America's teachers: professional and entrepreneurial opportunities and more chances to be involved with school policymaking and planning. From our surveys we can deduce that not only do teachers come to charter schools primarily for educational reasons, but they also feel that their charter schools are successful educationally.

Longevity of Charter School Attendance

Of course the truest marketplace test of whether a charter school is successful is whether families choose to attend them—and stick with their choices. Longevity is an important dimension of school choice, because it reveals much about parents' satisfaction with their decisions. If parents withdraw their children from regular schools in favor of charter schools, that makes a bold statement about the quality of the schools they are leaving, but only a tentative statement about the quality of the programs they are choosing. But if parents choose charter schools and stay there, that reveals more about charter school quality and parent satisfaction.

When parents were asked, "How long have your children been in their charter schools?" their responses were first year 40.2 percent, second year 29.1 percent, third year 12.8 percent, fourth year 5.3 percent, and more 6.4 percent. Seven out of ten were in their first or second year, whereas only a quarter were in their third year or beyond. (Student-reported data are similar.) We know that the charter movement is still in its infancy and most charter schools are new. Many face a wide variety of start-up problems. Yet according to our 1997 survey, nearly 80 percent of parents seem determined to keep their children in them. Fewer than 4 percent intend to go elsewhere.

Who Chooses Charter Schools?

In our sample half (49.6 percent) of the students were members of minority groups (see table 8-15): 25 percent were Hispanic, 15.7 percent were African American, 4.1 percent were Asian, 3.7 percent were Native American, and 1.1 percent were "other."[9] The first-year report on charter schools published by the Department of Education had very similar numbers for a larger sample: 48.4 percent were minority students, among whom 24.8 percent were Hispanic, 13.8 percent African American, 6.3 percent Asian or Pacific Islander, 3.5 percent American Indian or Alaskan Native.[10] (In American public schools, in contrast, about 34 percent of students are minority students.[11]) This close match between the two data sets would seem to confirm that charter schools enroll a significantly higher percentage of minority students than do conventional public schools.[12] (Note, too, that the federal study reported on 1995–96 enrollments, whereas our data are for 1996–97.) One might suppose that the "cream skimming" allegation could now be laid to rest. Put simply, a third of public school students nationally are minority students, whereas half of charter school students nationally are.[13]

According to the charter schools in our sample, 63.1 percent of their students had previously attended public schools, 10.7 percent had gone to private schools, 3.0 percent had been home schooled, 1.4 percent attended another charter school, 16.8 percent were not in school (e.g., pre-K), and 5 percent were former dropouts. The schools in our sample reported that 40.5 percent of their students are eligible for the federal free or reduced-price

Table 8-15. *Student Demographics*[a]

Characteristic	Response	Percent
Race-ethnicity	White	49.8
	African American	15.7
	Hispanic	25.0
	Asian	4.1
	Native American/Alaskan Native	3.7
	Other	1.1
Previous schooling	Regular public school	63.1
(immediately before this	Another charter school	1.4
charter school)	Private school	10.7
	Home school	3.0
	Former dropout	5.0
	Did not attend school	16.8
Gender	Male	48.0
	Female	52.0
Identified special needs	Eligible for free/reduced-price lunch	40.5
	Limited English proficiency	13.1
	Formal individualized education plan (currently)	7.7
	Formal individualized education plan (previously)	3.5
	Other serious learning impediments	1.4

a. Sample D school-reported data from forty-nine charter schools across nine states; n = 15,931 students (October 1996); percentages may not add to 100 percent due to invalid responses and nonresponses.

lunch program. According to the U.S. Department of Education, a third (33.8 percent) of students enrolled in their charter school sample were eligible for the federal free or reduced-price lunch program, which is similar to the 36.6 percent of all students in the ten charter states who are eligible for this program.[14] Also, 13.1 percent of the students in our sample had limited English proficiency (LEP). This contrasts with the federal charter school report, which claims that about 7 percent of charter school enrollment was comprised of students with LEP, compared to the 6.8 percent of students nationally who are classified as having LEP.[15] The fact that the schools in our sample enroll such a large percentage of poor children and children with LEP (a significantly higher percentage than the national average) makes the high levels of satisfaction apparent in these surveys all the more impressive.

With regard to students with disabilities, our sample indicates that charter schools are pulling their weight. According to data reported by the charter

Table 8-16. *Students' Educational Challenges (as Noted by Their Parents)*[a]
Percent

| Challenge | Race/ethnicity | | | | | |
	White	Black	Hispanic	Asian	Native American	Total
Interested in some subjects, but not others	38.5	32.5	34.4	23.4	26.9	35.6
Fast learner; often bored	34.5	37.8	24.2	29.8	26.9	32.3
No special challenges	27.7	19.8	29.4	25.5	15.4	26.6
Does not learn quickly; needs extra help	17.6	27.9	23.4	17.0	19.2	20.9
Too social; not academic enough	13.2	18.3	16.3	6.4	15.4	14.7
Behavior problems	9.1	16.2	15.0	14.9	7.7	11.5
Learning disability	10.4	6.3	7.7	6.4	19.2	9.1
Has few friends	7.9	6.6	7.6	12.8	11.5	8.2
Other	9.5	6.9	3.5	8.5	3.8	7.3
Does not speak English very well	0.7	2.5	15.0	8.5	3.8	5.0
Physical disability	1.8	2.5	1.5	0.0	0.0	1.8

a. Sample C parent survey respondents from thirty charter schools across nine states; $n = 2,978$ (February 1997); percentages may not add to 100 percent due to invalid responses and nonresponses.

schools in our sample, 7.7 percent of their students had formal individualized education plans (IEPs), 3.5 percent did not have current IEPs but probably would have had them in their former public schools, and 1.4 percent were students with other serious learning impediments. Altogether, these charter schools reported that 12.6 percent of their students had disabilities that affected their education. According to parents, 9.1 percent of their children had learning disabilities and 1.8 percent had physical disabilities. In addition, 11.5 percent of parents said their children had behavior problems and 20.9 percent said their child "does not learn quickly—needs extra help" (see table 8-16).

According to the U.S. Department of Education, 7.4 percent of charter school enrollments in 1995–96 were comprised of students who had received special education services prior to enrolling at their charter schools, compared to the 10.4 percent nationally who received services under the Individuals with Disabilities Education Act (IDEA) in 1994–95.[16] Charter schools are clearly serving a significant portion of children with special needs, but questions remain regarding the exact numbers compared to those in traditional public schools. More research is plainly needed on

Table 8-17. *Parent Demographics*[a]

Characteristic	Response	Percent
Total number of children in charter school	One	52.1
	Two	29.3
	Three	10.0
	Four or more	4.1
Length of time at least one child in charter school	First year	40.2
	Second year	29.1
	Third year	12.8
	Fourth year or more	11.7
Highest educational level	Did not complete high school	12.0
	High school, but no college	18.8
	Some college, no degree	28.6
	College graduate	18.7
	Postgraduate/professional degree	12.2
Total family income	Less than $10,000	11.0
	$10,000–$19,999	16.0
	$20,000–$39,999	26.0
	$40,000–$59,999	18.0
	$60,000–$99,999	13.0
	More than $100,000	4.8

this area. Of course obtaining an accurate count requires consistent application of a definition of which children are part of the special universe. The numbers are elusive because some families will not submit to having their children labeled, sorted, and treated differently and some schools are reluctant—for financial, staffing, and philosophical reasons—to identify students who need special education.

With regard to parent demographics (see table 8-17), we found that fewer than a third (30.9 percent) of charter school parents have college degrees or higher education, and 12 percent did not complete high school. Family incomes vary widely. About a quarter (27 percent) of charter parents in our sample reported incomes below $20,000, 26 percent between $20,000 and $40,000, 18 percent between $40,000 and $60,000, and 17.8 percent over $60,000. (As expected, a number of parents declined to answer income questions.)

Conclusion

Our data sets reveal satisfaction levels that were wide and deep. There seems to be consensus among all primary constituents that charter schools are living up to their expectations and delivering a high-quality product (or at least improving on the alternative). But of course it is one thing for charter school students to feel they are getting a good education and another to demonstrate it (in a statewide assessment, for example). Individual schools are reporting improved student scores, but no national or state summary reports exist yet. Clearly there is a gap in our knowledge base when it comes to achievement data. The whole point of charter schools is to answer today's call for bold school reform by injecting freedom, choice, and accountability into school systems, thereby providing a better education for America's children. Test scores will be an important part of the story, and collection of this information is underway in various parts of the country. Meanwhile, another chapter of the story is being written by families and teachers who are choosing these independent public schools, reporting much learning within their walls, and sticking with them.

The surveys regarding to charter schools paint a statistical portrait that is compelling: There are striking levels of satisfaction among all the constituents of charter schools, their focus is on education (without frills), their students are flourishing academically, and they are havens for children—of all races, backgrounds, and abilities—who were not thriving in conventional schools.

Appendix: Methodology and Project Description

Data

Our study yielded four sets of quantitative data, one each from students, parents, teachers, and schools:

—Sample A = student-reported data for grades five and up (n = 4,954 from thirty-nine schools in ten states). For this sample *student* was defined as a child enrolled in fifth grade or above. In ungraded or mixed-age schools a student was someone ten years of age or older. For the data to be included, we required that at least 70 percent of a school's students respond to the survey. It is worth noting that 35.6 percent of the student data came from California, 18.7 percent from Arizona, and 16.7 percent from Colorado.

—Sample B = parent-reported data (n = 2,978 from thirty schools in nine states). *Parent* was defined as a parent, guardian, or responsible adult with one or more children in any grade in the participating charter school. When siblings attended the same school, their parent filled out only one survey, using the oldest child as the "subject." We required that at least 40 percent of a school's parents respond. It is worth noting that 49.2 percent of our data came from California, 15.4 percent from Michigan, and 12.7 percent from Colorado.

—Sample C = teacher-reported data (n = 521 from thirty-six schools in ten states). *Teacher* was defined as a full- or part-time professional instructional employee of the school, in any grade, teaching any subject. (This did not include aides, tutors, and parent volunteers.) We required that at least 80 percent of a school's teachers respond. It is worth noting that 32.8 percent of our teacher data came from California, 22.3 percent from Arizona, 14.0 percent from Michigan, and 12.9 percent from Colorado.

—Sample D = school-reported data on students and teachers (number of schools = 49; number of states = 9; number of students = 15,931; number of teachers = 1,005).

Samples A, B, and C were obtained by the Hudson Institute and processed and tabulated by the Brookings Institution, whereas sample D was obtained exclusively by the Hudson Institute via self-reporting of data by the schools themselves. We did not use data that did not meet the response rates we required. In a couple of instances surveys were translated by schools so that parents with limited English proficiency could also participate. Individual identities were kept confidential. Surveys from Samples A, B, and C were coded. No names were ever written on them. The Hudson Institute never had access to the identities of any of the individuals filling out surveys. Each school assumed responsibility for internal confidentiality. Also, individual school data were kept confidential, although tabulations were provided to participating schools themselves. Our analysis and reporting were by state, by type of school (rural/urban, elementary/secondary, and so on), and for our full national sample of fifty schools. We did not publicly report data on individual schools.

Project Description

Charter Schools in Action was a two-year study by the Hudson Institute's Educational Excellence Network. Supported by the Pew Charitable Trusts, it began in July 1995 and concluded in July 1997. Through extensive site visits, phone interviews, and surveys the project team gathered and analyzed information about participating schools, communities, and states. The results are meant to enhance public understanding of the benefits and limits of charter schools as an education reform strategy—and of significant issues related to their implementation.

The project had several goals: to illuminate the practical and policy issues surrounding the creation and successful operation of charter schools (including finances, governance, regulations, facilities, enrollment, and personnel); to begin to gauge the educational impact of these schools; and to inform people involved in creating and operating charter schools—both practitioners and policymakers—of strategies devised elsewhere.

During the first project year (1995–96) site visits were made to 43 charter schools in seven states: Arizona, California, Colorado, Massachusetts, Michigan, Minnesota, and Wisconsin. Detailed information was collected on 35 of them, a cross-section of the approximately 225 charter schools then operating nationwide. Over 700 interviews were conducted with individuals in these schools and communities.

During the second year (1996–97) site visits were made to 45 charter schools in thirteen states; 17 schools that were visited for the second time; and 18 schools that were visited in 1995–96 participated in follow-up interviews via telephone. The research team obtained direct information from a total of 50 charter schools in ten states, a reasonable cross-section of the almost 500 charter schools nationwide. (The three states with operating charter schools that were added in the project's second year were Florida, Texas, and the District of Columbia.) Additionally, visits were made to New Jersey, North Carolina, and Hawaii to study the implementation of those states' new charter laws. Over 600 interviews were conducted, bringing the two-year total to well over 1,300.

During the second project year surveys were conducted of parents, students, and teachers in charter schools that agreed to participate—and whose response rates satisfied the project's minimum participation levels. The project team developed the three questionnaires in consultation with charter school experts nationwide and the Information Technology Services unit of the Brookings Institution, which also provided data processing and analysis. Results were tabulated from 4,954 students (fifth grade and above) attending 39 schools; from 2,978 parents of students attending 30 schools; and from 521 teachers in 36 schools.

Project staff members during the first year were Hudson senior fellows Chester E. Finn, Jr., Bruno V. Manno, and Louann A. Bierlein. Joining the project staff in its second year was Hudson research fellow Gregg Vanourek. They were advised by knowledgeable individuals in the participating jurisdictions.

Both the full text of the project year one and project year two reports are available by calling (800)HUDSON-0 or may be found on the Internet at http://www.edexcellence.net. Copies of the questionnaires are on the web site or can be obtained by calling (202) 223-5450.

Notes

1. The recently released federal study is called *A Study of Charter Schools: First-Year Report* (Washington, D.C.: U.S. Department of Education, Office of Educational Research and Improvement, 1997). Our first-year report was called *Charter Schools in Action: What Have We Learned?* (Indianapolis: Hudson Institute, 1996).

2. Essentially all the Native Americans in our sample attend one school, which happens to be a "conversion" school. Therefore, the teachers in their charter school are likely to be the same as the teachers in their previous school, so one would expect the "about the same" response to occur with great frequency. Also, a slightly higher percentage of black students did not answer these questions. When invalid responses and nonresponses are factored out, 62.5 percent of black students said they liked their teachers better and 56.1 percent said that they were more interested in their schoolwork at their charter schools than they were at their previous schools.

3. The only exception is for parents of LEP children when it comes to parental involvement. In that case, just over half think the charter school is better than their previous school.

4. See Center for Applied Research and Educational Improvement, *Minnesota Charter Schools Evaluation: Interim Report* (University of Minnesota, December 1996); Pioneer Institute, *Massachusetts Charter School Profile, 1995–96 School Year* (Boston: Pioneer Institute, July 1996); Pioneer Institute, *Massachusetts Charter School Profile, 1996–97 School Year (Interim Report)* (Boston: Pioneer Institute, March 1997); and Mary Gifford and Timothy Keller, "Arizona's Charter Schools: A Survey of Parents," Phoenix, Goldwater Institute, Arizona Issue Analysis 140, April 1996.

5. Jean Johnson and John Immerwahr, *First Things First: What Americans Expect from the Public Schools* (New York: Public Agenda, 1994), p. 41.

6. Jean Johnson, *Assignment Incomplete: The Unfinished Business of Education Reform* (New York: Public Agenda, 1995), p. 19.

7. Johnson, *Assignment,* pp. 11 and 13.

8. U.S. Department of Education, *A Study of Charter Schools: First-Year Report* (Washington, Office of Educational Research and Improvement, 1997), p. 65.

9. Since we have demographic data from three sources, we are presenting demographic data from our sample with the largest number (our school-reported data from sample D).

10. U.S. Department of Education, *A Study of Charter Schools,* p. 16. The data are for 58,620 students in 214 charter schools (1995–96). Apparently minority enrollment is especially high in "conversion" schools (especially for Hispanics). In addition, conversion schools that were formerly private schools enroll a surprisingly large percentage of blacks (p. 69).

11. U.S. Department of Education, *Digest of Education Statistics 1996* (Washington, National Center for Education Statistics, 1996), p. 60. The data are for fall 1994.

12. It should be noted that 63 percent of the children in our sample in 1995–96 were members of minority groups. See Chester Finn, Bruno Manno, and Louann Bierlein, *Charter Schools in Action: What Have We Learned?* (Indianapolis: Hudson Institute, 1996).

13. Of course, there are important state variations in minority enrollment patterns that warrant attention. For example, charter schools in Michigan and Minnesota have a significantly higher percentage of blacks and charter schools in Massachusetts have a higher percentage of Hispanics (than regular public schools in the state), whereas

charter schools in Georgia have a significantly lower percentage of blacks than other public schools in the state.

14. U.S. Department of Education, *A Study of Charter Schools,* p. 23.
15. U.S. Department of Education, *A Study of Charter Schools,* p. 22.
16. U.S. Department of Education, *A Study of Charter Schools,* p. 20.

NINE

The Performance of Privately Managed Schools: An Early Look at the Edison Project

John E. Chubb

THE EDISON PROJECT is the nation's largest private manager of public schools and, since its launch in 1991, one of the most closely watched and hotly debated initiatives in the world of education reform. Edison is of interest in its own right because of its prominent leadership, ample resources, and ambitious plans for growth. Edison also is of general interest because it provides a sizable test of some of the more innovative—and controversial—ideas in school reform today: not only the private management of schools, but also charter schools, public schools of choice, schools with longer days and years, schools with ubiquitous technology, schools with tougher academic standards, and more. Edison now has twenty-five schools in operation throughout the nation and is on the verge of opening many more. Interest in Edison's performance understandably runs high.

But that interest should be tempered with patience. Edison is implementing a comprehensive model for schools serving students in kindergarten through twelfth grade. It will be another ten years before any students will have moved all the way through the program and the effects of the program on student achievement can be measured fully. In the meantime, even short-term achievement gains take two or three years to measure properly. Then there are questions regarding how the Edison schools will affect other schools in a system: Will the competitive pressure of an Edison school in a school system stimulate other schools to improve, or will that pressure cause schools to stratify further as the best schools drain students and funds from the worst? These effects, much like the effects of deregulation on other sectors of the economy, will take years to come into focus. Finally, it is important to keep in mind that although Edison began its research and development phase in 1991, it did not begin operating schools until 1995. And even then the project started with only four schools, as it sought the experience to open increasing numbers each year thereafter: eight in 1996 and thirteen in 1997.

So what can be said about Edison's performance at this early point in its operating experience? Actually, two things of some importance. First, we can say what the facts about that experience really are. This is especially important for controversial initiatives such as the Edison Project, where debate often generates more heat than light and facts are adduced selectively to fuel the fire. Edison's operating experience may be limited, but a large number of hard data are available to document it. Those data, all publicly available, and assembled here for the first time, make it possible to say something else of some importance: Only time will tell how the Edison schools ultimately perform, but they are generally off to promising starts.

Research and Development

The Edison Project began work as a research and development effort. Chris Whittle, a leading media entrepreneur and Edison's founder and now chief executive officer, raised $45 million in private capital to support the effort, a very large sum by the standards of education research. Whittle also recruited Benno C. Schmidt, Jr., the current chairman of Edison, to leave the presidency of Yale University to head the research and development effort as Edison's first president. In the summer of 1992 Schmidt led a prominent team of researchers, educators, experts in technology and finance, journalists, and others on a two-year mission: to design the first national system of K–12 schools providing world-class education for all types of students within public school budgets, as a profitable business.[1] The project's leadership, resources, and ambition generated immediate interest and controversy, conditions that have persisted to this day.

In 1994 the Edison Project published its *Partnership School Design* and announced its plans to implement the design in public schools around the country.[2] The design includes nine key elements. First is an organization that will provide much better support to students. Schools are reduced in size so that students can be better known and attended to more closely by adults. Schools are divided into academies spanning two or three traditional grade levels: a primary academy for kindergarten through grade two, an elementary academy for grades three through five, a junior academy for grades six through eight, a senior academy for grades nine through ten, and a collegiate academy for grades eleven through twelve. Within academies students are organized into multigrade houses of 100 to 150. The students in each house are taught by a team of four to six teachers who stay with the house of students for the duration of their two- or three-year academy experience.

The second element is a curriculum both rich and ambitious. Schools need to restore to a place of importance music, visual arts, drama, dance, and foreign languages. Science needs to be taken seriously in elementary school and pursued by all students through high school graduation. History, ancient as well as more recent, needs to be understood in depth. Economics needs an important place in the curriculum. The development and nurture of character and ethics are legitimate and vital concerns for any school that aims to be successful, and Edison schools pursue them seriously. Edison defines a world-class education in classically liberal terms. In a fast-changing world, the best preparation is not an education that is narrowly practical, but one that cultivates the mind to make a student ready for opportunities of every kind. A world-class education must also be taught to clear and demanding standards. Accordingly, each field of Edison's curriculum is guided by student academic standards that specify what students must know and be able to do to satisfy the expectations of each academy.

The third element of the Edison design is research-based and purposeful instruction. A great deal is known about effective instruction, both in general terms and in specific areas such as reading and mathematics. Edison has adopted or created instructional programs and training to help teachers work as skillfully as possible. For example, all Edison schools implement a K–5 reading program, *Success for All,* developed at Johns Hopkins University and fine-tuned through dozens of experimental studies over the last ten years.[3] For mathematics Edison schools use programs developed through the University of Chicago School Mathematics Project,[4] also based on years of systematic research. In general, Edison provides teachers not with the tools to teach but with the tools to cause students to learn. This applies, moreover, to the full range of students, including those requiring special education services or learning English as a second language.

The fourth element is assessment that provides real accountability. It is often observed in education reform circles that what gets tested is what gets taught. And this creates a potential problem. Most assessments now used by states and school districts are multiple-choice exams that measure basic skills. Such exams do not gauge most of the knowledge and skills in a curriculum, including such vital ones as the ability to set up and solve a complex problem, conduct research, or write more than a few paragraphs. Even worse, standardized tests virtually invite schools to focus instruction on basic skills precisely as they are formatted for testing. Edison has designed an assessment system to avoid this debasement of the curriculum. The Edison project designs custom performance assessments to measure students' progress toward the more ambitious standards of the curriculum and trains teachers to use the whole curriculum to prepare students for standardized tests. Assessment thereby provides accountability for learning that really matters.

The fifth element of the Edison school design is technology for the information age. Edison believes that information technology can make students, teachers, and schools more effective—but only if it is used properly. This means technology is used as a tool to facilitate communication, research, writing, and analysis, as it is in the world outside of education, and not as a teaching machine as it is often used in education, typically in computer labs. Education and technology should be fully integrated. To make this to happen, Edison makes information technology readily available. Edison provides every teacher a laptop computer and classroom telephone, every classroom with several computers as well as a television and VCR, every school with scanners, printers, cameras, and a local area network connecting teachers and students to each other and to Edison's national network. This network makes possible interactions among Edison school sites and between school sites and Edison's headquarters in New York. Finally, each family of an Edison student in grade three and up is provided a home computer so that the student can work on the computer at home and the family can be in closer touch with the school.

The sixth element is professionalism as a priority. The Edison project provides teachers with four to six weeks of training before Edison schools first open. Teachers have two periods every day free for their own professional development. School calendars provide at least five days for ongoing training every year. Each teaching team is headed by a lead teacher who is responsible for mentoring other teachers on the team. Every school has senior teachers who receive special training to serve as resident experts in each of the content areas of the curriculum. Teachers learn from one another through Edison's online professional development network, the Pedagogy Project. Finally, teachers are paid more like professionals, earning more annually in Edison schools than they would otherwise, and are given opportunities to earn additional pay for shouldering additional professional responsibilities.

The seventh element of the Edison design is families who are treated as partners. Every school understands the vital role that support at home plays in students' success. But obtaining that support is extremely hard work. Families have plenty of problems and demands of their own without taking on the school's challenges as well. Edison helps its schools bring families into the fold. Home computers bring families into the school for training and help teachers bring the classroom into their students' homes. A special narrative report card called a Quarterly Learning Contract gives parents a more thorough understanding of their children's progress than they may be accustomed to receiving and brings parents into the school for regular conferences—all the way through high school. A Family and Student Support Team designed by researchers at Johns Hopkins University works with those families whose problems may be interfering with learning. A fulsome arts program gets parents to school the old-fashioned way, welcoming them to see and hear their children perform.

The eighth element is time to succeed. For the last generation this country has been raising the bar on schools and students, asking them to meet higher academic standards. Yet nowhere in this country are schools and students being given more time to meet them. Edison believes this is literally an impossible situation. Edison schools therefore have eight-hour days for all students beginning in grade three, seven-hour days for students in kindergarten through grade two. The extra time permits them to spend more time daily on fundamentals (for example, ninety minutes on reading and sixty minutes on math), more time for hands-on experiences such as science experiments, and more time for the arts, foreign language (which all students take beginning in kindergarten), and special subjects that are squeezed out of the daily schedules of most public schools. Moreover, Edison schools have a longer school year—200 to 205 days, which is four to five weeks longer than the national norm. The longer year adds time for learning and promises to cut down on summer forgetting, an especially serious problem for disadvantaged students whose summers often do not provide much academic reinforcement. Over a thirteen-year school career an Edison student will spend the equivalent of four additional years in school as compared to a student in most any other American school.

The final element is a system that serves. Edison is trying to create a national system of schools that are bound together in ways that make each school much stronger than it would be on its own. Edison pursues this goal in various ways. An electronic network allows principals, teachers, families, and students to share valuable information. Edison prepares and employs teachers as certified trainers to work with new schools and teachers as they join the system. It promotes teachers and principals into leadership positions in new schools to give educators opportunities to grow professionally without leaving the school buildings. Edison's system supports every function at each school site, whether it is curriculum, technology, or business services. And Edison must provide this support very efficiently. Edison's program costs more at the school sites than traditional public education programs. Edison's system must therefore operate at a lower cost per student than traditional school systems to function on the same overall level of financial support. The system strives to accomplish this by relying heavily on information technology, professionals in the schools, and economies of scale.

Public School Partnerships

In 1994 the Edison Project began talking with communities around the country about implementing its school design through a program that Edison calls Public School Partnerships. The program aims to bring Edison into a community through a contractual partnership agreement. The agreements forged through this program include five major elements. First, Edison assumes complete responsibility for opening and operating a school for a public board of education, a public charter school board of trustees, or another public body authorized to operate a public school. Among the responsibilities Edison assumes are controlling all funds to which the school is entitled; hiring all school personnel except the principal, whom Edison and its partner hire together; management and compensation of all personnel according to Edison's school design and work rules, except as limited by collective bargaining agreements or other state or local regulations that have not been waived in the contracting process; and delivering the entire education program as described in the *Partnership School Design*.

Before the school opens Edison works with the local partner to customize the school design to the needs of the local community. This customization process may involve, for example, providing a course in a particular state's history or adjusting Edison's academic standards to include content demanded by a particular school district. Customization might also be required by collective bargaining agreements, class size requirements, special education or bilingual education regulations, and the like.

Edison commits to invest its capital in the start-up of the school. It invests roughly $1.5 million in each new school of approximately 600 students. The money pays for all new instructional materials for each school, the wiring of the school and the installation of the computer network, and the training of the school's leadership and instructional staff. The investment enables a school to adopt Edison's model completely from opening day.

The school board or charter board of trustees pays Edison for each student enrolled at the school the amount that the board has in its operating budget per pupil overall. Edison is paid only for students who attend the school. The board of education or trustees in practice deducts some small percentage from the per-pupil allocation to cover certain administrative costs of the partnership. Edison may buy back certain district services, such as transportation and food services. Edison receives no funds from board capital budgets for its operating expenses. Generally Edison seeks to work with the same operating funds that boards have available for operating schools themselves.

Finally, the Edison Project is held strictly accountable by its partners for school performance. If a partner is dissatisfied with the performance of an Edison-operated school, the partner may cancel the contract before its expiration, which is normally after five years. Edison is specifically accountable for student achievement, which must show growth on state, local, and Edison assessments; customer satisfaction, as measured by annual surveys of parents, staff members, and students; implementation of the school design, as measured by Edison's *School Performance Standards* and observed by board and Edison officials;[5] and financial management as reported in annual audited financial reports.

The First Schools Open

In late 1994 and early 1995 The Edison Project signed contracts with its first partners.[6] Edison also raised the additional capital that it required to open its early schools. This funding resulted in a reorganization of Edison's own board of directors and added to the project a major institutional

investor, the Sprout Group, a division of the large investment bank Donald-
son, Lufkin, and Jenrette. Over the next three years Edison would raise
capital two additional times, once in 1996 and again in early 1998. These
investments raised the total invested in Edison since its inception to $161
million, and brought representatives of other major institutions to Edison's
board, among them J. P. Morgan, the venerable American investment
house, and Investor A. B., one of the largest holding companies in Europe.
As of 1998 Edison was capitalized to open several new annual cycles of
schools.

The schools that Edison opened during its first three operational years
are listed in table 9-1. Edison's first four schools were elementary schools,
the grades that Edison generally insists on opening first in any partnership
agreement. The first schools included three operated under contracts with
local school districts and one charter school, the Boston Renaissance Charter
School, currently the largest charter school in the nation. Boston Renaissance was started from scratch—new building (actually an old renovated
one), new students, and new staff members. Students were selected through
a lottery prescribed by state law after applications far outstripped openings.

Edison's other 1995 openings were conversion projects. Schools that
existed previously were renovated or retrofitted, restaffed, and reenrolled.
Many of the students who had attended school in the buildings before the
partnership began chose to remain. Attendance at the schools was governed
by the rules of neighborhood magnets, meaning children in the neighborhood had the first right to enroll; the remaining slots were filled by a lottery
among applicants. Each of Edison's initial district schools opened with
significantly more students than it had enrolled the previous spring.

In 1996 Edison added middle or intermediate schools to each of its first
four partnerships, an indication of partners' satisfaction with the year one
experience. Edison also opened four new elementary schools. In 1995,
enrollment in Edison schools had been about 2,000 students. In 1996
enrollment climbed to around 6500. The fall of 1997 brought a mixture of
expansions, including the opening of Edison's first senior academy, and
new elementary schools. Edison's third year of operation also saw the
project reach most regions of the country. From California to New England
and Florida, from Texas to Minnesota, and places in between, Edison had
established a total of twenty-five schools enrolling nearly 13,000 students.
About half of Edison's schools were operated under district contracts and
the other half were charters—or, more precisely, contracts with charter
school boards of trustees. Edison expects to grow to at least forty schools in
the fall of 1998 and to enroll about 22,000 students at that time.

Table 9-1. *Edison Project Partnership Schools, Spring 1998*

Name	Location	Date opened	Grades served	Enroll- ment	Charter or contract
Boston Renaissance Charter School	Boston, Mass.	1995	K–5	664	Charter
Dodge-Edison Elementary	Wichita, Kans.	1995	K–5	642	Contract
Martin Luther King, Jr., Academy	Mount Clemens, Mich.	1995	K–5	555	Contract
Washington Elementary	Sherman, Tex.	1995	K–4	472	Contract
Boston Renaissance Junior Academy	Boston, Mass.	1996	6–8	412	Charter
Dillingham Intermediate	Sherman, Tex.	1996	5–6	299	Contract
Jardine-Edison Junior Academy	Wichita, Kans.	1996	6–8	907	Contract
Mid-Michigan Public School Academy	Lansing, Mich.	1996	K–5	684	Charter
Mount Clemens Junior Academy	Mount Clemens, Mich.	1996	6–8	402	Contract
Reeves Elementary	Miami, Fla.	1996	K–5	1070	Contract
Roosevelt-Edison Elementary	Colorado Springs, Colo.	1996	K–5	678	Charter
Seven Hills Charter School	Worcester, Mass.	1996	K–7	446	Charter
Detroit Academy of Arts and Sciences	Detroit, Mich.	1997	K–5	692	Charter
Duluth Central Junior Academy	Duluth, Minn.	1997	6–8	192	Charter
Elm Creek Elementary	San Antonio, Tex.	1997	K–5	551	Contract
Emerson-Edison Elementary	Colorado Springs, Colo.	1997	6	129	Charter
Feaster-Edison Elementary	San Diego, Calif.	1997	K–6	1000	Charter
Garfield-Edison Elementary	Flint, Mich.	1997	K–6	499	Contract
Ingalls-Edison Elementary	Wichita, Kans.	1997	K–5	654	Contract
Isely-Edison Elementary	Wichita, Kans.	1997	K–5	277	Contract
Kenwood-Edison Elementary	Duluth, Minn.	1997	K–5	326	Charter
Mid-Michigan Public Junior Academy	Lansing, Mich.	1997	6–8	242	Charter
Mount Clemens Senior Academy	Mount Clemens, Mich.	1997	9–10	110	Contract
Seven Hills Junior Academy	Worcester, Mass.	1997	6–8	221	Charter
Williams-Edison Elementary	Flint, Mich.	1997	K–6	475	Contract

Source: Data supplied by individual schools to the Edison Project.

Who are these students? At this juncture Edison serves students who are lower in family income and higher in racial and ethnic diversity than students nationwide. Generally, students in Edison schools are representative of the communities in which the schools reside. Edison offers a comprehensive education program designed to work for students of all types, from those who struggle with school to those for whom success comes easily. So far the communities with the greatest interest in the Edison Project have been communities with significant educational need. Specifically, 60 percent of all Edison students are eligible for the federal government's free or reduced-price lunch program, a standard measure of economic disadvantage. The majority of Edison schools qualify as school-wide Title I projects, a designation that the federal government reserves for schools with at least 50 percent of all students eligible for free or reduced-price lunches. Schools that do not qualify still have significant levels of need; the lowest percentage of children receiving free and reduced-price lunches at any Edison school is 27 percent.

Edison schools are racially and ethnically diverse, both in the aggregate and within most every school. As a system Edison serves students who are 45 percent African American, 32 percent Caucasian, 18 percent Hispanic, 2 percent Asian, and 2 percent other. Edison's minority population is roughly three times the national average. Only four Edison schools have more than 70 percent of their students from a single racial or ethnic group. Edison students have more opportunity to interact with students from other backgrounds than most students in public schools nationwide.

Finally, Edison serves students with a range of educational needs. Fifteen percent of all Edison students receive English as a second language or bilingual education. This percentage represents a very wide range, from 94 percent in Chula Vista, California and 42 percent in Sherman, Texas, to single-digit percentages in several schools in Michigan and Minnesota. Special education is also a substantial part of Edison schools, with 9 percent of all students receiving services. This figure is slightly below the national average of 12 percent, but close to the percentages of students receiving special education in the respective communities of which Edison schools are part.

Because all Edison schools are filled through a parental choice process of some kind, it may come as a moderate surprise that Edison schools serve such disadvantaged and diverse student bodies. A frequently expressed concern about choice programs is that advantaged parents will do most of the choosing, leaving disadvantaged parents behind.[7] Edison students, however, are generally not advantaged.

There are good reasons for this. Edison schools in particular, and charter schools more broadly, are brand-new enterprises that are still trying to prove their mettle. Parents whose children are already succeeding in school may not be the first to try them out. Indeed, anecdotal reports from Edison schools suggest that many parents choose Edison schools because their children have not been successful elsewhere. Data on charter schools nationally indicate that such schools have attracted student bodies much like those at Edison schools: diverse and disadvantaged.[8] This does not mean that there are not even more needy families who fail to choose. But Edison tries to reach those families who do not choose as well: The majority of Edison schools are neighborhood magnets placed in disadvantaged communities by school districts determined to offer families the opportunity to send their children to an Edison school without making an affirmative choice.

Measuring School Performance

Edison schools are accountable to public authorities for performance in four areas: student achievement, customer satisfaction, program implementation, and financial management. If Edison schools perform well in these areas, the Edison Project will have fulfilled its obligations to the authorities that hired the company. Edison also expects that such performance will enable it to succeed as a business, attracting a growing number of clients and producing enough volume to provide a return to investors. The four criteria that public authorities use to evaluate the Edison Project are also appropriate for evaluating Edison as an education reform strategy.

Edison is asking for autonomy from conventional public authority to deliver a program, to produce results, and to be held strictly accountable for both while working with the same students and the same funds as public schools run conventionally. This is much the same approach to innovation promised by charter schools or, to a lesser extent, magnet schools and public schools of choice. Edison brings one crucial difference, which is private business. But this is a difference in which Edison's clients are interested as well—and the reason Edison must account for its management of public monies. Looking at the measures of performance for which Edison is contractually accountable is therefore a reasonable way to look at Edison as a strategy for education reform.

To be clear, the data that follow are also the data that are most readily available about the project. They are the data that the project must report regularly to boards of education and trustees. The data are not always available in ways that permit rigorous analysis or statistical tests. The data vary in quality, quantity, and format from one school to another. The data generally are not the product of formal research designs—though some data are. The data are, however, extensive. They summarize the bulk of the quantitative or otherwise systematic data available on the performance of Edison schools in the spring of 1998, providing a picture that is detailed and well rounded. They provide opportunity for a particularly thorough look at student achievement, the most important performance criterion by far.

Program Implementation: The Edison School Design

Edison's school design is comprehensive; it changes virtually everything that schools do. Even the most experienced teachers and administrators find the learning curve in new Edison schools to be steep. The Edison Project therefore works with schools through a developmental process that takes several years to complete. The process is guided by explicit school performance standards that guide schools through four stages of development: beginning, developing, proficient, and exemplary. The standards set exacting performance criteria for every area of the school design—nearly fifty areas in all. If schools are making good progress, they start showing genuine proficiency in the third year of a partnership.

Overall, Edison schools are on schedule in meeting these performance standards. In end-of-year reports to local boards of education, charter school boards, and state oversight agencies, Edison scores its schools on each school performance standard and documents the reported scores. On average, Edison schools register 1s and 2s, meaning beginning or developing, at the conclusion of their first year of operations and 2s and 3s, meaning developing and proficient, at the end of their second years of operation. Naturally there has been some variation around these averages. At least two schools, Dodge-Edison and Seven Hills, have moved more rapidly than other schools toward proficient implementations. Two other schools, Washington and Reeves, experienced difficult first years, necessitating changes in building leadership, and did not move beyond beginning levels of proficiency until their second years of operation. As might be expected, variations in implementation seem to be dampening as Edison gains experience as a system: The thirteen schools that started up in the fall of 1997 so far exhibit more implementation consistency than schools that started up during Edison's first two years of operation.

These patterns of implementation summarize a host of difficult but familiar challenges faced by any school working to improve itself; for example, learning new instructional programs in reading, writing, math, science, or social science. But the patterns also reflect efforts of Edison schools to meet challenges that are unusual or unique. Several of these accomplishments are distinctive enough to mention separately. All schools have implemented Edison's unique school organization characterized by multiyear academies, students organized in multiage houses, teachers working in teams and remaining with students for the duration of an academy experience, and a schoolwide Leadership Team that assists the principal in setting and carrying out schoolwide policy.

More time has been provided for instruction. A longer school day and year than in typical public schools (one hour longer in the Primary Academy and two hours longer in every other academy, 205 instructional days on average) provide 1,435 to 1,640 hours per year in Edison schools. The national norm is 1,080 hours, about 50 percent less. Moreover, only about 100 other schools across the country offer a school year as long as Edison's—an innovation educators widely believe America should adopt.

Teachers are implementing Edison's unique assessment system, including annual performance assessments in four academic fields designed by Edison and administered and scored by all Edison teachers nationwide; structured portfolios that document students' progress toward academic standards in every field and evaluate progress against explicit rubrics; and Quarterly Learning Contracts, Edison's original report cards that summarize students' progress toward standards with formal marks and extensive commentary and commit students and families to quarterly goals in regular conferences.

Edison's ambitious technology plan is on course. Schools are fully networked, with computers in every classroom and a laptop for every teacher. Televisions and telephones are also in every classroom. VCRs, scanners, printers, digital cameras, and more sophisticated technology are distributed generously throughout every school. Families of Edison students have received fully loaded home computers according to individual rollout plans agreed on at each site. As of spring 1998 over 8,000 families had been trained in computer use and received computers. Finally, Edison's technology curriculum, Technology as a Second Language®, is being embraced by classroom teachers and is helping to integrate technology use into the regular curriculum.

Edison schools have implemented a program of responsible inclusion for students with disabilities. These schools offer a continuum of services, with most services provided by special educators working with students in regular classrooms. Special educators also co-plan with and regularly visit the classrooms of all general education teachers to ensure that students with special needs benefit as much as possible from the general education program. Edison serves more than 1,000 students with special needs. These children bring the full range of disabilities to Edison schools; some children require full-time teaching aides. Edison's special needs students are served by a staff of more than fifty special educators nationwide. This program has been perhaps the most difficult innovation that Edison has implemented, for it is not easy to get all school staff members—and not just special education staff members—to take responsibility for special education students and to know how to serve them. In one school, Boston Renaissance, the difficulties resulted in a federal Department of Education investigation and findings of process violations. Today Boston Renaissance has a special education program that has been cited as a model of quality.[9] No other Edison site has experienced such extreme difficulties, but all have found responsible inclusion a serious challenge.

Edison schools have implemented English as a second language (ESL) and bilingual programs with special effectiveness. Because all students in Edison schools study Spanish beginning in kindergarten, the schools provide an environment in which speaking and learning new languages is widely encouraged. The daily schedule facilitates ESL instruction by enabling students with limited English proficiency to receive extra support while other students are taking Spanish. Edison's reading program, *Success for All,* has an excellent record in supporting both ESL and bilingual instruction.[10]

All Edison staff members have been provided a full program of professional development, beginning with four to six weeks of training prior to the opening of each new school and continuing throughout the first and second years of operation. In addition, the partnership school schedule provides teachers daily professional development time with their teams, usually ninety minutes a day.

Financial Management

In addition to its original research and development, Edison has invested, on average, $1.5 million per school to fund technology implementation, purchase all new curriculum materials, provide comprehensive professional development, and improve facilities. With twenty-five schools now operating, Edison has invested more than $40 million in public education.

Edison has also invested unique financial power in each of its schools. In recent years there has been much talk in education reform circles about the need for providing real decisionmaking power at school sites. Schools need to control their resources if they are to be held accountable for their performance. Some progress has been made, through "site-based decision-making" initiatives, to give schools more authority. But this authority is still quite circumscribed, especially when it comes to spending money. Edison schools are truly unusual in the wide latitude Edison gives to principals for financial management. Each principal, in addition to being the instructional leader of the school, is given accountability for properly stewarding millions of dollars in financial resources devoted to the school and its students. This accountability, while resting ultimately with the principal, permeates the school and is managed, at the principal's direction, by the business services manager of the site.

Edison's site leaders are learning to handle this responsibility rather well. After the 1995–96 school year, when Edison and its first four principals were struggling together to create a workable financial management system, Edison schools began to handle their own finances comprehensively and successfully. All but a very few Edison schools have remained within budgets established at the beginning of each fiscal year. This is no small accomplishment. Edison's program is not inexpensive. The richer curriculum and the unique technology program require extra staff members. Teachers are compensated for the longer school year. The sizable investment in each school's start-up must be repaid. The private capital that Edison continues to attract is testimony to the success that principals are having in delivering budgets that work financially as well as educationally.

Customer Satisfaction

Edison and its partners use a range of indicators to gauge the satisfaction of parents, students, and staff members. Some indicators, such as formal surveys, are broad and quantifiable. Other indicators, such as success stories, unfortunate "incidents," or the "buzz" in the school community, are narrow or impossible to summarize. The latter indicators often show up in early journalistic reports on Edison schools and have a valuable story to tell.[11] Here we focus on the broader and more quantifiable indicators that are available only after schools have operating experience.

Customer Satisfaction Surveys

The school districts and charter boards with which Edison works do not routinely measure customer satisfaction with well-designed surveys. Edison therefore contracts with the Gordon S. Black Corporation to provide all Edison schools with detailed information about the likes and dislikes of parents, students, and staff members. Black is a pioneering company in the field of total quality management surveys; it has worked for twenty years with some of the most respected private companies in American industry, including Xerox, where Black got its start. In more recent years Black has developed surveys and analytical frameworks to help public schools understand their constituencies and improve their services. In Edison schools the Black data are used primarily for this purpose, as principals and teachers focus on measures of satisfaction with every element of the school program. The data are also useful for reporting on satisfaction overall, and Edison and its partners track the Black data for this purpose as well.

At the most general level, the surveys administered by the Black Corporation every spring ask parents and students to rate their schools overall on a scale of A to F. By this measure Edison schools are performing well. In figure 9-1 parent satisfaction is summarized for the four schools that

Figure 9-1. *Overall Satisfaction of Parents, Percentage Grades, 1997*

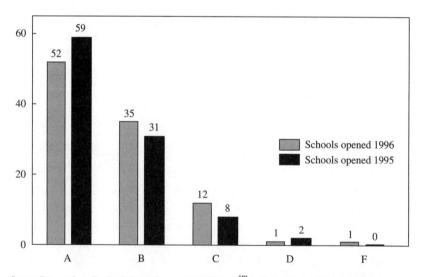

Source: Data are from Gordon S. Black Corporation. "CSmpact^sm for Edison Project Schools," 1997.

Figure 9-2. *Overall Satisfaction of Students, Percentage Grades, 1997*

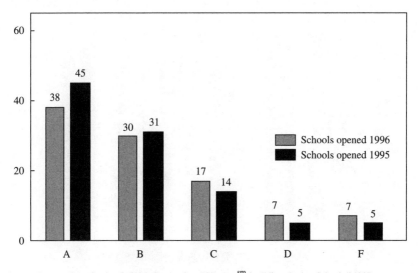

Source: Data are from Gordon S. Black Corporation. "CSmpact[sm] for Edison Project Schools," 1997.

opened in 1995 and the eight that opened in 1996. More than 50 percent of all parents have given the schools a grade of A, and about 90 percent have given a grade of A or B. These are high grades by national standards. In annual Gallup surveys, parents give their local schools considerably lower grades.[12] And the satisfaction level of Edison parents is high in schools that have just opened as well as in schools that have been open for two years.

The picture for students (figure 9-2) is essentially the same as that for parents, except that students are somewhat tougher critics of their schools—a logical and well-known phenomenon. Even among students, between two-thirds and three-fourths give their schools an A or B, with an A clearly the most popular grade.

Satisfaction among teachers is measured somewhat differently from that of parents and students, at least on the overall measures. Figure 9-3 shows ten-point scales of satisfaction for key areas of school operations. With scores averaging in the eight-point range for their immediate work environments (their houses, their lead teachers, and their careers) to the 7 point range for their supervisory structures (leadership teams, principals, and involvement in decisionmaking), teachers generally are satisfied with their new roles. The Black measurement process summarizes results on a revised scale that does not use ten points as the maximum possible score on most items: A low nine is the more common ceiling. Scores such as Edison

Figure 9-3. *Satisfaction Indicators for Teachers, Ten-Point Scales, 1997*

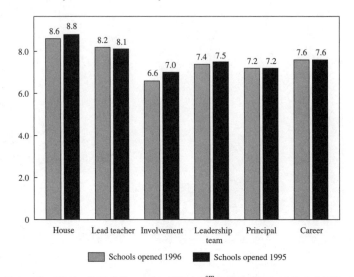

Source: Data are from Gordon S. Black Corporation. "CSmpact[sm] for Edison Project Schools," 1997.

teachers posted in twelve very different schools during 1997 are good in terms of the scale of measurement. They are even better when used as a gauge of the very different professional environment Edison is asking teachers to embrace.

Family Support

School success depends, perhaps more than anything else, on the full investment of families and students in the ambitious mission of their schools. Edison schools work hard to ensure that students and families are engaged. For example, parents came to quarterly conferences with teachers to discuss their children's quarterly learning contracts (QLCs) at a rate of 94 percent per quarter. This is a very high attendance rate, especially considering that many of the students are in middle school, where parent conferences are not even held in many of this nation's schools.

In addition, parents are getting their children to school, a phenomenon that is especially significant in the low-income neighborhoods that Edison schools sometimes serve. Student attendance at Edison schools averages 94 percent as well. Moreover, Edison families are keeping their children in Edison schools over time. Many schools struggle to educate children who regularly come to and go from the program. Edison has reduced annual turnover at its schools below 10 percent annually—a strikingly low figure and a clear measure of the value that families already place on an Edison education.

Finally, Edison schools have long waiting lists. For example, more than 1,800 students are waiting to enroll in Boston Renaissance, 600 at the Detroit Academy of Arts and Sciences, and 400 at Dodge-Edison. The average waiting list at an Edison School is 175.

Teacher Turnover

It should be noted that year-to-year turnover among teachers in Edison schools is about 23 percent annually—a figure that is higher than the norm in public education of about 12 percent.[13] The Edison average is a bit deceiving. Two Edison schools had teacher turnover rates that were quite a bit higher than the systemwide average due to problems in site leadership and program implementation early in their first years of operation. Those problems have been solved, and the schools' staffs have since stabilized. Obviously, without their high numbers, Edison's average turnover rate would be lower. Even so, the Edison program is a very rigorous one, with clear views about how schools should operate, and it demands much of teachers, especially as they decide whether the program is right for them. Edison does not expect the turnover rates of its new schools to match the public school average. The fact that close to 80 percent of all Edison teachers returned to their positions, especially after the challenging start-up years, is an indicator of satisfaction with the program.

Student Achievement

The Edison Project gauges and guides student achievement using three kinds of instruments: its own performance assessments and "structured portfolios" of students' work, group-administered state and district standardized tests, and, where they can be arranged, individually administered standardized tests of reading. The standardized tests, whether administered to students in groups or as individuals, are the most valid and reliable measures for evaluating student achievement at this juncture. Those tests come with state and national norms; Edison's own assessments are still in the process of establishing valid and reliable norms. This look at student achievement therefore focuses on standardized tests.

Table 9-2. *Individually Administered Reading Tests, Students Entering Primary Reading Studies in Kindergarten or First Grade, Edison Averages versus Control Averages and Effect Sizes, Spring 1996 and 1997*

| | Kindergarten | | | First grade | | | Second grade | | |
| | Grade equivalent | | | Grade equivalent | | | Grade equivalent | | |
Test	Control (n = 144)[a]	Edison (n = 190)[b]	Effect size[c]	Control (n = 228)[a]	Edison (n = 282)[b]	Effect size[c]	Control (n = 97)[a]	Edison (n = 114)[b]	Effect size[c]
Durrell Oral Reading	.96	1.16	.60	1.84	2.12	.39	2.62	3.07	.42
Woodcock Word Identification	1.05	1.25	.58	1.80	1.95	.32	2.50	2.95	.34
Woodcock Word Attack	.80	1.15	.71	1.55	1.88	.50	2.15	2.40	.30
Woodcock Passage Comprehension	1.00	1.15	.44	1.72	1.85	.28	2.35	2.65	.28

Sources: Data from Robert Mislevy, "Reading Achievement Test-Score Analysis: 1995/96, King-Edison vs. Control Schools, Grades K–2 Mount Clemens Community Schools," 1996; "Reading Achievement Test-Score Analysis: 1995/96, Dodge-Edison vs. Control Schools, Grades K–2 Wichita Unified School District #259," 1996; "Reading Achievement Test-Score Analysis: 1996/97, King-Edison vs. Control Schools, Grades 1–3 Mount Clemens Community Schools," 1997; "Reading Achievement Test-Score Analysis: 1996/97, Dodge-Edison vs. Control Schools, Grades 1–3 Wichita Unified School District #259," 1997.

a. Wichita and Mount Clemons.

b. Dodge and King.

c. Mean difference in scale score/control standard deviation.

Primary Reading Studies

The Edison Project places unusually strong emphasis on getting all children reading by the end of second grade, providing more time for reading in the daily schedule, offering small reading classes, frequently regrouping students based on progress, one-on-one tutoring, and a detailed instructional program, *Success for All.* Edison accordingly wants to know as precisely as possible how well primary reading is going. State and district testing programs usually omit kindergarten and first-grade students or provide data of limited reliability. To provide better data on the achievement of its early readers, Edison arranged for third-party studies of primary reading in five of the schools opened during the first two years of operation. The studies used a battery of reading tests administered to students, one by one, by trained testers working independently of the Edison Project. The students tested in the first year of the study are to be retested every spring for five years. In four schools being studied the district attempted to provide samples of students, in similar schools and with matching demographic characteristics, to be tested, compared to Edison students, and followed over time. The data for all of these studies are analyzed each year by Dr. Robert Mislevy, distinguished research scientist at the Educational Testing Service. The studies, paid for by Edison, follow a standard evaluation methodology agreed to by both Edison and its partners. The studies provide the best controlled evidence of how Edison students are achieving.[14]

Studies of two sites with control groups have been completed for their first two years of operation: Dodge-Edison in Wichita and King Academy in Mount Clemens. The results for the youngest two cohorts studied in each city are summarized in table 9-2. These cohorts entered the study as kindergarten or first-grade students; they are the cohorts for which Edison's reading program, *Success for All,* is most tailored. They are just beginning to acquire reading skills and are most likely to benefit from intensive instruction and relentless efforts to prevent early failure.

In every reading skill area—oral reading, word identification, word attack, and passage comprehension—and in kindergarten as well as first and second grades, Edison students are achieving more than students with the same characteristics and the same initial test scores in other district schools. The differences are moderate on average. Edison students are achieving nearly three months more in grade equivalents than control students on average. The differences tend to be larger the younger students are when they enter the program—an effect evident in the sizable differences for kindergarten students. It is too early to tell whether the youngest cohorts in Edison schools will build on their early advantage, simply maintain it, or perhaps even give it back. The data thus far do not show a consistent pattern. All that can be said with confidence is that students who entered these Edison schools in kindergarten or first grade are evidencing consistently stronger reading skills in grades K–2 than students from comparable backgrounds with comparable initial levels of achievement. In other *Success for All* schools that have been studied using the same methodology, early leads by students in the program grew steadily and reached a full grade equivalent by the end of fifth grade.[15]

The differences between Edison and comparable students can also be described by "effect sizes," a measure used frequently in formal evaluations of education programs. Effect sizes provide a common scale for comparing program effects that are originally measured on different scales. The common scale is standard deviation units. In the universe of education evaluation studies, an effect size of 0.5 is considered moderate. *Success for All* has averaged moderate effect sizes in its first years of implementation in other schools and larger effect sizes after five years of implementation. Edison's effect sizes are averaging nearly 0.5 for its early years of implementation as well. Effect sizes of 0.2 or greater generally represent statistically significant differences for the samples reported in table 9-2. The average effect size for every reading skill at these three grade levels exceeds the significance threshold.

Based on the experience of two of Edison's first schools, students beginning Edison's program in kindergarten or first grade can expect to be achieving at higher levels in reading than comparable students after one and two years in the program. As table 9-2 also shows, those students can expect to be reading on or above grade level in kindergarten and first grade, but somewhat below grade level in grade two—important accomplishments for the generally disadvantaged populations that the Dodge and King schools serve.

It must be said, finally, that students who began at these Edison schools in second grade are not achieving consistently more or less than comparable students after two years. *Success for All* has no independent data on the achievement of students who begin the reading program so late, so there is no way to determine whether Edison's performance with these students is typical. Mislevy will continue to follow Edison's late beginners, and Edison offers other forms of instruction to ensure that all students become strong readers, regardless of when they enter the program. On the reading measures in Mislevy's studies these older students are so far progressing no differently than comparable students in other schools. On other measures, as we shall see, older students do seem to be making good progress.

Dodge and King are not the only schools that Mislevy studied. But they are the only schools where the methodology permitted appropriately controlled comparisons. In the two other school districts where control groups were established and tested—Sherman, Texas, and Colorado Springs, Colorado—the control groups turned out to be noncomparable to the students in the Edison schools. In Colorado Springs the control group posted pretest scores that exceeded those in the Edison school by two-thirds of a standard deviation at every grade level. In Sherman the control group posted higher pretest scores at some grade levels and included far fewer students with limited English proficiency at every grade level. The reports from Mislevy concluded that achievement comparisons, even with statistical controls, cannot be used to draw strong conclusions.

Nevertheless, comparisons can be made. The most straightforward compare the differences in unadjusted pretest scores to the differences in unadjusted post-test scores. Because the tests are different and use different scales, this is most easily done by comparing effect sizes. Table 9-3 reports the differences in effect sizes, between the Edison schools and the control schools for the three grades included in the first-year studies.[16] The differences in table 9-3 indicate whether the Edison students improved their reading achievement more than the control groups improved theirs. Specifically, if the effect size at the post-test favors the control group less than the effect size at the pretest favored the control group, it can be inferred that the Edison students reduced the initial gap in reading achievement favoring the control group: The Edison students posted greater achievement gains.

At Roosevelt Elementary in Colorado Springs, students outgained the control groups at every grade level, ranging from an effect size difference of .70 in kindergarten to a difference of .20 in second grade. At Washington Elementary in Sherman, all three grade levels gained more than the control groups, but not by statistically significant amounts. The pre- and post-test differences in Colorado Springs and Sherman do not provide as rigorous a test of program effects as the statistical analyses and matched control groups in Wichita and Mount Clemens. However, the differences observed in Colorado Springs follow precisely the same pattern as those seen earlier—the younger the cohort, the larger the difference—and the differences in Sherman, though below the .20 threshold of significance, are at least in the same direction seen earlier. It is impossible to say from the Colorado Springs and Sherman data whether Edison students are in fact outgaining comparable students in other local schools: The data simply do not permit strong conclusions. But the Colorado Springs and Sherman data add some

Table 9-3. *Individually Administered Reading Tests, All Grade Levels in Primary Reading Studies, Unadjusted Effect Sizes for Pretests and Post-Tests, Edison versus Control, Washington and Sherman 1995–96, Roosevelt and Colorado Springs 1996–97*

Test	Kindergarten[a]			First grade[b]			Second grade[c]		
	Effect size[d]			Effect size[d]			Effect size[d]		
	Pretests[e]	Post-tests[f]	Difference[g]	Pretests[e]	Post-tests[f]	Difference[g]	Pretests[e]	Post-tests[f]	Difference[g]
Washington minus control	-0.41	-0.32	0.09	-0.67	-0.54	0.13	-0.26	-0.21	0.05
Roosevelt minus control	-0.64	0.06	0.70	-0.73	-0.36	0.37	-0.68	-0.48	0.20

Sources: Data are from Robert Mislevy, "Reading Achievement Test-Score Analysis: 1995/96 Washington-Edison School, Grades K–2 Sherman Independent School District," 1996; Reading Achievement Test-Score Analysis: 1996/97, Grades K–2, Roosevelt-Edison School, Colorado Springs, CO," 1997.

a. *ns* = 103 Washington, 87 Sherman control, 95 Roosevelt, 100 Colorado Springs control.

b. *ns* = 77 Washington, 80 Sherman control, 103 Roosevelt, 125 Colorado Springs control.

c. *ns* = 77 Washington, 80 Sherman control, 86 Roosevelt, 99 Colorado Springs control.

d. Effect size = mean difference in scale score/control standard deviation.

e. Pretest given in fall of study inception is Peabody Picture Vocabulary Test.

f. Post-tests are Durrell Oral Reading and Woodcock Word Identification, Word Attack, and Passage Comprehension tests.

g. Difference = post-test − pretest.

Table 9-4. *Individually Administered Reading Tests, All Grade Levels in Primary Reading Study, Boston Renaissance Charter School (BRCS) versus Dodge and King Averages, Gain Scores Spring 1996 to Spring 1997*

Test	Kindergarten to first grade[a]		First grade to second grade[b]		Second grade to third grade[c]	
	BRCS	Dodge and King	BRCS	Dodge and King	BRCS	Dodge and King
Durrell Oral Reading	1.10	1.10	1.00	1.10	0.90	0.85
Woodcock Word Iden.	0.80	0.75	0.90	1.05	0.90	0.90
Woodcock Word Attack	0.90	0.70	0.90	0.50	0.50	0.35
Woodcock Passage Comprehension	0.70	0.75	0.70	0.85	0.50	0.80

Source: Data are from Robert Mislevy, "Reading Achievement Test-Score Analysis: 1995/96 Boston Renaissance Charter School," 1996; "Reading Achievement Test-Score Analysis: 1996/97 Boston Renaissance Charter School," 1997.

a. 1997 Boston $n = 83$, Dodge and King $n = 112$.
b. 1997 Boston $n = 82$, Dodge and King $n = 123$.
c. 1997 Boston $n = 93$, Dodge and King $n = 112$.

weight to the reliable data in the other sites, indicating that Edison is making a significant difference for young readers.

This conclusion is lent final support by Mislevy's studies of Boston Renaissance in its first two years of operation. Because this school is a state-chartered public school, it has no school district from which comparison students might be drawn. Nevertheless, Edison and the Renaissance trustees want to follow primary reading progress at the school closely, and the youngest students are given the individual reading tests every spring. Mislevy analyzes the Boston Renaissance scores for patterns similar to those found in the controlled studies at other sites. Table 9-4 reports the average gain scores at Boston Renaissance, Dodge, and King for the 1996 and 1997 studies.

Boston Renaissance shows very similar gains to those posted at the other two schools. Mislevy concludes that reading progress at Boston Renaissance is likely to be of the same quality as that seen at Dodge and King, which is to say moderately better than local norms. As in the case of the Colorado Springs and Sherman schools, the Boston Renaissance data should not be overinterpreted; they say much more about the progress of students in that school than about progress relative to other students. The Boston data also reinforce the conclusion that Edison is so far making a meaningful difference in helping the youngest students in its schools learn to read.

Group-Based Standardized Tests

Most standardized tests are not administered to students individually, as the tests in the Primary Reading Studies are administered. Most standardized tests are administered to groups of students using written test booklets and multiple-choice answer sheets. These tests fall far short of measuring what students in good schools are learning. Typical standardized tests do not address much of Edison's curriculum. But standardized tests do provide valid and reliable measures of essential skills, particularly in reading and mathematics, and for groups of students.

Standardized tests come in several basic forms. Some are norm referenced, comparing tested students to a representative sample of students at the national, state, or local level. The Stanford Achievement Test is one example. Other tests are criterion referenced, comparing students to a standard of accomplishment—usually defined as a passing score—established by education experts. The Texas Academic Assessment System (TAAS) is a criterion-referenced test.

Edison students take whatever tests are customary or required for students in their local communities. If standardized tests are not normally taken, which is extremely rare, Edison asks schools to administer the Iowa Test of Basic Skills—every year and at every grade level from grade three to grade ten. When the same test, with increasing levels of difficulty, is administered to students in every grade level every year, it is easiest to gauge progress in student achievement: A cohort of students or even individual students can be followed over time. Many tests are given this way, but many are not. For example, some tests are given each year to only a single grade level. This approach only allows the comparison of different cohorts of students over time, which is an inferior way to gauge student progress: Different but successive cohorts must be assumed to have identical ability.

The standardized tests that Edison students take do not always make it easy, then, to measure achievement growth. The tests also do not provide any regular way to compare Edison students to similar students in similar schools. One reason the Primary Reading Studies are conducted is to guarantee at least one body of data that facilitates such comparisons in a rigorous manner. Standardized tests are given to every student in a state or district; data on similar students or schools are available only if test publishers or school authorities make them available. It will usually be possible, therefore, to judge whether Edison students are making good academic progress, but not whether that progress is better than that of comparable students. This analysis must work with whatever data are readily available.

So what do the standardized tests show? Table 9-5 reports the change scores for every grade cohort at an Edison school that has taken the same nationally normed standardized test in two consecutive years. The table reports on four widely used national tests—the Stanford Achievement Test, editions 8 and 9 (SAT-8, SAT-9); the Metropolitan Achievement Test, edition 7 (MAT-7); and the Iowa Test of Basic Skills (ITBS)—at seven Edison Schools. The reported score is not exactly the same for each test, as the table notes describe: The reports from the testing companies vary in the information they provide, and Edison must sometimes depend on abridged score reports provided by district officials. In any case, all of the measures report 100-point scales based on national norm groups. Some of the scores are means and others medians. Some are national percentile scores, and others are normal curve equivalent scores. Because the same kind of score is used at each point in time for a particular test and grade cohort, measurement does not interfere with the key inference about whether the cohort of students improved its achievement relative to national norms during the time between the two tests.

To strengthen this inference the table reports, whenever possible, the grade-level averages for only those students who took tests at both points in time. This method of reporting ensures that a school is not assigned responsibility for gains or declines that are due to students' moving into or out of the cohort being studied. Where Edison has access to the individual-level data, students entering or leaving a school between test points are removed from the averages. The sample sizes in each grade cohort are about 100 students on average. Generally speaking, differences in scores over time need to be about five points on a percentile scale and two points on a normal curve equivalent scale to be statistically significant. Results of tests of statistical significance are not reported in this table or subsequent ones, because the individual-level data needed to perform such tests are generally not available. The sample sizes and the magnitudes of the empirical differences, however, make inferences reasonable without formal statistical tests.

One very clear pattern emerges in table 9-5. Edison students appear to be making consistent academic progress in reading and in math—with one glaring exception: the students in Reeves Elementary in Dade County, Florida. At the six schools besides Reeves, fifteen different grade-level cohorts have been tested, and thirteen out of the fifteen have shown progress in reading and in math. All but one of the gain scores, moreover, would likely be statistically significant if formal tests were possible. Of the four negative changes, two in reading and two in math, only one is large

Table 9-5. One-Year Changes in Nationally Normed Standardized Test Scores, Same Cohorts

School	Test	Grade levels	Years	Reading			Math		
				Year one	Year two	Change	Year one	Year two	Change
Boston Renaissance[a,e]	SAT-9	3rd to 4th	1996–97	50	53	3	48	52	4
	SAT-9	5th to 6th	1996–97	47	51	4	47	52	5
Dodge-Edison[b]	MAT-7	3rd to 4th	1995–96	39	48	9	39	52	13
	MAT-7	4th to 5th	1995–96	47	60	13	37	65	28
	MAT-7	3rd to 4th	1996–97	47	53	6	58	63	5
	MAT-7	4th to 5th	1996–97	48	62	14	52	71	19
King Academy[c,e]	ITBS	3rd to 4th	1995–96	40	51	11	42	53	11
	ITBS	4th to 5th	1995–96	39	46	7	42	46	4
	ITBS	3rd to 4th	1996–97	27	47	20	28	44	16
	ITBS	4th to 5th	1996–97	51	49	–2	53	52	–1
Washington[c]	ITBS	1st to 2nd	1996–97	38	41	3	15	49	34
Jardine[b]	MAT-7	6th to 7th	1996–97	51	50	–1	34	43	9
	MAT-7	7th to 8th	1996–97	41	42	1	41	35	–6
Reeves[d,e]	SAT-8	1st to 2nd	1996–97	54	32	–22	67	48	–19
	SAT-8	2nd to 3rd	1996–97	26	21	–5	43	28	–15
	SAT-8	3rd to 4th	1996–97	21	18	–3	40	37	–3
	SAT-8	4th to 5th	1996–97	21	21	0	44	31	–13
Roosevelt[c]	ITBS	3rd to 4th	1997–98	27	43	16	20	23	3
	ITBS	4th to 5th	1997–98	41	44	3	23	29	6

Source: Data are from test publishers or school districts, provided by individual schools to the Edison Project.
a. Scores are national normal curve equivalent of mean standard score.
b. Scores are national percentile of median normal curve equivalent score.
c. Scores are national student percentile of mean standard score.
d. Scores are national percentile rank.
e. Includes only students tested in both years.

enough to be significant. On the positive side, finally, many of the gains are double digit—by any standard, truly large. These indicators of success contrast sharply with the evidence from Reeves, which is consistently negative. The data in table 9-5 suggest that Edison has been generally successful in boosting the achievement of elementary students, but not everywhere Edison has worked: The results at one school for at least one year appear disappointing.

These largely positive results are reinforced by those in table 9-6. There the tests just considered are used to follow cohorts of students over two full years. There are not many entries in table 9-6 because Edison has only a few schools that have been open long enough to be tested three times and post two-year gains. These measures are nonetheless important, because learning is a process that spans many years; whatever early successes Edison might produce need to be sustained and extended. This is particularly true for Edison's work in disadvantaged communities. Edison is beginning with many students achieving below national norms. It is not enough to help such students reach national averages, at least if Edison is going to fulfill its commitment to its partners. A world-class education should mean much more than average levels of achievement, even in communities where the national average has long been out of reach.

The two-year gains at Edison schools indeed show the promise of great accomplishment. At Boston Renaissance two cohorts have moved forward over ten normal curve equivalent points, which is excellent progress for two years time. King Academy moved its one two-year cohort over ten percentiles—also substantial. Finally, Dodge-Edison has produced remarkable results: gains exceeding twenty percentiles in reading and thirty percentiles in math have moved this group from well below the national average in 1995 to well above it in 1997. To be sure, these are only three schools and a handful of student cohorts. But they give at least an indication that Edison may be beginning to make meaningful and enduring improvements in student achievement.

Table 9-7 summarizes a different set of indicators. State and local education authorities are making increasing efforts to raise student achievement standards. These efforts often result in unique state and local assessments, as authorities conclude that nationally normed tests do not gauge either the right standards or sufficiently tough standards. The proliferation of state and local tests creates another challenge for Edison, as its program must help students succeed on a wide range of measures. The measures reported in table 9-7 are for state and local tests the Edison students have taken twice, the minimum number of observations needed to make any inferences about progress.

Table 9-6. *Two-Year Changes in Nationally Normed Standardized Test Scores, Same Cohorts*

School	Test	Grade levels	Years	Reading			Math		
				Year one	Year two	Change	Year one	Year two	Change
Boston Renaissance[a]	MAT-7	3rd to 5th	1995–97	45	54	9	37	49	12
	MAT-7	4th to 6th	1995–97	42	52	10	29	46	17
Dodge-Edison[b]	MAT-7	3rd to 5th	1995–97	39	62	23	39	71	32
King Academy[c]	ITBS	3rd to 5th	1995–97	39	49	10	38	52	14

Source: Data are from test publishers or school districts, provided by individual schools to the Edison Project.

a. Scores are national normal curve equivalent of mean standard score.

b. Scores are national percentile of median normal curve equivalent score.

c. Scores are national student percentile of mean standard score.

Table 9-7. *One-Year Changes in State or Local Assessments, Same or Successive Cohorts*

School	Test	Grade levels	Years	Reading			Math		
				Year one	Year two	Change	Year one	Year two	Change
Dodge-Edison[a]	Kansas	3rd to 3rd	1996–97	51	54	3	...	...	...
	Kansas	3rd to 3rd	1996–97	46	52	6	...	...	...
	Kansas	4th to 4th	1996–97	...	...	...	44	46	2
King Academy[b]	MEAP	4th to 4th	1995–96	40	46	6	57	55	–2
Washington[b]	TAAS	3rd to 3rd	1996–97	68	67	–1	67	–57	–10
	TAAS	4th to 4th	1996–97	52	67	15	31	47	16
Roosevelt[c]	DALT	3rd to 4th	1996–97	184	191	7	178	188	10
	DALT	4th to 5th	1996–97	196	201	5	192	202	10

Source: Data are from test publishers or school districts, provided by individual schools to the Edison Project.

a. Scores are state percentile ranks of mean score

b. Scores are percent meeting minimum expectations—that is, passing

c. Scores are fall-to-fall scale scores and gains, where an annual gain of 10 points is expected.

Table 9-8. *Edison Gain Scores or Level Scores versus State or Local Comparison Groups, All Tests Except Primary Reading Studies*

School	Test	Grade levels	Years	Reading Comparison group	Reading Edison	Reading Difference	Math Comparison group	Math Edison	Math Difference
Boston Renaissance	MEAP[a]	4th	1996	1275	1350	75	1270	1320	50
	ITBS[b]	3rd	1997	36	45	9	…	…	…
Dodge-Edison	MAT-7[c]	3rd to 4th	1995–96	3	5	2	3	7	4
	MAT-7[c]	4th to 5th	1995–96	5	7	2	3	15	12
	MAT-7[c]	3rd to 4th	1996–97	5	3	–2	7	3	–4
	MAT-7[c]	4th to 5th	1996–97	3	6	3	5	9	4
	MAT-7[c]	3rd to 5th	1995–97	5	11	6	6	16	10
	Kansas[d]	3rd to 3rd	1996–97	6	3	–3	…	…	…
	Kansas[d]	3rd to 3rd	1996–97	5	6	1	…	…	…
	Kansas[d]	4th to 4th	1996–97	…	…	…	1	2	1
King Academy	MEAP[e]	4th to 4th	1995–96	–4	6	10	–14	–2	12
Dillingham	TAAS[f]	5th	1997	25	33	8	28	36	8
	TAAS[f]	6th	1997	39	45	6	36	47	11
Reeves	SAT-8[g]	1st to 2nd	1996–97	–15	–22	–7	2	–19	–21
	SAT-8[g]	2nd to 3rd	1996–97	–4	–5	–1	–6	–15	–9
	SAT-8[g]	3rd to 4th	1996–97	0	–3	–3	5	–3	–8
	SAT-8[g]	4th to 5th	1996–97	–1	0	–1	–1	–13	–12
Roosevelt	DALT[h]	3rd to 4th	1996–97	6	7	1	12	10	–2
	DALT[h]	4th to 5th	1996–97	6	5	–1	10	10	0

Source: Data are from test publishers or school districts, provided by individual schools to the Edison Project.

a. Scale is 1600 points; differences of 50 points are statistically significant. Comparison group is similar students statewide.

b. Scale is 100 percentiles. Comparison group is Boston Public Schools, a district with demographic characteristics similar to Boston Renaissance Charter School.

c. Scale is 100 percentiles. Comparison group is six neighborhood or neighborhood magnet schools with demographic characteristics similar to Dodge-Edison.

d. Scale is 100 percentiles. Comparison group is seven neighborhood or neighborhood magnet schools with demographic characteristics similar to Dodge-Edison.

e. Scale is 100 percentiles. Comparison group is other district elementary schools with demographic characteristics similar to King Academy.

f. Scale is 100 percentiles. Scores are percentage of students increasing their Texas Learning Indexes by 5 points or more. Comparison group is all other students at Dillingham Intermediate School; Edison program is a school within a school.

g. Scale is 100 percentiles. Comparison group is a random sample of district students with demographic characteristics similar to Reeves.

h. Scale assumes 10-point gain annually. Comparison group is district students with demographic characteristics that indicate they are less advantaged than Roosevelt students.

Edison's progress on state and local assessments is uneven, but generally positive. On the Kansas state assessments, successive cohorts at Dodge-Edison improved two to six percentile points. To spur improvement, Kansas asks schools to raise scores one to two points per year. Dodge has done so. The King Academy raised its passing rate on the Michigan Educational Assessment Program (MEAP) test of reading by six percentiles; the school's passing rate on the math test fell by two percentiles. These outcomes, as we shall see, are better than they appear.

Washington Elementary had a mixed experience on TAAS, with third grade passing rates down but fourth grade passing rates up rather sharply. This performance, however, is more disappointing than it might appear: The fourth grade scores are still far short of where they need to be, and the scores for both grades reflect school performance well into the school's second year of operation. Edison is encouraged by the strong upward trend of the fourth grade data, but the scores clearly reflect the difficulties that the school experienced in year one implementing the Edison model. Finally, there is the District Achievement Levels Test (DALT) for Roosevelt Elementary. Scores by the same cohort of students are up ten points in math and five to seven points in reading. The district expects scores to go up ten points per year—which Roosevelt accomplished in mathematics—but disadvantaged schools, such as Roosevelt, have traditionally not met this standard.

When it comes to student achievement, Edison's partners are concerned first and foremost with this question: Are students in Edison schools making clear academic progress and raising their standard of performance over time? The answer to this question for most Edison students and schools is clearly yes. On nationally normed tests Edison students at various grade levels and in numerous schools plainly are moving forward and sometimes by impressive amounts. The only real exception to this generalization is Reeves Elementary, where a failure to implement Edison's model or any consistent alternative to it caused test scores to go down.[17] On state and local assessments the picture is not quite so clear, but on balance it is positive. Inconsistencies are confined mostly to a single campus.

These conclusions are reinforced by the answer to another achievement question: Are students in Edison schools making greater academic progress than similar students in similar schools, either statewide or locally? The answer generally is yes. Table 9-8 summarizes all data currently available that permit comparisons between Edison students and students roughly comparable to them. The data are typically not available in a form that would permit demographic characteristics or differences in test scores to be modeled and tested statistically. But the patterns in the data are fairly strong and clear.

Boston Renaissance topped a statewide demographic comparison group by a significant margin on the state assessment, Massachusetts Educational Assessment Program, in reading and in math. Renaissance also bested the Boston Public Schools by nine percentiles on the state-mandated ITBS reading test, though the two groups of students are close but not identical demographically. Dodge-Edison's annual gain scores on the MAT-7 exceeded those posted by similar Wichita schools in three out of four cases; Dodge-Edison's two-year gain scores easily outdistanced the gains of similar schools and would easily be significant. On the Kansas state assessments, the gains of Dodge-Edison and the comparison schools are not very different, though Dodge-Edison is slightly ahead in two out of three instances.

King Academy fared much better on the state assessment than the other Mount Clemens elementary school, whose demographic characteristics are very similar to King's; the differences of ten and twelve percentiles would certainly be significant. Edison's school-within-a-school program at Dillingham Intermediate School had a higher percentage of students increasing their Texas Learning Indexes by five or more points—a recognized standard of strong academic progress—than the traditional district program at Dillingham.

The Reeves scores look somewhat better when compared to the scores of similar Dade County students than when compared to national norms. In reading, except for grade two, Reeves students performed similarly to the district comparison group. In math Reeves had its clear failure; its students progressed far less than comparable students. Finally, Roosevelt's DALT gains turn out to be virtually identical to the gains in the Colorado Springs district overall. The district is not as disadvanatged as Roosevelt, but it is a necessary point of comparison. The DALT scores are not reported on a scale that makes progress easy to evaluate. The fact that Roosevelt kept pace with the district, which serves a less disadvantaged population, suggests that Roosevelt had a relatively strong first year.

Comparative data such as these should be interpreted with care. First, the data are not subject to statistical controls or tests. Second and more important, the comparisons oversimplify the issue of school performance. Edison's partners want to know if students in Edison schools are making clear progress toward higher academic standards. Edison's partners are less interested in whether students in Edison schools are doing better than students in other schools. In fact, local authorities that contract with Edison generally hope that an Edison school will stimulate improvement in all schools—and achievement in the Edison school will not stand out. From a policy standpoint, such hopes make perfect sense. They represent the benefits of healthy competition for a system of schools rather than just the benefits of private management for a single school. From an evaluation standpoint, however, such hopes make matters complex. If an Edison school raises its achievement level, but other local schools do as well, is Edison succeeding more or less? Fortunately, the current data do not force us to grapple with the issue. By and large, achievement is up in Edison schools, and up more than in the schools with which these schools compete.

Conclusion

The Edison Project now operates twenty-five public schools in eight states and thirteen cities across the United States. With the 1997–98 school year marking the third year since the Edison Project began operating partnership schools, Edison is beginning to accumulate substantial data on school performance. Most significantly, information based on standardized tests is accumulating on the two-year experiences of the first four partnership schools opened in 1995 and on the one-year experiences of the eight partnership schools opened in 1996. These experiences represent only the initial stages of school change processes that Edison and its partners continue to carry out.

Although the early data examined here should not be overinterpreted, they indicate that Edison schools are off to promising starts. All schools are not doing equally well, and two plainly got off to shaky starts. Several years must yet go by before it will be possible to judge more than initial results. But the early returns are clearly positive. Student achievement is up pretty consistently, and sometimes impressively. Parents, students, and staff members are generally very satisfied. Edison's ambitious school design is being implemented faithfully. Edison is making good on one of its key commitments as a private company, to invest its capital in local public school improvement. Communities are partnering with Edison at an increasing rate, a sign of America's growing openness to new ideas in education.

Notes

1. I was a member of the original Edison design team.
2. The Edison Project, *Partnership School Design* (New York, 1994).
3. Robert E. Slavin, Nancy A. Madden, Lawrence J. Dolan, and Barbara A. Wasik, *Every Child, Every School: Success for All* (Thousand Oaks, Calif.: Corwin Press, Inc., 1996).

4. *Everyday Mathematics: Student Achievement Studies* (Chicago: Everyday Learning, 1997).

5. The Edison Project, *School Performance Standards* (New York, 1997).

6. A full account of Edison's early history, from the reasearch and development period through the first operating year, can be found in John E. Chubb, "Lessons in School Reform from the Edison Project," in Diane Ravitch and Joseph P. Viteritti, eds., *New Schools for a New Century* (Yale University Press, 1997), chap. 4.

7. Concerns about the inequity of school choice are well presented in Edith Rasell and Richard Rothstein, eds., *School Choice: Examining the Evidence* (Washington, D.C.: Economic Policy Institute, 1993).

8. Chester Finn, Louann A. Bierlein, Gregg Vanourek, and Bruno Manno, *Charter Schools in Action* (Washington, D.C.: Hudson Institute, 1997).

9. Julia Landau, Massachusetts Advocacy Center attorney and Scott Hamilton, associate commissioner for charter schools, Massachusetts Department of Education, as quoted in "OCR: Charter School Discriminated Against Student with Disability," *Section 504 Compliance Advisor* (LRP Publications, October 1997), pp. 5–6.

10. Slavin and others, *Every Child, Every School,* pp. 205–10.

11. For example, see Kevin Fedarko, "Starting from Scratch," *Time Magazine,* October 27, 1997; and Peggy Farber, "The Edison Project Scores—and Stumbles—in Boston," *Phi Delta Kappan,* March 1998, pp. 506–11.

12. The figure in recent years has been about 70 percent A or B. *The Annual Phi Delta Kappa Gallup Poll of the Public's Attitudes Toward the Public Schools* (Bloomington, Ind., 1994).

13. United States Department of Education, *Digest of Education Statistics 1996* (Washington: Government Printing Office, 1997).

14. The studies generally follow protocols established in Slavin and others, *Every Child, Every School,* chap. 8. The studies can be obtained from Dr. Mislevy at the Educational Testing Service, Princeton, NJ.

15. Slavin and others, *Every Child, Every School,* pp. 198–205.

16. The Sherman study dropped the control group in its second year because Edison and the district agreed that the control group was too different to be of serious use; the Colorado Springs study, only in its first year, will continue to employ the control group.

17. In its second year Reeves made a major turnaround, formally recognized by the Miami-Dade Board of Education in March 1998, after reviewing a series of formal program reviews conducted by Dade district staff members in November 1997 and February 1998.

TEN

Charter Schools: Politics and Practice in Four States

Bryan C. Hassel

Despite what the words seem to imply, "charter schools" is not basically about the schools. For the teachers who found them and the students who enroll in them, true, it is the schools that are important. But for others, from the beginning, "charter schools" has been about system-reform . . . a way for the state to cause the district system to improve.[1]

—Ted Kolderie

SINCE THE AUTHOR of the above quotation helped his home state of Minnesota adopt the nation's first charter school law in 1991, more than half the states have followed suit. As of fall 1997, more than 700 charter schools educated well over 150,000 students across the United States. In the flurry of press coverage that these fledgling public schools have generated, though, the talk has remained decidedly about the schools. In the battle for headlines, the trials and triumphs of educational entrepreneurs have seemed a more promising weapon than wonkish discussions of the diffusion of innovations or breaking local school boards' "exclusive franchise" over public education. No one would begrudge these new schools their moments in the spotlight; certainly the work they are doing is newsworthy. But if we are to take Kolderie's vision of charter schools' system-changing potential seriously, the talk must move beyond the schools. This chapter represents a preliminary effort to do just that. After exploring how charter schools might transform public education for the better, I look to the actual experience of charter school programs to assess their potential for having a positive impact on the broader system.

In theory, charter schools might make an impact on the school system through three mechanisms. First, they might serve as laboratories. Freed up from law and regulation, this argument goes, charter schools will experiment with new educational practices. Ideas that work on a small scale in charter schools can be replicated on a broader scale in many public schools. Second, charter schools might serve as competitors to school districts. Since money follows children from the district schools they leave to the charter schools they choose, districts will face a financial incentive to persuade families not to exit. Consequently, it is argued, districts will respond to the presence (or even the potential presence) of charter schools by improving their offerings in the hope of stanching any outflow of students (and money). Third, charter schools might, over time, simply replace district schools as the primary purveyors of public education. As more and more families choose charter schools, conventional district schools will serve a smaller and smaller fraction of the public school population.

These three mechanisms differ from one another primarily in their assessments of conventional school districts' ability to change for the better. The laboratory thesis is the most optimistic, positing that the mere demonstration that some idea or another works will persuade many school districts to adopt the innovation. The replacement thesis is the least optimistic, reasoning that conventional districts will muddle along in their familiar fashion until they fade into oblivion. The competition thesis lies in between, hypothesizing that conventional districts can change for the better, but only with the introduction of a quasi-market for public education.

Do charter school programs as they are now constructed have the potential to transform public education in any of these ways? This chapter, based on a larger study of charter school programs across the country, presents a fairly pessimistic answer. In part, this assessment responds to the fact that state legislatures across the country have departed substantially from the "charter school idea" in the charter laws they have adopted. These departures limit the ability of charter school programs to have the system-changing impact their proponents envision. But political compromise is not the only culprit. Experience also suggests that charter proponents need to think more carefully about how the three mechanisms for making an impact might work in practice. Though in this chapter I draw on information from across the country, most of the empirical material comes from case studies of charter programs in four states: Colorado, Georgia, Massachusetts, and Michigan.[2]

The Politics of Charter School Programs

One of this chapter's central contentions is that, in passing charter school laws that look quite different from "pure" charter programs, legislators have limited the capacity of charter schools to produce systemwide improvement. But what would a pure charter school program look like? First, a wide range of individuals and groups would have the opportunity to propose charter schools. The application process would be open to parents, teachers, business people, community organizations, and diverse combinations of all of these groups. There would be no cap on the number of schools that could open, or at least a very high cap. Second, prospective organizers could apply to more than one potential authorizer or sponsor, including at least one other than the local school board. Third, charter schools would operate very autonomously, freed up from state laws and regulations as well as district policies and collective bargaining agreements. Only a core of essential public school laws and regulations (such as prohibitions on tuition, selective admissions, religious instruction, unsafe conditions, and discrimination) would remain. Fourth, full per-pupil funding would follow children. If a family opted to move a child from a district school to a charter school, per-pupil funding would move along with the child. Finally, charter schools would sign "charters," contracts obligating them to meet specified performance targets. Schools that failed to measure up could be closed.

All of these provisions would make it possible for charter schools to have a broader impact on the public education system. But the politics of charter schools has made it difficult for state legislatures to pass charter laws that include all five. Charter school programs tend to attract bipartisan support wherever they are proposed. Many Republicans see charter schools as a first step toward introducing choice and competition into public education. Many Democrats see them as a way to offer educational opportunities to the underserved or to stave off less desirable forms of school choice, such as voucher plans. With both Democrats and Republicans on board, charter school proposals typically gain momentum quickly in state legislatures. As a result, legislators and interest groups that might ordinarily oppose charter schools altogether begin to think about fallback positions—compromised versions of charter laws that can satisfy charter advocates while protecting the status quo.

If charter proponents had the votes to pass pure laws, these calculations would not matter. But in education policymaking, as in so many other domains, proponents of significant system-challenging reform rarely have the clout to achieve their legislative goals without compromise.[3] Eventually they sit down with charter opponents and hammer out a deal. The legislation that emerges includes compromises, deviations from the ideal charter law proponents had in mind. And since those deviations were insisted on by interests that would prefer no charter law at all, they have the potential to undermine the program's ability to achieve the purposes envisioned by charter proponents.

Of course these processes have unfolded differently in each state legislature. Some states have passed relatively uncompromised laws; others have deviated from almost every component of the ideal charter law. But at least some such compromises have emerged in every state that has passed charter legislation. The next three sections detail some of the most common, explaining their impact on charter schools' potential to serve as laboratories, competitors, and replacements for existing public school systems.

The Laboratory Thesis

For charter schools to serve as laboratories they must be autonomous, relatively free to differentiate their practices from the conventional ways of doing things. But legislative compromises have undermined the autonomy enjoyed by charter schools in many states. First, some charter laws have created operating environments that limit the independence and freedom of charter schools. For example, some laws require charter schools to be legally part of local school districts rather than independent organizations. Since the idea of charter schools is to provide options that are different from (and competitive with) those offered by school districts, one would expect district control of charter schools to limit the amount of differentiation that takes place. Some laws also limit the scope of exemptions charter schools receive from state laws and regulations or require them to request exemptions on a case-by-case basis. Second, some charter laws construct selection processes for charter schools that have the effect of limiting charter schools' autonomy. For example, some laws place decisionmaking authority over the approval of charter schools in the hands of local school boards, but the other schools these boards govern are the very organizations from which charter schools are supposed to differentiate themselves and with which they are supposed to compete. Other laws limit the range of individuals or organizations that are eligible to propose charter schools, effectively limiting the range of ideas that enter the arena.

Table 10-1 presents information about how charter school laws treat these issues in the twenty states that had passed charter schools by January 1996. The four rows of the table correspond to the four examples of key legislative provisions listed in the previous paragraph. A bullet in one of these rows indicates that a state law includes a provision likely to favor autonomy and independence for charter schools.

As table 10-1 reveals, quite a few state charter laws appear likely to restrict charter schools' autonomy. Eleven of twenty make charter schools part of local school districts rather than independent entities. Twelve sharply restrict the exemptions charter schools can receive from state law or require schools to request exemptions on a case-by-case basis. In nine of the twenty states, no entity other than local school boards may issue charters. In six of the twenty, only public schools may apply for charter status; groups of parents, teachers, community organizations, or businesses are excluded. Eleven of the state laws include two or fewer of the autonomy-enhancing provisions; only three contain all four. In one of the case study states, Georgia, these kinds of compromises are so severe that charter schools have almost no more latitude than conventional public schools enjoy in the core elements of school decisionmaking.

Still, not all of the states have so heavily compromised on issues of autonomy. In the three other case study states, despite some apparent statutory constraints on autonomy, charter schools enjoy wide latitude in most important areas of school decisionmaking. To be sure, charter schools find themselves enmeshed in many of the regulations that entangle regular public schools. They labor to meet detailed building codes, to fulfil byzantine reporting requirements, to follow countless procedures for everything from special education to food service. But most of the regulation about which charter officials complain lies on what we might think of as the periphery of school management. In interviews charter school officials have reported little if any restriction in the core elements of school decisionmaking: what and how they teach, whom they hire and fire, how they organize and govern themselves, and how they spend money. Perhaps the prospects for the laboratory thesis are brighter in these states and others with more permissive laws.

But even in those states it is important to be clear about the kind of laboratory work we should expect from charter schools. Discussions of

Table 10-1. *Autonomy in Twenty State Charter School Laws in 1996*

Components of state laws	Alaska	Ark.	Ariz.	Calif.	Colo.	Del.	Ga.	Hawaii	Kans.	La.	Mass.	Mich.	Minn.	N.H.	N.J.	N.M.	R.I.	Tex.	Wisc.	Wyo.
Operating environment																				
Charter school may be legally and fiscally independent of local school board	...	...	✓	✓	...	✓	...	...	...	...	✓	✓	✓	✓	✓	...	...	✓	...	...
Charter school receives automatic exemption from many state and local policies	...	...	✓	✓	...	✓	...	✓	...	✓	...	✓	...	✓	...	...	...	✓	...	...
Selection process																				
Entity other than local board may authorize a charter school	...	...	✓	✓	✓	✓	...	...	...	...	✓	✓	✓	...	✓	✓	✓	✓	...	✓
Wide range of people and organizations may start a charter school	✓	...	✓	✓	✓	✓	...	...	✓	✓	✓	✓	✓	✓	✓	...	...	✓	✓	✓

charter schools as laboratories tend to focus on experimentation at the school level. Charter schools, it is argued, will pioneer new curricula, teaching methods, disciplinary systems, organizational structures, contracting arrangements, and budgetary allocations. Other public schools can adopt the innovations that work. But this kind of school-to-school replication appears unlikely for reasons that have less to do with legislative compromises than with two questionable assumptions underlying the school-level laboratory thesis.

The first assumption is that charter schools will use their latitude to engage in activities to which school districts would have had no exposure, giving districts the chance to adopt practices that otherwise would have been unknown to them. But charter schools in Colorado, Massachusetts, and Michigan are generally not engaging in activities that conventional districts would regard as completely new and pathbreaking. To be sure, charter schools are doing interesting and varied things with their curricula, their instructional practices, their staffing, their budgets, and their governance. But the innovations that charter schools are undertaking are by and large innovations that have been proposed elsewhere and, to a limited extent, carried out by existing public schools.[4] Of the eighty schools in operation in these states in 1995–96, some 54 percent reported either a "basics" approach, a standard vocational education model, a subject-focused curriculum (focused on subjects such as arts or science and math), or a general or nonidentifiable educational approach. Some 9 percent followed culture-centric models which, though unusual, have certainly been well publicized in the national education press and literature. The remaining 36 percent indeed listed alternative educational approaches. But many of these, though "alternative," are based on widely known models such as Montessori.[5] As a result, it seems unlikely that many school districts would adopt the practices of charter schools solely on their merits. Most school districts have already been exposed to the ideas charter schools are implementing and have chosen not to adopt them.[6]

There is a second questionable assumption underlying the school-level laboratory thesis: the assumption that new ideas will diffuse once shown to be successful. Elmore convincingly argues that even highly organized and well-funded efforts to take "good ideas" to scale in American education have foundered, largely because existing institutions and personnel lack incentives to adopt new ideas, no matter how good.[7] Elmore chronicles the history of many such efforts and the limited impact on practice they have had. For example, he describes the work of several National Science Foundation (NSF)–funded curriculum development projects in the 1950s and

1960s: "Hundreds of thousands of teachers and curriculum directors were trained in summer institutes. Tens of thousands of curriculum units were disseminated. Millions of students were exposed to at least some product or by-product of the various projects." But though some schools undertook major efforts to transform their curricula in response, the overall results were minimal: "A weak, diluted, hybrid form emerged in some settings in which new curricula were shoe-horned into old practices, and, in most secondary classrooms, the curricula had no impact on teaching and learning at all."[8]

A more recent case in point is the New American Schools project, which has funded several teams to develop whole-school designs and then work with schools and districts to implement them.[9] This strategy shares some kinship with the charter idea, focusing as it does on designing entire schools on paper, piloting them, and then taking the designs to scale. Though many observers are enthusiastic about the designs that have emerged and several school districts (and some entire states) are working with New American Schools to implement them, the experience of the effort has shown how daunting is the task of taking good ideas to scale. Efforts to implement the designs have fallen victim to everything from lack of local capacity to political infighting.[10]

If projects like the NSF curriculum development initiative and New American Schools have difficulty diffusing good ideas on their merits, it is difficult to imagine charter schools' ideas spreading widely, purely on the basis of their success. New American Schools is a deliberate effort to diffuse whole-school innovations, complete with a national staff and a multi-million-dollar annual budget. Charter schools, in contrast, tend to be independent organizations whose leaders may or may not be interested in diffusion. Even those that are committed to diffusion generally find themselves with limited time to devote to spreading the word about what they are doing, much less provide existing public schools with the kind of hands-on technical assistance New American Schools offers.

Since district-based public schools are already awash in new ideas and seem less than inclined to transform themselves, it seems unlikely that the ideas issuing forth from charter schools will by themselves spark much change at the school level. But charter school programs have the potential to be laboratories in a different respect—laboratories testing a new way to organize a system of schools. When one analyzes the charter world carefully, what looks most unique is not the specific practices of charter schools, but the overall system in which they work. Where conventional public schools emerge from district bureaucracies, charter schools arise from self-organized teams of people who may sit outside the system. A charter school sets a mission that can be more targeted and specific than that of a conventional public school, which must strive to be all things to all people. To open, it must convince some public body that its mission has merit, that it has a plan to achieve it, and that it has the capacity to enact the plan. It deploys the design in an environment that allows broad latitude within the constraints of the marketplace and a core of public school law. And it signs a contract that obligates it to meet performance standards, facing the revocation of the charter if it fails. It is this constellation of institutional arrangements that is most clearly being tested in the charter school laboratory.

Conventional school districts could adopt some version of this institutional regime within their own systems. They could invite proposals from the community (or beyond) for the design and management of schools. They could judge these proposals and award contracts to the most promising. They could give schools more flexibility than they now enjoy, combined with the accountability that arises from the threat of the contracts' revocation. To be sure, districts would face some constraints in state law. But most have considerable latitude within these constraints. And in an increasing number of states, districts can request waivers of state laws or regulations.[11]

Still, merely demonstrating the efficacy of a new institutional form is not likely to spark widespread change in the way school districts relate to their schools, for the same reasons that demonstrating the value of new educational approaches has failed over the years to spur changes in practice. Without some alterations in the incentives facing public school districts, no amount of good news from the charter world—at the school or system level—can be expected to result in systemwide change. Such changes in incentives are, in fact, the basis for the second potential mechanism for impact: establishing charter schools as competitors.

The Competition Thesis

Can charter schools have a broad impact on American education by competing with districts for students, and thus funds? As with the laboratory thesis, the mechanism of competition appears unlikely to work its magic at the moment because of legislative compromises. And, as with the laboratory thesis, more careful thinking about how competition might work in practice reveals some additional problems with the thesis.

Legislative compromise might undermine competition in one of three ways. First, legislators might impose limits on the number of charter

Table 10-2. *Competitive Impact in Twenty State Charter School Laws in 1996*

Components of state laws	Alaska	Ark.	Ariz.	Calif.	Colo.	Del.	Ga.	Hawaii	Kans.	La.	Mass.	Mich.	Minn.	N.H.	N.J.	N.M.	R.I.	Tex.	Wisc.	Wyo.
Entity other than local board may authorize a charter school	…	…	✓	✓	✓	✓	…	…	…	…	✓	✓	✓	…	✓	✓	✓	✓	…	…
Law enables many charter schools to open	✓	✓	✓	…	✓	…	✓	✓	…	…	…	✓	…	✓	✓	…	…	…	…	✓
Full per-pupil operating funds follow the child	…	…	✓	✓	…	✓	…	✓	…	✓	✓	✓	✓	…	…	…	✓	✓	…	…

schools in a state or district, statutorily capping scale and, as a consequence, response and impact. Second, legislation might cushion the financial blow to existing districts when students choose charter schools, lessening the incentive to respond. Finally, even if legislation imposes no numerical limits on charter schools, it can institute de facto caps by making the business of running a charter school less viable or by placing exclusive decisionmaking authority over charter schools in the hands of school districts.

Table 10-2 shows the extent to which state laws have capped the number of charter schools or deviated from the idea of full per-pupil funding following the child. Ten of these states place strict caps on numbers. Six of the ten that do not do so impose de facto caps by granting local school boards veto power over whether charter schools open. That leaves only four states where a large number of charter schools can open without local approval. And all of these still cap the number of schools; the limits are just higher than in the other states profiled. Though virtually no state offers charter schools full per-pupil funding inclusive of capital spending, full per-pupil operating funding follows the child in nine states. In the other eleven, charter schools either receive less than 100 percent of per-pupil operating money or districts are reimbursed for their losses.[12] Of these twenty states, only Arizona and Michigan allow nonlocal sponsorship, have relatively high limits on numbers, and require full per-pupil operating funding to follow the child.

Even without these compromises, though, there are reasons to believe the competition mechanism would not work as the proponents of charter schools expect. The assumption that underlies this mechanism is that school districts will not only respond to competition, but will respond in a particular way: that is, by improving the quality of the education they offer to students. Evidence from the four state case studies, however, suggests that districts have a whole array of possible responses to the introduction of competition. Many of these have little to do with improving the quality of public education; some, perversely, are likely to have the opposite effect. Here are five sets of prominent examples from the four states in this study.

—1. Districts can use the courts to derail or restrict charter schools. In the three states with strong laws, districts and other opponents of charter schools have filed lawsuits challenging the charter laws or specific applications of these laws. The most successful case was a lawsuit filed in Michigan by a range of individuals and organizations, including the Council About Parochiaid (a broad coalition of education interest groups), three members of the state board of education, a member of a local board of education, the Michigan Education Association, and the Michigan branch of the American Civil Liberties Union (ACLU). The plaintiffs argued that the law violated the state constitution's ban on spending public money on private schools and that it usurped the state board of education's rightful authority over public education. In October 1994 an Ingham County Circuit Court judge enjoined the state from releasing state funds to the ten charter schools currently open; he struck down the law the next month. In response, the legislature rewrote the charter law to clarify the state board of education's ultimate authority over charter schools, their public nature, and the constraints they faced as public schools.[13]

—2. Districts can use subsequent legislation to derail or restrict charter schools. Districts and other opponents of charter schools, rather than competing constructively, can also attempt to persuade the legislature to scale back a charter program or minimize its impact on existing schools. Massachusetts represents the most striking example of this phenomenon. As noted above, Massachusetts districts persuaded legislators to reimburse many of them, at least partially and temporarily, for funds they lost to charter schools. In Michigan as well, districts and their allies have prompted legislators to weaken the law in important respects. The 1995 school code revisions in that state, for example, made charter schools subject to virtually all public school law. In an attempt to restrict the chartering activity of prolific Central Michigan University, the new law also prohibited any one sponsor from chartering more than half of the state's charter schools (initially an effective limit of fifty, eventually to rise to seventy-five).

—3. Districts can use other means to make life difficult for charter schools. Districts and other charter opponents have also responded to charter schools by using various tactics to undermine charter schools individually. In a study of eight new charter schools in Massachusetts, Loveless and Jasin reported that many of Massachusetts' first charter schools repeatedly faced severe hostility from local districts.[14] Hostile tactics used against the schools included alleged harassment of charter school organizers as well as prospective students and parents, reported by Loveless and Jasin;[15] refusal to provide student records to a charter school until well after school started, complicating the school's efforts to divide students into classes, choose appropriate materials, and devise plans for special education students;[16] and one school system's efforts to persuade a congregation to lease space to it instead of the local charter school, which had been housed in a motel.[17]

Some responses along these lines came not from school districts per se, but from other opponents of charter schools. In Michigan a local office of the Michigan Education Association (MEA) raised a stir by writing a letter to a university president threatening various actions if the university chartered schools that did not meet the MEA's standards. These included close cooperation with the local school district and adherence to all provisions of relevant collective bargaining agreements. If the university chartered schools that fell outside these guidelines, the letter said, union members would not accept university students as student teachers, would not donate money to the university, and would not participate in university graduate or training programs.[18] In another incident a school district seeking to sell a vacant school building placed a restriction in the deed preventing its use as a school—a provision apparently aimed at blocking a local charter school from making use of the facility.[19]

—4. Districts can respond to fiscal stress not by improving, but by cutting back on popular programs (the Washington Monument strategy). One school district in Massachusetts announced that because of a charter school the district would have to eliminate art and advanced placement courses, reduce sports programs, suspend after-school services, and end tutoring programs.[20] In Colorado Jefferson County's school board president told the *Denver Post,* "For every charter school I approve I may have to tell someone that this will cut their student's sports program or bus ride, or renegotiate teacher salaries. To give to one place you have to take from another."[21] In 1995 the Denver Public Schools proposed a raft of budget cuts to apparently popular programs. In part in response to charter schools' costs, officials said, marching bands, sports, libraries, and enrichment activities would get the ax, and class sizes would rise.[22]

—5. Districts can ignore or peacefully coexist with charter schools. All of the responses already described typify the reaction expected of a monopoly supplier to the presence of competition. But in his famous discussion of monopoly Albert Hirschman makes a provocative suggestion, which is worth excerpting at some length because of its relevance here: "There are many other cases where competition does not restrain monopoly as it is supposed to, but *comforts and bolsters* it by unburdening it of some of its more troublesome customers. . . . If, as is likely, the mobile customers are most sensitive to quality, their exit, caused by the poor performance of the local monopolist, permits him to persist in his comfortable mediocrity. . . . Those who hold power in the lazy monopoly may actually have an interest in *creating* some limited opportunities for exit on the part of those whose voice might be uncomfortable."[23]

Based on this analysis one might conclude that, as long as charter schools remain a relatively small force, they may prove useful to school districts as safety valves. Instead of taking up time at school board meet-ings, harassing teachers and administrators, and making disparaging re-marks about the districts in the press, disgruntled parents and voters can occupy themselves with starting charter schools. School districts may also regard charter schools as an avenue through which to off-load students they regard as undesirable. Certain students may impose high financial costs on school districts because they have disabilities or require intensive assistance of other kinds. Certain students may drag down average district test scores. If charter schools are willing to serve high-cost and low-performing stu-dents, districts might regard their presence as a blessing rather than a curse.

Districts may gain other benefits from charter schools as well. In Douglas County, Colorado, for example, officials are contending with 10 percent annual enrollment growth (about 2,000 students per year), stim-ulating the need for massive capital expansion. In that context the district does not mind having 500 to 1,000 students housed in charter schools, which are responsible for finding their own facilities.[24] That factor more than any other may explain the different response charter schools have met in growing districts like that of Douglas County versus more stable-enrollment districts such as Denver.

The point of all these examples is that even if a charter school stimulates a response from its local school district, that response may not be aimed at improving education for the district's young people. In fact, in all five cases district actions might have the opposite effect. In the first four, districts divert resources from potentially quality-enhancing activities. In the fifth, to the extent that districts' most vocal critics exit, pressure on the districts to change for the better is reduced, not increased.

To be sure, anecdotes have surfaced in which districts have responded to the presence (or anticipated presence) of charter schools by improving their educational offerings. The most noted example is Boston's creation of "pilot schools," charterlike schools that operate within the Boston system but are free of many of the constraints imposed by district policy or collective bargaining agreements. Since the school system established pilot schools very shortly after the passage of charter legislation, its action has been widely cited by charter advocates as an example of the "ripple effects" charter schools can produce.[25] Similarly, Boulder Valley School District in Colorado established "focus schools," quasi-independent schools with a charterlike application process.[26] Also in Colorado, parents in Jefferson County, the state's largest school district, had long clamored for the expan-sion or replication of an oversubscribed alternative school established by the district many years ago. Despite the presence of 1,000 students on the waiting list and numerous such calls for expansion, including one by an internal committee of the district, the school board refused. After the charter law passed and parents began organizing a charter school, however, the district agreed to establish a new alternative program governed in part by those organizing the charter school. By spring of 1994 the district had more than doubled the number of alternative schools: some charter, some district run.[27] Many other such anecdotes populate the charter school literature.[28]

But these stories are much less common than the collection of other possible responses described above. One possible explanation, of course, is that the legislative compromises that limit competition have made these other strategies possible. Only because the potential for competition is so minimal have districts chosen to respond to charter schools in ways that do nothing to improve—and may in fact degrade—the quality of the education they offer. If charter schools were allowed to compete more intensely with public districts, threatening to attract a large percentage of students, districts might be forced to change for the better. Evidence that this kind of formidable competition might work comes from recent experience in Albany, New York, where the school system replaced staff members and financed new equipment and training at a school in which at least a sixth of the students had opted for private schools when given scholarships to do so.[29]

This response certainly applies to the fifth example: Hirschman's lazy monopolist wants "limited opportunities for exit," not the possibility of mass exodus. The Washington Monument response, too, assumes a rather limited loss of funds to charter schools. Faced with a massive loss of funds, one could argue, school districts could no longer afford to play public relations games with popular programs. But the first three responses—using the courts, the legislature, and nuisance tactics—seem likely only to intensify as competition grows more substantial. Even faced with many potential charter schools, a district still might find these responses more cost-effective than a wholesale revamping of its practices.

The reason districts might respond in these ways, even in the face of significant competition, is that reworking an entire school district for high performance is a very difficult piece of work. It is difficult in the technical sense that devising and implementing wide-ranging reforms are extremely complex and daunting tasks. This is true even for organizations completely immersed in highly competitive markets, as recent studies of corporate efforts to "reengineer" their operations have shown.[30] Wholesale change is also difficult because of the same political forces that make it difficult to pass relatively pure charter laws at the state level. Those with an interest in the status quo are likely to resist change even in the face of a loss in a district's competitive position. If wide-scale reform were easy to effectuate, surely it would already be more common in light of the now-incessant criticism of public schools and political pressure for significant improvement. Competition from charter schools may not be substantial enough to change the basic calculations most districts appear to have made.

The Replacement Thesis

For those who believe districts are unlikely to respond constructively to the presence of charter schools, the replacement thesis stands as the last hope of systemic impact. Perhaps charter schools will transform public education by gradually withdrawing students and funds from conventional districts until charter schools are in fact the primary vehicles for the delivery of public education. At this juncture, of course, the legislative compromises described in the previous section make the replacement hypothesis unrealistic. Nowhere in the country are charter schools approaching implementation on a scale on which one would regard them as replacing public schools.[31]

Like the other two mechanisms, though, the replacement mechanism might have trouble working even if the charter idea were enacted fully and without compromise by a state legislature. Replacement requires a massive increase in the independent supply of public education. The United States currently has some 88,000 public schools. Even if typical charter schools were the same sizes as the regular public schools they replaced, more than 40,000 would need to be created (or converted) just to half-replace the public system. Since charter schools are in fact typically about half the sizes of their conventional public school counterparts, half-replacement would actually require the creation or conversion of some 80,000 charter schools.

The prospects for the creation of that many completely new schools are bleak. Evidence from this study and other studies of charter school programs makes it clear that starting a new charter school from scratch requires an extraordinary effort.[32] Primary among the difficulties is locating a suitable facility and financing its purchase, lease, or renovation to meet the stringent requirements of school building codes. Charter school legislation does not generally provide any funds for this purpose, though some laws require school districts to make vacant space available to approved charter schools. In addition to preparing a facility, charter operators have numerous other tasks to perform before school opens: advertising for and filling teaching positions; marketing their schools to prospective families; conducting a selection process; fleshing out curricula and instructional strategies; learning about the various laws and regulations to which all public schools, including charter schools, are subject; acquiring equipment and furniture; and finding contractors and negotiating contracts for food services, custodial services, special education administration, bilingual education, and the like. All or most of this activity must be completed before public funds begin to flow. As a result, hundreds of volunteer hours go into everything from writing the application to staffing the school up front.

To cover the costs of start-up (and to compensate for a lack of economies of scale once open), many charter schools are raising substantial amounts of funds beyond the per-pupil public funds they receive. In Massachusetts private funds amounted to about 12 percent of charter schools' revenues in 1995–96. In Michigan nonstate funds accounted for almost 16 percent of charter schools' revenues in the same year. Fully fifteen of the twenty-four schools chartered by Central Michigan University for which full data are available would have been insolvent in 1995–96 without the infusion of nonstate funds.[33] Interviews with charter officials suggest that the existing crop of charter schools has been successful in mobilizing volunteers and tapping nonpublic funds. But would thousands of charter schools be able to do the same? Philanthropic resources and volunteer efforts that are available to a few high-profile schools might not stretch to cover a larger sector of charter schools.

It would appear, then, that the conversion of existing public or private schools would have to play a major role in this expansion of charter schools. Otherwise, the "charterization" of public schools would be akin to deregulating local telephone service by allowing dozens of companies to lay separate fiber optic networks throughout a city rather than arranging for would-be competitors to tap into the existing monopolist's infrastructure. It also seems unlikely that such a massive endeavor would be accomplished by 80,000 unconnected groups of individuals. More plausible is the scenario under which a handful of large organizations—whether for-profit outfits like the Edison Project or nonprofit efforts like New American Schools—would each sponsor a large number of charter schools nationwide. Whether such developments would be positive or negative is beyond the scope of this study. But it seems clear that the resulting charter school sector would look very little like today's fledgling band of charter schools.

Conclusion

As they are now constituted, charter school programs will have difficulty achieving the system-changing impact their proponents envision. In part they are limited by legislative compromises that diminish charter schools' ability to act as effective laboratories, competitors, or replacements for existing district schools. To give charter schools a real chance of motivating broader system reform, state legislatures will have to strengthen most charter laws substantially by allowing a wide range of groups to apply for charters, removing caps on the number of schools that may open, empowering bodies other than local school boards to issue charters, making charter schools legally autonomous from local school districts and freeing them up from state laws and regulations, and ensuring that full per-pupil funding follows children to charter schools.

In addition to advocating these policy changes, though, charter proponents also need to consider other ways to bolster charter schools' potential for impact as laboratories, competitors, and replacements. Since charter schools appear unlikely, even with legislative victories, to serve as laboratories for changes in practice at the school level, attention should be focused on charter school programs as laboratories for the design of new ways to organize systems of schools. We should use the charter experience to learn as much as we can about stimulating good proposals for school design from the field, reviewing those proposals effectively, exempting schools from most public school law while retaining a core of constraints, and designing systems of results-based accountability.

Legislative changes may make charter schools more viable competitors, but districts may continue to respond to competition with nonconstructive activities, such as court battles and nuisance tactics. Policymakers and advocates intent on beefing up charter schools' competitive potential would benefit from thinking about ways of making these responses less attractive—or even impossible. For example, one potential nuisance tactic is for districts to tie up funds that are destined to go to charter schools. Having the state education agency directly fund charter schools would make this tactic impossible.

Finally, for charter schools to act as competitors or replacements, policymakers and advocates need to pay attention to the supply of charter schools. Even with a pure charter law, the charter movement faces significant challenges in scaling up. Outside of government, educating potential charter operators about the opportunity, targeting philanthropic dollars to help prospective organizers plan, and providing technical assistance to applicants and schools should be priorities, functions that private resource centers for charter schools are performing in many states. Policy can also help make the supply of charter schools more robust by retooling administrative systems to minimize costly red tape and ensuring that charter schools have fair access to facilities funds, federal categorical programs, and other special funding streams.

Of course a small-scale, low-impact charter school sector may still be worth cultivating. If charter schools provide excellent educations to even a small number of students who would otherwise be ill served, they play a valuable role in American education. Perhaps the only way to develop the higher-impact variety of charter program is to begin with the version so common now in American states. But the real promise of the idea—what justifies the attention charter schools now receive from the media, policymakers, and academics—surely rests on the prospect of more systemic impact. At this stage in the development of charter programs, that potential remains untapped.

Appendix: Sources of Empirical Data for the Study

This study relied on in-depth field research in four states with charter school laws: Colorado, Georgia, Massachusetts, and Michigan. Since these states passed such different charter school laws, they provide an opportunity to analyze how different state laws have played out in practice. All four states adopted charter school legislation in 1993, and this study traced the implementation of the programs through the end of the 1995–96 school year. By that time charter schools in all four states had been operating for at least one year; some schools in Michigan and Colorado had been open for two years.

Three primary sources of information informed the analysis of charter school implementation in these states. First, a series of interviews was conducted in each state. Those interviewed in each state included the state government official or officials responsible for implementation of the charter school program; representatives of other public bodies responsible for approving and overseeing charter schools, if different from those responsible for implementation; representatives of at least three randomly selected charter schools; representatives of one or more organizations dedicated to supporting the development of charter schools (so-called friends' groups); and political leaders and staff members involved in crafting and monitoring charter legislation (governors' aides, legislators, and legislative staff members). Altogether, fifty-one individuals were interviewed for the study.

Second, public documents regarding charter schools were reviewed. Because the process of charter school selection and oversight differs from state to state, the nature of these documents differed from state to state as well. In general, though, these documents included charter school regulations; materials documenting the charter school selection process, such as application materials and scoring rubrics; charter school applications; records of proceedings of bodies charged with reviewing charter school applications; official documents produced in the review of charter school applications; profiles of approved charter schools; actual "charters," or contracts between charter schools and their authorizing agencies; official correspondence sent by authorizing agencies to all charter schools explaining policies and procedures; reports by authorizing agencies on the progress of the charter school program; reports by outside agencies on the progress of the charter school program; and annual reports prepared by charter schools on their finances and operations.

Last, over 400 news stories on the progress of charter school programs were reviewed. Stories were identified by conducting a NEXIS search for newspaper and magazine articles containing the word *charter* in close proximity to some variant of *school*.

Notes

1. Ted Kolderie, "The Charter Idea: Update and Prospects, Fall '95" (Public Services Redesign Project, Center for Policy Studies, University of Minnesota, Saint Paul, Minn. 1995).

2. Bryan C. Hassel, "Designed to Fail? Charter School Programs and the Politics of Structural Choice," Ph.D. diss., Harvard University, 1997. See appendix of this chapter for some details on the research design.

3. Terry M. Moe, "The Politics of Bureaucratic Structure," in John E. Chubb and Paul E. Peterson, eds., *Can the Government Govern?* (Brookings, 1989), pp. 267–329; Terry M. Moe, "The Politics of Structural Choice: Toward a Theory of Public Bureaucracy," in Oliver E. Williamson, ed., *Organization Theory: From Chester Barnard to the Present and Beyond* (New York: Oxford University Press, 1990), pp. 116–53.

4. It is important to make a distinction between *innovative* and *distinctive*. Charter schools are often quite distinctive from neighboring public schools. But they still might not be innovative if they resemble other schools elsewhere. Therefore, to say a school is not innovative is not to say it is providing a service that would be otherwise available locally. As one report on charter schools noted: "If you crave tea and all the local restaurant serves is coffee, the opening of a cafe stocked with Darjeeling and Oolong

can look like an extraordinary breakthrough." See Chester E. Finn, Jr., Bruno V. Manno, and Louann Bierlein, *Charter Schools in Action: What Have We Learned?* (Washington, D.C.: Hudson Institute, 1996), p. 21).

5. Colorado Department of Education, "Colorado Charter Schools, November 15, 1995, Charter Schools Approved and Operating," Memorandum; Massachusetts Department of Education, *The Massachusetts Charter School Initiative, 1996 Report* (Boston, 1996); Michigan Department of Education, *A Description of Michigan Public School Academies: 1995–96 Report to the House and Senate Committees in Education* (Lansing, 1996).

6. Perhaps one reason charter schools' curricula and practices do not look radically different from prevailing norms is their ultimate accountability to parents. It might be that, although parents who choose charter schools are looking for options different from conventional public schools, most are not eager to have their children become the subjects of drastic experiments.

7. Richard Elmore, "Getting to Scale with Good Educational Practice," *Harvard Educational Review* 66, no. 1 (1996), pp. 1–26.

8. Elmore, "Getting to Scale with Good Educational Practice," p. 13.

9. New American Schools. *Getting Stronger and Stronger. New American Schools Annual Report* (Arlington, Va., 1996).

10. Susan J. Bodilly and others, *Lessons from the New American Schools' Scale-Up Phase* (Santa Monica, Calif.: RAND, 1998).

11. Susan H. Fuhrman and Richard F. Elmore, *Ruling Out Rules: The Evolution of Deregulation in State Educational Policy* (New Brunswick, N.J.: Consortium for Policy Research in Education, 1995).

12. All four case study states cushion the financial impact on school districts in some respect. In Massachusetts subsequent legislation has appropriated funds to reimburse most districts at least partially for the losses they incur when students choose charter schools (see Robert Antonucci, "Charter School Reimbursement," memorandum to State Board of Education, January 3, 1997). In Georgia funding does not follow the child in any meaningful respect. Charter schools remain fiscally part of the school districts and are only conversions of public schools in any case. In Colorado initial legislation sought to limit the fiscal impact on districts by requiring charter schools to negotiate funding with districts, perhaps receiving as little as 80 percent of per-pupil operating revenues or 52 percent of actual per-pupil costs (see "State Average Per-Pupil Spending," memorandum to Bill Windler, August 22, 1995). Since districts presumably realize some cost savings when children leave, though, this amount still may represent a minimal net fiscal impact on districts. Michigan is the only state in this study where districts feel nearly the full financial effects of students' choices. Even there charter schools are not entitled to a share of district funds for capital expenditures.

13. Joan Richardson, "Lawsuit Targets Charter School; Academy Would Run Home School Network," *Detroit Free Press,* August 18, 1994 p. 1B; Joan Richardson, "Judge Halts Charter School Funding; Foes Say Support for Nonpublic Schools May Defy Constitution," *Detroit Free Press,* October 20, 1994 p. 2B; Joan Richardson, "Judge Strikes Down Charter-School Law; Engler, Supporters Promise to Fight," *Detroit Free Press,* November 2, 1994, p. 1A; Joan Richardson, "Charter School Funds Approved; Lawmakers also Revise Law to Try to Address Judge's Concerns," *Detroit Free Press,* December 15, 1994, p. 1B. In Massachusetts and Colorado parents filed lawsuits challenging the charter laws or specific actions taken pursuant to them. These lawsuits were not successful, and they were not filed

by districts. In fact, a school district was the defendant in the Pueblo, Colorado, case after closing two existing public schools and simultaneously opening a charter school. On the Massachusetts case see Jordana Hart, "Lawsuit Challenges Charter Schools," *Boston Globe,* June 23, 1995, p. 22; Paul Langner, "Charter School Foes Lose Court Ruling," *Boston Globe,* July 1, 1995, p. 20.

14. Tom Loveless and Claudia Jasin, "Starting from Scratch: Political and Organizational Challenges Facing Charter Schools," *Education Administration Quarterly* 34, no. 1 (1998), pp. 9–30.

15. Loveless and Jasin, "Starting from Scratch."

16. John Correiro, interview by author, Fall River, Mass., November 17, 1995.

17. Brendan Farrington, "Temple Defends Decision on Lease," *The Patriot Ledger,* May 13, 1996.

18. Joan Richardson, "Union Pressures State University over Charter Schools," *Detroit Free Press,* June 4, 1994.

19. Joan Richardson, "District Won't Sell a Building for Charter School," *Detroit Free Press,* September 27, 1994.

20. Loveless and Jasin, "Starting from Scratch," p. 23. In the federal government this perverse practice of cutting successful programs first has become known as the Washington Monument strategy after the Department of the Interior's "offer" to trim its budget by closing the Washington Monument, stimulating calls and letters from would-be tourists.

21. Janet Bingham, "Charter School Money a Trade-off; Public Education Could Suffer When Funds Spent on Alternatives," *Denver Post,* February 15, 1994.

22. Mark Stevens, "Programs May Be Cut by DPS; Grim Budget Picture Shown to School Board," *Denver Post,* May 19, 1995.

23. Albert O. Hirschman, *Exit, Voice, and Loyalty: Responses to Decline in Firms, Organizations, and States* (Harvard University Press, 1970), pp. 59–60 (emphasis in original).

24. Patrick Grippe, interview by author, Castle Rock, Colo., January 12, 1996.

25. Joe Nathan. *Charter Schools: Creating Hope and Opportunity for American Education* (San Francisco, Jossey-Bass, 1996), pp. 85–87.

26. William Windler, "Colorado's Charter Schools: A Spark for Change and a Catalyst for Reform," (Colorado State Department of Education, Denver), pp. 3–4.

27. Mary Ann Raywid, "The Struggles and Joys of Trailblazing," *Phi Delta Kappan* 76, no. 7 (1995), pp. 555–60. An interesting feature of all of these anecdotes is that they are all examples of districts emulating the institutional arrangements under which charter schools work rather than specific curricula or instructional approaches. This experience makes sense in light of the previous section's argument that the institutional arrangements under which charter schools function are the programs' most significant innovations, the ones most likely to diffuse.

28. Nathan, *Charter Schools,* pp. 88–92; Pioneer Institute for Public Policy Research, "Charter Schools: Fears and Facts," *Policy Directions* 1 (1995); Finn, Manno, and Bierlein, *Charter Schools in Action.*

29. Jeff Archer, "Voucher Proponents Claim Victory in Albany," *Education Week,* February 11, 1998, p. 5.

30. For example, James Champy, *Reengineering Management: The Mandate for New Leadership* (New York: HarperBusiness, 1995).

31. Exceptions to this generalization are most likely to emerge in school districts with very low enrollments, such as rural districts. In these areas a good-sized charter school could indeed overtake the district as the leading provider of public education. In

larger systems, where most students attend school, many more charter schools would have to open for replacement to occur.

32. For example, Finn, Manno, and Bierlein, *Charter Schools in Action.*

33. The Massachusetts Department of Education reports that $2 million in private donations were raised by charter schools in 1995–96 (*The Massachusetts Charter School Initiative*). Michigan calculation based on data from twenty-four schools chartered by Central Michigan University. Total revenue data from Michigan Department of Education, *A Description of Michigan Public School Academies.* State revenue data from Central Michigan University Resource Center for Charter Schools, *Annual Report Period Ending June 30, 1996* (Mount Pleasant, Mich., 1996).

Part Four

VOUCHERS FOR PRIVATE SCHOOLS

ELEVEN

Comparing Public Choice and Private Voucher Programs in San Antonio

R. Kenneth Godwin, Frank R. Kemerer, and Valerie J. Martinez

IN THIS CHAPTER we assess the impacts of school choice programs in San Antonio, Texas. We use the results of that assessment, along with results of other research, to examine equity concerns about school choice. In the last section of the chapter we present an outline of a school choice proposal that we believe will increase equity across income classes and improve academic performance.

San Antonio is a good site for investigating the consequences of school choice on low-income minority families. More than 70 percent of San Antonio's urban school children are Hispanic, and approximately 85 percent are from minority ethnic groups. Given that Hispanics have the highest school dropout rate in the nation, have a poverty level that surpasses that of African Americans, and are more segregated in schools than African Americans, our study has significant implications for that population group.[1] In 1991, 18 percent of low-income families residing in the San Antonio Independent School District (SAISD) sent their children to private schools,

Research reported in this chapter was supported by grants from the U.S. Department of Education, the Spencer Foundation, and the Walton Family Foundation.

and an additional 2 percent participated in the district's thematic choice program called the multilingual program. In Fall 1992 the Children's Educational Opportunity (CEO) Foundation increased the availability of private school choice for low-income families by providing partial scholarships to children throughout the San Antonio metropolitan area.

The CEO scholarship program offers tuition scholarships to low-income families in San Antonio so that they may enroll their children in private or public schools of their choice in grades one through eight.[2] Each scholarship covers half of a school's tuition, with a maximum of $750. Although low by private school standards in many parts of the country, the CEO scholarship has real value in San Antonio, where the average elementary school tuition is less than $1,500.

In the 1992–93 school year the CEO Foundation provided 936 students with scholarships. The foundation awarded scholarships on a first-come, first-chosen basis. Approximately half of the scholarships went to families whose children had attended public schools the previous year. By design, the other half of the scholarships were granted to eligible families whose children were already enrolled in private schools. Approximately 60 percent of CEO students enrolled in Catholic schools, 20 percent in nondenominational religious schools, 10 percent in Baptist schools, 1 percent in secular schools, and the remainder in religious schools of various denominations. The scholarship program was and remains heavily oversubscribed. During the duration of this study, there were more than 800 students on the waiting list, all of whom were enrolled in private schools.[3]

SAISD has an enrollment of 61,000 students; 81 percent are Hispanic, 12 percent are African American, and 7 percent are Anglo or Asian. Approximately 80 percent of the district's students receive free or reduced-price meals. SAISD initiated its multilingual choice program in the early 1980s to enhance the district's foreign language offerings. The multilingual program begins in the sixth grade. It includes instruction in the same essential elements required in all Texas public school districts, as well as special language enrichment through honors classes, accelerated pacing, and individualized instruction. Superior academic performance—as evidenced by test scores, grades, and teacher recommendations—determines admission.[4] Two middle schools and one high school house the multilingual program. For the 1992–93 school year SAISD admitted 675 students to the multilingual program. Due to enrollment limitations, SAISD rejected 307 students who applied and were eligible for the program. The presence of these rejected students allows us to partially compensate for the selection bias problem that faces almost all evaluation studies. However, because the selection process was not random, there may be differences between accepted and rejected students.[5]

Study Methodology

In August–September 1992 we used mail and telephone surveys of parents to collect baseline data on five categories of children:[6] (1) those who enrolled in the public multilingual program, (2) those who applied to the multilingual program, but could not enroll due to limited enrollment space, (3) those who received CEO scholarships and moved from public to private schools, (4) those who were already in private schools and applied to the CEO program, and (5) nonchoosers, those SAISD students who did not attempt to choose alternatives to their "attendance-zone" schools.[7] The response rate for the choosing families, categories one through four, was 48.5 percent. The response rate for the nonchoosers was 40 percent.[8]

The survey instruments requested standard socioeconomic and demographic information as well as opinions regarding children's past educational experiences, the extent of parental involvement with their children's education, and the importance of education relative to other values and goals. To maximize comparability with the evaluation of the Milwaukee public voucher program, we used survey instruments adapted from those used by John Witte and his colleagues in their evaluation of the Milwaukee Parental Choice Program.[9] In January 1994 we surveyed baseline respondents a second time. Eighteen months later (September 1995) we contacted the families for the final time. The response rates for these surveys were 64 percent and 61 percent, respectively. To better understand the educational decisions of choosing and nonchoosing families, we selected at least eight families from each group to participate in separate focus group sessions. These sessions were held in May 1995. The families selected included both two-member families and single heads of households. Families received $50 for their participation.

Student Data

The research team administered written questionnaires to students in grades six through eight during site visits to nine schools in 1993. We obtained completed questionnaires from 1863 students, approximately 54 percent of those eligible. The schools included the two SAISD multilingual schools, two comparable SAISD attendance-zone schools, and five private schools with the largest number of CEO students enrolled—three Catholic, one Baptist, and one nondenominational Christian school. Of the 1,863 respondents, 945 were from the multilingual schools, 588 from the attendance-zone public middle schools, 234 from Catholic schools, and 96 from the non-Catholic private schools. The survey requested standard demographic information and student opinions concerning school climate and the character of the instructional program.

We asked SAISD and the private schools to provide nationally normed standardized test scores for all students included in the study. The scores requested included those for the year prior to the study (1991–92) and each subsequent year of the study. Obtaining this information proved difficult for several reasons. First, students do not start testing until the third grade. Second, some private schools did not administer standardized tests in 1991–92, and many discontinued testing after 1993. Third, SAISD discontinued using a nationally normed test after 1993. This eliminated test scores for SAISD attendance-zone students, multilingual students, and students rejected by the multilingual program.

Teacher Data

In spring 1993 and fall 1994 we distributed written questionnaires to 1,113 teachers at 74 schools—34 SAISD public schools and 49 private schools with CEO students enrolled. The response rate was 46 percent. The survey requested information concerning a teacher's ethnicity, age, gender, education completed, and teaching experience. It also requested data concerning school goals, administrative style, teacher autonomy and influence, and pedagogical approaches. Finally we carried out structured group interviews with teachers at the nine schools from which we have student surveys.

Comparing Choosing Families with Nonchoosing Families

Our research shows that there are significant differences between choosing and nonchoosing families and between public and private choosing families.[10] Choosing families, whether public or private, have more years of education, higher incomes, higher employment levels, fewer children, a lower probability of being on welfare, a lower probability of being African American, and a higher probability of being two-parent families. Families who choose have much higher educational expectations for their children

Table 11-1. *Comparisons of Mean Scores for Characteristics of Nonchoosers, Multilingual Choosers, and Private School Choosers*

Variable	Nonchoosers	Public school choosers	Private school choosers
Demographic characteristics			
Female parent education	2.82	3.74	4.32**
Male parent education	2.89	3.81	4.24**
Family income	4.22	4.71	4.45
Female parent employment	0.35	0.57	0.45**
Male parent employment	0.73	0.80	0.80
Receiving federal assistance	0.35	0.16	0.15
Two-parent family	0.48	0.61	0.61
Number of children	3.51	3.00	2.90
Anglo	0.03	0.06	0.18**
Latino	0.62	0.73	0.71
African American	0.10	0.14	0.06**
Family values			
Educational expectations	3.47	4.43	4.43
Importance of religion	1.58	1.80	1.95**
Importance of ethnic values	1.50	1.60	1.70*
Tolerance score	11.42	13.82	15.21
Parental involvement in education			
Help with schoolwork	5.43	5.23	8.15**
Activity in child's school	1.85	1.98	3.09**
Child's education			
Child's test score	36.05	54.80	46.75**
N	1,375	424	1,001

*Differences between multilingual and private school choosers are significant at $p < .01$.

**Differences between multilingual and private school choosers are statistically significant at $p < .001$.

and are more active in their children's education both at home and at school. Finally, children who attempted to enroll in choice programs have higher standardized test scores.

Table 11-1 shows the differences between private school parents and parents whose children participate in a public choice program. Private school parents have more education but less income than parents of children who applied to the multilingual program. Private school choosers are more likely to be Anglos and less likely to be African Americans. Not surprisingly, private choosing families are significantly more religious. In addition, in the year prior to our survey parents of children who used the

CEO scholarships to move from public to private schools were more involved in their children's education than were parents of multilingual students. However, students using the CEO scholarships have substantially lower test scores and lower family incomes than students who applied to the multilingual program. The differences between public and private school choosers largely reflect the differences in program design. The CEO program emphasizes giving low-income children private school opportunities, whereas the SAISD program emphasizes past academic performance and future academic potential.

Changes over Time in Satisfaction with Schools

A critical factor in the decision to choose a private school is parents' perceptions of the quality of public schools. When asked to rate their children's past public schools, 64 percent of CEO parents assigned a grade of C or worse. In sharp contrast, only 18 percent of SAISD parents assigned grades this low to their children's public schools. The critical components of this grade were parents' satisfaction with how much their children learned and with the school's safety and discipline. Table 11-2 shows the evaluations of these factors by CEO parents who moved their children from public to private schools. The table provides ratings for the year prior to moving their children to private schools, after one year in private school, and after three years in private school. When parents used the CEO vouchers to move their children from public to private school, their satisfaction with both the amount their child learned and with school discipline increased dramatically. Although this satisfaction diminishes slightly by the end of the

Table 11-2. *CEO Parents' Ratings of Children's Learning and of Discipline in the Schools*[a]

Percent

Parents' rating	Amount child learned			School discipline		
	1991–92	*1992–93*	*1994–95*	*1991–92*	*1992–93*	*1994–95*
Very satisfied	19	60	41	12	56	41
Satisfied	40	31	51	40	33	54
Dissatisfied	24	5	7	27	8	2
Very dissatisfied	18	4	6	21	2	2
N	351	326	61	344	327	61

a. The question asked was, "How satisfied were you with the following last year?" Because response rates in the final year of the survey were low, great care should be taken in making generalizations from these data.

third year, parents' satisfaction remained much higher with their child's private school than with past public schools.

Among CEO parents, if a child could not enroll in one school, there typically were other private school alternatives. This was not the case for families who applied to the multilingual program but were not admitted because of space limitations. Our sample of SAISD choice families included not only 319 families whose children enrolled in the thematic multilingual program, but also 94 families whose children met the program's qualifications but who did not enroll because the program lacked space for them. We compared these groups with each other and with our random sample of SAISD attendance-zone students.

Parents whose children enrolled in the multilingual program were pleased with their schools. As table 11-3 indicates, more than 90 percent indicated that they were either very satisfied or satisfied with the amount their children learned in the multilingual program and with the schools' discipline. However, table 11-3 also shows that the satisfaction level dropped precipitously for parents whose children were eligible for the choice program but who were not admitted. Among the parents of rejected children, the percentage of those who were dissatisfied with the amount their children learned increased from 13.8 percent to 24.4 percent, whereas the percentage of those who were dissatisfied with school discipline jumped from 10.5 percent to 20.6 percent. The scores for other sets of SAISD parents remained essentially unchanged.

Our focus group interviews showed that many parents whose children were rejected by the multilingual program were bitter about this decision. Some believed that the enrollment criteria were unfair and biased. Parents of students rejected by the public choice program reported not only a substantial drop in their satisfaction with and involvement in their children's schools, but also a significant decline in their participation in their children's education at home.

Surveys of parents with children in private schools typically showed that the parents were more satisfied with their children's schools and more involved with their children's education both at home and at school than were parents of students in attendance-zone schools. An important issue in the debate over expanding choice to private schools, however, is whether involved parents become private choosers or whether having children in private schools increases parental involvement. In September of the first year of the study we questioned parents concerning their satisfaction and involvement with their children's schools during the previous year and the frequency with which they participated in at-home learning activities. We

Table 11-3. *SAISD Parents' Ratings of Children's Learning and of Discipline in the Schools*
Percent

Parents' rating	Amount child learned						School discipline					
	Nonchoosers		Thematic enrollees		Thematic rejected		Nonchoosers		Thematic enrollees		Thematic rejected	
	91–92	92–93	91–92	92–93	91–92	92–93	91–92	92–93	91–92	92–93	91–92	92–93
Very satisfied	26.7	34.5	54.7	49.6	56.4	31.7	22.5	29.4	50.8	47.9	44.2	30.8
Satisfied	58.3	52.3	42.1	43.8	29.8	43.9	63.3	57.7	41.0	44.6	45.3	48.7
Dissatisfied	12.1	10.3	2.5	5.0	13.8	22.0	9.9	8.4	5.4	3.3	10.5	10.3
Very dissatisfied	2.9	2.4	0.6	1.7	0	2.4	4.3	4.5	2.9	4.1	0	10.3
N	1,346	493	318	121	94	41	1,346	493	318	121	94	41

Table 11-4. *Average Scores on Parents' Involvement and Participation*

Measure	SAISD attendance zone families			CEO families whose children moved from public schools		
	1991–92	1992–93	1995–96	1991–92 (to public schools)	1992–93 (to private schools)	1995–96 (to private schools)
School grade[a]	87	87	87	77	88**	89
Average school involvement[b]	2.62	2.84	2.70	4.52	4.43	4.02*
Average participation at home[b]	5.53	5.68	4.66*	7.82	7.08*	4.33**
N	1,144	398	290	351	207	61

a. A grade of 90 or above = A, 80–89 = B, 70–79= C, 60–69 = D, and below 60 = F.
b. Scores could range from 0 to 11.
*The change from the previous year's score is statistically significant at the .05 level.
**The change from the previous year's score is statistically significant at the .01 level.

repeated these questions eighteen months later and then again two years after that. Table 11-4 shows that nonchoosing parents tended to give their public schools very high ratings and that these ratings continued throughout the period studied. On the other hand, the families who moved their children from public to private schools rated their previous public schools significantly lower than nonchoosing families. Once their children had changed to private schools, these parents rated their new schools highly. This satisfaction ratings remained high for parents whose children remained in the program. Table 11-4 shows that in the final year of our study the number of CEO respondents dropped dramatically.[11] We do not know whether the responses of those remaining in the study reflect the opinions of those who did not respond to the final survey.

Although choosing a private school increases the satisfaction level of choosing parents, it does not increase their participation levels. Compared to nonchoosing parents, CEO parents who moved their children from public to private schools involved themselves significantly more in their children's schools. However, moving from a public to a private school does not increase involvement. As a child grows older, whether the child enrolls in a public or a private school, school involvement drops. This decline is greater for private school parents than for public school parents, but the reason for this is the much higher level of initial involvement of CEO parents.

Student Attrition from Choice Programs

Employing a combination of focus group interviews, surveys, and school records, we examined student attrition from both school choice programs. Among families who used the CEO scholarships to transfer their children from public to private schools, the student dropout rate over the three-year period was 49.6 percent. Students were most likely to drop out of the program during their first year and when they moved from middle school to high school. Catholic students, students whose parents attended church more frequently, and students whose parents had attended private schools were significantly less likely to drop out of the CEO program. Our focus groups found that families whose children remained in the CEO program typically made their decisions to send their children to religious schools either before or shortly after the children were born. In contrast, parents of students who dropped out made their decisions in response to frustration with public schools. Almost all parents who moved their children from public to private schools thought that the CEO scholarships were too small. In addition, transportation to the private schools proved to be a greater problem than these parents expected.

The multilingual program also has a high dropout rate. Less than a third of the students who entered the SAISD multilingual choice program remained there for all seven years. We examined possible factors that encouraged student retention by comparing students who remained in the program at least one year with students who dropped out during their first year. Three variables strongly affected student retention in the public choice program: a student's participation in the decision to join the multilingual program, whether the student's closest friend attended the same school, and the student's standardized math score. Using the three factors we could correctly predict who would remain in the program with 79 percent accuracy.

Impact of School Choice on Student Achievement

As already indicated, SAISD discontinued using a nationally normed test for its students in 1993, and the CEO program did not enforce its requirement of standardized testing for its scholarship students. These factors make comparisons between public and private school students difficult. SAISD helped overcome this problem by providing 1992 test results for all students in grades three through eleven. Figure 11-1 shows that in the third grade the average math and reading rankings for SAISD students were the forty-fifth

Figure 11-1. *SAISD Nationally Normed Standardized Test Scores*

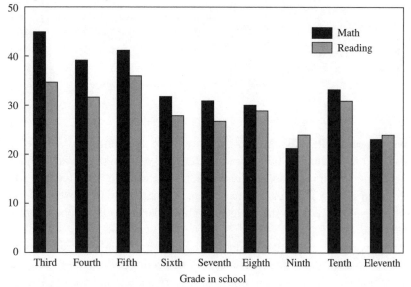

Mean percentile ranking

Source: San Antonio Independent School District.

and thirty-fifth percentiles, respectively. By the eleventh grade the average scores had fallen to the twenty-third and twenty-fourth percentiles. These results are consistent with our own findings for SAISD test scores. At almost every grade level the average standardized test scores for SAISD attendance-zone students dropped from 1992 to 1993.

We have shown elsewhere that, after controlling for past academic performance and socioeconomic and demographic characteristics of the students, students in both public choice and private schools have more positive changes in test scores than do students in attendance-zone schools.[12] As table 11-5 makes clear, however, regardless of the type of school a student attends, the inner-city environment of San Antonio is not conducive to educational achievement. The students who fare worst are those who applied to the multilingual program and were rejected.

We have standardized test scores for 263 CEO students in the baseline academic year. The high dropout rate from the CEO program and the failure of many private schools to continue giving nationally normed standardized tests reduced the number of students for whom we have baseline and final year standardized test scores to eighty-eight. For these few students the

Table 11-5. *Average Middle School Students' Changes in Nationally Normed Math and Reading Scores from 1992 to 1993*

Subject	CEO private school	Enrolled in multilingual program	Rejected by multilingual program	Public attendance-zone school
Change in math scores	−0.06	−1.17	−4.49	−2.11
Change in reading scores	2.14	1.16	−3.67	−0.16
N	70	306	51	433

average percentile rankings improved over the entire period by 0.79 in math and 0.35 in reading. In other words, after four years in the private schools there was essentially no difference in test scores. As the students who remained in the CEO program may not be comparable to those who dropped out, to generalize from these eighty-eight students to other populations is risky.

To overcome the limitation created by the small number of students for whom we have 1991–92 scores and 1995–96 scores, we counted each year for which a student had both that year's score and the previous year's test score as a separate case. For example, the scores of a student who received a CEO scholarship in the fourth grade, remained in the program all four years, and took a nationally normed test each year constituted four cases. Counting each year's change as a case gave more than 700 observations for both math and reading. Because schools do not give standardized tests until the third grade, students who first received CEO scholarships in the second grade could not have changes in test scores until the final two years of our study. Students who began the first grade in 1992 could have scores only for the last year of the program. The drawbacks of this procedure were that cases and their error terms were not independent, the scores of older students were given greater weight than those of younger students, and students who remained in the program counted more than those who dropped out. The advantages of the procedure were that it included students who dropped out after the first year and it increased the number of cases by more than 800 percent. Using this procedure we found that, on average, for each year a student was in the program the student's percentile ranking dropped by 0.12 in math and increased by 0.44 in reading. Neither the test score results for the multilingual program students nor those for private school students were substantively significant until we compared them with the substantial drop in test scores that occurred for SAISD attendance-zone students. Figure 11-1 showed that SAISD students, on average, lost 2 percen-

Table 11-6. *Teacher Credentials and Experience*
Percent

Credential or experience	Private elementary school	SAISD elementary school	Private middle school	SAISD multilingual middle school	SAISD attendance-zone middle school
State teacher certification[a]	53	100	50	86	96
Master's degree	12	30	18	51	44
Less than five years' experience	38	15	44	23	4
N	140	160	73	79	54

a. The question asked of respondents was whether they were certified. It was not about temporary or provisional certification. Some teachers who fell into the latter category may have responded negatively.

tile rankings per year in math and 1.4 rankings in reading for every year they remained in attendance-zone schools. In contrast, neither multilingual nor CEO students experienced significant declines in test scores.

What accounts for the differences between the outcomes of choice and attendance-zone schools? In the case of San Antonio, it certainly is not because of smaller class sizes, greater teacher training, or higher teacher salaries. Texas state law mandates that elementary schools have teacher-student ratios of one to twenty-two, and fewer than 10 percent of the SAISD teachers reported having classes larger than twenty-five. In contrast, 27 percent of private school teachers reported class sizes larger than twenty-five. As table 11-6 indicates, private school teachers are less likely than SAISD teachers to have graduate degrees, to hold certification, and to have lengthy teaching experience. Similarly, multilingual teachers are less likely than attendance-zone teachers to hold certification and have less experience than attendance-zone middle school teachers. Our examination of the physical facilities found that the public schools, on average, have better facilities and better equipment than private schools. And, to the extent that tuition represents most of the actual costs of private schools, SAISD spends, on average, more than twice as much per pupil as private schools.

What Accounts for the Success of Choice Schools?

There are three general explanations of the success of choice schools. The first is that market forces compel choice schools, particularly private schools, to outperform their competitors and to respond to the demands of their customers.[13] In order to respond, choice schools give principals and teachers greater authority and autonomy, and they are less controlled by centralized bureaucracies. Bryk, Lee, and Holland provide the second explanation of the greater success of choice schools.[14] They argue that choice schools are more successful because they are smaller, they have a stronger sense of mission, and parents, students, and teachers feel part of a community. All of these factors facilitate learning, particularly by at-risk students. Although Bryk and his colleagues studied Catholic schools, there is no a priori reason that their findings are not generalizable to other schools. The third explanation of the success of choice schools concerns the composition of the student bodies in those schools. Education is a good that those who consume it also help to produce. Not only do teachers teach students; students teach themselves and each other. And more motivated and higher-achieving classmates, on average, make better teachers.[15] The self-selection of more highly motivated and higher-achieving students for choice schools encourages students to teach each other and to set peer group norms that emphasize academic achievement. Having better students and more involved parents also encourages schools to require more demanding curricula, and it leads teachers to have higher expectations of their students.

Notice that although the three explanations of the success of choice schools are not mutually exclusive, the policy implications of the first and second explanations differ from those of the third. If competition is the primary reason for the success of choice schools, a publicly funded voucher plan should improve the education of all categories of students in all types of schools. Competition will force low-performing schools out of business and encourage less effective schools to adopt the techniques of those that are more effective. If Bryk and his colleagues are correct, governments should adopt policies that encourage smaller schools where parents, teachers, and students agree on each school's mission. Increasing the number of charter schools and thematic schools as well as instituting a voucher program would improve educational outcomes. And, if having a sectarian mission encourages community and learning in schools, choice policies should include public funding for sectarian schools.

What happens if characteristics of the student bodies rather than characteristics of the schools explain the better outcomes of choice schools? If the success of choice schools depends on having student bodies composed largely of higher-achieving students and more involved parents, there are likely to be only a limited number of successful schools in the inner cities. Not all students can be above average, and many parents are not involved in their children's educations. Because different social classes have different sets of educational preferences and because many parents are unwilling or unable to participate vigorously in the choice process, expanding school choice could increase inequalities among students.

If the previous paragraph describes the probable outcomes of increasing choice, public policy must decide what distributional outcomes it prefers and choose the educational policies that are most likely to lead to those outcomes. For example, if government wishes to maximize the total test scores of students in an area, research must identify the mix of high-, medium-, and low-achieving students that will achieve that goal. Then the government should implement the choice plan that would lead to that mix. If society wishes to maximize outcomes for the most motivated and talented students, education policy should include large subsidies for programs for gifted and talented students and encourage schools to group students by expected achievement levels. Many argue that increasing choice will achieve exactly this result. Choosing a school is complicated, and parents who do it best are those with well-formed educational expectations, greater education, and a strong achievement orientation. Allowing these families to cluster in a few schools will segregate children according to the socioeconomic characteristics of their parents as well as the talents of the children.[16] Finally, society could choose to reduce inequalities of educational outcomes by prohibiting most forms of choice and integrating all students in a geographic area. Government could achieve this by busing students across districts and using the motivation and talents of students as the bases for equally allocating students who have the most positive impacts on their classmates.

Evidence from San Antonio

The interview data from San Antonio's choice programs provide some support for all three explanations of why students in choice schools outperform students in attendance-zone schools. Those who advocate a market approach to education predict that private schools will be more responsive to parents, give greater autonomy to teachers, and be less bureaucratic. Our interviews showed that parents who moved their children from public to private schools became much more satisfied with school performance (see table 11-2). Private school teachers have greater autonomy and influence in their schools. Fifty-six percent of private school teachers compared with 43 percent of public school teachers reported having moderate or great influence over school goals. Private schools also have fewer regulations and less bureaucratic intervention than their public school counterparts.

The interviews with teachers and students supported the hypothesis that private schools have a stronger sense of community. Eighty-seven percent of teachers at private schools reported working together as a team compared to 58 percent of teachers at school attendance-zone. Similarly, fewer than 10 percent of private school teachers compared to 36 percent of teachers at attendance-zone schools reported that their schools were not conducive to learning. Private school teachers were much more likely than public school teachers to know and agree with their schools' missions. In addition, students in private schools held more positive attitudes toward their schools, classmates, and teachers than did students in either multilingual or attendance-zone schools.[17]

Table 11-1 shows that choice schools have higher-achieving students and more educated and involved parents. The question is whether the characteristics of the student body or the characteristics of the school account for the changes in test scores. Our San Antonio data support the importance of peer influence (see table 11-5). The largest changes in standardized test scores occurred among students who experienced the greatest changes in the academic characteristics of their peers. Students who moved from attendance-zone schools to private schools showed the largest increase in test scores, 4.62 points in reading. Students whom the multilingual program rejected and who lost many of their academic peers to the multilingual schools experienced the largest decline in scores, 4.49 points in math and 3.67 points in reading.[18] As our data include a relatively small number of students from a single city, we are unwilling to generalize confidently from these data. As we shall show in the next section, however, the San Antonio data are consistent with those of larger national studies.

All three explanations of the greater success of choice schools include the expectation that choice schools will have higher standards and goals for students. This certainly was the case in San Antonio. More than 60 percent of teachers at private middle schools and at the multilingual middle schools assigned more than fifteen minutes of homework a class period. In comparison, only 35 percent of the teachers at SAISD attendance-zone schools assigned more than fifteen minutes of homework. Student surveys confirmed teachers' reports. Sixty-four percent of private school students said that their teachers assigned a lot of homework, compared with 49 percent of the students at SAISD multilingual schools and only 34 percent of students at attendance-zone schools. Students at choice schools were also more likely to complete their homework than were students at attendance-zone schools. Approximately 60 percent of private school students and students participating in the multilingual program reported that they usually did their homework. This compares with 42 percent of students at attendance-zone schools.[19]

As anticipated, teachers in the multilingual program expected their students to perform at or above grade level. The same was true of private schools, where a majority of teachers expected that 90 percent or more of their students would be performing at or above grade level by the end of the year. In contrast, only 35 percent of attendance-zone middle school teachers foresaw even half of their students performing at grade level by the end of the year. While the expectations of all three sets of teachers accurately reflected the standardized test performance of their students, the expectations of teachers may become self-fulfilling prophecies.

Results from Other Studies of Educational Outcomes

The San Antonio study, because it included only one school district, could not test the importance of competition to school performance. Hoxby's study came closest to testing the impacts of competition among producers.[20] She examined the effects of public school choice as measured by the enrollment concentrations of students within school districts in metropolitan areas. She reasoned that having many school districts within a metropolitan area makes it easier for families to exercise school choice by changing school districts. It is also easier for upper-income families to cluster together. To analyze student outcomes Hoxby used the National Longitudinal Survey of Youth (NLSY), a panel study of 12,676 men and women fourteen to twenty-two years of age in 1979 who had been surveyed every year since 1979. These data allowed Hoxby to control for each respondent's ethnicity, sex, number of siblings, birth order, parents' education, and religious affiliation. NLSY students took the Armed Forces Qualifications Test (AFQT), and Hoxby used those scores, high school graduation, highest grade of school attained, and wage at age twenty-four as her measures of educational outcomes.

Hoxby's results show that increasing the number of school districts did increase ethnic and income segregation. However, it also decreased educational costs and improved all student outcome variables. The greatest improvements occurred among the more advantaged students. When Hoxby added data on private schools to her study, she found that increasing enrollment in private schools in a metropolitan area improved the educational outcomes for public school students.[21] These results indicate that competition among educational producers decreases costs and improves educational outcomes. Because Hoxby's data include only information on the metropolitan area in which students resided rather than on the schools they attended, we must be careful in generalizing from her results. She could not examine the effects of student body composition or other school effects on individual students or sets of students. Nevertheless, her results suggest that competition and decentralization improve learning outcomes.

Factors such as competition, rigor of the curriculum, amount of homework, teacher expectations, and sense of community explain some of the difference between the performance of students in choice and attendance-zone schools. However, a large and growing body of literature shows that the characteristics of students' classmates may be the most important factors in explaining the success of students in choice schools. Using data from the studies of High School and Beyond (HSB), the National Education Longitudinal Survey (NELS), the National Longitudinal Survey of Youth (NLSY), and case studies of choice programs in several cities, numerous authors have found that peer effects are critical influences on academic performance. Although students in choice schools tend to outperform students in attendance-zone schools, controlling for student body composition eliminates most of the observed difference in changes in standardized test scores.[22] For example, although Bryk and his colleagues argue that a sense of community is an important factor in the success of Catholic schools, their data show that student body composition variables have the largest impacts on student outcomes.[23] Other studies using different data sets and different statistical techniques have had similar results. There are many reasons that student body composition influences academic achievement, but the most important are that students teach other students and that, especially after the fifth grade, students rather than teachers set the norms for academic achievement.[24]

Unfortunately, although most studies show that being in choice schools helps the students who attend them, there are few data on whether school choice harms the most disadvantaged students who are left behind. Again, Hoxby's research comes closest to answering this question. Her analysis of the effects of competition in a metropolitan area showed that it not only increased the average AFQT scores of more advantaged students, it *decreased* the probability that a student in a metropolitan area would rank in the lowest quartile on the AFQT. Having more school districts in a metropolitan area also increased the high school graduation rates of disadvantaged students.[25]

There is an extremely important exception to the generalization that controlling for student body characteristics eliminates the differences between public and private schools. That exception is the increase in the performance of low-income and minority students who attend Catholic schools. Even after controlling for student body composition and the number of math courses, Bryk and his colleagues found that Catholic schools increase test scores for at-risk students.[26] Using high school graduation and the probability of attending college as outcome measures, several authors have found that attending Catholic high schools makes a statistically and substantively significant impact on the performance of minority students.[27] Neal found that after controlling for students' socioeconomic character- istics, Catholic school students were 45 percent more likely to graduate from high school than public school students and 245 percent more likely to graduate from college.[28] As in studies using test scores as the outcome variable, the greatest gains in graduation rates occurred for students whose achievement test scores were in the bottom half of the distribution.

Steinberg and his colleagues provide a possible cause for the positive performance of minority students in Catholic Schools.[29] Their research on peer group influence in attendance-zone schools found that peer pressure by fellow African-American and Latino students coerces minority students to do poorly. Good grades mean that the student has sold out and surrendered to the "white culture." This pressure is so strong that the steps parents take to facilitate their children's school success are severely undermined. Stein- berg argues that the positive results of Catholic schools occur because in parochial schools minority students are exposed to a higher proportion of minority peers with high educational aspirations and good study habits.

Equity and Choice

The potential of school choice to sort students by ethnicity, social class, motivation, and achievement raises three important equity issues. First, if putting the higher-performing students together enhances their education, skimming them from neighborhood schools may harm those left behind. Valerie Lee summarizes this view: "By allowing more motivated and better informed families to seek out what they see as better educational environ- ments for their children, the environments from which they exit are certainly impoverished in some fundamental way."[30] From this perspec- tive, increasing school choice increases social inequality and injustice. Students who are sufficiently lucky to have exceptional academic skills or parents who value education highly will be winners as greater school choice will cluster these students in a few schools where the environments en- courage learning. Students whose academic talents are insufficient to be chosen by magnet schools or whose parents either are not involved or face severe information or language barriers become losers. Choice will leave these students in low-performing schools; schools made worse by the exit of higher-performing students and more involved parents.

Opponents of increased choice, especially choice that includes private schools, are fond of quoting Albert Hirschman's justly famous book *Exit, Voice, and Loyalty.*[31] They maintain that education policy should stress not the private benefits of education to individuals, but its benefits to the common good of the community. To achieve this common good, policy should make it more difficult for more motivated students and more involved parents to exit the inner-city public schools. Forcing more involved parents to keep their children in attendance-zone schools will make the voices of parents more effective and will force public schools to become more responsive, effective, and efficient. Keeping more motivated students in neighborhood schools will improve the educational opportunities of the more disadvantaged students. Reducing the opportunities to exit will improve public schooling without creating the increased inequality that choice may promote.[32] From this perspective the composition of a school's student body is a social resource that government should control and allocate. A fair allocation of these resources is one that keeps resources in neighborhood public schools by reducing parents' educational choices.

This perspective, however, raises a second equity issue: Why should the children of poor but motivated parents in the inner city have fewer opportunities than children of parents who live in the suburbs? The argument for denying exit to inner-city families ignores the inequalities of educational opportunity that segregated neighborhoods and segregated public schools cause. More than two-thirds of all African-American students and almost three-fourths of all Latino students in the public schools attend predominantly minority schools. More than a third of these students are in schools where more than 90 percent of students are from minority ethnic groups.[33] A student in an intensely segregated minority school is fourteen times as likely to be in a high-poverty school as a student in a school with fewer than 10 percent black or Latino students. This powerful link between racial segregation and poverty is a central element in perpetuating the educational inequality of minority students.[34] Massey and Denton document that segregation concentrates the consequences of unemployment, welfare dependency, and teenage childbearing in inner-city schools. This creates a culture that devalues schooling and stresses attitudes and behaviors hostile to educational success.[35] Therefore, the currently dominant institution of choice—selection of housing—clusters students in exactly the ways that the opponents of choice decry. To reduce the exit opportunities of low-income minorities without forcing children of higher-income families to share the burden of being a resource to the most disadvantaged seems inconsistent and unjust. We believe that it is inequitable for society to allow upper- and middle-income families to segregate their children from the students in the inner cities while denying that option to highly motivated inner-city families who cannot afford housing in the suburbs or enrollment in private schools.[36]

The third equity issue concerns the right of parents to choose the values that their children will learn. Stephen Gilles's chapter in this volume provides an excellent justification of public funding for a voucher program based on this right. Simply put, the absence of public funding for private schools denies distributive justice to low-income families whose values are inconsistent with those taught in the public schools.[37] School choice, including the choice of sectarian schools, was once the liberal solution to the problem of seeing that every student received a good education. John Stuart Mill urged the state to require a good education for every child, but he denied the right of the state to provide it. Arguing for many competing experiments in education, Mill referred to state-controlled education as "a mere contrivance for molding people to be exactly like one another."[38] In more recent times critics of the state's monopoly on publicly funded education have argued that it violates the fundamental separation of powers, is inconsistent with the values advanced by the First and Fourteenth Amendments, denies distributive justice, and discourages a free and open society.[39] Proponents of publicly funded private school choice maintain that societies that cherish freedom of expression will provide educational options to all families, not just the wealthy.[40]

The preceding discussion of the first and second equity issues assumes that choice will sort students in ways that harm the most disadvantaged in society. But is this necessarily true? Is it possible to design choice programs where sorting occurs, but it does not exacerbate existing social inequalities? Might not the improvements that choice can effect through competition and the development of a sense of community outweigh any harms that sorting may cause? Certainly Hoxby's chapter in this book suggests that the benefits of competition among educational producers outweigh the educational costs of sorting, even for those students who are most disadvantaged. In addition, how much weight should a society based on liberal democratic principles give to the increases in parental rights that a voucher program would provide? In the following section we briefly summarize existing choice programs and their benefits and harms.

Public Choice and Equity

Housing segregation has concentrated many social pathologies in the inner cities and has deprived the students who live there of equal educational opportunity. To what degree do public choice programs reduce these inequities? After residence selection, magnet schools represent the most common form of public school choice. They enroll an average of 20 percent of high school students in large urban districts, often skimming those students who have greater talents and skills than do other students in the district.[41] Better-educated parents tend to select magnet schools because of perceived academic excellence. Even when a student's past academic performance is not a selection criterion, magnet schools tend to underrepresent low-income, African-American, Latino, bilingual, and low-test-score students.[42] Our analysis of thematic schools in San Antonio indicates that their effects are similar to those of magnet schools. Therefore, for nonchoosers magnet and thematic schools reinforce the negative effects of residential patterns by removing higher-achieving students and more involved parents from neighborhood schools.

Several states have hoped to increase choice for inner-city families by allowing open enrollment within and across school districts and by encouraging charter schools. Open enrollment allows students to attend any public school in the state.[43] Charter schools reduce bureaucratic regulations while encouraging innovation. Proponents of charter schools expect them to increase educational opportunities for less advantaged students. Unfortunately, the outcome of open enrollment program has been greater segregation. As with magnet schools, families of higher socioeconomic status are more likely to participate in these programs because they have greater resources to pay for transportation and greater access to information.[44] In addition, interdistrict open enrollment will not significantly increase educational equity because students in the receiving districts have first priority for enrollment in their districts, and the current incentive structures facing suburban schools mean that they will accept few inner-city students. Intradistrict open enrollment has limited effects, because most attendance-zone schools within the inner-city districts face all the problems that a society segregated by ethnicity and income has created.

It is too early to tell what effects charter schools will have on the educational outcomes of high-risk students. Bruno Manno suggests that charter schools do not skim the best students from neighborhood schools. However, a comprehensive analysis of the charter school program in Texas found that although many high-risk students enroll in charter schools, they do not enroll in the same charter schools as students from families of higher socioeconomic status.[45] In other words, charter schools may increase educational options, but they also increase sorting by socioeconomic status.

In summary, public school choice appears to have exactly the effects that opponents of choice fear: it sorts students by socioeconomic status and student achievement. Although public school choice may help choosers in the inner cities, it may harm nonchoosers. Public choice does not increase opportunities for low- and middle-income families to choose the values their children will learn in school. Can private choice improve this situation?

Private Choice and Equity

The most comprehensive data on private school choice come from experiences in other countries. Research concerning publicly subsidized private choice programs in Great Britain, France, and the Netherlands indicates that subsidized private choice tends to have effects similar to those of public choice programs. Middle- and upper-middle-class families are more likely than working-class families to participate in these programs. Subsidized private choice also encourages ethnic and religious segregation. Unless policy design strongly encourages income integration, subsidized private choice reinforces and perpetuates existing class structures.[46]

As discussed by Jay Greene and his colleagues in this volume, the Milwaukee and Cleveland voucher programs show that public funding of private school choice need not skim the best students from attendance-zone schools, nor must it reinforce existing class structures. Who participates in voucher programs depends upon, among other things, who is eligible to receive a voucher, its size, the types of private schools that participate, whether or not the program pays for transportation, and access to information about the program. The Afro-centric and bilingual orientation of the private schools that participate in the Milwaukee program discourages participation by Anglos. The availability of religious schools in Cleveland and San Antonio encourages participation by families who value religion highly. The requirement in San Antonio that the participating families pay at least half the tuition and all transportation costs leads to participation by students with higher average family income in San Antonio than in Milwaukee and Cleveland. These experiments with vouchers show that although publicly subsidized private choice in other countries has increased ethnic and class segregation, it is possible for policymakers to design voucher plans that do not have this effect.

Table 11-7. Comparison of Choice Alternatives and Their Likely Outcomes

Type of choice	Mechanism	Liberty rights	Equity of choice	Educational benefits	Educational costs
A. No publicly supported choice except through school district and housing market	Housing prices and ethnic segregation	For those families who can pay for private schools	Ability to choose depends upon family income and the level of housing integration in the area.	Benefits children attending schools with high-SES student bodies	Harms low-income and minority students by segregating them into inner-city schools
B. Magnet and thematic schools	Enrollment by interest, past achievement, or random selection. Family, student, or teacher may initiate.	Same as A	Provides greater choice to active, educated parents and to high-achieving children	Benefits students who attend choice schools. Improves integration if the policy mandates this	May harm the students left behind when more skilled students and more active parents exit
C. Open enrollment within and across districts	Families initiate requests. Some states limit to changes that do not harm racial balance.	Same as A	Same as B; especially helpful to families who can pay transportation costs	Benefits students who transfer to schools with higher-SES student bodies	Same as B. The policy increases segregation unless regulations prevent it.
D. Charter schools (schools started for particular sets of students or curricula)	Same as B	Same as A	Some "creaming" may occur, but also may increase access to special programs for high-risk students	Same as B and C. Also can reduce regulations and encourage innovation	Same as B and C. Charter schools may disadvantage students with disabilities because of relaxed regulations
E. Equal partial voucher to all students	Subsidies for students who attend private schools or out-of-district public schools	Increases for all, but especially for higher-income families	Favors higher-income families and families with children currently attending private schools	Can improve outcomes of low-income or high-risk students who attend choice schools	Same as B, C, and D

In summary, society wants excellence, efficiency, and equity in education. However, these goals often are in conflict. The research discussed in this chapter shows that, although smaller school districts increase efficiency, they also may increase racial and economic segregation.[47] Existing research indicates that choice schools improve the outcomes of those who attend them. It may be, however, that removing more highly motivated and higher-achieving students from attendance-zone schools harms those whom choice leaves behind. Society wishes to increase the equality of parents' rights across income groups, yet to do so might encourage further socioeconomic, religious, and ethnic segregation. Table 11-7 summarizes the likely effects of various choice programs and the benefits and harms that they are likely to produce.

A Proposal

Do the inconsistencies we have pointed out among social goals mean that policymakers should do nothing? Our research in San Antonio convinces us that the educational opportunities for low-income inner-city students must be expanded and improved. To do this, however, policymakers must choose between increasing intraclass equity or interclass equity. It is not possible to simultaneously give priority to both. Currently low-income inner-city families face problems that none of us want children to confront. Parents who are poor and whose children do not qualify for magnet schools have little opportunity to remove their children from undesirable environments. Parents in other income categories are not so constrained. We think that a just society must improve the opportunities for the currently disadvantaged and create greater interclass equity in educational opportunities and in parental rights.

We offer the following outline of a proposal for school choice.[48] It gives priority to removing interclass inequities by structuring incentives to make public use of private interest. We suggest that a state choose one or more metropolitan areas and create a pilot voucher program. The program would have the following characteristics.

—Every student would be eligible for a voucher, but its size would vary with household income. Low-income students who attend private schools would receive vouchers equal to 80 percent of the average per-pupil expenditure in the public schools in the area. As family income increased, the size of the voucher would decrease to a minimum of 50 percent of the average per-pupil expenditure. If a school was oversubscribed, new students would be randomly selected from the applicants.[49]

—For every low-income student attending an out-of-district public school the voucher would equal the full cost of attending the school. If the tuition in the receiving district was higher than that of the student's home district, the state government would make up the difference in cost.[50]

—Any school that accepted vouchers would be required to enroll and maintain at least a set percentage of students who qualified for federally assisted school lunches. The quota would be phased in over three years. Schools that maintained their quotas for a minimum of two years would be eligible for a one-year grace period if their enrollments of low-income students dropped below the targeted level. We suggest setting the initial minimum quota equal to a third of the percentage of students in the metropolitan area who are eligible for federally assisted school lunches. Over time this quota would be increased to half of those eligible for federally assisted lunches.[51]

—Every specially challenged student would receive a larger voucher. The size of this voucher would equal 100 percent of the public costs to educate a child with similar disabilities.

—The state would provide information centers to assist parents in choosing among schools.

—Each school accepting vouchers would be required to have a minimum of twenty-five students.

—No school accepting vouchers would be allowed to advocate unlawful behavior, teach hatred, or provide deliberately misleading information about the school.

—All existing regulations on private schools would continue in force.

—All schools and families participating in the voucher program would also be required to participate in a full-scale outcomes evaluation.

—The state government would require the attendance-zone schools to gather the data necessary to allow evaluators to estimate the impacts of choice on students who remained in the public schools.

—The state would distribute voucher payments to schools each month. Every school would be required to file a monthly report to the state certifying each voucher student's attendance and continuing enrollment.

If the demand for vouchers exceeded the openings available at choice schools, the proposed program should allow evaluators to directly measure the effects of selection bias, student composition, and other variables on student performance. The benefits of public school education for the teaching of tolerance and support for democratic values also could be empirically tested.

How would this proposal change incentives and exploit private interest to achieve public benefits? It would provide large economic incentives to choice schools and parents to integrate choice schools. Private, charter, and out-of-district public schools would be likely to recruit low-income students because the vouchers they would receive would be larger than the marginal cost of educating an additional child. The proposal should increase parental demand for alternatives to attendance-zone schools and encourage the development of new schools, since the number of families that could afford them will increase substantially. For families who currently send their children to private schools and for families who wish to do so, the cost of private education would decline sharply if the private school of their choice recruited its quota of low-income children. Because of this, with the exception of those schools that cater only to families with the highest incomes, parents would pressure their choice schools to recruit less-advantaged students. This should increase the efforts of private schools to inform less-advantaged families of the benefits of attending their schools, and it would encourage schools to provide transportation and other benefits to low-income families. The result should be greater socioeconomic integration of private schools.

The policy proposed should reduce the correlation between family income and the level of resources devoted to a student's education, as more low-income students would attend schools in which the composition of the student-body encouraged learning. In this way the proposal would increase equality of educational opportunity across income classes. Because of the high correlation between ethnicity and poverty, the proposal should increase ethnic integration and increase the equality of opportunity across ethnic groups as well. These changes should improve the academic performance of high-risk students, particularly of those who choose to attend Catholic schools. The proposal should increase diversity by encouraging a diverse set of new schools. Finally, by basing the size of private school vouchers on income, the proposal should reduce current inequalities in parental rights. Families of all incomes could choose to send their children to schools that teach the values or use the pedagogies that the parents prefer.

There is a downside to this proposal. Children from low-income families who did not participate in the voucher program might be further disadvantaged if higher-performing students and more involved parents moved their children to private schools. We expect private schools to meet their low-income quotas by seeking out the highest-performing students and the most highly motivated parents. The students left in the public schools would likely be those whose parents do not value education highly or who face education or language barriers that would reduce their likelihood of seeking out choice schools. This situation highlights the necessity of having an information component in choice programs so that the most disadvantaged children will have an opportunity to achieve a better education. To prevent discrimination based on language, the state should provide bilingual individuals who go into neighborhoods to inform and assist parents who do not speak English or who are having difficulty understanding the choices that the vouchers would provide to them.

Conclusion

Racism in our society encourages residential segregation and urban ghettos, and it makes education policy politically difficult. Policies that rely on public school choice cannot resolve interclass inequities, because segregation prevents solutions. This judgment leads us to suggest that a state adopt a pilot voucher program in which a student's family income and disability status would determine the size of the voucher, but the state would provide a partial voucher to every student. The issues that this pilot program could address concern the level of benefits to choosers and the extent of harm, if any, to nonchoosers. A large pilot program also might identify the factors that lead to the superior performance of Catholic schools with high-risk students, and it could ascertain whether other sectarian schools achieve similar results.

Notes

1. See Gary A. Orfield, *The Growth of Segregation in American Schools: Changing Patterns of Separation and Poverty since 1968* (Alexandria, Va.: National School Boards Association, 1993); C. Goldberg, "Hispanic Households Struggle As Poorest of the Poor," *New York Times,* July 17, 1997, A-1.

2. Only students who qualify for free or reduced lunches under federal financial guidelines are eligible. The CEO program allows students to use their scholarships to attend out-of-district public schools. Several CEO students applied to those schools, but they did not receive admission.

3. The waiting list would have been much larger but the CEO did not advertise the program after first announcing it and discouraged applications once the initial scholarships were allocated.

4. Our data as well as our interviews with administrators of the program indicate that ethnicity also plays a role in admission decisions.

5. Perhaps the most difficult problem in school choice research deals with selection bias. Families who participate in choice programs differ in many respects from families who do not, and it is impossible to capture the effects of all differences through statistical controls. For example, assume that there are two families who live next door to one another. The parents in the two families are of the same ethnicity and have similar

jobs, educations, and incomes. In addition, the children in the families have similar academic abilities. Yet if the parents in one family spend time and money searching for the best educational opportunities for their child and the other parents do not, the two families differ in a way that is likely to affect their children's educational achievements.

Our study suffers from at least two types of selection bias. First, private school choosers differ from nonchoosers in ways not completely captured by controls for socioeconomic and demographic characteristics. Second, those who were rejected by the multilingual program may have differed in terms of teachers' expectations for success. Therefore, even though both those accepted and those rejected are choosers and are qualified for the multilingual program, there may be unmeasured differences between the two groups that relate to their academic success.

6. For all respondents both English and Spanish surveys were available.

7. We refer to schools that students attend because they have been assigned to them by the school districts, usually on the basis of where the students live, as attendance-zone schools. The vast majority of SAISD students enroll in attendance-zone schools.

8. Although the response rates may seem low, they are higher than average for mail surveys of comparable groups. See Gerado Marin and Barbara VanOss Marin, *Research with Hispanic Populations* (Newbury Park, Calif.: Sage, 1991). To identify possible sample bias we compared survey respondents with the total applicant population on key demographic variables and found only two statistically significant differences: Latinos and working mothers are slightly underrepresented among survey respondents.

9. For a full report on the findings of the Milwaukee Parental Choice Program, see John F. Witte and others, "Fourth Year Report: Milwaukee Parental Choice Program," University of Wisconsin–Madison, Department of Political Science and Robert M. La Follette Institute of Public Affairs, December 1993.

10. We use the terms *choosers* and *choosing* to designate families who either attempted to place their children in the SAISD multilingual thematic school program or applied for CEO scholarships. *Nonchoosers* and *nonchoosing* refer to families who did not attempt to have their children enrolled in choice schools and who were part of a large random sample of families with students in grades one through eight at attendance-zone schools.

11. Unfortunately, the CEO Foundation and the authors of this chapter disagreed substantially concerning the uses that the foundation could make of test score data. Because of this disagreement the foundation wrote the families involved in the study and informed them that they should not answer our final survey. Although it later rescinded this instruction, our response rate declined considerably.

12. Valerie Martinez, Kenneth Godwin, and Frank Kemerer, "Public School Choice in San Antonio: Who Chooses and with What Effects?" in Bruce Fuller, Richard F. Elmore, and Gary Orfield, eds., *Who Chooses: Who Loses? Culture, Institutions, and the Unequal Effects of School Choice* (New York: Teachers College Press, 1996); Valerie Martinez, Kenneth Godwin, and Frank Kemerer, "Private Vouchers in San Antonio: The CEO Program," in Terry Moe, ed., *Private Vouchers* (Stanford, Calif.: Hoover Institution, 1995).

13. John E. Chubb and Terry. M. Moe, *Politics, Markets, and America's Schools* (Brookings, 1990).

14. Anthony S. Bryk, Valerie E. Lee, and Peter B. Holland, *Catholic Schools and the Common Good* (Harvard University Press, 1993).

15. George Borgas, "Ethnic Capital and Intergenerational Mobility," *Quarterly Journal of Economics* 107 (1992), pp. 123–50.

16. Mark Schneider and others, "Shopping for Schools: In the Land of the Blind, The One-Eyed Parent May Be Enough," *Social Science Quarterly,* forthcoming, 1998; Stephen J. Ball, Richard Bowe, and Sharon Gewirtz, "School Choice, Social Class, and

Distinction: The Realization of Social Advantage in Education," *Journal of Education Policy,* 11 (1996), pp. 89–112; Richard. F. Elmore and Bruce Fuller, "Conclusion: Empirical Research on Educational Choice: What Are the Implications for Policymakers," in Fuller, Elmore, and Orfield, eds., *Who Chooses? Who Loses?*

17. For a full report of teacher and student attitudes in the San Antonio schools, see Frank Kemerer, Valerie Martinez, and R. Kenneth Godwin, *Comparing Pubic and Private Schools: Teacher Survey Results* (Denton, Tex.: Center for the Study of Education Reform, September 1996); and Frank Kemerer and Carrie Y. Ausbrooks, *Comparing Pubic and Private Schools: Student Survey Results* (Denton, Tex.: Center for the Study of Education Reform, November 1996).

18. Unfortunately we do not have data on students who moved from attendance-zone schools to the multilingual schools. Our multilingual population included only students who had been in the schools for one year when our research started.

19. Kemerer, Martinez, and Godwin, *Comparing Public and Private Schools: Teacher Survey Results;* Kemerer and Ausbrooks, *Comparing Public and Private Schools: Student Survey Results.*

20. Caroline Minter Hoxby, "Does Competition among Public Schools Benefit Students and Taxpayers?" Working Paper 4979, National Bureau of Economic Research, Cambridge, Mass., 1994.

21. Hoxby, "Does Competition Benefit Students?" p. 26.

22. For a review of this literature, see John F. Witte, "School Choice and Student Performance," in Helen F. Ladd, ed., *Holding Schools Accountable: Performance-Based Reform in Education* (Brookings, 1996).

23. Bryk, Lee, and Holland, *Catholic Schools and the Common Good,* p. 267.

24. Among the studies that show the importance of peer group effects are those of Laurence Steinberg, B. Bradford Brown, and Sanford M. Dornbusch, *Beyond the Classroom: Why School Reform Has Failed and What Parents Need to Do* (New York: Simon and Schuster, 1996); and William Sander and Anthony C. Krautmann, "Catholic Schools, Dropout Rates, and Educational Attainment," *Economic Inquiry* 33 (April 1995), pp. 217–33. For an alternative view, see William N. Evans, Wallace E. Oates, and Robert M. Schwab, "Measuring Peer Group Effects: A Study of Teenage Behavior," *Journal of Political Economy,* 100 (1992): 966–91.

25. Hoxby, "Does Competition Benefit Students?" p. 23.

26. Bryk, Lee, and Holland, *Catholic Schools and the Common Good.*

27. Jennie W. Chase, "School Choices: How Public and Catholic Schools Influence Their Students," Department of Economics, University of North Carolina, Chapel Hill, 1996; William N. Evans and Robert M. Schwab, "Finishing High School and Starting College: Do Catholic Schools Make a Difference?" Department of Economics, University of Maryland, College Park, Md., 1995; and Derek Neal, "The Effects of Catholic Secondary Schooling on Educational Achievement," *Journal of Labor Economics* 15 (1997), pp. 98–123.

28. Chase, "School Choices;" Evans and Schwab, "Finishing High School and Starting College;" and Neal, "The Effects of Catholic Secondary Schooling." See also Sander and Krautmann, "Catholic Schools, Dropout Rates, and Educational Attainment," for a study that found a smaller Catholic school effect on higher education after controlling for selection bias.

29. Steinberg, Brown, and Dornbusch, *Beyond the Classroom,* pp. 137–38, 155–58.

30. Valerie E. Lee, "San Antonio School Choice Plans: Rewarding or Creaming?" *Social Science Quarterly* 76 (September 1995), p. 520.

31. Albert O. Hirschman, *Exit, Voice, and Loyalty: Responses to Decline in Firms, Organizations, and States* (Harvard University Press, 1970). Examples of writers who make this argument are Amy Gutmann, *Democratic Education* (Princeton University

Press, 1987) and Jeffrey R. Henig, *Rethinking School Choice* (Princeton University Press, 1994).

32. See, for example, Carnegie Foundation for the Advancement of Teaching, *School Choice: A Special Report* (Princeton, N.J., 1992) and Lee, "San Antonio School Choice Plans."

33. Orfield, *The Growth of Segregation in American Schools*.

34. Orfield, *The Growth of Segregation in American Schools*, p. 22.

35. Douglas S. Massey and Nancy A. Denton, *American Apartheid: Segregation and the Making of the Underclass* (Harvard University Press, 1993), p. 13.

36. The Supreme Court decision *Milliken v. Bradley* 418 U.S. 717 (1974) rejected forced busing of children across school district boundaries for the purpose of achieving ethnic integration. This decision has made treating children in suburban school districts as a social resource for inner city children almost impossible.

37. For additional information on this topic, see Stephen Gilles's chapter in this volume as well as his "On Educating Children: A Parentalist Manifesto," *Chicago Law Review* 63 (1996), pp. 937–1034; and Kenneth Godwin and others, "Liberal Equity in Education: A Comparison of School Choice Options," *Social Science Quarterly*, forthcoming, 1998.

38. John Stuart Mill, *On Liberty* (New York: Hackett Press, 1978), pp. 104–06.

39. See Nathan Tarcov, *Locke's Education for Liberty* (Chicago: University of Chicago Press, 1984); Stephen Arons, *Compelling Belief: The Culture of American Schooling* (New York: McGraw Hill, 1982); and John E. Coons, "School Choice as Simple Justice," *First Things* (1992), pp. 15–22.

40. Opponents of vouchers respond that schools must create democratic citizens and that the public purpose of schools requires the state to socialize students to that purpose. Because private schools cannot guarantee this outcome, education must be controlled by public officials and provided by agents of the state. Schools must expose all students to a common educational experience that cannot be left to the vagaries of individual or family choice. To allow parents to use public funds to choose private schools might lead to prejudice, intolerance, and a failure to respect ways of life dissimilar to those of the students. Among those who make these arguments are Gutmann, *Democratic Education;* Henry M. Levin, "The Theory of Choice Applied to Education," paper presented at the Conference on Choice and Control in American Education, University of Wisconsin, Madison, 1989; and Henig, *Rethinking School Choice*.

41. Rolf Blank, "Educational Effects of Magnet High Schools," in William H. Clune and John F. Witte, eds., *Choice and control in American Education,* vol. 2 (New York: Falmer Press, 1990).

42. For discussions of the selection bias of magnet schools see Douglas Archbald, *Magnet Schools and Issues of Public School Desegregation, Quality, and Choice* (Palo Alto: American Institutes for Research, 1991); Rolf K. Blank, Roger E. Levine, and Lauri Steel, "After 15 Years: Magnet Schools in Urban Education," in Fuller, Elmore, and Orfield, eds., *Who Chooses? Who Loses?*

43. Some states do not allow transfers if they would adversely affect racial balance.

44. See the contribution of David J. Armor and Brett M. Peiser in this volume; M. Rubenstein, R. Hamar, and N. Adelman, *Minnesota's Open Enrollment Option* (Washington, DC: Policy Studies Associates, 1992); and J. Douglas Willms and Frank Echols, "Alert and Inert Clients: The Scottish Experience of Parental Choice of Schools," *Economics of Education Review* 11 (1992), pp. 339–50.

45. Bruno V. Manno, this volume; Delbert Taebel and others, *Texas Open Enrollment-Charter Schools: Year One Evaluation* (Austin, Tex.: Texas Education Agency, December 1997).

46. John S. Ambler, "Who Benefits from School Choice? Some Evidence from Europe," *Journal of Policy Analysis and Management* 13 (1994), pp. 454–76; Ball, Bowe, and Gewirtz, "School Choice, Social Class, and Distinction;" Sabrina Lutz, "The Impact of School Choice in the United States and the Netherlands on Ethnic Segregation and Equal Educational Opportunity," *Equity and Excellence in Education,* 29 (1996), pp. 48–54; Schneider and others, "Shopping for Schools."

47. Orfield, *The Growth of Segregation in American Schools;* and Gary Orfield, Mark Bachmeier, David R. James, and Tamela Eitle, "Deepening Segregation in American Public Schools," Harvard Project on School Desegregation, April 1997.

48. This proposal also appears in the September 1998 issue of *Social Science Quarterly.* The fully described proposal will appear in the forthcoming book by Kenneth Godwin and Frank Kemerer, *Competing Goals in School Choice: Liberty, Equity, and Law.*

49. We suggest removing only 80 percent of the per-pupil funding from the public schools for three reasons. First, if as their advocates argue private schools were more efficient, 80 percent should be sufficient to cover their costs. The 80 percent figure is much higher than the tuitions of most private schools. Second, leaving 20 percent of the funding with the public schools should ease the shock to these schools as they adjust to competition from private schools. Finally, public schools are more likely to have a greater proportion of high-risk and specially challenged students. The additional funds would help provide for their special needs.

50. We propose state funding for the pilot program to avoid potential problems with a sudden removal of funds from local districts. However, we believe that if the pilot program was successful in most of its objectives, at least half of the difference between a student's home district and the tuition of the receiving district should be paid by the sending district. This would provide incentives for districts to improve their own instruction.

51. Dismissing a student can present a problem for the school if the dismissal reduces the school's percentage of low-income students below the required quota. We believe it is wise to allow private schools to control their enrollment and retention. This means they must be able to dismiss their students for cause. At the same time, we believe schools should not be allowed to systematically use dismissals to reduce the number of low-income students enrolled. We suggest that when a dismissal drops a school below its quota, it be required to replace that student by the beginning of the following term. Having dismissals count against a school's quota would encourage schools to recruit higher numbers of low-income students so that the dismissal of a student for cause would not create problems for other students in the school and their families.

TWELVE

Evidence from the Indianapolis Voucher Program

David J. Weinschrott and Sally B. Kilgore

MOST SCHOOL CHOICE PROGRAMS restrict choice to public schools. The Educational Choice Charitable Trust (ECCT), however, uses private funds to help parents send their children to the private schools of their choice. Thus it provides a laboratory for ascertaining how extending choice to private schools affects students' performance. The results of the Hudson Institute's evaluation of the ECCT program are reported in this chapter. These results are encouraging: Although transferring students lost some ground in the early grades, they soon began to emulate the steady upward progress of students who had been in private schools all along. Moreover, parental satisfaction with and participation in their children's education increased significantly. Therefore, we can conclude that increasing parents' choice over how and where their children are educated gives parents a sense of ownership and enthusiasm that contribute directly to improvements in students' performance.

Choice and Educational Reform

Since 1983—when the National Commission on Excellence in Education issued a report warning that the nation was at risk because of poor

This chapter is based upon David J. Weinschrott and Sally B. Kilgore, "Education Choice Charitable Trust: An Experiment in School Choice," Hudson Briefing Paper 189 (Indianapolis: Hudson Institute, May 1996). Permission granted by the Hudson Institute.

student achievement—education reformers, public policymakers, and academics have refocused attention on the nation's elementary and secondary schools. The report and subsequent attention also helped trigger a substantial education reform movement that continues today. As Chubb and Moe note, this education reform movement is characterized by efforts to raise education standards and expectations for students and teachers and to inject into all the nation's public schools many of the attributes commonly associated with more successful schools (both private and public).[1]

While the focus of the education reform debate was shifting from inputs to outcomes, school choice policies gained increasing support. Coons and Sugarman note that the idea of government's purchasing education services as well as providing them directly is not new.[2] It is popularly attributed to Milton Friedman, who applied economic theory to John Stuart Mill's brief analysis of education policy. Friedman notes that the usual justification for government interest in mandating and even assisting in the financing of a minimum level of education is widely understood and supported. But he argues that government management of schools is much more difficult to justify.[3] Jencks proposed vouchers as a way to improve equality of educational opportunity in the United States.[4]

Recent reform efforts have sought ways to hold providers of education responsible for achieving desirable outcomes (i.e., acceptable levels of achievement as measured by some objective means, such as standardized tests). For such expectations to be realistic, incentives must be established so that providers respond to performance results. Also, the providers must have sufficient control over the institutions they run so that they can institute appropriate innovations to bring on performance improvements. Each step in this chain of conditions has encountered problems of definition and implementation. In particular, it has become clear that many public educational systems have significant barriers to change from within, including bureaucratic structures, teachers' unions, and centralized authority.

In response to the growing perception that public schools are encumbered by complex bureaucratic structures that impede organizational responsiveness, proponents of school choice such as Chubb and Moe suggest that such policies might give more parents an increased measure of control over their children's education and, by doing so, force schools to become more responsive to their students' educational needs.[5] Chubb and Moe also argue that private schools, because they are controlled by market forces rather than bureaucratic institutions, place a premium on responding to family needs and produce superior education results. Others, such as Coleman, have suggested that school choice policies might help form nongeographic communities that would establish and enforce desirable norms of behavior.[6] Scholars have also asserted that public funding and support of private schools are more conducive to pluralism.[7] Still others have argued that traditional economic cost-benefit analyses support school choice. Peterson, for example, notes that the ability of private schools to educate for less cost would be important evidence supporting school choice policies.[8] Finally, Bryk, Lee, and Holland argue that, in contrast to what many school choice critics claim, private schools promote educational equality better than public schools do.[9]

Critics of school choice policies fear that choice will increase educational inequality. Kozol, for example, questions whether all people will receive adequate information regarding their education options.[10] He also asserts that school choice will probably increase school segregation by race and class. Other critics of school choice argue that public schools would be placed at a competitive disadvantage if forced to compete with private schools for scarce education funds, partly because private schools have wider flexibility in selecting students and a broader ability to expel problem students.[11] Others contend that the administrative burdens and associated costs incidental to establishing and maintaining school choice programs and providing the oversight needed to protect against waste and fraud are considerable and might overcome any benefits attributable to school choice.[12]

While the academic and public debate surrounding school choice increases in tone and tenor, state legislatures—the governmental units primarily charged with the constitutional duty to educate Americans—continue to explore and implement various school choice policies. Already twenty states have implemented programs described as school choice. Fifteen of those states have done so in the past five years, including Michigan and Ohio.[13] In addition to these state-led efforts, scores of individual school districts have introduced choice plans.[14]

Most school choice programs restrict the choice to schools within or among public school districts. In essence, these programs redirect some public funds to follow the child within the public school sector. Often the range of choice lies only within the home district of the child. Therefore, until quite recently school choice programs did not include private schools and thus did not affect the government's or even the district's role as the dominant supplier of education services. In contrast, the experiment under investigation here uses private funds to enable children to attend private schools. The Educational Choice Charitable Trust program and similar programs address the broader issue of government and district dominance and therefore should yield important data that will better enable researchers and others to understand issues that have important consequences for education policy.

Overview of the ECCT Program

The Educational Choice Charitable Trust was created in 1991 to provide education vouchers to low-income families in the Indianapolis Public Schools (IPS) district. Eligible families were able to select any private schools located within the IPS district, including religious schools. The trust was initially funded by Golden Rule Insurance Company. Grants covering half of a private school's annual tuition, up to a maximum of $800, were available to eligible families and were awarded on a first-come, first-served basis. To be eligible for funds a family had to reside within the corporate boundaries of IPS and qualify for free or reduced-price lunch programs. Half of the money available from the trust was reserved for families whose children were enrolled in private schools before the creation of the trust program. No other criteria, such as student grades or behavior, were considered in the selection process. Eligibility for admission to a chosen private school was determined by that school. The trust began aiding families in September 1991, and in the first year of its three-year commitment children from the 744 participating families attended fifty-eight different private schools. Among the 744 students who participated during the trust's first year were more than 350 students who transferred from IPS schools.

The Hudson Institute, with researchers at Butler University in Indianapolis, oversaw a multiyear evaluation of the experiment. The evaluation, partially funded by the Lilly Endowment, Inc., and the Smith Richardson Foundation, consisted of focus interviews and parent, teacher, and administrator surveys. This chapter is based upon the evaluation's final report.

Toward Evaluation of Choice Experiments

The opening section of this chapter identified school performance as the dominant issue driving the school choice movement of which the ECCT program is an embodiment. Although it might appear that the ultimate "bottom line" in an evaluation of a choice experiment would be standardized test score results, reflecting on the process of schooling calls for evaluation in a wider context. Test scores are a component, albeit an important one, of a multifaceted set of behaviors of students, parents, and teachers that make for better schooling. Because of the subtleties involved in comparing students' achievement, it might also be expected that an experimental framework should be established that would randomly assign students to different settings to control the variety of background and covariate relationships associated with students' performance. Such a design would permit an analyst to identify unambiguously the separate contributions of parental, student, and school factors in outcome evaluations. Ethical and expense considerations, however, ruled out the use of such an experimental design.

The framework for evaluation of the ECCT program proceeded along more informal lines. Our treatment group included students who transferred from public schools to private schools under the ECCT program. The control group included students who had applied for ECCT vouchers, but had not yet been able to enroll in private schools due to lack of sufficient funding or because their families wished them to transfer at a semester or year-end break.[15] The treatment and control groups were alike in the sense that their parents both met the income limits for participation and were sufficiently motivated about their children's education (a) to seek application to the program and (b) to be willing to pay a portion of their private school tuition. The two groups were different in that the treatment group included those actually enrolled in the program, whereas the control group was comprised of those who were not yet enrolled because of funding constraints and therefore were placed on a waiting list. Many of those on the waiting list eventually did enroll in the program at a later date. It is important to note that conditions (a) and (b) may have distinguished these parents from other low-income parents who did not seek application to the program.

Comparison Dimensions

The main source of information supporting our evaluation of the program was a parent survey administered in the fall of each year to families who had applied for enrollment in the program. At that point the status of an applicant could be one of the following: a new student from the public sector, a new student from the private sector, a continuing student, a student on the waiting list who had previously attended a public school (or would have, for first grade students), a student on the waiting list who had previously attended a private school, or a student previously in the program who had left the program. The surveys administered to all these groups were essentially the same in any given year, except for a set of additional questions appended to the survey of students who had ended their participation.

In general, the content of the questionnaire addressed two sets of issues. The first set related to issues preceding application and enrollment, such as what factors characterized parents of children seeking application (such as income, education attainment, marital status); what sources of information were relevant (such as media, institutional sources, word of mouth); and what considerations motivated the decision to seek enrollment or leave the program. The second set related to issues following enrollment in private school, such as what were parents' attitudes about the choice after the first year (such as satisfaction with school curriculum, student effort, teachers) and what were self-reported behavior changes in parents after the first year (such as interaction with their children's study and participation in school activities). The first set of issues might be regarded as marketing issues in the sense that they describe the population seeking enrollment and the sources and kinds of information influencing their decisions to enroll. Therefore the analysis of this set of responses is applied to new private and public enrollees and persons on the public waiting list (the control group). The focus of the second set of issues is on the "school" effect resulting from a transfer from the public to the private sector. Therefore, the analysis is limited to second- and third-year continuing ECCT students who originally came from IPS.

Plan of the Study

In the next section we identify the components of the survey database used for various parts of the analysis, describe the characteristics of the ECCT participant population, and identify factors associated with enrollment and leaving the program. Then we examine parents' reasons for enrolling their children and characteristics of families that chose to leave the program. Next we evaluate the "customers' perspective," including parents' satisfaction, parents' assessment of their children's performance, and the involvement in the schooling process of parents who have moved their children from the public (IPS) system to private schools under the ECCT program. In our analysis we compare parent responses to the survey regarding their experience in the public school setting to their responses regarding their experience in the private school setting. Finally we compare standardized test scores for four groups of children: students who previously attended private schools, those who transferred from public to private schools, a group of students attending public schools who are matched in important ways to those who transferred, and all IPS students.

Characteristics of the ECCT Participant Population

The number of completed parent surveys for the first three years of the project was 1,515. This total included multiple observations of students who remained in the program for two or three years. Table 12-1 shows the number of surveys by year and by sample group. Year 1 refers to the school year beginning in 1991, year 2 to the school year beginning in 1992, and year 3 to the school year beginning in 1993. There are three main groups of respondents: students enrolled in the ECCT program who had been in private schools before enrollment in the program, students enrolled in the ECCT program who had been in public schools before enrollment in the program, and the control group, which comprised students originally from public school who applied for ECCT grants but were put on a waiting list. Therefore, the total number of students from the public sector includes both the former public school students and the control group. Actually, most members of the control group were eventually placed in private schools through the ECCT program. Overall, enrollees in the program were drawn evenly from private and public schools; there were 744 private school students and 750 public school students.

Table 12-2 shows the number of surveys by category (at the time of the survey) and by year. Under each year the first column gives the percentage of surveys sent out that were usable for analysis. For example, the 268 surveys of new enrollees available for analysis in year one constituted 36 percent of the surveys sent out. The number of usable surveys received increased to 45 percent in year two. The number of students in the program in any year included new enrollees plus continuing students minus those who left the program plus those on waiting lists. These categories are identified in the left-most column of table 12-2. The analyses that follow draw from various portions of these data. For example, the marketing studies that examine why parents enrolled their children in the program

Table 12-1. *Number of Surveys, by Year on Sample Group*[a]

Year	Private	Public	Control	Total public	Total
Year 1	157	107	0	107	264
Year 2	311	212	94	306	617
Year 3	276	284	53	337	613
Total	744	603	147	750	1494

a. Excludes twenty-one records with missing public or private value.

Table 12-2. *Number of Surveys, by Category and Year*

	Year 1		Year 2		Year 3		Total
Category	Percent usable surveys	Number of records	Percent usable surveys	Number of records	Percent usable surveys	Number of records	Records
Returning students	. . .	. . .	37	191	. . .	119	310
New students	36	268	57	209	. . .	164	641
Total enrollees	. . .	268	45	400	. . .	283	951
Private waiting list	. . .	. . .	64	105	. . .	185	290
Public waiting list	. . .	. . .	50	94	. . .	84	178
Total waiting	. . .	268	49	599	. . .	552	1419
Left program	. . .	. . .	21	35	. . .	61	96
Total surveys	36	268	45	634	. . .	613	1515

focus on new students for each year. The studies comparing parent satisfaction between those with students in public and private schools focus on surveys of parents whose children originally came from public schools and who remained in the program at least two years. Analysis of reasons for leaving the program focused on the "left program" category.

The ECCT program provides subsidies to families with low incomes, defined as families eligible for the subsidized school lunch program. Figure 12-1 depicts the income distribution for families of students entering the program as private school, public school, and "control" students. The modal incomes for all three groups were between $10,000 and $20,000, but there were some differences across groups. In particular, the public school and control groups had higher percentages of families with incomes below $10,000 than the private school group, and families of students previously in private schools included a higher percentage of families with incomes over $20,000. There is also evidence that longevity in the program was weakly associated with higher incomes: a higher percentage of families of both public and private school students who had been in the program for three years had incomes in the $30,000-plus range. We used the term *weakly associated* because it is not dominant. For instance, very low income students were well represented in the public school third-year group.

Because parents must supply as much as half of the students' private school tuitions, it is of interest whether low income affects the ability of families to sustain participation in the program. Figure 12-2 shows the income distribution of three cohorts of families in the program: those new to the program, those returning for a second or third year, and those who

Figure 12-1. *ECCT Enrollees, by Income of Parents and Prior School Setting*

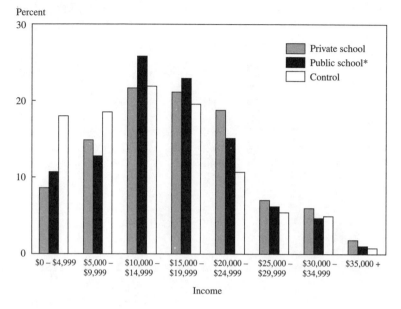

*Differences are significant at 5 percent.

Figure 12-2. *Students' Enrollment Status, by Income of Parents*

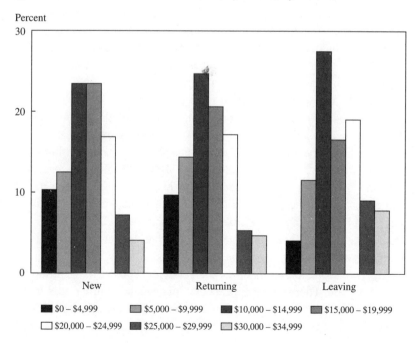

Figure 12-3. *ECCT Enrollees, by Income and Marital Status of Parents*

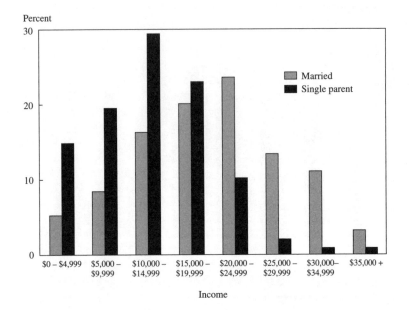

had ended their participation. Although differences in these distributions are not significant statistically, there is a slightly higher percentage of families in the $10,000–$15,000 bracket among those who had left the program. But there are also higher percentages of families in the $25,000–$30,000 range. Therefore, at this level of analysis it does not appear that income is a dominant reason for leaving the program.

One might also question whether the burdens of single parenthood pose a barrier to participation in the program, because single parents usually have lower incomes. Figure 12-3 confirms that single-parent families in the ECCT program generally have lower incomes than two-parent families. The modal income of single-parent families is $10,000–$15,000, whereas the modal income for married families is $10,000 higher. The next question is whether lower income and other factors in single-parent households are related to a higher incidence of leaving the program.

Our data indicate that the percentage of single-parent families was not particularly elevated in any of the participation cohorts. In particular, the percentage of single-parent families was relatively smaller in the group that left the program. Therefore, it appears that income and family status are not barriers to program participation, and these factors are not significantly related to leaving the program. These comparisons are simple single-variable

Figure 12-4. *ECCT Enrollees, by School of Origin and Ethnic Group*

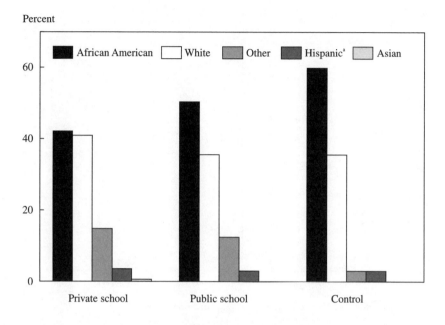

a. Hispanic is not technically an ethnic group like African American or white, because it may include members of each of these groups. Because the survey was constructed in this fashion and some persons responded in this category, however, the results are included here.

comparisons; more evidence based on multivariable comparisons is presented later.

Figure 12-4 portrays the distribution of ethnicity in the three student groups. The public and control groups had higher percentages of African-American students and correspondingly lower percentages of white students. In addition, the control group was comprised of almost exclusively African-American and white students, with virtually no members of other ethnic groups.

The data contain some interesting information regarding the levels of educational attainment of parents in the public and private groups. The public families showed a higher percentage of mothers with some college training than the private group. The two sectors showed little difference in educational attainment of fathers. Note that there were 1,203 responses regarding the mother's educational attainment and only 623 responses regarding the father's educational attainment; the difference reflected the number of single-parent households.

Figure 12-5. *Parents' Educational Goals for Students, by School of Origin*

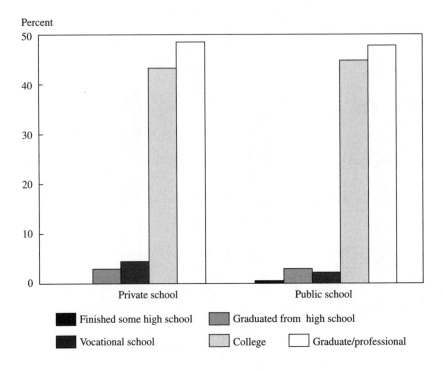

Percent

Finished some high school   Graduated from high school

Vocational school   College   Graduate/professional

The data also provide evidence regarding the proposition that parents' educational attainment might be associated with longer participation in the program. Public school students whose mothers have some college education, appear more likely to continue to the second year. But mothers with only a high school education comprise a high percentage of those in the third year of participation. A similar pattern exists for fathers' educational attainment, although there is a higher percentage of fathers with some college education among those sustaining longer participation in the program. This result may be associated with the previously noted relationship between income and longer program participation.

Figure 12-5 depicts parents' educational aspirations for their children by the school sector the children attended before the study began. Both groups of parents had high aspirations for college and professional or graduate school education for their children. Figure 12-6 indicates that these aspirations remained consistent for families that stayed with the program.

Most of the private schools receiving students under the ECCT program are either Catholic parochial schools or are supported by church organiza-

Figure 12-6. *Parents' Educational Goals for Students, by School of Origin and Time in Program*

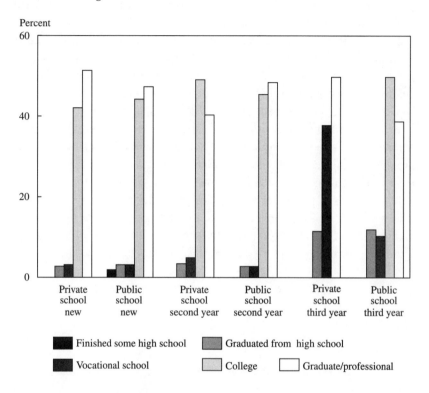

Percent

Finished some high school   Graduated from high school

Vocational school   College   Graduate/professional

tions. Approximately two-thirds of the ECCT participant population claim membership in a church or synagogue, and nearly three in five report attending religious services at least weekly.

Factors Influencing Parents' Decisions to Enter or Leave the ECCT Program

This section connects various features of the ECCT program to the characteristics of the participating families. We begin with what might be called "marketing" information, which identifies how families found out about the program and what factors were important in their decisions to apply for enrollment. Because critics of the choice movement argue that under choice programs parents will not be able to make informed choices among schools, this section examines the factors parents considered in deciding to participate in the ECCT program.

Marketing Information

Information about the ECCT program was distributed through formal and informal channels. Parents were asked to indicate on the survey which sources of information reached them. Figure 12-7 indicates that most families received information on the program by way of informal networks of families and friends. This was especially true among parents whose children were in public schools. The other major sources of information were the private schools themselves and the newspapers.

We noted that nearly two-thirds of the ECCT population were church members. Because the information from friends and relatives might come through worship communities, we examined the sources of information for persons who did not claim membership in churches. Figure 12-8 shows that higher fractions of public school families gained information directly from private schools and that private school families gained more information directly from churches or synagogues than did the entire population in figure 12-7 (where two-thirds of the population belonged to churches or

Figure 12-7. *Sources of Information about ECCT, by Prior School Sector*

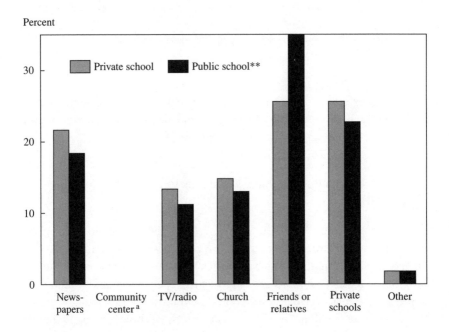

Percent

**Differences are significant at 1 percent.
a. Less than 0.10 percent.

Figure 12-8. *Sources of Information for Parents Not Associated with Churches or Synagogues*

Percent

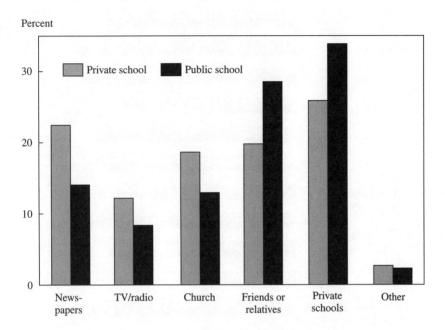

synagogues). It may seem paradoxical that those with no church membership were more likely to gain information directly from churches. Upon reflection, however, it appears that parents who are less likely to attend church services seek information directly from the church or synagogue offices about what are mostly parochial schools, whereas parents more deeply involved in congregations obtain their information from fellow congregation members.

The survey asked parents to indicate the importance of various reasons for joining the program. Figure 12-9 shows the responses for first-year parents across the three years of the program. The responses are differentiated by whether the students were already attending private schools or were transferring from IPS public schools. The most important issue for all groups was safety; nearly all respondents in both groups ranked it as important or very important. Other relatively important issues (80 percent response or better) were religious values, general atmosphere, discipline, the availability of the choice, financial considerations, and the educational quality of the new school. The presence of another child at the school was

Figure 12-9. *Reasons to Participate in ECCT Program, by School of Origin*

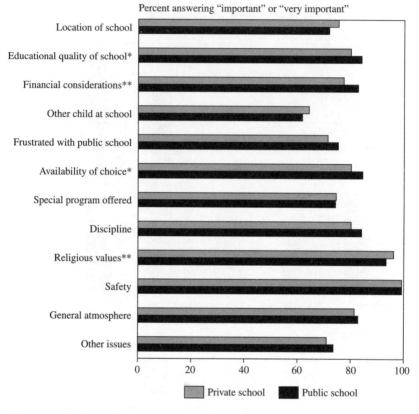

Percent answering "important" or "very important"

Location of school
Educational quality of school*
Financial considerations**
Other child at school
Frustrated with public school
Availability of choice*
Special program offered
Discipline
Religious values**
Safety
General atmosphere
Other issues

0   20   40   60   80   100

Private school   Public school

*Differences are significant at 5 percent.
**Differences are significant at 1 percent.

least important. Interestingly, the location of the school was one of the least important factors in the choice. Frustration with the public school was not one of the more important reasons for enrolling in the program.

Characteristics of the Population Leaving the Program

Over the course of the program, ninety-six families responded to a questionnaire regarding why they removed their children from the program, thirty-five in the 1992–93 academic year and sixty-one in 1993–1994. The split between public and private schools was about even: thirty-seven public, forty-two private. Table 12-3 shows the responses of parents who

Table 12-3. *Parents' Reasons for Leaving the Program*
Percent

Reason	Response	
Part A	*Yes*	*No*
Income too high	15.6	84.4
Moved from IPS	14.8	85.2
Poor student performance	1.3	98.7
Poor behavior	5.1	94.9
Part B	*Important/very important*	*Not/somewhat important*
Frustrated with school	28.1	70.9
Financial considerations	80.3	19.7
Poor academic quality	39.3	60.7
Sought different program	28.6	71.4
Poor discipline	35.1	64.9
Disliked atmosphere	42.1	57.9

removed their children from the ECCT program. In general, these response patterns did not differ significantly between students coming from private or public schools. Most parents answered "no" or "not important" to these possible reasons for withdrawing from the program. Financial considerations emerged as the most prominent reason for leaving.

The analysis of figure 12-3 suggested that income was not a barrier to continuation in the program, but this evidence suggests that income or other financial considerations might be important in decisions to leave the program.[16] To examine this issue further, we conducted a probit regression analysis designed to identify factors affecting the choice. This confirms our earlier result with univariate comparisons.

Parent Satisfaction and Participation

Evaluation of the relative success levels of private and public education ultimately rests on two pillars: the satisfaction of parents with the educational process for their children and objective performance results measured by standardized tests. In this section we examine the perceptions of parents whose children made the transition from public schools to private ones. The analysis is limited to those parents who had enrolled their children in public schools before enrolling in the ECCT program and whose children have completed two to three years in the program. Since the survey "looks back" one year, successive years of the survey record parents' perception of their children's experience in the public setting and then the private setting. The surveys were given at the beginning of the school year so that the parents would make their evaluations of their public school experience before accumulating much private school experience. The analysis compares responses regarding parents' satisfaction with the public and private schools, how they evaluated their children's performance and the schools' performance, and to what extent they participated in their children's educational programs.

Parents' Satisfaction with Private and Public Settings

In the first analysis in this section we examine the change in parents' satisfaction as their children switched from public to private schools. The results are displayed in Figure 12-10. Looking across all issues, it is clear that parents prefer the private school experience to its public counterpart. In all dimensions more than 90 percent of respondents were satisfied or very satisfied with the private school environment. Satisfaction in the second year of private school dropped in some categories, but in most cases 80 percent of the respondents were at least satisfied with the private school setting. Whereas more than 90 percent of parents were satisfied with teachers' performance, principals' performance, discipline, instruction, textbooks, the amount their children learned, school location, and parent input in the private schools, fewer than 60 percent of parents were satisfied with these factors when the same parents had their children in public schools. There was less dissatisfaction with the value of homework, academic standards, and the children's effort, enjoyment, and safety. There seems to be some conflict between priorities for joining ECCT and reported satisfaction after enrolling. In particular, parents ranked safety as the most important factor in seeking admittance to the ECCT program, but they did not report that they were significantly dissatisfied with safety in their actual public school settings. A possible resolution of these responses is that parents were not dissatisfied with their previous experience in the public schools, but feared the future.

Subjective Performance Evaluation

The survey asked parents to recall their children's overall grade performance in school the previous year and give an overall grade to their schools. The heading of this section identifies the comparisons here as subjective because of the difficulty in making firm comparisons of performance based

Figure 12-10. *Change in Parents' Satisfaction from Public to Private School Experience*

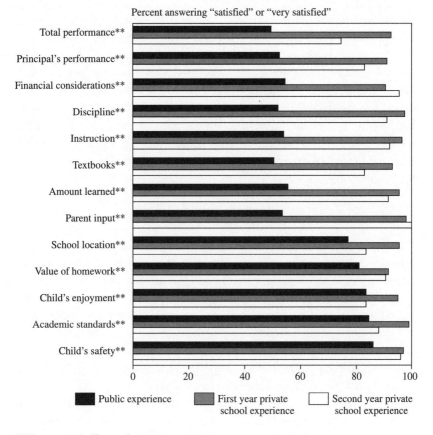

Percent answering "satisfied" or "very satisfied"

*Differences are significant at 5 percent.
**Differences are significant at 1 percent.

on the students' grades in quite different environments and the recollection of parents of those grades. It is best to understand these comparisons as a rough index of how successful parents think their children were in the two settings. Moreover, it must be remembered that the judgments were recorded in two different surveys a year apart. The data show that parents see their children earning more A and C grades in their first and second years in private schools and fewer D or F grades in their third year in private schools. Most parents recalled that their children received B grades in the public school settings, but about 4 percent recalled their receiving D grades or lower. Again, the reader must be cautioned about reading too much into these comparisons, because the grading systems and scope of the work in the two settings may have differed considerably.

The results of the survey also indicate that parents generally rated private schools superior to public schools. Nearly half the parents rated private schools with an A, but only some 35 percent rated public schools with an A or B. These comparisons are more likely to reflect correct information than parents' recollection of their childrens' grades, because the parents were making the judgments about the quality of the schools in both cases. In the second year of their children's attendance at private schools, parents were more likely to give the schools a B grade than in the first year, but the fraction giving A or B grades still exceeded the fraction giving those grades to the public school experience, and the fraction giving D or F grades was much smaller for private schools than for public schools.

Parents' Involvement in Students' Education

It is widely understood that parental involvement in a child's education produces improvement in outcomes. In the parent survey we investigated a number of these issues, asking each parent to indicate the extent of his or her own involvement in the child's education in the previous year. In the following analyses we compare parents' responses in the first year of their ECCT program participation to those in their second year. The survey asked parents to reflect on their previous year's experience; therefore, the first year refers to the parents' experience in the public schools and the second year to their experience with the private schools.

The first set of responses was derived from a series of questions focused on contacts between the schools and parents on students' performance, class schedules, school fund-raising efforts, parents' requests concerning information in school records, behavior problems, and opportunities for the parents to help in the school classrooms or other volunteer efforts. Separate questions requested information regarding whether the parents contacted the schools or the schools contacted the parents. In virtually every category there was more interaction, on average, between the schools and parents in the private school experience. Because of individual variation in responses, however, most categories did not show differences that reached statistical significance. On requests for volunteer activity and involvement in school fund-raising activities, however, the level of contact was significantly higher in the private schools. A similar pattern emerged for cases in which a school contacted a parent, and again the difference between the public and private cases was significant.

The survey asked parents about five different aspects of parent involvement with regard to which parents answered yes or no. In the case of four of the categories, the parents reported more personal involvement when their children were in private schools. These categories were belonging to a parent-teacher organization, attending parent-teacher organization meetings, being active in a parent-teacher organization, and belonging to some other parent-teacher organization. In the case of the fifth category, attending parent teacher conferences, the parents' involvement was significantly greater than during their public school experiences.

In the first section we noted that student performance derives from a multifaceted set of student and parent behaviors in conjunction with the school setting. The results in this section confirm that parents are more involved in the private school setting than in the previous (IPS) setting. This finding has implications that extend beyond parent participation; it also means that parents are more knowledgeable about what is occurring in the schools and more likely to be "on top" of the students' progress and effort. Parental involvement also means that the parents are excited about what the children are doing; therefore, the student and parent components of the equation are mutually reinforcing. We expect this result to have cumulative effects and ultimately to lead to better student performance.

Student Achievement: Comparisons between Public and Private Schools

We have left comparison of student achievement until last to ensure that the broader issues of parent preference and involvement are understood, because they provide the context in which to evaluate progress in student achievement. Analysis of standardized test scores must be carefully structured, because there are a variety of ways in which inappropriate or misleading comparisons can be presented. In the first place, different standardized tests measure different philosophies of education—with different weights attached to different components of curriculum or priorities of items included to measure knowledge or skills. These different underlying philosophies make comparisons between major testing systems such as the California Achievement Test, the Iowa Basic Skills Test, and the Indiana Statewide Testing for Educational Progress (ISTEP) battery highly questionable or even impossible.

Second, not all measurement systems used in reporting test scores are directly comparable. Commonly reported percentile rankings or grade equivalents cannot be added up across individuals in a classroom to obtain averages that can then be used for comparisons across time or school settings.[17] In the case of other measures such as stanines and normal curve equivalents the scores of individual students on a single test can be added up and compared over time or across settings.

Before engaging in the following analysis we examined the test instruments and procedures in IPS and the private schools to which students transferred. IPS uses the state-mandated ISTEP test instrument for students in grades two, three, six, and eight. This instrument is based on a commercially prepared test by CTB, a division of McGraw-Hill. A subset of the ISTEP, the Comprehensive Test of Basic Skills/4 (CTBS/4) instrument, is used in grades other than grades two, three, six, and eight. Many private schools use different test instruments such as the Iowa Basic Skills Test and the California Achievement Test. Seven Catholic schools, however, use the ISTEP/CTBS combination on a schedule similar to that of IPS—even giving the tests at the same point in the school year. Therefore, to maximize the comparison value we limited our analysis to these schools. It must be noted at the outset that these seven schools are located in the IPS district and are not wealthy suburban schools by any measure. Indeed, many have severe limits on resources.

Because of the schedule for administering the test, the sample sizes for comparison shrink quickly if one attempts to stratify results by parent characteristics such as income or if one attempts to follow an individual child over time. This is because the ECCT students have entered in different years and at different grade levels, and therefore the number in any participation/grade category in a single year is likely to be small. Moreover, because individual test scores can be quite volatile, it is advisable to restrict comparisons to relatively large groups to get the statistical benefits of the "law of large numbers."

For this evaluation we compared four groups of students: IPS students who had transferred to private schools via the ECCT program, all IPS students, private school students who had been in private schools before becoming involved in the ECCT program, and a group of IPS students who had applied to the ECCT program, but who had not yet transferred.

The first group was our "treatment" group—those students who were expected to improve their performance because of the choice opportunity. The second group was a broad "control" group representing the environment from which the transferring students came. They do not represent a control group "matched" to the treatment group, because they were not restricted by the income limitations of the ECCT program. Moreover, one could argue that parents who elect to transfer their children are a self-selected group that may exhibit higher motivation to support their children's education. The lack of income limitations could be construed as biasing the performance of this group of students upward relative to the treatment group, as the richer economic means of the parents could be expected to provide positive support. On the other hand, the fact that these parents did not all exhibit the self-selection characteristic of seeking to transfer their children might bias the performance of this broad control group down relative to that of the treatment group. On balance it is impossible to ascertain the net effect of these two factors.

The third group represented the environment the transferring group entered—that is, private school students who were in private schools before the beginning of the ECCT program. These students were also enrollees in the ECCT program. They met the income limitations of the transferring students, and they also received up to half their tuition from the program. The fourth group was a narrower control group that was matched to the treatment group in terms of income level and the parents' motivation to transfer their children. This group was taken from the waiting list of public school students who had not yet transferred to private schools. This group was broader than the group of surveyed waiting list students identified as the control group in the first section of this report. Not enough students in that group were in the appropriate grade to make for a valid comparison with the treatment group. Therefore, we augmented the waiting list students who had been surveyed with students and families on the 1995 waiting list who were in IPS schools and were in grades two and above. This provided us with a matched control group of 250 students for whom we were able to obtain ISTEP and CTBS/4 scores for tests given in the IPS system in 1992–95. Unfortunately, no students above the seventh grade had applied to the ECCT program, so we were not able to obtain any IPS eighth-grade ISTEP scores. We also did not have parent survey information for this group, but the data we did have enabled us to make comparisons with sufficient numbers to obtain the benefits of large samples in suppressing statistical noise.

To obtain the benefits of larger samples, we combined test scores within each of the four groups across all years for which we had data. That is, test scores for the IPS total are average scores for four years across all schools by grade level and subject (reading, math, and language). Similarly, for the treatment group, the private school group, and the augmented control group we calculated the average ISTEP score by grade level and by subject.

The first two vertical bars in figure 12-11 represent, respectively, the average scores of IPS students who had transferred to private schools and of the private students who had previously been enrolled in the private

Figure 12-11. Average *ISTEP Total Reading Scores, 1990–93*

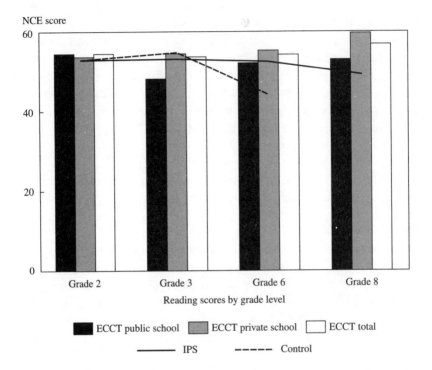

schools. The third bar is the average score of these two groups of students combined. The solid line represents the aggregate scores of all IPS students in the IPS system. The dotted line represents the matched control group of students who were on the waiting list to transfer to private schools, but were still in the IPS system. The scores are ISTEP scores converted to the normal curve equivalent (NCE) format so that they are comparable across schools and time. The difficulty of the test increases with each grade, so a student who earns, for example, a score of 60 in grade two and also in grade three would be expected to have made progress of one grade level. Therefore, scores are comparable across grades as measures of progress.

The first thing to notice is the marked decline in IPS ISTEP scores in grades six and eight. This pattern of declining standardized scores is quite common in urban areas and is not limited to IPS—although it might be more severe in that district. In contrast to this pattern, the scores of the ECCT private school group do not display this decline in the middle school years. The question

Figure 12-12. *Average ISTEP Total Math Scores, 1990–93*

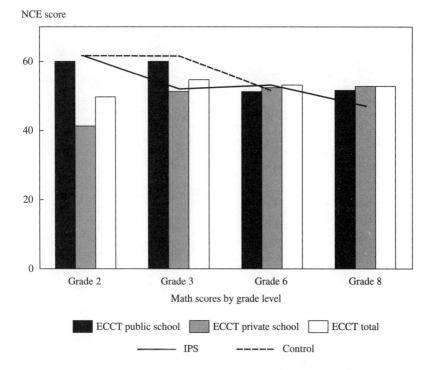

NCE score

Math scores by grade level

is how did the treatment group fare in the new environment? Although the reading scores of the ECCT public school group dropped between the second and third grades, they began to track the general upward trend of the private ECCT students in grades six and eight. The scores of the matched control group were similar to the IPS aggregate except that there was a more severe decline in grade six. (There are, as mentioned, no eighth-grade scores for this group.)

It is important to note that the comparisons between successive grades are not longitudinal in the sense that the students in the grade two group are the same as in the grade three group one year later. Although there are some cases of the same individuals' appearing in the grade two data and in the grade three data for the next year, there are not enough of those individuals to make a valid comparison. Moreover, there are no individuals who spanned the time period from third grade to the sixth grade.

Figure 12-12 depicts the math scores for the four groups. Again a decline in IPS ISTEP scores is evident, and the matched control group seems to have followed the same pattern. There also was a decline in scores in the

Figure 12-13. *Average ISTEP Total Language Scores, 1990–93*

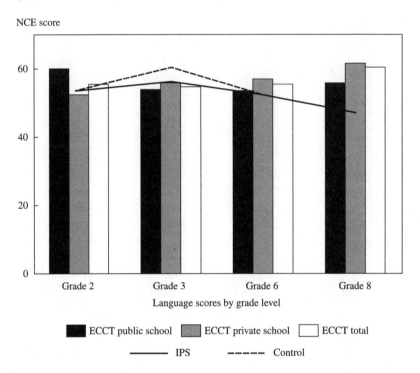

NCE score

Language scores by grade level

ECCT public school   ECCT private school   ECCT total

——— IPS   ----- Control

treatment group as they progressed from grades two through six. Although the treatment group's math scores exceeded the private school scores in grades two and three, they were approximately the same in grade six. In grade eight the IPS scores continued to decline, but the ECCT students' scores remained the same. Because we have no eighth-grade scores for the matched control group, we do not know whether they would follow the IPS scores. It seems reasonable to assume that they would.

Figure 12-13 depicts the language ISTEP scores for the four groups. The IPS scores again show a decline in grades six and eight; the matched control group followed suit in grades two through six. The ECCT public and private school scores were similar to the IPS scores in grades two and three, but then began to exceed the IPS scores in grades six and eight.

Remembering that these are not longitudinal results showing progress from year to year, it nevertheless seems fair to conclude that students in private schools, including those who have transferred under the auspices of the ECCT program, do as well as IPS students in the earlier grades and seem to be doing better in the middle school grades.

Conclusion

We compared four groups: students who had previously been in private schools, students who had transferred from public schools, students who expected to transfer but were on waiting lists, and the entire population of the public IPS system. Although transferring students lost some ground in the early grades, especially in mathematics, in middle school they began to track the steady upward progress of the students who were in the private schools all along. The broad population of IPS middle school students, on the other hand, experienced a severe drop in performance in the sixth and eighth grades.

Reasonable observers could disagree about the meaning of these standardized test comparisons and to what extent they tell us anything about the impact of the availability of school choice. The results are descriptive and not definitive because of the small sample and narrow model. In addition, they are based on a comparison with the Indianapolis public schools, which many regard as a poor public-school system. Had the comparison group attended higher quality public schools, the results might have been different. But when information from the standardized tests is combined with the results of the parent survey in the previous section—which showed that parents whose children were in the ECCT program were more satisfied with and more involved in their children's education—the evidence of positive benefits arising from expanded choice is strengthened. We conclude that giving parents a choice over how and where their children are educated also gives them ownership and enthusiasm that contribute directly to improvement of their children's performance outcomes.

Notes

1. John E. Chubb and Terry M. Moe, *Politics Markets, and America's Schools* (Brookings, 1990).

2. John E. Coons and Stephen D. Sugarman, *Education by Choice: the Case for Family Control* (University of California Press, 1978).

3. Milton Friedman, *Capitalism and Freedom* (University of Chicago Press, 1962).

4. Christopher Jencks, *Inequality* (New York: Basic Books, 1972).

5. Chubb and Moe, *Politics, Markets, and America's Schools.*

6. James S. Coleman, *Foundations of Social Theory* (Belknap Press of Harvard University Press, 1990).

7. John E. Coons and Stephen D. Sugarman, *Family Choice in Education: A Model State System for Vouchers* (University of California, Institute of Governmental Studies, 1971).

8. Paul E. Peterson, "Monopoly and Competition in American Education," in William H. Clune and John F. Witte, eds., *Choice and Control in American Education: The*

Theory of Choice and Control in American Education, vol. 1 (London: Falmer, 1990) pp. 47–78.

9. Anthony Bryk, Valerie E. Lee, and Peter B. Holland, *Catholic Schools and the Common Good* (Harvard University Press, 1993).

10. Jonathan Kozol, *Savage Inequalities: Children in America's Schools* (New York: Crown, 1991).

11. Albert Shanker, "Do Private Schools Outperform Public Schools?" *American Educator* 15, no. 2 (1991), pp. 8–15, 40–41.

12. Carnegie Foundation for the Advancement of Teaching, *School Choice: A Special Report* (Princeton, N.J.: The Carnegie Foundation for the Advancement of Teaching, 1992); Henry M. Levin, "The Economics of Educational Choice," *Economics of Education Review* 10 (1988), pp. 137–58.

13. Carnegie Foundation for the Advancement of Teaching, *School Choice: A Special Report.*

14. Carnegie Foundation for the Advancement of Teaching, *School Choice: A Special Report,* p. 1.

15. Actually, the analysis includes results from two different control groups, both defined in the same way but at different points in time. The first control group completed surveys in the fall of 1994, describing their characteristics and reasons for joining the program; these results are discussed later in this chapter. We were unable, however, to obtain test scores for this group of students; therefore, a second control group was established in the spring of 1995. This second control group was used in the comparisons of standardized test scores presented in the section on student achievement.

16. Our measure of income is static. It might be that persons reporting financial considerations as the reasons for withdrawing experienced a reduction in their incomes. This change could have been the operational factor leading to a decision to leave regardless of the average level of income.

17. Percentile rankings and grade equivalents suffer from a mathematical problem: They do not represent an "equal interval" scale. Simply put, this means that a 5 percent gain in the middle of the distribution represents a different interval of growth from those in outer portions of the distribution. Therefore, it is not possible to "add up" gains from students at different points in the distribution to obtain an overall average.

THIRTEEN

School Choice in Milwaukee: A Randomized Experiment

Jay P. Greene, Paul E. Peterson, and Jiangtao Du

SCHOOL CHOICE OR VOUCHER plans in which parents could use public funds to select the public or private schools that their children would attend have been receiving serious consideration as a means of improving the quality and efficiency of educational services. Although there are theoretical reasons to believe that choice and competition in schooling might be beneficial, evidence from a randomized experiment has not been available to substantiate or refute those theories. The evidence presented in this chapter from the school choice program in Milwaukee provides an opportunity to learn more about the effects of voucher programs from experimental data.

The Milwaukee experiment is unique in that it is the first publicly funded voucher program in the country and the only one with several years of results. The Milwaukee experiment is also unique in that vouchers were assigned by lottery when classes were oversubscribed. Analysis of data from a randomized experiment avoids the selection bias of comparing choosers to nonchoosers that has plagued other studies of choice in education. The Milwaukee experiment is of further interest in that it offers a hard test of choice theories because of the numerous constraints under which the program has operated.

Scholars have suggested that privatization may enhance efficiency in education in three different ways. First, competition among providers may reduce the cost and improve the quality of services.[1] Second, government-financed services may more closely match consumer preferences if the latter are given opportunities to sort themselves among an array of options.[2] Third, private producers may more easily enlist the participation of consumers in the co-production of the services, thereby enhancing service quality and effectiveness.[3]

If school choice could significantly improve the quality of education, the political and social benefits would be more than trivial. Apart from cash-transfer services, education is the largest part of the gross national product (GNP) of any publicly provided service.[4] In 1990 the cost of publicly financed education services constituted $305.6 billion, or 5.6 percent of the GNP.[5] Yet public confidence in public schools remains very low. In 1993 only 19 percent of the population was willing to give schools a grade of A or B, a fall of 8 percentage points since a decade earlier.[6]

Weak confidence in our public schools may be due to their failure to keep pace with rising public expectations. Estimated real costs within the educational sector, adjusted for inflation, rose by 29 percent or at an annual rate of 1.5 percent between 1974 and 1991.[7] Meanwhile, students' performance as measured by test scores, an important educational outcome, remained fairly constant.[8] Between 1970 and 1992 elementary and secondary students averaged no more than a gain of .1 of a standard deviation in mathematics and reading on the National Assessment of Educational Progress, generally thought to be the best available measure of student achievement. Meanwhile, their scores in science fell by .24 of standard deviation.[9] Increasing costs with at best slight gains in student achievement suggest that the public school system has become less efficient.

Opportunities for efficiency gains are particularly large in central cities. Whereas competition among small school districts exists in suburban parts of many metropolitan areas,[10] most city schools are governed by a single school board that does not ordinarily allow schools to compete for students.[11] Schools in rural areas often function as community institutions, facilitating co-production of educational services, but city schools have more limited ties to their immediate neighborhoods. Perhaps for these reasons, educational outcomes in the city lag those outside the central city.[12]

It has been argued that any efficiency gains are unlikely to result in higher levels of student achievement, because cognitive skills are either inherited or set in place at an early age, making them hardly susceptible to manipulation by educational processes.[13] But the weight of the evidence is in the opposite direction; numerous studies have found that school characteristics affect student achievement.[14] If these findings are correct, it may be hypothesized that if government grants are made available to families so they can purchase educational services for their children, efficiency gains accompanying privatization will result in enhanced student achievement.[15] Under such arrangements, competition among producers increases. Inasmuch as consumers' educational preferences vary and entry into the educational market is not prohibitively large, many producers will attempt to meet a demand for a range and variety of services. Co-production by consumers and providers (families and the schools) is more likely if families have a choice of schools.[16]

Yet efficiency gains that facilitate academic achievement may not be as great as these considerations suggest. Consumers may not have the information necessary to discern schools' academic quality.[17] Or consumers may choose schools on the basis of the schools' nonacademic characteristics, such as proximity, religiosity, sports facilities, or social segregation.[18]

Potential gains in student achievement as a result of privatization are much disputed, in part because empirical research has left the issue unresolved. Although two different research traditions have sought to estimate the comparative efficiency of private and public schools, neither has provided a definitive answer. The first research tradition has relied on data from national samples (High School and Beyond, the National Longitudinal Study of Youth, and the National Education Longitudinal Study) to estimate the achievement effects of attending public and private schools. Most of these studies have found that students who attend private schools score higher on achievement tests or are more likely to attend college than those who attend public schools.[19]

Because private schools are generally less expensive than public schools, these studies suggest greater efficiency in the private sector. But these findings may be contaminated by selection bias: Students in private schools, who come from tuition-paying families, may have unobserved characteristics that increase the likelihood of their scoring higher on achievement tests, regardless of the schools they attend.[20]

The second research tradition consists of studies that evaluate the test performance of students from low-income or at-risk backgrounds who have received scholarships that give them the opportunity to move from public to private schools.[21] Although these evaluations also have reported that private schools produce higher levels of student achievement with less expenditure per pupil, their findings may also be contaminated by unobserved background characteristics of scholarship recipients. In almost all the programs studied, scholarships have been distributed on a first-come, first-served basis. They also require additional tuition payments by families, increasing the likelihood that scholarship recipients have unobserved characteristics (such as motivation) correlated with higher test scores.

A previous evaluation of the Milwaukee choice program reports no systematic achievement effects of enrollment in private schools.[22] But this evaluation compared students from low-income families with public school students from more advantaged backgrounds, leaving open the possibility that unobserved background characteristics could account for the lack of positive findings.[23] In sum, with the exception of the Milwaukee evaluation, most studies have found efficiency gains from the privatization of educational services. Yet all studies have suffered from potential selection bias, because they have relied on nonexperimental data that have included unobserved but possibly relevant background characteristics that could account for reported findings.

One way to improve on previous research is to conduct an experiment that avoids selection bias by randomly assigning students to treatment and control groups. With random assignment the members of the two groups can be assumed to be similar, on average, in all respects other than the treatment they receive. Differences in average outcomes can be reasonably attributed to the experimental condition. Only a few studies of school effectiveness have been able to draw upon data from randomized experiments, probably because it is difficult to justify random denial of access to apparently desirable educational conditions.[24] The results from the Milwaukee choice program reported here are, to the best of our knowledge, the first to estimate from a randomized experiment the comparative achievement effects of public and private schools.

Some results from the randomized experiment in Milwaukee were reported by Witte and associates in 1994,[25] but that study concentrated on a comparison of students in choice schools with a cross-section of students attending public schools. Data from the randomized experiment were underanalyzed and discussed only in passing.[26] In addition to our initial report,[27] two other studies have reported results from the randomized experiment in Milwaukee,[28] but all three studies relied on inaccurate test score data.

Subsequent to issuing our report in 1996, we discovered that the Milwaukee test score data available on the world wide web did not adjust for the fact that some students were not promoted from one grade to the next. For example, students in both test and control groups who were held back for a year at the end of third grade were scored as third graders when they otherwise would have been scored as fourth graders. When this happens, a student can receive a much higher percentile score than is appropriate. Other students are allowed to skip a grade, and if this promotion is not taken into account, it produces an error of the opposite kind. We were able to eliminate both types of error by adjusting test scores to the correct grade level by means of conversion tables.[29]

A Hard Case

The Milwaukee choice program, initiated in 1990, provided vouchers to a limited number of students from low-income families to be used to pay tuition at their choice of secular private schools in Milwaukee. The program was a hard case for testing the hypothesis that efficiency gains can be achieved through privatization, because it allowed only a very limited amount of competition among producers and choice among consumers.[30]

The number of producers was restricted by the requirement that no more than half of a school's enrollment could receive vouchers. Because this rule discouraged the formation of new schools, no new elementary school came into being in response to the establishment of the voucher program. Consumer choice was further limited by excluding the participation of religious schools (thereby precluding use of approximately 90 percent of the private school capacity within the city of Milwaukee). Co-production was also discouraged by prohibiting families from supplementing the vouchers with tuition payments of their own. (But schools did ask families to pay school fees and make voluntary contributions.) Other restrictions also limited program size. Only 1 percent of the Milwaukee public schools could participate, and students could not receive a voucher unless they had been attending public schools or were not of school age at the time of application.

These restrictions significantly limited the amount of school choice that was made available. Most choice students attended fiscally constrained institutions with limited facilities and poorly paid teachers.[31] One school, Juanita Virgil Academy, closed a few months after the program began.[32] Although the school had existed as a private school for a number of years, it was eager to admit sixty-three choice students in order to alleviate its enrollment and financial difficulties. Even with the addition of the choice students, the school's problems persisted. To comply with the requirement that schools offer secular curricula, the school had to drop its Bible classes. Parents complained about the food service, overcrowded classrooms, a shortage of books and materials, and a lack of cleanliness and discipline. The executive director had hired a new principal away from the public schools, but she had to be relieved of her responsibilities two months into the school year. The school withdrew from the choice program the next semester, giving as its reason the desire to "reinstate religious training in the school." A few weeks later the school closed altogether.[33]

Given the design of the Milwaukee choice program, more school failures might have been expected. The three schools that together with Juanita Virgil Academy admitted 84 percent of the choice students in 1990 had modest facilities and low teacher salaries. Bruce Guadalupe Community School was in particular difficulty. Established in 1969, it sought to preserve Latino culture and teach children respect for both English and Spanish. Many teachers had once taught in Central American schools. Instruction was bilingual, often more in Spanish than English. Despite its distinctive educational mission, the school had difficulty making ends meet. Even finding an adequate school building seemed a never-ending problem; the school moved from one location to another on several occasions during its first two decades. By January 1990 things had become so desperate that the school was on "the verge of closing." But enactment of the choice program gave the school "new hope for the future," a hope that "otherwise had been snuffed out."[34] A tuition voucher of more than $2,500 per student was a boon to a school that had had trouble collecting $650 from each participating family.

Despite the arrival of choice students in the fall of 1990, the school, still in financial distress, was forced to cut its teaching staff by a third. The school's difficulties were fully reported in the *Milwaukee Journal:* "Two staff aides were fired, the seventh and eighth grades were combined, the second grade was eliminated with children put into the first or third grade, and the bilingual Spanish program was cut. . . . Two teachers were transferred. . . . The former eighth grade teacher [was] teaching fourth grade. . . . Overall, the teaching staff was reduced from 14 to 9."[35] The school's principal described staff morale as "low."

The two other community schools with large choice enrollments, Harambee Community School and Urban Day School, had better reputations, but still suffered from serious financial difficulties.[36] Like Bruce Guadalupe, they catered almost exclusively to a low-income minority population. Established in the 1960s in former Catholic parish schools, they tried to survive as secular institutions after the archdiocese closed the parochial schools. Named for the Swahili word meaning "pulling together," Harambee presented itself as "an African American–owned school emphasizing the basics through creative instructional programs, coupled with a strong cultural foundation."[37] Urban Day was said to place "a heavy emphasis on African history and culture."[38]

Like Bruce Guadalupe, these schools could ask families to pay only a very modest tuition. Though they set their annual rates at somewhere between $650 and $800, only a few families whose children were attending the schools actually paid full tuition. Tuition scholarships were the norm, not an exceptional privilege. But parents were expected to participate in fund-raising activities. Teacher salaries were much lower than those paid by the Milwaukee public schools. As one principal observed, "The teachers who stay here for a long time are either very dedicated or can afford to stay on what we pay."[39]

The quality of the physical plant provided a visible sign of the school's modest financial resources: "Recess and physical education facilities were relatively poor in the schools. One school had easy access to a city park for recess, one relied on a blocked off street, two others asphalt playgrounds with some wood chips and playground equipment. All the schools had some indoor space for physical education, but it often served multiple purposes."[40] One of its hardest-working supporters was asked what she would most wish for the school. She said, "I'd like to see the school financially self-sufficient."[41]

To repeat, the Milwaukee choice program is a hard case to test the hypothesis that privatization can result in efficiency gains. If one finds efficiency gains under considerably less than ideal circumstances, one is likely to find gains under more opportune conditions.

School Costs

The relative costs of the public and private schools in Milwaukee remained approximately the same throughout the four years of the experiment. In the 1991–92 school year payments per pupil to schools participating in the choice program schools were $2,729. Based on interviews with school administrators, it is estimated that schools received an additional $500 per student through fees and fund-raising activities. Therefore, the total costs per pupil are estimated to have been $3,229. Per-pupil costs for the Milwaukee public schools at this time averaged $6,656, somewhat higher than the $5,748 cost of educating the average public school student in the United States as a whole.[42]

Although it appears that the cost of educating a pupil in a choice school was only 48 percent of the cost of educating a student in the Milwaukee

public schools, the actual difference was not this large. Choice school
students were provided transportation by the Milwaukee public school
system if they needed it. In addition, the reported per-pupil expenditures for
the Milwaukee public schools included the costs of educating secondary
school students (which may be more expensive than elementary education)
as well as students receiving special services. But even after taking these
considerations into account, the per-pupil costs of the private schools were
lower.

The Milwaukee Randomized Experiment

The Milwaukee school choice program was a randomized experiment.
To ensure equal access to the choice program among eligible applicants, the
legislature required choice schools, if oversubscribed, to admit applicants at
random. In the words of the original evaluation team, "Students not selected
into the Choice Program in the random selection process represent a unique
research opportunity. . . . If there are any unmeasured characteristics of
families seeking private education, they should on average be similar between those in and not in the program."[43] The legislature asked the state's
Department of Public Instruction to evaluate the Milwaukee choice experiment. Data were collected on family background characteristics and
student performance on the Iowa Test of Basic Skills in reading and
mathematics. These data were made available on the world wide web in
February 1996.

Students did not apply to the choice program as a whole; instead, they
applied each year for a seat in a specific grade in a particular school. They
were selected or not selected randomly by school and by grade. Because the
random assignment policy was implemented in this way, in our analysis we
used a fixed effects model that took into account the grade to which a
student applied and the year of application.[44] Our analysis was unable to
ascertain the particular school to which a student applied,[45] but it took this
factor partially into account by adjusting for the ethnicity of the applicant.
More than 80 percent of the choice students attended one of three schools,
and of these three schools virtually all students applying to one school were
Hispanic, and almost all students applying to the two others were African
American. Though the analysis took the two predominantly African-
American schools as a block, it otherwise distinguished among schools by
adjusting for whether the applicant was Hispanic or African American.
Because the number of white students and other minority students for

whom information was available was so sparse that no reliable results could be obtained, these students were removed from the analysis.

By using a fixed effects model that took into account each point at which randomization occurred, together with a control for gender, it was possible to estimate the effects of enrollment on test scores in choice schools.[46] This procedure treated each point at which randomization occurred as a dummy variable. The measures of test score performance were the students' normal curve equivalent (NCE) scores for math and reading on the Iowa Test of Basic Skills. The NCE is a transformation of the national percentile rankings that arranges the scores around the fiftieth percentile in a manner that can be described by a normal curve. A standard deviation for NCE is 21 percentile points.

Separate ordinary least squares regressions produced an estimate of the effect of one, two, three, and four years of treatment on math and reading scores. The analysis of the Milwaukee randomized experiment conducted by Rouse constrained the effects of treatment to be linear in order to estimate the effect of each year in a single regression for math and reading, respectively.[47] Because the effects of treatment do not seem to have been linear, our approach of estimating each amount of treatment separately avoided this source of potential bias.

Coefficients for each dummy representing the points of randomization and the constant are too cumbersome to present in a book of this nature, but are available from the authors upon request, as are the coefficients for all substantive variables employed in the models. We controlled for gender in every regression, because it was available for virtually all students and produced a more precise estimate of the effect of treatment.

Our data are limited by the fact that test data were available for only 78 percent of those assigned to the treatment group and 72 percent assigned to the control group. The percentage of test scores available decreased to 40 percent of the treatment group and 48 percent of the control group by the third or fourth year following application to the program (see table 13-1).

Our results depend on the assumption that the missing cases did not differ appreciably from those remaining in the sample.[48] One way of estimating whether this assumption is reasonable is to examine the observed characteristics of students in the treatment and control groups. As can be seen in table 13-2, the background characteristics of the two groups do not differ in important respects. In the words of the original evaluation team, "In terms of demographic characteristics, non-selected . . . students came from very similar homes as choice [students did]. They were also similar in terms of prior achievement scores and parental involvement.[49]

Table 13-1. *Students for Whom Data Are Available*

Student category	Choice students	Control students
Percent with test scores available (table 13-3, columns 1–4)	79	72
Total number who applied, 1990–93	908	363
Percent with test scores three or four years after application (table 13-3, column 5)	40	48
Total number who applied in 1990 or 1991, making it possible to have scores three or four years after application	592	166

Table 13-2. *Background Characteristics of Students in Treatment and Control Groups*
Total numbers of cases in parentheses

Characteristic	All students in the study			All students with scores three or four years after application		
	Choice students	Control students	p value[a]	Choice students	Control students	p value[a]
Math scores before application	39.7 (264)	39.3 (173)	.81	40.0 (61)	40.6 (33)	.86
Reading scores before application	38.9 (266)	39.4 (176)	.74	42.1 (60)	39.2 (33)	.35
Family income	10,860 (423)	12,010 (127)	.14	10,850 (143)	11,170 (25)	.84
Mothers' education 3 = some college 4 = college degree	4.2 (423)	3.9 (127)	.04	4.1 (144)	3.8 (29)	.15
Percent married parents	24 (424)	30 (132)	.17	23 (145)	38 (29)	.11
Parents' time with children 1 = 1–2 hours/week 2 = 3–4 hours/week 3 = 5 or more	1.9 (420)	1.8 (130)	.37	1.9 (140)	1.7 (27)	.26
Parents' education expectations of children 4 = college 5 = graduate school	4.2 (422)	4.2 (129)	.85	4.2 (142)	3.7 (27)	.01

a. The tests of significance are suggestive of the equivalence of the two groups. Technically, tests of significance should be done at each point of random assignment, but the number of cases at each point is too few for such tests to be meaningful.

Results

Using the analytical procedures discussed above, we estimated the effects of choice schools on students' performance after one, two, three, and four years of attending choice schools.[50] Table 13-3 reports the results of our main analysis, in which we estimated the difference in test scores between students attending choice schools and those in the control group after controlling for gender using a fixed effects model that takes into account the points of randomization in the experiment.

The estimated effects of choice schools on mathematics achievement were slight for the first two years students were in the program. But after three years of enrollment students scored 5 percentile points higher than the control group; after four years they scored 10.7 points higher. These differences between the two groups three and four years after their application to choice schools are .24 and .51 standard deviation of the national distribution of math test scores, respectively. They are statistically significant at accepted confidence levels.[51] Differences on the reading test were between 2 and 3 percentile points for the first three years and increased to 5.8 percentile points in the fourth. The results for the third and fourth years are statistically significant when the two are jointly estimated.[52]

Table 13-3. *The Effect of Attending a Choice School on Test Scores, Controlling for Gender, Using Fixed Effects Model*
NCE Percentile points[a]

Effect and subject	1 year of treatment	2 years of treatment	3 years of treatment	4 years of treatment	3 or 4 years jointly estimated
Differences in mathematics scores between choice students and control group					
Effect on math scores	1.31	1.89	5.02**	10.65**	6.81**
Standard error	1.98	2.05	3.07	4.92	2.97
N	772	584	300	112	316
Differences in reading scores					
Effect on reading scores	2.22*	2.26	2.73	5.84*	4.85**
Standard error	1.74	1.78	2.63	4.22	2.57
N	734	604	301	112	318

* = p < .10 in one-tailed t-test
** = p < .05 in one-tailed t-test
a. Normal curve equivalent

Controlling for Family Background

The results in the main analysis in table 13-3 provide the best estimate of the achievement effects of attendance in private schools, because this analysis had the fewest missing cases. But because these results do not take into account family background characteristics, they depend on the assumption that students were assigned at random to the test and control groups. Inasmuch as even the main analysis had many missing cases, it was possible that the two groups were no longer similar in relevant respects, despite their similar demographics (see table 13-2). To explore whether this possibility contaminated our results, We performed a fixed effects analysis that took into account gender, mother's education, and parents' marital status, income, education expectations, and time spent with the child. Table 13-4 reports the results.

This analysis depended on information provided in response to a written questionnaire which, unfortunately, many parents did not complete. Background information was available for only 47 percent of the selected students and 36 percent of the control group. The number of cases available for analysis was therefore considerably reduced, and the point estimates are less reliable. Nevertheless, all point estimates are positive, and six of the eight are actually larger than those reported in the main analysis.

Table 13-4. *The Effect of Attending a Choice School on Test Scores, Controlling for Gender, Education Expectations, Income, Marital Status, Mother's Education, and Time Spent with Child, Using Fixed Effects Model* NCE percentile points[a]

Effect and subject	1 year of treatment	2 years of treatment	3 years of treatment	4 years of treatment
Differences in mathematics scores between choice students and control group				
Effect on math scores	6.01**	5.36*	8.16*	7.97
Standard error	3.39	3.39	5.82	9.85
N	378	289	149	57
Differences in reading scores				
Effect on reading scores	4.72**	1.17	8.87**	15.00*
Standard error	2.88	2.99	5.27	9.45
N	358	293	150	55

a. Normal curve equivalent.
* = p < .10 in one-tailed t-test
** = p < .05 in one-tailed t-test

Controlling for Prior Test Scores

The main analysis did not control for students' test scores before entering into the choice program. It is not necessary to control for pre-experimental test scores when comparing a treatment group and a control group in an experimental situation, because the two groups, if randomly assigned to each category, can be assumed to be similar. But because of the sizable number of missing cases it is possible that the two groups we compared had different pretest scores before the experiment began. This potential source of bias did not appear, however. The average pretest scores at the time of application for the two groups were essentially the same. The average math and reading pretest scores for those selected choice for the program were the NCE equivalents of 39 and 38 percentile rankings, respectively; for those not selected they were the NCE equivalents of a 39 percentile ranking for reading and a 40 percentile ranking for math (see table 13-2).

Inasmuch as the students' pretest scores at the time of application were essentially the same, it is unlikely that controls for this variable would alter the result. We nonetheless tested for the possibility, and the results are reported in table 13-5. Because pretest scores at the time of application were available for only 29 percent of the selected students and 49 percent of the control group, the sample size for this analysis is smaller and the results are generally not statistically significant. Yet five of the eight point es-

Table 13-5. *The Effect of Attending a Choice School on Test Scores, Controlling for Gender and Test Score before Application, Using Fixed Effects Model*
NCE percentile points[a]

Effect and subject	1 year of treatment	2 years of treatment	3 years of treatment	4 years of treatment
Differences in mathematics scores between choice students and control group				
Effect on math scores	2.34	3.46*	7.40**	4.98
Standard error	2.32	2.71	4.08	9.16
N	286	185	83	31
Differences in reading scores				
Effect on reading scores	1.50	3.24*	5.28*	−3.29
Standard error	2.07	2.46	3.74	7.46
N	303	189	84	31

a. Normal curve equivalent.
* = p < .10 in one-tailed t-test
** = p < .05 in one-tailed t-test

timates are larger than those in the main analysis, and all but one have positive signs.

Effects on All Students Accepted into the Choice Program

The results reported so far compare students who attended private schools with students who had applied for choice but were assigned to the control group. Some students, however, were accepted into the program but chose not to participate for the full four years. Some students immediately turned down the opportunity, but others left sometime during the four-year period.

To see the effect of the choice program on all those admitted, regardless of their subsequent enrollment decisions, we conducted an analysis identical to the main analysis, except that analysis compared all students initially assigned to treatment and control groups, regardless of the schools they chose to attend. This type of analysis is known in medical research as an intention-to-treat analysis. In many medical experiments subjects may be more or less faithful in complying with the treatment. For example, some forget to take their pills three times a day as instructed. An intention-to-treat analysis answers this question: Is the treatment effective even when compliance is less than 100 percent? Those who refused enrollment in the private schools or left before the end of the experiment can be thought of as not having complied with the treatment.

This approach had the important disadvantage of including in the treatment group many students who either did not attend the private schools or attended the private schools for less than the full period under study. But it had two advantages. First, departure from an ideal randomized experiment was less in this case than in the main analysis. All cases were preserved except instances in which test data were not collected. The percentage of intention-to-treat cases in the analysis was 89 percent; sixty-three percent of the intention-to-treat cases three or four years after application remained in this analysis (see table 13-6).[53] (There were fewer missing cases because the students who left private schools but were tested in the Milwaukee public schools were not excluded from the intention-to-treat analysis.) Second, this analysis may have better captured what might happen if choice between public and private schools were generalized; students can be expected to migrate back and forth between the two systems.

Are there efficiency gains when comparisons are made between all those randomly assigned to the intention-to-treat group and the control group?

Table 13-6. *Percentage of Students in Intention-to-Treat Analysis for Whom Data Are Available*

Student category	Selected students	Control students
Percent with test scores available (table 13-7, columns 1–4)	89	72
Total number who applied, 1990–93	908	363
Percent with test scores three or four years after application	63	48
Total number who applied in 1990 or 1991, making it possible to have scores three or four years after application	592	166

The answer to this question is given in table 13-7. The effects do not differ in any significant way from those reported in the main analysis. Slight positive effects are found for the first three years after application to the program, and moderately large effects are found after four years. Students who were given a choice of schools performed better than did the control group, regardless of the public or private schools they attended. All results but one are statistically significant at the .1 level; fourth-year results are significant at the .05 level.

Table 13-7. *The Effect of Being Selected for a Choice School (Intention to Treat) on Test Scores, Controlling for Gender, Using Fixed Effects Model* NCE percentile points[a]

Effect and subject	1 year of treatment	2 years of treatment	3 years of treatment	4 years of treatment
Differences in mathematics scores between choice students and control group				
Effect on math scores	2.68*	2.59*	3.83*	11.00**
Standard error	1.89	1.94	2.87	4.14
N	854	728	435	175
Differences in reading scores				
Effect on reading scores	2.46*	2.57*	2.10	6.26**
Standard error	1.71	1.68	2.48	3.65
N	816	738	441	175

a. Normal curve equivalent.
* = p < .10 in one-tailed t-test
** = p < .05 in one-tailed t-test

These results suggest that some of the achievement effects produced by choice may be due to a closer match between school qualities and student needs. When families are given a choice between public and private schools, they may be choosing the options best suited to their children. It is possible that public schools induced some families with students in the treatment group to return to the public schools by providing them with better public school alternatives. The Milwuakee public school system had the ability to respond in this manner because it had a number of magnet schools. It also had the incentive to react, because the system could regain funds equivalent to the size of the voucher if a student returned to the public school system.

Conclusions

The Milwaukee choice experiment suggests that privatization in education may result in efficiency gains. This finding emerges from a randomized experiment less likely to suffer from selection bias than studies dependent on nonrandomized data. The consistency of the results is noteworthy. Positive results were found for all years and for all comparisons except one. The results reported in the main analysis for both math and reading are statistically significant for students remaining in the program for three to four years when these are jointly estimated.

These results after three and four years are moderately large, ranging from .1 of a standard deviation to as much as .5 of a standard deviation. Studies of educational effects interpret effects of .1 standard deviation as slight, effects of .2 and .3 standard deviation as moderate, and effects of .5 standard deviation as large.[54] Even effects of .1 standard deviation are potentially large if they accumulate over time.[55] The average difference in test performances of whites and minorities in the United States is one standard deviation.[56] If the results from Milwaukee can be generalized and extrapolated to twelve years, a large part of between-group reading differences and all of between-group math differences could be erased.

Without data beyond the Milwaukee program's first four years, one can only speculate as to whether such generalization and extrapolation are warranted. But if they are, the effectiveness of government-financed education could be greatly enhanced. These moderately large effects on student achievement were observed even though the Milwaukee plan offered students and families only a slightly enlarged set of educational choices. These achievement effects were produced at lower per-pupil cost than that of a Milwaukee public school education.

One must be cautious concerning the universe to which these results are generalized. Efficiency gains may be greater in Milwaukee and other central cities than in suburban areas where competition among school districts is greater. They may also be greater in cities than in rural communities where opportunities for co-production in public education may be more prevalent. The magnitude of the gains reported here may not be generalizable beyond central cities.

In addition, the study was limited to students from low-income families. Other studies suggest that private schools have a larger positive effect on the achievement of disadvantaged students.[57] Perhaps the results found in Milwaukee are restricted to low-income minority populations. Finally, the results are for families who applied for vouchers. It may be that the benefits of privatization are greater for those families who desire alternatives to the public schools serving them. Their children may have been particularly at risk in public schools, and they may be more willing to engage in co-production than all other families.

The conclusions that can be drawn from our study are further restricted by limitations of the data made available on the world wide web. Many cases are missing from this data set. The percentage of missing cases is especially large when one introduces controls for background characteristics and preexperimental test scores. But given the consistency and magnitude of the findings as well as their compelling policy implications, they suggest the desirability of further randomized experiments capable of reaching more precise estimates of efficiency gains through privatization.

Randomized experiment are under way in New York City, Dayton, and Washington, D.C.[58] If the evaluations of these randomized experiments minimize the number of missing cases and collect preexperimental data for all subjects in both treatment and control groups, they could, in a few years' time, provide more precise estimates of potential efficiency gains from privatizing the delivery of educational services to low-income students. Similar experiments should be conducted in a variety of contexts, but especially in large central cities, where potential efficiency gains seem particularly likely.

Notes

1. Kenneth Arrow, "An Extension of the Classical Theorems of Welfare Economics," in *Proceedings of the Second Berkeley Symposium on Mathematical Statistics* (Berkeley: University of California Press, 1951); Jacob Schmookler, *Invention and Economic Growth* (Harvard University Press, 1966); and James Dearden, Barry W. Ickes,

and Larry Samuelson, "To Innovate or Not to Innovate: Incentives and Innovation in Hierarchies," *American Economic Review* (December 1990), pp. 1105–06.

2. Charles M. Tiebout, "A Pure Theory of Local Expenditures," *Journal of Political Economy* 64 (October 1956), pp. 416–24; Robert L. Bish, *The Public Economy of Metropolitan Areas* (Chicago: Markham, 1971).

3. Elinor Parks, Roger B. Parks, and Gordon P. Whitaker, *Patterns of Metropolitan Policing* (Cambridge, Mass.: Ballinger Publishing, 1978).

4. Cash-transfer programs are larger but do not involve direct service provision. Although publicly funded medical services are more costly than publicly-funded schools, most medical services are provided by private vendors. In recent years the cost of defense has fallen below the cost of state-provided educational services.

5. Paul E. Peterson, *The Price of Federalism* (Brookings, 1995).

6. *Public Perspective,* Roper Center Review of Public Opinion and Polling (November-December 1993), p. 13.

7. Some of these increased school costs are due to improved services for students with disabilities and those who are otherwise disadvantaged.

8. Helen F. Ladd, ed., "Introduction," in Ladd, ed., *Holding Schools Accountable: Performance-based Reform in Education* (Brookings, 1996), p. 3; Richard Rothstein and Karen Hawley Miles, *Where's the Money Gone? Changes in the Level and Composition of Education Spending* (Washington: Economic Policy Institute, 1995), p. 7.

9. Larry V. Hedges and Rob Greenwald, "Have Times Changed? The Relation between School Resources and Student Performance," in Gary Burtless, ed., *Does Money Matter? The Effect of School Resources on Student Achievement and Adult Success* (Brookings, 1996), pp. 74–92; information cited on p. 78.

10. Caroline Minter Hoxby, "When Parents Can Choose, What Do They Choose? The Effects of School Choice on Curriculum," in Susan Mayer and Paul E. Peterson, eds., *When Schools Make a Difference* (forthcoming).

11. Paul E. Peterson, "Monopoly and Competition in American Education," in William H. Clune and John F. Witte, eds., *Choice and Control in American Education,* vol. 1 (New York: Falmer, 1990), pp. 47–78.

12. Pam Belluck, "Learning Gap Tied to Time in the System: As School Stay Grows, Scores on Tests Worsen," *New York Times,* January 5, 1997, p. B1; George A. Mitchell, *The Milwaukee Parental Choice Plan* (Milwaukee: Wisconsin Policy Research Institute, 1992); and Paul E. Peterson, "Are Big City Schools Holding Their Own?" in John Rury, ed., *Seeds of Crisis* (University of Wisconsin Press, 1993).

13. Richard J. Herrnstein and Charles Murray, *The Bell Curve: Intelligence and Class Structure in American Life* (Free Press, 1994).

14. David Card and Alan B. Krueger, "Does School Quality Matter? Returns to Education and the Characteristics of Public Schools in the United States," *Journal of Political Economy* 100 (February), pp. 1–40; Hedges and Greenwald, "Have Times Changed?"; Christopher Jencks and Meredith Phillips, "Does Learning Pay Off in the Job Market?" in Mayer and Peterson, eds., *When Schools Make a Difference*; Jay Girotto and Paul E. Peterson, "Do Hard Courses and Good Grades Enhance Cognitive Skills?" in Mayer and Peterson, eds., *When Schools Make a Difference;* Susan Mayer and David Knutson, "Early Education Versus More Education: Does the Timing of Education Matter?" in Mayer and Peterson, eds., *When Schools Make a Difference;* Robert Meyer, "Applied versus Traditional Mathematics: New Evidence on the Production of High School Mathmatics Skills," in Mayer and Peterson, eds., *When Schools Make a Difference.*

15. John E. Chubb and Terry M. Moe, *Politics, Markets, and American Schools* (Brookings, 1990).

16. Anthony Bryk, Valerie E. Lee, and Peter B. Holland, *Catholic Schools and the Common Good* (Harvard University Press, 1993).

17. Kevin B. Smith and Kenneth J. Meier, *The Case Against School Choice* (Armonk, N.Y.: M. E. Sharpe, 1995), p. 126; but also see Hoxby, "When Parents Can Choose, What Do They Choose?"

18. Richard F. Elmore, "Choice As an Instrument of Public Policy: Evidence from Education and Health Care," in Clune and Witte, eds., *Choice and Control in American Education,* vol. 1; Carnegie Foundation for the Advancement of Teaching, *School Choice* (Princeton, N.J., 1992); and Amy Gutmann, *Democratic Education* (Princeton University Press, 1987).

19. James S. Coleman, Thomas Hoffer, and Sally Kilgore, *High School Achievement* (New York: Basic Books, 1982); James S. Coleman and Thomas Hoffer, *Public and Private Schools: The Impact of Communities* (Basic Books, 1987); Chubb and Moe, *Politics, Markets, and American Schools;* Bryk, Lee, and Holland, *Catholic Schools and the Common Good;* William N. Evans and Robert M. Schwab, "Who Benefits from Private Education? Evidence from Quantile Regressions," Department of Economics, University of Maryland, 1993; and Christopher Jencks, "How Much Do High School Students Learn?" *Sociology of Education* 58 (April 1985), pp. 128–35. But for different results, see Douglas J. Wilms, "School Effectiveness within the Public and Private Sectors: An Evaluation," *Evaluation Review* 8 (1984), pp. 113–35; Douglas J. Wilms, "Catholic School Effects on Academic Achievement: New Evidence from the High School and Beyond Follow-up Study," *Sociology of Education* 58 (1985), pp. 98–114.

20. Arthur S. Goldberger and Glen G. Cain, "The Causal Analysis of Cognitive Outcomes in the Coleman, Hoffer, and Kilgore Report," *Sociology of Education* 55 (April-July 1982), pp. 103–22; Peter W. Cookson, Jr., *School Choice: The Struggle for the Soul of American Education* (Yale University Press, 1994); John F. Witte, "Understanding High School Achievement: After a Decade of Research, Do We Have Any Confident Policy Recommendations?" paper prepared for the 1990 annual meeting of the American Political Science Association; and John F. Witte, "Private School versus Public School Achievement: Are There Findings That Should Affect the Educational Choice Debate?" *Economics of Education Review* 11 (1992), pp. 371–94.

21. Terry M. Moe, ed., *Private Vouchers* (Stanford University Press, 1995); Valerie Martinez, Kenneth R. Godwin, and Frank R. Kemerer, "Private School Choice in San Antonio," in Moe, ed., *Private Vouchers*; Janet R. Beales and Maureen Wahl, *Given the Choice: A Study of the PAVE Program and School Choice in Milwaukee,* Policy Study 183, Reason Foundation, Los Angeles, January 1995.

22. John F. Witte, "First Year Report: Milwaukee Parental Choice Program," Department of Political Science and the Robert M. La Follette Institute of Public Affairs, University of Wisconsin-Madison, November 1991; John F. Witte, Andrea B. Bailey, and Christopher A. Thorn, "Second Year Report: Milwaukee Parental Choice Program," Department of Political Science and the Robert M. La Follette Institute of Public Affairs, University of Wisconsin-Madison, December 1992; John F. Witte, Andrea B. Bailey, and Christopher A. Thorn, "Third Year Report: Milwaukee Parental Choice Program," Department of Political Science and the Robert M. La Follette Institute of Public Affairs, University of Wisconsin-Madison, December 1993; John F. Witte and others, "Fourth Year Report: Milwaukee Parental Choice Program," Department of Political Science and the Robert M. La Follette Institute of Public Affairs, University of Wisconsin-Madison, December 1994; John F. Witte, Troy D. Sterr, and Christopher A. Thorn, "Fifth Year Report: Milwaukee Parental Choice Program," Department of Political Science and the Robert M. La Follette Institute of Public Affairs, University of Wisconsin-Madison, December 1995; and John F. Witte, "Achievement Effects of the

Milwaukee Voucher Program," paper presented at the 1997 annual meeting of the American Economics Association.

23. Jay P. Greene, Paul E. Peterson, and Jiangtao Du, with Leesa Berger and Curtis L. Frazier, "The Effectiveness of School Choice in Milwaukee: A Secondary Analysis of Data from the Program's Evaluation," Occasional Paper, Program in Education Policy and Governance, Harvard University, 1996.

24. But see the evaluation of the Tennessee randomized experiment in Frederick Moesteller, "The Tennessee Study of Class Size in the Early School Grades," *The Future of Children* 5 (1995), pp. 113–27. This study found that class size has a positive affect on student achievement, contrary to many econometric studies. For the latter, see Eric Hanushek, "The Economics of Schooling: Production and Efficiency in Public Schools," *Journal of Economic Literature* 24 (September 1986), pp. 1141–77.

25. Witte and others, "Fourth Year Reports."

26. Paul E. Peterson, "A Critique of the Witte Evaluation of Milwaukee's School Choice Program," Occasional Paper, Center for American Political Studies, Harvard University, February 1995.

27. Greene and others, "Effectiveness of School Choice."

28. Witte, "Achievement Effects of the Milwaukee Voucher Program"; Cecilia Rouse, "Private School Vouchers and Student Achievement: An Evaluation of the Milwaukee Parental Choice Program," Department of Economics and the National Bureau of Economic Research, Princeton University, 1997.

29. A. N. Hieronymous, *Teacher's Guide Multilevel Battery Level 9–14: Iowa Test of Basic Skills Forms G/H* (Chicago: Riverside Publishing, 1986); H. D. Hoover and others, *Iowa Tests of Basic Skills: Norms and Score Conversions, Form K, Complete and Core Batteries, Levels 5–14* (Chicago: Riverside, 1993).

30. The Milwaukee choice program is described as it was in its initial years, because the data on student achievement are available for only the first four years. In subsequent years the program was expanded somewhat, but the important expansion in 1995 to include religious schools has yet to be implemented due to court challenges. For a fuller discussion of the program, see Paul E. Peterson, Jay P. Greene, and Chad Noyes, "School Choice in Milwaukee," *Public Interest* (Fall 1996), pp. 38–56; and Paul E. Peterson and Chad Noyes, "Under Extreme Duress, School Choice Success," in Diane Ravitch and Joseph Viteritti, eds., *New Schools for a New Century: The Redesign of Urban Education* (Yale University Press, 1997.)

31. The number of students attending each school was made available by the State Department of Public Instruction and reported in the *Milwaukee Journal* ("Court Time on Choice Extended," October 3, 1991) and a report by the Wisconsin Legislative Audit Bureau (*An Evaluation of Milwaukee Parental Choice Program,* February 1995, table 2, p. 22, table 3, p. 23). In addition to the schools discussed in the text, a Montessori school serving a middle-class constituency admitted three students the first year and four the next. Woodland School, formerly a laboratory school for a local Catholic college, enrolled between twenty and forty choice students each year. After the first year three other private elementary schools admitted a small number of students. Test performances of a small number of students attending the high schools participating in the program were not analyzed because no appropriate control group was available. These schools were initially established to serve at-risk students referred to them by the Milwaukee public schools.

32. The students attending this school are not included in the main analysis because they were not in a choice school at the end of the first year; nevertheless, they are included in the intention-to-treat analysis in table 13-7.

33. Witte, "First Year Report: Milwaukee Parental Choice Program."

34. Amy Stuart Wells, "Milwaukee Parents Get More Choice on Schools," *New York Times,* March 28, 1990, p. B9.

35. Barbara Miner, "'Choice' School in Turmoil Because of Staff Cuts, Changes," *Milwaukee Journal,* November 23, 1990, p. B5.

36. Four of the original choice schools were said to be in "serious financial difficulty" and, in addition to Juanita Virgil, two more were said to be "on the verge of closing in the Spring of 1990" (Witte, Bailey, and Thorn, "Third Year Report: Milwaukee Parental Choice Program").

37. *Milwaukee Community Journal,* Special Supplement, May 4, 1994.

38. Paul Taylor, "Milwaukee's Controversial Private School Choice Plan Off to Shaky Start," *Washington Post,* May 23, 1991, p. A3.

39. Witte, "First Year Report: Milwaukee Parental Choice Program," p. 12.

40. Witte, "First Year Report: Milwaukee Parental Choice Program," p. 13.

41. *Milwaukee Community Journal,* Special Supplement.

42. U.S. Department of Education, *Digest of Education Statistics* (Washington, Office of Educational Research and Improvement, 1991), table 158.

43. Witte and others, "Fourth Year Report."

44. Siblings were exempt from the random assignment rule. We were unable to identify siblings from the information made available on the world wide web.

45. To protect the confidentiality of students, the data on the world wide web do not identify the schools they attended. To obtain this information we offered to protect students' confidentiality, but we were unable to obtain access to these data.

46. Inasmuch as there were nine grades, two racial groups, and four years in which students applied, analyses could potentially include seventy-two dummy variables representing all possible points of randomization. In practice, the number of dummy variables or "blocks" included in the analyses reported in table 13-3 varied between eleven and sixty-five, the precise number depending on the number of grades for which students applied in particular years. See W. G. Cochran, "The Planning of Observational Studies of Human Populations," *Journal of the Royal Statistical Society,* Series A, 128 (1965), pp. 234–65, and D. B. Rubin, "William Cochran's Contributions to the Design, Analysis, and Evaluation of Observational Studies," in Podurl S. R. S. Rao, ed., *W. G. Cochran's Impact on Statistics* (New York: John Wiley, 1984).

47. Rouse, "Private School Vouchers and Student Achievement."

48. Many factors contributed to the large number of missing cases: Milwaukee public schools administered tests intermittently; students were absent on the days the tests were administered; students left the city, left the choice program, or were excluded from testing; test scores were lost; and so forth. One can speculate that the large number of missing cases may bias results in one direction or another. Low performers may be more likely to be tested (because of federal requirements) or may be less likely to be tested (designated as special students); they may be more likely to have moved (live in mobile homes) or less likely to have moved (do not have many options). If the initial assignment to test and control groups was random, one may reasonably assume that all extraneous factors operate with equal effect on both treatment and control groups. The fact that most observable characteristics of the treatment and control groups do not differ significantly is consistent with such an assumption.

49. Witte and others, "Fourth Year Report."

50. These data are from the first four years of the choice school experiment. Test score information on the control group was not available on the world wide web for subsequent years.

51. We prefer the one-tailed t-test to estimate the statistical significance of the findings, because theory and prior research both suggest that students should perform better in private schools.

52. Results for three and four years after application were jointly estimated by averaging scores for students who were tested in both years and by using the single score available for each of the remaining students. Dummy variables were included for those who had only third-year or fourth-year scores.

53. The background characteristics of students who are included in the intention-to-treat category are virtually identical to those who actually enrolled, as reported in table 13-2.

FOURTEEN

Lessons from the Cleveland Scholarship Program

Jay P. Greene, William G. Howell, and Paul E. Peterson

DOES SCHOOL CHOICE WORK? If so, who benefits? Choice critics say private schools do not appear to serve students' academic needs any better than public schools. They further argue that the few detectable benefits of school choice accrue mainly to students who need the least assistance. Parents who are already involved with their children's education will capitalize on choice. What is more, private schools are disinclined to accept students with special needs. And after choice students gain admission to private schools, the argument goes, the weakest will be weeded out.

In addition to the funds made available by the Ohio State Department of Education, PEPG received financial support for this evaluation from the Kennedy School of Government's Taubman Center on State and Local Government and the John M. Olin Foundation. We wish to thank William McCready, Robin Bebel, and the staff of the Social Science Research Institute at Northern Illinois University in Dekalb, Illinois, for preparing and conducting the parent survey. We thank Mark Hinnawi for research assistance and Michelle Franz for her expert administrative support. We would also like to thank Bert Holt and her staff at the Cleveland Scholarship and Tutoring Program for compiling information on applicants to the program and providing us with the information needed to conduct the parent survey. We also appreciate the assistance provided by Francis Rogers at the Ohio Department of Education and the principal and staff at the Hope schools.

The Cleveland Scholarship and Tutoring Program (CSTP), which began in the fall of 1996, provides new evidence that sheds light on these issues.[1] CSTP is the first program in the country to offer state-funded scholarships that can be redeemed at both secular and parochial schools. During the 1996–97 school year 1,996 scholarship recipients attended fifty-five private schools in kindergarten through grade three. For the 1997–98 school year CSTP offered scholarships to 3,000 students from kindergarten through fourth grade.

At the time the data reported in this chapter were collected, CSTP had been in place for only one year. Consequently, the data do not speak to the long-term effects vouchers will have on student test scores, how many and what kinds of schools will emerge in response to new demand, or whether vouchers will stimulate reform within the Cleveland public schools. But it is not too soon to begin to evaluate important aspects of the program. In the summer of 1997 Harvard's Program on Education Policy and Governance (PEPG) commissioned a survey of 2,020 voucher applicants in order to find out who participated in the program, who did not, and how satisfied the parents of both groups were with the schools their children attended. PEPG also analyzed the test scores of students attending two new choice schools. The evidence collected has important implications for the contemporary school choice debate.

We present five main findings. First, parents reported that their decisions to apply for scholarships were largely motivated by academic concerns. Second, a relatively small proportion of nonrecipients claimed that inability to secure admission to preferred private schools was an important reason for their decisions not to participate in the program. Third, parents of scholarship recipients who previously attended public schools were much more satisfied with every aspect of their choice schools than applicants who did not receive scholarships, but attended public schools instead. Fourth, choice schools did well at retaining students in the program, both within the school year and from one school year to the next. Fifth, preliminary test score results in mathematics and reading show moderate gains for students attending two new schools set up in response to the establishment of the scholarship program (the Hope schools). Overall, third graders in choice schools seem to be acquiring more language skills and learning more science.

Origins of the Program

In March 1995 the Ohio General Assembly appropriated funds expected to be sufficient to provide 1,500 scholarships worth as much as $2,250 each. Scholarship recipients were to be chosen by lottery. Each scholarship covered up to 90 percent of a school's tuition, with the balance to come from the child's family or another private source. The maximum amount provided was little more than a third the per-pupil cost of Cleveland public schools, which in 1997 was $6,507.[2] This simple comparison of costs, however, omits the additional costs of transportation, special education, and any additional aid to choice schools from public or private sources.

The legislation establishing CSTP allowed as many as 50 percent of all scholarships to be used by students already in private schools. The Ohio Department of Education, however, reduced the figure to 25 percent. Of the 6,244 applications received in the fall of 1995 by CSTP, 29 percent or 1,780 came from students already attending private schools. In January 1996 CSTP awarded 375 scholarships to these applicants. As of April 3, 1997, CSTP had awarded 21 percent (427 of 1,996) of the scholarships to students previously matriculated in private schools. CSTP granted the remaining 79 percent of the scholarships to students who had previously been attending public schools or who were beginning kindergarten.[3]

In two respects the Ohio Department of Education gave preference to poor families. First, students from low-income families received larger scholarships. Students from families whose incomes were below 200 percent of the poverty line received 90 percent of their schools' tuition, up to $2,250, whereas students coming from families whose incomes were at or above 200 percent of the poverty line were eligible to receive $1,875 or 75 percent of their schools' tuition, whichever was less. Second, low-income students had a better chance of winning the initial lottery. The first lottery, held in January 1996, was limited to those applicants (58 percent of the sample) whose families' incomes were below the poverty line. And because this lottery received considerable attention from the local press, low-income families were more likely to find out that they had won scholarships.

Many of those offered scholarships did not accept them, either because the CSTP office could not reach them or because they did not come to the CSTP office to verify their incomes or, if they did, were found to be ineligible. By the summer of 1996 CSTP also discovered that tuition at Cleveland private schools was less than originally estimated, making it possible to increase the number of scholarship recipients to nearly 2,000. To accommodate more applicants the Ohio Department of Education then relaxed the rules, making eligible any family with an income below 200 percent of the poverty line. But by the time of the second, less visible, lottery CSTP was in the midst of a court challenge, making it unclear whether the program would actually begin in the fall of 1996. Also, CSTP reported that it was becoming increasingly difficult to locate applicants (due to changes of telephone numbers and addresses). As a result, the acceptance rate declined sharply, and CSTP claimed it eventually offered scholarships to all low-income applicants it was able to contact.[4]

CSTP planning and administration were seriously hampered by a lawsuit brought by the Ohio Federation of Teachers (an affiliate of the American Federation of Teachers) and other interest groups and individuals. The court case dragged on into August 1996, and it was not until two weeks before the beginning of the school year that the lower court ruled in favor of CSTP.[5] In addition, private schools reported difficulties obtaining student records from the Cleveland public schools. What is more, CSTP did not convince the Cleveland public schools to arrange transportation until well into the school year, making it necessary to shuttle many scholarship students by taxi. In short, the program began with enough uncertainty and confusion that parental satisfaction could not be taken for granted.

Data Collection

During the summer of 1997 Harvard University's Program on Education Policy and Governance conducted a telephone survey of 2,020 CSTP applicants and analyzed available test score data. PEPG interviewed 1,014 scholarship recipients and 1,006 applicants who did not enroll in the program. The 2,020 interviews required 3,437 telephone attempts. As shown in table 14-1, only 5 percent of the attempts resulted in refusals to participate in the survey; other interviews were not completed because no contact could be made, usually because a respondent was no longer at the telephone number provided PEPG by CSTP.

The survey completion rate for the households of scholarship recipients (74.1 percent) was higher than for those who applied but did not receive scholarships (48.6 percent). Therefore, the survey better represents scholarship recipients than nonrecipients. As can be seen in table 14-2, the incomes and ethnicities of recipients new to choice schools who responded to the survey (column 3) did not differ significantly from the incomes and ethnicities of all such recipients (column 4), though they came from slightly smaller families. As compared to the universe of nonrecipients (column 8), however, the nonrecipients responding to the survey (column 7) had higher family incomes and were more likely to be white and come from smaller families. If these demographic characteristics are positively correlated with parental satisfaction, the effects reported below underestimate CSTP's actual programmatic impact.

Table 14-1. *Breakdown of Survey Response Rates*

	Scholarship recipients			
	Yes			
Response	Previous public school	Previous private school	No	Total
	(1)	(2)	(3)	(4)
Frequencies				
Interviewed	726	288	1,006	2,020
Could not contact[a]	240	69	933	1,242
Refused to be interviewed	37	8	130	175
Total contacts attempted	1,003	365	2,069	3,437
As a percentage of contacts attempted				
Interviewed	72.4	78.9	48.6	58.8
Could not contact	23.9	18.9	45.1	36.1
Refused to be interviewed	3.7	2.2	6.3	5.1
Total	100.0	100.0	100.0	100.0

CSTP was not set up as a randomized experiment. Although a lottery was initially used to determine scholarship recipients, CSTP eventually attempted to give scholarships to all low-income applicants. As a result, those receiving scholarships may have been the applicants CSTP could easily reach and who were willing to have their incomes verified.

The demographic characteristics of recipients new to choice schools and nonrecipients remaining in the public schools were nonetheless quite similar, perhaps because CSTP initially used a lottery to award scholarships. When demographic differences can be observed, the scholarship recipients are the more disadvantaged group. Though the two groups may also have unobserved characteristics that distinguish them, if such differences are correlated with demographic differences the comparisons are likely to be biased against finding positive programmatic effects.

Background Characteristics of Applicants

Many of those critical of school choice fear that disadvantaged families will be excluded from either the program itself or from the private schools to which they apply. In the words of a recent Twentieth Century Fund report, if school choice "becomes a strategy to . . . restrict lower-income

Table 14-2. Examining the Possibility of Response Bias, Grades K–3

Characteristic	All applicants		Choice (previous public)[a]		Choice (previous private)[b]		No scholarship	
	Survey	Universe	Survey	Universe	Survey	Universe	Survey	Universe
	(1)	(2)	(3)	(4)	(5)	(6)	(7)	(8)
Average income (dollars)	16,279***	14,754	12,533[c]	12,045	11,923**	10,698	20,748***	16,251
Average family size	3.77***	4.03	3.77**	3.89	3.83***	3.97	3.92***	4.09
Ethnicity (percent)								
African American	59.5*	62.8	68.6	68.8	49.3	48.7	55.9***	62.4
White	31.7*	27.4	23.8	22.0	38.2	37.3	35.8***	28.1
Hispanic	3.9*	5.0	3.0	3.5	6.9	7.3	3.5*	5.2
Multiracial	3.5	3.2	3.5	3.8	3.8	4.4	3.3	2.9
Other	1.3	1.6	1.1	1.9	1.7	2.0	1.3	1.4
Total	100.0	100.0	100.0	100.0	100.0	100.0	100.0	100.0
N	1,896	6,050	719	1,493	288	496	887	4,548

* Differences between adjacent columns are statistically significant at .05 level.

** Differences between adjacent columns are statistically significant at .01 level.

*** Differences between adjacent columns are statistically significant at .001 level.

a. Those individuals who received a scholarship and previously attended a public school, including kindergartners.

b. All individuals who received a scholarship and previously attended a private school, including kindergartners.

c. See note 8.

students of color to an inferior education, then the divisions between rich and poor in this country, and the attendant social problems, will only increase."[6] But a Heritage Foundation report counters that "school choice programs benefit minority inner-city students the most."[7] The parental survey described in this chapter permits an evaluation of these rival claims.

Survey results indicate that it is possible for choice programs to award scholarships to low-income recipients. Table 14-3 shows that the average family income of scholarship recipients new to choice schools (column 1) was less than that of nonrecipients in public schools (column 2). Similarly, the average family income of scholarship recipients from private schools (column 3) was less than that of nonrecipients attending private schools (column 4).[8] All of these differences are statistically significant.

In other respects, recipients new to choice schools resembled nonrecipients in public schools. Differences in terms of their mothers' education, their mother's employment, their family size, their family living arrangements, their residential mobility, and their religious affiliations were not statistically significant. These findings generally do not change when we isolate kindergartners.[9]

Educational differences were somewhat more pronounced. Scholarship recipients new to choice schools were less likely to have received special education than were nonrecipients in public schools (10.7 percent as compared to 17.6 percent). But recipients were also less likely to have been in classes for gifted students (7.7 percent compared to 18.3 percent).[10] It does appear, though, that some students who had special education needs or who had been suspended for disciplinary reasons had difficulty obtaining placement in private schools. Of the respondents who said they could not obtain admission in desired private schools, 25 percent said their children had been receiving special services related to disabilities or learning problems, and 12 percent said their children had been suspended for disciplinary reasons. In the conclusion to this chapter we discuss the policy implications of these findings.

Reasons for Seeking Choice School

School choice advocates say they wish to empower parents by giving them a choice among schools. But some critics have suggested that families, especially low-income families, do not choose schools on the basis of school quality. The Carnegie Foundation for the Advancement of Teaching has claimed that "when parents do select another school, academic con-

Table 14-3. *Demographic Comparisons among All CSTP Applicants, Grades K–3[a]*

Percent

Demographic characteristics	Scholarship recipient, previous public school	Nonrecipient, attending public school[b]	Scholarship recipient, previous private school	Nonrecipient, attending private school[c]
	(1)	(2)	(3)	(4)
Income (dollars)				
0–10,999	29.8	23.0	25.0	4.3
11,000–24,999	40.6	22.2	43.2	14.9
25,000–39,999	20.2	23.7	22.4	28.4
40,000–49,999	5.4	12.7	4.2	16.6
More than 50,000	3.9	11.0	5.1	24.8
Total	100.0	100.0	100.0	100.0
Average income (dollars)[d]	20,091[***T]	25,545	21,099[###]	39,108
Mother's education				
Some high school or below	8.6	13.9	6.6	4.9
High school graduate (or GED)	30.6	29.4	29.3	26.0
Some college	49.9	43.5	50.4	44.3
College graduate and above	10.9	13.3	13.6	19.2
Total	100.0	100.0	100.0	100.0
Average education[e]	3.6[T]	3.6	3.7[##]	3.9
Mother's employment status				
Full-time	49.2	51.6	49.4	56.4
Part-time	20.9	17.1	20.7	21.9
Looking for work	12.4	15.6	10.8	4.5
Not looking	17.5	15.6	19.1	17.2
Total	100.0	100.0	100.0	100.0
Average employment[f]	3.0	3.1	3.0[###]	3.2
Family size				
2	17.4	17.4	17.6	12.9
3	29.7	28.2	32.4	23.7
4	29.5	24.8	23.0	34.4
5	13.2	16.4	13.3	17.5
6+	10.2	13.2	13.7	11.5
Total	100.0	100.0	100.0	100.0
Average size	3.8	3.9	3.8[#]	4.0

Table 14-3 (*continued*)

Demographic characteristics	Scholarship recipient, previous public school	Nonrecipient, attending public school[b]	Scholarship recipient, previous private school	Nonrecipient, attending private school[c]
	(1)	(2)	(3)	(4)
Living arrangement				
Mother and father	37.0	36.6	37.5###	67.2
Only mother	57.1	54.8	54.7###	29.2
Only father	1.3	1.2	0.8	1.5
Grandparent	3.2	3.8	3.9###	0.4
Other	1.3*	3.4	2.7	1.7
Total	100.0	100.0	100.0	100.0
Mobility (time at current residence)				
0–1 year	8.2*	5.9	7.5#	4.2
1–2 years	16.4*	13.4	13.8###	6.1
2+ years	75.4	78.8	78.7###	88.7
Total	100.0	100.0	100.0	100.0
Ethnicity				
African American	66.8*TTT	76.1	48.4###	35.1
White	25.0TTT	15.5	37.9###	56.7
Hispanic	3.2TTT	3.2	7.4##	4.0
Multiracial	3.8	3.8	4.3	3.0
Other	1.2	1.4	2.0	1.3
Total	100.0	100.0	100.0	100.0
Religious affiliation				
Baptist	40.4TTT	43.0	29.4##	22.1
Other Protestant	13.8	17.4	12.6	15.7
Catholic	24.8***TTT	13.4	43.1#	49.8
Other religion	13.2TTT	14.3	5.9	7.2
No religion	7.9	10.2	9.0##	4.8
Total	100.0	100.0	100.0	100.0
N	533	416	236	426

a. Values of *n* signify the smallest number of cases represented by a group among the selected items; consequently, one cannot infer the value of certain frequencies by taking the product of a percentage and the value of *n*. Of those students who did not receive scholarships and attended public schools in 1996–97, 7.4 percent had attended private schools the year before. Data on ethnicity and family size were compiled from CSTP office records. All kindergarteners who were scholarship recipients are included in column one.

b. Of those students who did not receive scholarships and attended public schools in 1996–97, 28.4 percent had attended public schools the year before.

c. Of those students who did not receive scholarships and attended private schools in 1996–97, 7.4 percent had attended private schools the year before.

cerns often are not central to the decision."[11] A Twentieth Century Fund report claims that low-income parents are not "natural 'consumers' of education. . . . [Indeed], few parents of any social class appear willing to acquire the information necessary to make active and informed educational choices."[12] Similarly, the American Federation of Teachers (AFT) report on the Cleveland program suggests that parents sought scholarships not because of "failing public schools," but "for religious reasons or because they already had [another child] attending the same school."[13]

Not much support for such criticisms can be found in the parent survey (see table 14-4). Asked why they applied for scholarships, 85 percent of parents new to choice schools said they wanted to improve the academic quality of their children's education.[14] Second in importance was the greater safety to be found at choice schools, a reason given by 79 percent of the recipients. Location was ranked third. Contrary to AFT's suggestion, religion was ranked fourth, said to be very important by just 37 percent of recipients. Finally, friends were said to be very important by fewer than 20 percent of the scholarship recipients. Nonrecipients who remained in public schools ranked the reasons in the same order, but did not give them the same degree of importance.[15]

Reasons for Nonparticipation

Nonrecipients were asked their reasons for not participating in the program. According to CSTP officials, the office made strong efforts to reach all applicants, so nonrecipients may have had substantive reasons for not

Table 14-3 (*notes continued*)

---

d. When calculating average income, responses of "over $50,000" were set at $60,000.

e. This index is scaled from 1 to 6, where 1 signifies less than high school, 2 some high school, 3 high school graduate (including GED), 4 some college, 5 college graduate, and 6 more than college.

f. This index is scaled from 1 to 4, where 1 signifies not looking for work, 2 looking for work, 3 part-time employment, and 4 full-time employment.

[*] Differences between columns 1 and 2 are statistically significant at .05 level.

[**] Differences between columns 1 and 2 are statistically significant at .01 level.

[***] Differences between columns 1 and 2 are statistically significant at .001 level.

[#] Differences between columns 3 and 4 are statistically significant at the .05 level.

[##] Differences between columns 3 and 4 are statistically significant at .01 level.

[###] Differences between columns 3 and 4 are statistically significant at .001 level.

[T] Differences between columns 1 and 3 are statistically significant at .05 level.

[TT] Differences between columns 1 and 3 are statistically significant at .01 level.

[TTT] Differences between columns 1 and 3 are statistically significant at .001 level.

Table 14-4. *Reasons for Applying for Scholarships, Grades K–3ᵃ*

Important consideration in decision to apply	Scholarship recipient, previous public school	Nonrecipient, attending public school	Scholarship recipient, previous private school	Nonrecipient, attending private school
	(1)	(2)	(3)	(4)
Improved academic quality	2.85**	2.69	2.79###	2.56
Greater safety	2.78***	2.55	2.75###	2.51
Location	2.47	2.44	2.52###	2.33
Religion	2.12***,TTT	1.80	2.40##	2.27
Friends	1.63T	1.62	1.70	1.68
N	597	459	255	415

a. Average scores. Indexes scored from 1 to 3; averages reported: 1 signifies not important, 2 important, and 3 very important. Also, see notes to table 14-3.

accepting scholarships. The recent evaluation of CSTP by the American Federation of Teachers explained nonparticipation this way:

> It is clear that the [CSTP] Office made repeated efforts to make vouchers available to low-income public school families. However, some families who had originally applied for a voucher never followed up, as evidenced by the fact that families representing 34 percent of public school students in the voucher lottery did not visit the Office and verify their income. More significantly, many families who did verify their income and thus wanted vouchers could not find an available seat in a private school, at least not in the private school of their "choice." . . . About half of public school students who wanted vouchers most likely could not find an open seat in the private school or schools of their "choice."[16]

Why did many people apparently offered scholarships by CSTP turn them down? The most important reason, from the parents' point of view, was inadequate communication between CSTP and the applicants. As shown in table 14-5, 44 percent of the nonrecipients whose children remained in public schools said they were never offered scholarships. This figure is

Table 14-5. *Reasons for Not Participating in CSTP, Grades
K–3[a]*

Reason for not participating	Percent responding "important"
Did you receive a scholarship this year?	
Believed not offered a scholarship[b]	44.1
How important was each of the following in your decision not to participate in the scholarship program?	
Transportation	36.5
Offered admission to desired public school	35.3
Financial reasons	31.2
Refused admission to private school	21.1
Moved from area	13.1
N	460

a. Possible responses to survey question were dichotomous. Also, see notes to table 14.3.

b. These results combine answers to two questions. Those who believed they were not offered scholarships were not asked the second question. Consequently, although individual respondents who believed they were offered scholarships could claim that multiple reasons influenced their decision not to accept a scholarships, those who believed they were not offered scholarships in the first place could indicate only the one reason.

probably much larger. We estimate that a clear majority of those our survey team could not contact were also not reached by CSTP.

Low-income families are highly mobile and often depend on friends and relatives for telephone and mail services. They can be extremely difficult to reach. Even when contacted, many families may not have understood that in order to receive scholarships they had to verify their incomes. Moreover, Ohio Department of Education rules, which first limited eligibility to applicants with incomes below the poverty line, may have discouraged many of those above the poverty line from giving the program further consideration, despite the fact that eligibility requirements were subsequently relaxed. Families with incomes above 200 percent of the poverty line were not eligible until November 1997, two months after the school year had begun.

Possible communication problems, compounded by the uncertainty caused by court challenges and the small staff charged with conducting the lotteries, made it less than surprising that half or more of the nonrecipients thought that they had not won scholarships. More surprising is the fact that nearly 2,000 applicants did receive scholarships and were placed in choice schools within a short period of time—under difficult and continuously changing circumstances.

We asked the remaining 56 percent of nonrecipients their reasons for not accepting scholarships. Three reasons were mentioned with roughly equal frequency: transportation, financial considerations, and the offer of admission to desired public schools (see table 14-5). Apparently the initial difficulties in setting up travel arrangements may have affected parental decisionmaking. In mentioning financial considerations, parents may have been referring to the fact that they needed to supplement the scholarships with tuition payments (10–25 percent of the cost) or to eligibility requirements, which initially limited scholarships to those below the poverty line. The third major reason, said to be important by over a third of the nonrecipients in public schools, was their success in gaining admission to desired public schools. Observers reported that the Cleveland public schools responded to the scholarship program by giving applicants access to the city's magnet schools or enrichment programs. If so, this suggests that CSTP increased the choices of CSTP applicants within the Cleveland public schools.

The fourth most important reason for nonparticipation, given by the parents of 21 percent of those remaining in public schools, was the inability to secure admission to their desired private schools. Many private schools were already oversubscribed. Also, the choice program was being set up in a context seriously complicated by the court suit filed by the Ohio Federation of Teachers, creating a great deal of uncertainty. As we have already seen, scholarship recipients also were more likely to have special education needs than their counterparts in public schools. For any of these reasons, it is entirely possible that some private schools might have been reluctant to accept a large number of scholarship recipients from public schools.

Parental Satisfaction

Many economists think that customer satisfaction is the best measure of a product's quality. According to this criterion there is little doubt that Cleveland's choice schools outperformed the city's public schools. Recipients from public schools were much more satisfied with every single

Table 14-6. *Parent Satisfaction with School Their Child Is Attending, Grades K–3*[a]

Characteristic	Scholarship recipient, previous public school	Nonrecipient, attending public school	Scholarship recipient, previous private school	Nonrecipient, attending private school
	(1)	(2)	(3)	(4)
Academic quality	3.56[***,T]	3.06	3.64[#]	3.57
Safety	3.51[***,TT]	3.02	3.66[#]	3.58
Discipline	3.49[***,TT]	2.91	3.59[##]	3.49
Teaching of moral values	3.66[***]	3.02	3.69	3.68
Private attention to child	3.42[***]	2.80	3.42	3.36
Parent involvement	3.44[***]	3.03	3.47	3.44
Class size	3.37[***]	2.75	3.35[##]	3.23
Facility	3.38[***,T]	2.85	3.47[###]	3.30
N	592	483	254	465

a. Average scores. Indices scored from 1 to 4; averages reported. 1 signifies very dissatisfied; 2 dissatisfied; 3 satisfied; and 4 very satisfied. Also, see notes to table 14-3.

[*] Compares columns 1 and 2.

[#] Compares columns 3 and 4.

[T] Compares columns 1 and 3.

aspect of their children's choice schools. The results shown in table 14-6 may be substantively understood in the following way: Two-thirds of parents new to choice schools (column 1) reported being very satisfied with the academic quality of their children's school, as compared to fewer than 30 percent of parents with children in public schools (column 2). Nearly 60 percent were very satisfied with school safety, as compared to just over a quarter of nonrecipients with children in public schools. With respect to discipline, 55 percent of recipients from public schools, but only 23 percent of nonrecipients in public schools, were very satisfied. The differences in satisfaction rates were equally large when parents were asked about the school's private attention to the child, parent involvement, class size, and school facility. The most extreme differences in satisfaction pertained to teaching moral values: Seventy-one percent of the recipients with children in public schools were very satisfied, as compared to only 25 percent of the nonrecipients with children in public schools.

It also is worth inquiring whether scholarship families in public schools were as satisfied as those who had already been enrolled in private schools. The AFT, in its report on the program, suggests that scholarship recipients from private schools were given important advantages. In the words of the report, "Voucher students who had previously been enrolled in private schools held a 'monopoly' on placements in the established private schools. In contrast, almost half of the voucher students who moved from public to private schools were enrolled in four schools with little or no educational and financial track record."[17]

There is some evidence from the survey in support of the AFT suggestion that scholarship recipients in public schools had less satisfying educational experiences than those who had already been in private schools. However, the differences between the two groups, in most cases, are modest. For example, 67 percent of recipients with children in private schools (table 14-6, column 3) said they were very satisfied with the academic quality of the schools, compared to 63 percent of those with children in public schools (table 14-6, column 1). For school discipline the figures were 62 percent and 55 percent, respectively. The biggest difference concerned school safety, with 69 percent as compared to 59 percent reporting they were very satisfied. But despite these small differences, the overall pattern is quite the opposite to that suggested by the AFT report: Choice parents, whether or not they were new to choice schools, expressed much higher levels of satisfaction with their children's schools than did families with children still in public schools.

What factors contributed to the differences between choice-school and public school parents? To answer this question we employ multivariate regression analysis. We build a composite measure of school satisfaction, which is simply the sum of the responses given for each category, rescaled from zero to 100 to facilitate interpretation.[18] We then regress this summary satisfaction measure on each child's educational characteristics, the type of school attended, and demographic characteristics. In table 14-7 we examine the determinants of satisfaction for all applicants; in table 14-8 we consider scholarship recipients; in table 14-9 we focus on nonrecipients. In each table model 1 controls for the most significant demographic factors; model 2 includes the full range of demographic factors. The baseline of the regression in table 14-7 against which other categories are compared consists of those individuals who actively chose to attend public schools. These

Table 14-7. *Explanations of Scholarship Applicants' Satisfaction with Their Own Schools, Grades K–3*[a]

	Parental satisfaction[b]	
Determinant	Model 1	Model 2
Educational experiences		
Involuntarily in public school	–6.7[***]	–6.6[***]
Type of school[c]		
Private (no scholarship)	15.5[***]	15.0[***]
Established parochial school (scholarship)	16.0[***]	15.9[***]
New parochial school (scholarship)	0.5	0.3
Established secular school (scholarship)	15.7[***]	16.1[***]
New secular school (scholarship)	6.5[***]	6.6[***]
Demographics		
Special needs	–2.6[**]	–2.7[**]
Minority	–3.3[**]	–3.0[***]
Income	0.2	0.2
Kindergarten	2.8[**]	2.4[**]
Family size	. . .	0.4
Mother's education	. . .	0.7
Mother's employment status	. . .	–0.6
Residential mobility	. . .	0.2
Constant	69.4[***]	66.9[***]
Adjusted R^2	0.24	0.23
N	1,586	1,585

[*] significant at .05 level.

[**] significant at .01 level.

[***] significant at .001 level.

a. Unstandardized coefficients from ordinary least squares regressions

b. Index of satisfaction, summarizing eight dimensions listed in table 14-3. See text for description.

c. The baseline group includes those individuals who were offered scholarships, but refused them, and claimed that being refused admission to desired private schools was not an important reason for choosing to attend public school.

individuals knew they were offered scholarships and refused them, and they claimed that being refused admission to preferred private schools was not an important reason for making decisions to attend public schools.

The results reported in table 14-7 are quite striking. The most prominent finding is that parents with students attending established private schools were as much as 16 percentage points more satisfied than parents whose children voluntarily decided to remain in public schools.[19] The findings indicate much higher satisfaction with established choice schools; they do

Table 14-8. *Explanations of Scholarship Recipients' Satisfaction with Their Own Schools, Grades K–3*[a]

| | Parental satisfaction | |
Determinant	Model 1	Model 2
Educational experiences		
Previous public school	−0.3	−0.5
Religious compatibility	−0.4	−0.2
Type of school[b]		
Established parochial school	15.0***	15.0***
Established secular school	14.9***	15.4***
New secular school	5.6**	5.9***
Demographics		
Special needs	−3.0*	−3.0*
Minority	−4.2**	−3.5**
Income	−0.1	−1.8
Kindergarten	2.3	2.3
Family size	. . .	0.7
Mother's education	. . .	0.5
Mother's employment status	. . .	−0.4
Residential mobility	. . .	0.1
Constant	76.3***	73.3***
Adjusted R^2	0.17	0.17
N	770	755

* Significant at .05 level.

** Significant at .01 level.

*** Significant at .001 level.

a. Unstandardized coefficients from ordinary least squares regressions.

b. The baseline group includes two parochial schools with a high number of new scholarship students.

not just tap the dissatisfaction felt by a small subset of public school parents who could not get their children into the program.

The level of satisfaction varies with the type of school scholarship recipients attended. As shown in table 14-8, parents whose scholarship students attended established parochial schools (which consisted mostly of Catholic schools) and established secular school (largely Montessori schools) were the most satisfied, the next most satisfied group of parents are those whose children attended those with children in new secular schools (the Hope schools), and the least satisfied of choice parents are those whose children attended new parochial schools (two religious schools that admitted a large number of scholarship students). The fact that the coefficient for new parochial schools in table 14-7 is indistinguishable from zero suggests that the satisfaction levels of parents who voluntarily sent their children to public schools and scholarship parents in the newly established parochial schools were essentially the same.

The parents of children who involuntarily ended up in public schools were approximately 7 percentage points less satisfied with the public schools than those of students who actively chose to attend public school. Children who involuntarily attended public schools include nonrecipients who either did not know they were offered scholarships or claimed that rejection by desired private schools was an important reason for not taking advantage of the scholarships.

Parents with special needs children were three percentage points less satisfied with their children's schools. This attribute is statistically significant when we examine the universe of applicants and not just scholarship recipients (tables 14-7 and 14-8), but not when we examine nonrecipients (table 14-9). The differences between the satisfaction rates of special needs recipients and nonrecipients, however, are not statistically significant. Nonetheless, there is some evidence that choice programs need to give additional attention to ensuring adequate services for this population.

Racial differences with respect to parental satisfaction between recipients and nonrecipients are somewhat more pronounced. Minority scholarship recipients, the vast majority of whom were African American, expressed, on average, about 3 percentage points less satisfaction with their schools than white parents (table 14-8); among nonrecipients no such differences can be detected (table 14-9). Differences between recipients and nonrecipients are statistically significant. It is possible that some minorities may have had a more difficult time either gaining admission to desired private schools or integrating into the schools once there.

With respect to income, a reverse effect can be detected. As shown in tables 14-8 and 14-9, income affected the satisfaction levels of only nonrecipients. Among nonrecipients, parents with incomes of more than $50,000 were about 6 percentage points more satisfied with their children's schools than parents with incomes of less than $10,000. The size of the coefficient appears small because the variable is coded from zero to 10.[20] No such differences are recorded among scholarship recipients. This finding suggests that voucher programs attenuate the influence of income, presumably by affording choice to all children.

Interestingly, religious compatibility seems to have had little or no effect on the satisfaction of scholarship recipients (table 14-8). It made no difference whether a student attended a parochial school that was of the same religion as his or her family. This finding includes families with no religious

Table 14-9. *Explanations of Nonrecipients' Satisfaction with Their Own School, Grades K–3*[a]

	Parental satisfaction	
Determinant	Model 1	Model 2
Educational experiences		
Prior public school	1.9	1.4
Involuntarily in public school	–3.8**	–3.6**
Type of school[b]		
Private school	19.1***	18.3***
Demographics		
Special needs	–1.5	–1.4
Minority	–0.8	–0.3
Income	0.5	0.6*
Kindergarten	3.4*	3.1
Family size	...	0.1
Mother's education	...	0.3
Mother's employment status	...	–0.8
Residential mobility	...	0.0
Constant	57.3***	56.0***
Adjusted R^2	0.20	0.20
N	813	736

* Significant at .05 level.

** Significant at .01 level.

*** Significant at .001 level.

a. Standardized coefficients from ordinary least squares regressions

b. The baseline group consists of those individuals who were offered scholarships but refused them and claimed that being refused admission to desired public schools was not an important reason for choosing to attend public schools.

affiliation, suggesting that children of many different religious backgrounds can have positive educational experiences, regardless of whether they attend compatible secular or parochial schools.

In summary, four principal findings are evident. First, scholarship recipients were far more satisfied with their children's schools than were nonrecipients with children in public schools. Second, parental satisfaction is especially high in well-established private schools. Third, among scholarship recipients minorities seemed less satisfied with their children's schools, but these differences are not statistically significant among nonrecipients. Finally, although the satisfaction of low-income parents with children in public schools nonrecipients is less (even when controlling for other demographics), no such relationship between income and satisfaction is apparent among parents with students in choice schools.

School Mobility Rates

Most educators think that, all things being equal, it is better that a student stay in the same school, especially during a single school year. Most of the time education works better when it is not subject to disruption. One evaluation of the Milwaukee choice experiment argued that "attrition" from the program was its "most troubling aspect."[21] Daniel McGroarty, in contrast, has argued that the students in Milwaukee's school choice program were less mobile than students in the city's public schools. Moreover, high rates of school mobility are to be expected given the high residential mobility rates that occur among low-income families in inner-city neighborhoods.[22] According to the U. S. census the annual residential mobility rate among female-headed central city households with children between the ages of six and seventeen is 30 percent for African Americans and 35 percent for Latinos.

The Cleveland choice schools seem to have done well at retaining their students. Only 7 percent of all scholarship families reported that their children did not attend the same schools for the entire year. Among recipients from public schools the figure was 10 percent. In Milwaukee's public elementary schools nearly 20 percent left even before the end of the school year in June.[23] By the following fall nearly 40 percent of the students changed schools.

As shown in column 1 of table 14-10, the most important reason recipients new to choice schools gave for changing schools midyear was admission to preferred private schools. Very likely, many of these changes were due to the fact that the CSTP program was delayed by the legal suit, so that some recipients did not receive their scholarships until after the school year had begun. If so, this cause of school mobility should decline over time. Another 1 percent of the students changed schools because they had been admitted to preferred public schools; perhaps the Cleveland public schools had given these students opportunities to attend magnet schools. Another 0.8 percent moved during the course of the year. And 0.8 percent changed schools for transportation reasons, perhaps a sign that the initial transport problems of the CSTP program posed difficulties for some parents.

Parents were also asked whether they planned on sending their children to the same schools the next year. Eighty-one percent of scholarship recipients from public schools gave positive responses, as did 88 percent of the recipients whose children already had been attending private schools (table 14-11). If the actual choices were consistent with these plans, the mobility rate in Cleveland from one year to the next was approximately the

Table 14-10. *School Mobility Rates of Scholarship Students, Grades K–3*
Percent

Whether child attended same school entire year	Previous public school	Previous private school	Total
Yes	91.0[***]	99.2	93.7
No (stated reason)			
Admitted to preferred private school	3.3[*]	0.0	2.3
Quality of schools	1.3	0.4	1.1
Admitted to preferred public school	1.0	0.0	0.7
Moved	0.8	0.0	0.6
Transportation difficulties	0.8	0.4	0.7
Administration	0.3	0.0	0.2
Disability/behavior problems	0.3	0.0	0.2
School closure/change	0.3	0.0	0.2
Financial reasons	0.2	0.0	0.1
Expulsion	0.2	0.0	0.1
Other	0.3	0.0	0.2
Total	100.0	100.0	100.0
N	600	256	856

[*] Compares columns 1 and 2. Also, see notes to table 14-3.

same as in Milwaukee's state-funded elementary choice program, which was about half the mobility rate in Milwaukee public schools.

Choice critics have suggested that private schools may routinely expel or not readmit students for a second year if they are not keeping pace with their peers. Defenders of school choice say that private schools use this discretion sparingly. To provide empirical information on this point, we asked why families planned on changing schools. As shown in table 14-11, fewer than half of 1 percent of recipients from public schools said their children could not be readmitted to their private schools. In other words, while admission refusals are not unknown, neither have they been practiced to any significant degree.

Parents instead gave a wide range of other reasons for planning to move their children to other schools in the fall of 1997. Six percent gave quite practical reasons, such as the families' moving from the area or their children's changing grade levels (necessitating a school change). Another 1.5 percent found other private schools they preferred, and 0.5 percent found preferable public schools. Either transportation difficulties or finan-

Table 14-11. *Matriculation Plans of Scholarship Students, Grades K–3*
Percent

Whether child plans to attend same school next year	Previous public school	Previous private school	Total
Yes	80.5[a]	87.7	82.8
No (stated reason)			
Quality of school	5.7[*]	2.1	4.5
Change of student's grade level	3.5[*]	0.4	2.5
Move from area	2.0	1.3	1.8
Prefer different private school	1.6	2.1	1.8
Transportation difficulties	1.4[*]	0.0	1.0
Cost	1.0	2.1	1.4
Disappointed with program	0.8	0.9	0.8
School or program closing down	0.8	0.8	0.8
Lack special education resources	0.4	0.0	0.3
Prefer different public school	0.4	0.0	0.3
Refused readmission/expulsion	0.4	0.4	0.4
Other	1.8	2.1	1.9
Total	100.0	100.0	100.0
N	507	244	751

[a] Tests on significance compares columns 1 and 2. Also, see notes to table 14-3.

cial costs posed an obstacle for another 2.4 percent. But 6.5 percent of all recipients from public schools planned on leaving because they were not satisfied with the quality of the schools or were disappointed in the way in which the CSTP program operated. For a small but still important fraction of scholarship recipients, CSTP was not a success, at least in its first year.

To examine reasons for school mobility more closely, we ran a probit model where the dependent variable was scored 1 if the child either changed school during the school year, changed over the summer, or both, and zero otherwise. All non-demographic variables were coded from zero to 1 to facilitate comparisons. After controlling for demographic and school characteristics, parental satisfaction proved to be far and away the most important factor affecting a scholarship recipient's decision to stay at a school. The more satisfied parents were with their children's school, the more likely they were to remain at the same school. Choice critics may see this as a sign of program failure, because not all families' expectations were

Table 14-12. *Explanations of Retention of Scholarship Recipients, Grades K–3*[a]

	Retention rate[b]		
Determinant	Model 1	Model 2	Model 3
Educational experiences			
Satisfaction	2.88***	2.24***	. . .
Prior public school	–0.17	–0.13	–0.14
Religious compatibility	–0.02	0.06	–0.02
Type of school[c]			
Established parochial school (scholarship)	0.46***	0.36*	0.84***
Established secular school (scholarship)	–1.01***	–0.74***	–0.46*
New secular school (scholarship)	–0.05	0.02	0.15
Demographics			
Special needs	0.11	0.09	–0.02
Minority	–0.22	–0.16	–0.29*
Income	–0.00	0.02	–0.00
Kindergarten	–0.07	–0.10	–0.06
Family size	–0.06	–0.07	–0.06
Residential mobility	–0.11	–0.09	–0.06
Mother's education	. . .	–0.09	–0.07
Mother's employment status	. . .	0.04	0.08
Single parent household	. . .	–0.07	–0.09
Constant	–1.05**	–0.62	0.99*
Degrees of freedom	753	737	763
Chi-square goodness of fit	785	899	776
N	766	753	778

* Significant at .05 level.

** Significant at .01 level.

*** Significant at .001 level.

a. Regression coefficients from a probit model.

b. Mobility is a dummy variable, scored 1 if the respondent changed school during the school year or planned to change school at the end of the school year.

c. The baseline group consists of students at two parochial schools, both of which were established in the early 1990s, with high numbers of new scholarship students.

fulfilled. However, school choice supporters may interpret this as evidence that choice allows parents to make a move when things do not seem to be working out.

Table 14-12 also corroborates some of the parental satisfaction findings. Students attending established parochial schools are significantly less likely to change schools, presumably because of the high parental satisfaction recorded for these schools; this inference is supported by the fact that as one moves from models 1 and 2 (which include the satisfaction measure) to model 3 (which does not), the size of the established-school coefficient doubles.[24]

Students who attended established secular schools were more likely to change schools. The reason for this, however, has little to do with parental satisfaction. Rather, this category largely includes students in Montessori schools, which usually terminate at kindergarten. The students who attended these schools were more likely to leave at the end of the year, not because they were less satisfied, but because these schools could no longer accommodate them. The high correlation between established secular school and kindergarten explains why the latter variable does not come up statistically significant in any of the three models.

Test Scores

Much doubt has been cast on the newly established secular schools. The AFT expressed concern that the Hope schools were "voucher-dependent" and had little or no "educational track record."[25] And parents of children at the Hope schools were only 6 percentage points more satisfied than those of children who voluntarily remained in public schools. An analysis of test scores from the Hope schools addresses the concerns raised by the AFT, and insofar as the satisfaction of parents with children at more established private schools was greater, provides conservative evidence about the performance of choice schools on the whole.

Three additional factors make this analysis particularly interesting. First, the Hope schools were the only schools formed in response to the adoption of CSTP. They therefore provide information on schools that develop in response to the introduction of a parental choice program. Second, the Hope schools announced that they would accept all students who applied for admission. Many of the poorest and most educationally disadvantaged students went to the Hope schools, making an examination of test scores from those schools a hard test case for the program as a whole. If gains are achieved schools, they are probably being achieved under better circumstances in other choice schools. And third, enrollment at the Hope schools constitutes approximately 15 percent of the total enrollment in the Cleveland scholarship program and approximately 25 percent of students who previously attended public schools.

Standardized test scores from Hope Academy and Hope Ohio City were made available to PEPG during the summer and fall of 1997. We examined scores from the California Achievement Test (CAT) for all students tested

Table 14-13. *Test Score Changes*[a]

Grade and subject	Fall 1996	Fall 1997	Change
Grades 1–3			
Math total	31.0	39.6	8.6*
	(97)	(97)	
Math concepts	30.2	37.3	7.1*
	(97)	(97)	
Language	38.1	37.8	–0.3
	(97)	(97)	
Reading	31.3	37.0	5.7*
	(95)	(95)	
Grades K–3			
Math concepts	34.0	36.8	2.8
	(156)	(156)	
Reading	30.5	36.6	5.1*
	(154)	(154)	

* Significant at .05 level.

a. Average national percentile rankings from the California Achievement Test are reported. Sample sizes are in parentheses. All students who attended Hope Central and Hope Ohio City when tests were administered were tested, including special needs students. This comparison includes all students who took both tests. The math total and the language tests were not administered to students when they were in kindergarten. Note that students in grades 1–3 are a subset of those in grades K–3; they are not mutually exclusive.

in both the fall of 1996 and fall of 1997.[26] The Hope schools' staffs reported that they tested all students in attendance, including those students identified as having special needs.

The scores of Hope school students show moderate gains in reading and math. Ninety-seven students in grades one to three were tested in the fall of 1996 and tested again in the fall of 1997. These students scored, on average, 8.6 percentile points higher on their math total tests and 5.7 points higher on their reading tests after one year in the Hope schools (see the top section of table 14-13, which indicates students' 1997–98 grade levels). An analysis that includes kindergarten students, who took only parts of the standardized test due to their age, shows that their reading scores gained 5.1 percentile points whereas their math concepts scores improved 2.8 points (see the bottom section of table 14-13). All of these gains, except those for math concepts, are statistically significant. Our previous analysis of test scores showed significant gains from fall to spring of the 1996–97 school year.[27] Contrary to doubts raised by the AFT, table 14-13 shows that these gains did not disappear over the summer.

Of the students who took the fall 1996 test, almost 90 percent were retested in the spring of 1997, making it very unlikely that these increases were caused by attrition of underperforming students. By the fall of 1997, however, only a little more than 50 percent of those tested a year earlier were retested. This greater attrition over the summer was probably exaggerated by several factors.[28] First, the continued operation of the Hope schools was jeopardized by an adverse appellate court ruling that threatened to end the program. Second, one of the two Hope schools changed location over the summer, possibly inconveniencing some parents. And third, the Hope schools serve extremely low-income families who normally experience high mobility.

To ensure that the test score gains from fall to fall were not simply a function of attrition, we compared the 1996 test scores of Hope school students who were tested again in the fall of 1997 with those who were not. If the gains shown from fall to fall were caused by high-performing students' returning and lower-performing students' leaving, we would expect the earlier scores of the returning students to be significantly higher than those of nonreturning students. This is not the case. As shown in the top section of table 14-14, there are no differences significant at the .05 level between the fall 1996 scores of the students who were retested a year later and those who were not. The bottom section of table 14-14 shows that the only significant difference between the spring 1997 scores of returning and nonreturning students favors the latter group. It does not appear that reported test gains are generated by differences between those who did and did not return to the Hope schools over the summer of 1997.

The gains achieved by Hope school students should be contrasted against the decline of 1 to 2 points that is typical of inner-city students. According to the office overseeing desegregation in Cleveland, Cleveland public school reading scores declined, on average, by 1 to 2 percentile points between both the first and second grades and between the second and third grades in the years 1994–95 to 1995–96. PEPG and other researchers have found a similar pattern in the Milwaukee choice experiment.[29] The decline in percentile rankings can be attributed to the fact that inner-city students learn at a slower rate than the national average and therefore, as they grow older, they fall further behind. The reverse effect observed at the Hope schools suggests that these students are learning at a faster rate, allowing them to close the gap with others nationwide.

In March 1998 the Indiana University School of Education released its evaluation of the Cleveland Scholarship Program.[30] The evaluation finds no

Table 14-14. *Missing Case Analysis*[a]
Percent

Test date and subject[b]	Students with no fall 1997 scores	Students with fall 1997 scores	Significance of difference
Fall 1996 tests	(1)	(2)	
Math total	23.5	31.0	0.12
	(70)	(97)	
Math concepts	28.0	34.0	0.06
	(131)	(156)	
Language	39.5	37.7	0.67
	(70)	(98)	
Reading	26.2	30.4	0.10
	(131)	(156)	
Spring 1997 tests			
Math total	27.6	31.0	0.49
	(49)	(97)	
Math concepts	30.3	34.0	0.29
	(97)	(156)	
Language	46.8	37.7	0.05
	(49)	(98)	
Reading	28.9	30.4	0.59
	(97)	(156)	

a. Sample sizes are in parentheses. Column 1 includes those students who took tests in either the fall of 1996 (the first set) or in the spring of 1996 (the second set); column 2 includes students who took tests in both the fall of 1996 and the fall of 1997 (the first set) or in the fall of 1996 and the spring of 1997 (the second set). Also, see notes to table 14-13.

b. Results for Hope school students who also took fall 1997 tests versus students with no fall 1997 tests.

effect of the first year of the scholarship program on student test scores. However, the evaluation suffers from the following limitations:[31]

1. The study analyzed only third-grade test scores; no information is available for students in kindergarten, first or second grades.

2. To control for student achievement prior to the beginning of the scholarship program, the evaluation relies upon implausible second-grade scores obtained from tests administered by the Cleveland Public Schools (CPS). These scores suggest that groups of students from central-city, low-income, largely one-parent families were performing in second grade, on average, at approximately the national average, obtaining 51.6 on the

vocabulary test and 47.0 on the test of reading comprehension. Yet one year later, the same group of students obtained, on average, scores in reading of 39.6 and language, 37.7. If the second-grade test scores are accurate, then students lost somewhere between 7 to 14 NCE points (equivalent to a decline of approximately 12 to 23 national percentile points) over a one year period.[32] This is an extraordinary decline far beyond the most pessimistic portraits painted about American education.

The second-grade test scores also had implausibly weak correlations with such family background characteristics as income and ethnicity. The more credible third grade test scores, collected by the evaluation team, had higher correlations with these variables.[33]

If the implausible second-grade scores are removed from the analysis, scholarship students score significantly higher than the comparison group in all subjects. Of course, it is ordinarily better for prior test scores to be included in an analysis of programmatic effects, but it is hardly self-evident that an analysis is improved by the inclusion of problematic ones. If poor-performing public schools are especially likely to teach to a test, and if scholarship applicants disproportionately come from such schools, then the inclusion of such tests as control variables will lead to an under-estimation of programmatic effects.

3. Scholarship students were compared with the third-grade classmates of public-school students who had received tutoring grants.[34] To see whether this comparison group came from typical Cleveland schools, we examined twenty-four measures of school characteristics, including student/teacher ratios, student attendance rates, and many other factors.[35] Using an analytical technique known as meta-analysis, we were able to determine whether the combined characteristics of the public schools attended by the students in the comparison group differed significantly from those of the typical Cleveland public school. When all twenty-four measures are considered together, the comparison group of students attended schools that were .14 standard deviations more advantaged than the typical public school. The odds that we would find advantages this large by chance are less than 1 in 20. In other words, the schools attended by the comparison group of students had a more advantageous learning environment than the one available to students in the typical Cleveland public school.

4. The evaluation does not include results from the Hope schools, even though, in the third grade alone, Hope-school students constituted 25 percent of all the choice students coming from public schools for whom test score information was available. The evaluation team states that it excluded

test results from the Hope schools from its analysis on the grounds that the California Achievement Test administered by the Hope schools differed from that taken by other students. While this difference does require statistical adjustment of scores, the maker of the test has provided a straightforward formula for making the adjustment.[36]

The evaluation team also excluded Hope test scores on the grounds that portions of the tests were administered on successive days, not all at one time. Yet CTB-McGraw-Hill says that its tests may be administered either all at once or on successive days without significantly altering the results.[37]

5. The statistical analysis chosen by the evaluation team—analysis of residuals of a regression equation (also known as sequential regression or step-wise least squares regression)—has been mathematically proven to underestimate positive effects of interventions.[38]

Since the data from this evaluation have been made available, it is possible to address two of the deficiencies of the original evaluation by: 1) incorporating the Hope school test results into the analysis; 2) using more appropriate statistical techniques; and 3) reporting results that both include and exclude the implausible second-grade test scores from the analysis.

When the implausible second-grade test scores are removed from the regression analysis (but all the family background characteristics are included), choice-school effects are positive in all subject domains.[39] Scholarship students scored 4.1 NCE points higher in language, 4.5 points higher in science, 2.5 points higher in reading, 2.5 points higher in social studies, and 0.6 points higher in math. Two of the results are statistically significant at the .05 level and two at the .01 level.

Even when the questionable second-grade test scores are included in the analysis, results remain positive in all domains except for math. However, their magnitude is not as great. The results of an ordinary least squares regression analysis that includes the second-grade test scores are reported in table 14-15. Although the effects in reading, math, and social studies are insignificant, modest, positive choice-school effects are still observed in two subject areas: language skills (2.4 points) and science (2.7 points).

The findings from this secondary analysis of the Indiana University evaluation can hardly be definitive, because the results depend upon a data set suffering from deficiencies mentioned in points one to three above. But even data biased against finding positive choice-school effects reveal positive choice-school effects in two subject domains.

Table 14-15. *Effect of Scholarship Program on Third-Grade Test Scores: A Reanalysis of Data from the Indiana University Evaluation*[a]

Determinant	Language	Science	Reading	Math	Social Studies
School effects					
Choice school	2.37*[b]	2.70*	0.38	-0.92	0.63
2nd grade test controls					
Vocabulary score	0.17***	0.18***	0.20***	0.14***	0.18***
Comprehension score	0.31***	0.27***	0.34***	0.32***	
			0.24***		
Demographic controls					
Caucasian	4.52**	5.12**	3.55*	6.30***	5.04***
Female	1.31	-1.01	1.34	0.36	0.60
Lives with mother only	-1.33	1.97	1.31	1.97	1.31
On free lunch program	-3.91**	-4.99**	-3.98***	-6.71***	-6.79***
R^2	0.41	0.35	0.45	0.29	0.45
N	574	574	574	574	574

a. One-tailed significance test.

b. Unstandardized coefficients reported.

* Significant at .05 level.

** Significant at .01 level.

*** Significant at .001 level.

It is also worth noting that the choice-school effects in Cleveland are of a modest order of magnitude comparable to those observed in Milwaukee after one year (as reported in the previous essay). As the authors of the Milwaukee essay pointed out, school choice is not a magic bullet. One cannot expect to observe more than modest learning gains in the first year of attendance at a choice school. It takes time for children to adjust to a new setting and take advantage of whatever opportunities a school can provide. It will be of interest to learn whether the effects in Cleveland, modest though they are in the first year, will cumulate over time, as happened in Milwaukee.

Conclusions

CSTP has been in operation for only one year, a period not long enough to allow researchers to evaluate an educational program fully. Test score results need to be monitored over several years before definitive results can be obtained. Also, CSTP was not set up as a randomized experiment that would enable investigators to compare participants with a control group of essentially similar parents and students. Therefore, the results from the parent survey reported in this chapter compare groups that may differ in respects that cannot be detected.

Despite these limitations, the quality of the data is sufficient to allow us to draw some preliminary conclusions. The parent survey included the responses of more than 70 percent of scholarship recipients the survey team attempted to reach, totaling 1,014, which was more than half of all recipients. The demographic characteristics of the sample of recipients are not significantly different from those of the universe from which they were drawn. The survey team was less successful in reaching nonrecipients, contacting 49 percent. The nonrecipients surveyed were from more advantaged backgrounds than those of the universe from which they were drawn; however, this simply biases the findings against the parental satisfaction results that were obtained. It is likely that even stronger results would have appeared had the response rate been higher.

Though the comparison groups were not created by a randomized experiment, neither did their background characteristics differ in important respects. Whenever demographic differences do appear, it is the scholarship recipients from public schools who are usually the more disadvantaged group. Kindergarten students are an exception to this generalization, but similar findings appear whether or not kindergartners are included in the analysis.

The results of the parent survey indicate that the educational opportunities afforded by CSTP have won a strong endorsement from those participating in the program. A majority of scholarship parents were very satisfied with nearly every aspect of the schools their children attended. The levels of satisfaction with the choice schools were much higher than the levels of satisfaction with the Cleveland public schools. This enthusiasm seems justified. Test scores in math and reading rose in the two schools newly established in response to CSTP, with which parents were less satisfied than with more established choice schools, and gains were made in third grade in the choice program as a whole.

Parents listed academic quality as the most important reason for their participation in CSTP, suggesting that educational objectives are paramount in their choice of schools. However, a fifth of the nonrecipients said one reason they did not participate was their inability to find desired private schools. And families whose children had special education needs found it more difficult to obtain desired private school placements; parents of special needs students were also less satisfied with their schools.[40] School choice plans clearly need to provide participating schools with the funds and incentives to deliver the necessary services to students with special needs. School mobility rates among CSTP schools were lower than those in central city public schools. Only a tiny fraction, less than half of 1 percent, of the parents new to choice schools reported that their children had been expelled from their private schools or refused admission for a second year.

The findings coming out of the Cleveland Scholarship Program further clarify a number of the claims and assumptions surrounding the spirited contemporary debate about school choice. Though CSTP encountered some difficulties establishing itself in its initial year, in good part because of the uncertainty surrounding a legal suit, both test score and parental survey data provide strong support for future choice initiatives. The data, however, suggest that special funding arrangements and further programming are necessary if students with disabilities and other special needs are to participate fully in school choice programs.

As similar programs proliferate in other cities, we will learn more about the ways in which school choice affects the education of inner-city children. In the fall of 1997, for example, roughly 1,200 New York students accepted scholarships to attend the private schools of their choice. This particular program has the added advantage of being set up as a randomized experiment, and therefore it will provide important data on who participates in choice programs and how choice influences the educational experiences of scholarship recipients as compared to nonrecipients. Hopefully, the debate over school choice will increasingly hinge on the examination of evidence, and less on ideology, allowing policy makers the opportunity to consider carefully the promise choice may offer in promoting educational reform for the inner-city residents who need it most.

Notes

1. We focus on the scholarship component of the program.

2. "The Equity Gap," *Cleveland Plain Dealer,* March 25, 1957, p. A9.

3. Paul T. Hill and Stephen P. Klein, "Toward an Evaluation Design for the Cleveland Scholarship Program," paper prepared for Ohio Department of Education, November 1996. Undoubtedly, some of the kindergarten students would have attended private schools even if they had not received scholarships.

4. However, 44 percent of the nonrecipients contacted in our survey thought that they had never been awarded scholarships.

5. The Ohio Federation of Teachers appealed the case, and in the spring of 1997 the appellate court ruled CSTP unconstitutional because it violated both the federal establishment of religion clause and an Ohio state constitutional requirement that general laws be equitably applied across the entire state. In July 1997 the Ohio State Supreme Court accepted the case for review and permitted CSTP to continue contingent on its decision on the merits.

6. Carol Ascher, Norm Fruchter, and Robert Berne, *Hard Lessons: Public Schools and Privatization* (New York: Twentieth Century Fund Press, 1996), p. 111.

7. Nina H. Shokraii and John S. Barry, "Two Cheers for the S. 1: The Safe and Affordable Schools Act of 1997," *The Heritage Foundation Issue Bulletin,* no. 232, p. 5.

8. The discussion in the text relies solely on data collected from the parent survey; these data differ significantly from the data collected by the CSTP office. According to the survey data the average family income for recipients from public schools was $20,091. According to official CSTP records taken from application forms submitted eighteen months earlier, the family income reported by this same group was $12,253. We do not think the explanation of the discrepancy is a remarkable increase in parents' earning power. More likely, respondents had incentives to give downwardly biased estimates of their incomes when reporting to an official government agency allocating benefits based on income; respondents may have had incentives to report upwardly biased estimates of their incomes when talking anonymously to survey researchers. Although all estimates of the income of a population are subject to error, the problem can be minimized by always making comparisons within a specific data set in which the same bias, whether upward or downward, is likely to exist across groups. We follow this procedure throughout this chapter.

9. See Jay Greene, William Howell, and Paul Peterson, "An Evaluation of the Cleveland Scholarship Program," Occasional Paper, Harvard University's Program on Education Policy and Governance, 1997.

10. These data are available in tables 1.2 and 1.3 of Greene, Howell, and Peterson, "An Evaluation of the Cleveland Scholarship Program."

11. Carnegie Foundation for the Advancement of Teaching, *School Choice: A Special Report* (Princeton, N.J.: Carnegie Foundation for the Advancement of Teaching, 1992), p. 13.

12. Ascher, Fruchter, and Berne, *Hard Lessons,* pp. 40–41.

13. Dan Murphy, F. Howard Nelson and Bella Rosenberg, 1997. "The Cleveland Voucher Program: Who Chooses? Who Gets Chosen? Who Pays?" A report by the American Federation of Teachers. p. 10.

14. See tables 1.4 and 1.5 in Greene, Howell, and Peterson, "An Evaluation of the Cleveland Scholarship Program."

15. What accounts for this difference? Two possibilities present themselves. On the one hand, nonrecipients might have appeared less enthusiastic about their original reasons for applying as post hoc rationalizations for not having taken advantage of the scholarships. Alternatively, one might hypothesize that the intensity of parents' reasons for seeking choice schools was an important factor in determining who actually received scholarships. Preliminary evidence suggests that the former is true. The responses of those whose children involuntarily were placed in public schools (either because they did not know they received scholarships, or because they claimed that being denied admission to preferred private schools was an important reason for refusing the scholarships) were largely indistinguishable from those of nonrecipients who actively chose to send their children to public schools. This suggests that the strength of parents' intentions did not have much impact on which applicants received scholarships.

16. Murphy, Nelson and Rosenberg, "The Cleveland Voucher Program," pp. 9–10.

17. Murphy, Nelson and Rosenberg, "The Cleveland Voucher Program," p. ii.

18. The zero order correlation among satisfaction categories ranges from .45 to .68.

19. These differences are large. The parents of students attending established parochial schools, for example, were four-tenths of a standard deviation more satisfied with the schools than those whose children voluntarily remained in public schools.

20. Differences with respect to satisfaction of the richest and poorest applicants is simply ten times the unstandardized regression coefficient.

21. John F. Witte, "Who Benefits from the Milwaukee Choice Program?" in Bruce Fuller, Richard Elmore and Gary Orfield, eds., *Who Chooses? Who Loses? Culture, Institutions and the Unequal Effects of School Choice* (New York: Teachers College Press, 1996), p. 133; see also Ascher, Fruchter, and Berne, *Hard Lessons,* p. 71.

22. Daniel McGroarty, "School Choice Slandered," *Public Interest,* Fall 1994, pp. 94–111.

23. Data on the mobility rates among students in low-income elementary schools in grades two through five are provided by John F. Witte, Andrea B. Bailey, and Christopher A. Thorn in "Second Year Report: Milwaukee Parental Choice Program," Department of Political Science and the Robert M. La Follette Institute of Public Affairs, University of Wisconsin-Madison, December, 1992, pp 19–20.

24. Note also that when moving from models 1 and 2 to model 3 the constant switches signs, again to compensate for the variance accounted for by parental satisfaction.

25. Murphy, Nelson and Rosenberg, "The Cleveland Voucher Program," p. ii.

26. The white paper "What Really Matters in American Education," put out by the Department of Education on September 23, 1997, makes a number of erroneous statements concerning our analyses of test scores. First, it says that we do not "control for the family background or prior achievement of the voucher students." This is not correct. By examining gains in achievement from the beginning to the end of the first year of exactly the same students in choice schools, we automatically take into account family background and prior achievement. Second, the white paper states, without documentation, that the Hope school test scores are based on an "old, invalid form of the California Achievement Test (CAT)." This is also incorrect. Officials at the company that makes the CAT, McGraw-Hill-CTB, confirm that the CAT 5, the version of the test taken by students in the Hope schools, continues to be sold and graded by the company in the belief that the results are valid. We do not know of any study that has shown their belief to be incorrect. Third, the white paper claims that our reporting of the scores "lumps together results for students in grades K through 3, suggesting that differences among grades are being masked." The scores reported in table 14-13, however, are generally

consistent across grade levels—with the exception of first grade students, who experienced a significant drop in language scores (see Greene, Howell and Peterson, "An Evaluation of the Cleveland Scholarship Program").

27. Greene, Howell, and Peterson, "An Evaluation of the Cleveland Scholarship Program."

28. We assume that the vast majority of students who were tested in 1996 but not in 1997 left the Hope schools over the summer. It is possible, nonetheless, that a fraction of these students did attend the Hope schools in 1997 but were not present on the day of testing.

29. The Cleveland public school test score decline is documented in "Cleveland City School District, Building Profiles, Data for 1995–96 School Year. Three-year Baseline Data, Elementary Schools," Assessment and Information Services, September 1996. For the comparable decline among Milwaukee students, see Jay P. Greene, Paul E. Peterson, and Jiangtao Du, "Effectiveness of School Choice: The Milwaukee Experiment," Occasional Paper 97–1, Harvard University, Program on Education Policy and Governance, March 1997; and Cecilia Elena Rouse, "Private School Vouchers and Student Achievement: An Evaluation of the Milwaukee Parental Choice Program," *Quarterly Journal of Economics,* forthcoming, figures 1 and 2.

30. Kim K. Metcalf, William J. Boone, Frances K. Stage, Todd L. Chilton, Patty Muller, and Polly Tait, "A Comparative Evaluation of the Cleveland Scholarship and Tutoring Grant Program: Year One: 1996–97," School of Education, Smith Research Center, Indiana University, March 1998.

31. The evaluation has other limitations as well. See Paul E. Peterson and Jay P. Greene, "Assessing the Cleveland Scholarship Program: A Guide to the Indiana University School of Education Evaluation," Occasional Paper, Harvard University, Program on Education Policy and Governance, March 1998.

32. This is only an approximate number. One cannot state an exact equivalence without knowing precisely where on the distribution of scores the comparison is being made.

33. When second grade test scores are regressed on all available family background characteristics, the R^2 for the vocabulary test is .044 and for reading comprehension, it is .056. When third grade test scores are regressed on the same family background characteristics, the R^2 for language is .079; for reading, it is .067; for math, .084; for science, .063; and for social science .098.

34. The evaluation was originally designed to test the effectiveness of a tutoring program; those receiving tutoring grants were to be compared to their classmates. This aspect of the evaluation has not been reported.

35. The twenty-four characteristics were as follows: attendance rate, percentage of bilingual students, scores on ten different tests, percentage of students not promoted from one year to the next, percentage female, number of school disturbance incidents reported, the mobility rate in and out of the school, the percentage of students eligible for free lunch, the percentage white, the percentage of students bused to the school, the percentage of the teaching staff that was white, the percentage of the students coming from single-parent families, the number of suspensions from the school, the student-teacher ratio, and the size of the school's enrollment. A characteristic was assumed to have a positive effect on a student's learning environment if it had a positive association with test scores.

36. The conversion tables are available from CTB-McGraw-Hill, the maker of both tests.

37. We are grateful to Professor Alex Molnar, University of Wisconsin-Milwaukee, for pointing out this feature of the test at a meeting of the Advisory Committee to the

Ohio Department of Education on the Indiana University evaluation on April 7, 1998. His observation was subsequently confirmed by CTB-McGraw-Hill.

38. Gary King, "How Not to Lie with Statistics: Avoiding Common Mistakes in Quantitative Political Science," *American Journal of Political Science* 30 (August 1986), pp. 665–86; Arthur S. Goldberg, "Stepwise Least Squares: Residual Analysis and Specification Error," *Journal of the American Statistical Association* 56 (December 1961), pp. 998–1000; Arthur S. Goldberger and D. B. Jochems, "Note on Stepwise Least Squares," *Journal of the American Statistical Association* (March 1961), pp. 105–110; Christopher H. Achen, "On the Bias in Stepwise Least Squares," unpublished manuscript, 1978.

39. Using tables provided by CTB-McGraw-Hill we converted test scores from the metric of the California Achievement Test metric to that of the Terra Nova. We use an ordinary least squares regression technique, including the treatment effect as a dummy variable, in an equation that includes all available co-variates.

Our analysis uses a one-tail test of significance, as recommended for this study by the statistical adviser to the Ohio Department of Education. See "Cleveland School Voucher Power Analysis: Determining the Value of Obtaining Fourth-Grade Standardized Test Scores to Measure Differences in Achievement between Participants and Public School Students," February 17, 1998.

A second estimation compared the scores of the third-grade choice-school students (included in the Indiana evaluation) with a matching group of public-school students (drawn from the Indiana evaluation comparison group) who had a similar propensity to test at a particular level. The two groups of students are matched on all characteristics, including second-grade test scores. These estimations confirm those reported in Table 14–15. Choice-school effects in language were 2.79; science, 2.89; reading, 1.95; math, -0.64; and social studies, 1.35. Because the matching design reduced the number of observations, the confidence levels for the choice school effects in language and science were .07 and .06. The point estimates indicate slightly stronger choice-school effects than the point estimates reported in table 14–14.

Jennifer Hill, a graduate student in the Department of Statistics, Harvard University, performed the propensity-score estimation; Donald Rubin provided helpful guidance and assistance. The technique is explained in Paul R. Rosenbaum and Donald B. Rubin, "Constructing a Control Group Using Multivariate Mathched Sampling Methods that Incorporate the Propensity Score," *The American Statistician* 39, no. 1 (1985), pp. 33–38; Donald B. Rubin, "Estimation from Nonrandomized Treatment Comparisons Using Subclassification on Propensity Scores," Paper presented at the German Cancer Research Center, Heidelberg, Germany, April 10, 1997; this paper is a modification and expansion of an article in *Annals of Internal Medicine* 127, no. 8 (1997), pp. 757–63.

40. Though, as we noted previously, parents of special needs children who attended private schools were not significantly less satisfied with their schools than parents of special needs children who attended public schools.

Part Five

CONSTITUTIONAL ISSUES

FIFTEEN

Why Parents Should Choose

Stephen G. Gilles

IN THIS CHAPTER, I analyze some of the theoretical and policy issues presented by voucher plans from a pro–parental rights standpoint. In the first section I describe the "liberal parentalist" approach to issues of educational authority and summarize the theoretical arguments for adopting it.[1] In the second section I lay out the parentalist case for vouchers, and in the final section I offer a parentalist rejoinder to some of the most common arguments against vouchers.

Liberal Parentalism in Brief

The central tenet of the liberal parentalist approach to allocating educational authority between individual parents and the state is that, as a matter of political theory, states should defer to parental decisions unless they are plainly unreasonable.[2] This is parentalism because it gives parents primary authority over and responsibility for their own children while relegating government to the important but secondary role of backstop against parental wrongdoing. It is liberal both because it sharply limits the state's role in the upbringing of children and because it limits parents' custodial authority as well. Parents may not abuse or neglect their children or deprive them of a basic education; and de jure parental control ends when a child becomes an adult.

Within these limits, however, liberal parentalism holds that custodial parents are more likely than the state or its agents faithfully to discover and pursue their children's welfare, which is defined by reference to some reasonable view of the good life and of the children's interest in living such a life. Liberalism's commitment to toleration ordinarily forbids the majority to impose its conception of the good life on persons who live by a different, but likewise reasonable, understanding of what is best for them.[3] So, too, the majority ought not substitute its educational judgment for that of a child's custodial parents merely because it disagrees with their reasonable conception of the child's educational good. States may override parental choices that subvert the child's basic interests (educational or otherwise), but when it comes to disagreements over what constitutes the child's best interests, the parents' judgment should prevail.

The main alternative to liberal parentalism is what I call liberal statism— the view that parental educational authority must ordinarily yield to the state's authority to define what constitutes children's best interests and the state's interest in educating children to be good citizens. Many liberal academics subscribe to one version or another of statism in education (though they generally call it by other names). Rather than seeking to displace parental educational authority altogether, educational statists envision the home as the realm of parental authority and the school as the realm of public authority.[4] Nevertheless, the contrast is clear, for whereas liberal parentalism affirms parents' traditional authority to direct the education of their children, liberal statism rejects that authority within the ever-expanding domain of formal schooling. Depending on which educational theorist one consults, the statist solution involves one or another mixture of constitutional, majoritarian, and governmental control of institutionalized education.[5] The state is thus in the educational driver's seat; parents are just along for the ride.

Liberal statists sometimes write as if their support for "children's rights" distinguishes them from defenders of parental rights, whom they see as antagonistic to the rights of children.[6] But this is wrong. Although parentalists and statists allocate educational authority very differently, there is general agreement that the presumptive benchmark in adult decisionmaking about a child's education should be the child's best interests (though of course the interests of families and of society may sometimes loom large). Moreover, parentalists and statists agree that young children should not be given conventional legal rights to control their own educations or their own lives, because they lack the maturity to exercise such rights in ways consistent with their long-run self-interest. Rather, children should have certain inalienable rights—rights that they may not waive and that are exercised on their behalf (and without the need for their consent) by their adult representatives.[7] We agree, in other words, that the child's best interests—not the child's wishes—should supply the basic standard for decisionmaking on the child's behalf. And insofar as this is so, both parentalists and statists are advocates of children's welfare, not of children's rights in the conventional sense.[8]

What divides us, then, is not whether adults should control children's educations and lives, but whose judgment should be controlling when parents and the state disagree about where the child's best interests lie. Which type of control—private and familial, or public and institutional—is more likely to be in the educational best interests of young children? The liberal parentalist answer is that parental control should be presumed superior unless the parents' choices are clearly unreasonable. The basis for that presumption is not the naive belief that parents unfailingly do what is good for their children. Rather, it is the comparative judgment that the fallible human agents through whom government must act are less likely to do what is good for other people's children than fallible individual parents are to do what is good for their own.

This judgment rests on a number of considerations and arguments. There are good reasons why parents have better incentives to be faithful agents for children than public officials do, and why routinely overriding parental educational authority at the behest of the state would more often harm than help children. Unlike teachers, social workers, and bureaucrats, who deal with large numbers of children for relatively short times, most parents are linked to their children both by nature and by long-run custodial relationships. Consequently, as everyday experience confirms, parents normally identify strongly with the interests of their children, and that identification is reinforced by powerful social norms about good parenting. Of course the expertise of teachers and other educators is often a useful complement to the efforts of parents. But parents have superior knowledge of a different and less readily transferable kind: knowledge of their children's character and development. Knowledge and incentives both suggest, then, that the parents' role should be a decisionmaking one, with educators assigned to an advisory capacity.

Moreover, we have every reason to think that stable, loving, responsible parenting makes a huge difference in helping children to become stable, loving, responsible adults. This parental nurturing encompasses the whole of a child's life; it cannot be arbitrarily confined to the sphere of home education as distinguished from democratically controlled formal schooling. That is why parents seek schooling that meshes with and reinforces what they are trying to do at home. To require parents to accept schooling that contradicts and undermines their own values, teaching, and example would jeopardize the foundational, paradigmatic loving relationships in a child's life. In a society in which it is increasingly obvious that both good parents and good substitutes for parents are in short supply, undermining parental authority is an exceedingly peculiar strategy for advancing the well-being of children.

The disagreement between liberal parentalists and liberal statists has a second dimension as well. Our judgments diverge concerning how the interests of society and of individual parents ought to influence the allocation of educational authority over children in general, as well as decision-making about any particular child's education. Statists give greater weight to the liberal state's interest in ensuring that children become good liberal citizens than they do to the interests of individual parents in nurturing and rearing their children by their own best lights. They think it is both legitimate and necessary to use the coercive power of the state to mandate that certain civic values and virtues be part of every child's formal education. The state cannot force maturing children to conform to its conception of good citizens. But it can at least require that they be exposed to regular classroom instruction that promotes this understanding of what citizenship means.[9]

Parentalists reverse these priorities. We start with liberalism's core commitment to the flourishing of individual human beings and with the fact that most people in our society define their individuality primarily in terms of loving relationships with family and friends—above all, with spouses and children. The workplace and the public square have their satisfactions. But millions of committed parents understand that the most rewarding work—and the most important public service—they will ever do is to teach their children, as best they can, to become virtuous, caring, flourishing men and women. Liberal societies have a far more vital interest in maximizing the number of parents like these (and helping them succeed) than they do in imposing any particular conception of citizenship on every family and its children. Parentalists think the risk that majorities (or bureaucrats) will needlessly run roughshod over the values of many dissenting families is much more likely to materialize than the risk that large numbers of parents will inculcate perverse notions of citizenship in their children. Using the coercive power of the state to promote an official version of citizenship will inflame parental resentment and teach children to distrust authority. Not only is this strategy not necessary to liberal democracy, it is bound to weaken it. We should eschew mandatory civic education and allow (indeed encourage) parents to choose how—and as part of what larger scheme of values—their children should be taught the basics of liberal citizenship.

The Liberal Parentalist Case for School Vouchers

These parentalist first principles lead straight to the conclusion that we should rethink our entrenched practice of providing free education only at state-run "public" schools. It is far from obvious why we need a universal entitlement to subsidized K–12 education, as opposed to a more modest program of educational assistance for poor families.[10] The conventional wisdom, however, is that the public is wedded to universal education subsidies for the foreseeable future.[11] On that assumption, the choice is between the current system of selective funding, in which only public schools are tuition free, and some form of tuition subsidy that includes private and religious schools, too. In parentalist terms the decision is an easy one. Selective funding puts major financial pressure on parents to send their children to state-run schools even if they disagree with much of what is being taught. True, the public school monopoly on free education is not as bad as the infamous mandatory public schooling law struck down by the Supreme Court in *Pierce v. Society of Sisters*.[12] But as Stephen Arons has long argued, for many nonaffluent families the financial coercion associated with selective funding is practically as irresistible as the penal coercion in *Pierce*.[13] Selective funding forces many parents to act against their better judgment about what kind of education their children need, and forces many others to pay heavily for the privilege of differing with the majority about their children's educational best interests. In that way it runs directly counter to the parentalist axiom that government should defer to and facilitate parents' reasonable educational judgments.

The majoritarian response to all this, of course, is that the voting public should be free to decide which versions of a basic education it wishes to subsidize—just as it is free to decide, say, which forms of transportation to underwrite. Nor does the existence of local democratic control deprive parents of a reasonable range of educational options. Individual parents, the argument goes, have an exit option (paying for private education), a transfer option (moving to a community whose public schools they like), and a political option (organizing at the grassroots level to change whatever they dislike about their local schools). Especially in a democratic society, why isn't this array of choices enough?

It would be wrong to deny that these choices are reasonably satisfactory to many (though by no means all) parents. Public schools have lots of satisfied customers, some of whom moved to those schools or helped transform them to their liking through politics. Given that our educational system is for the most part democratically controlled, it would be surprising if most families were deeply dissatisfied with it. But why is this the right benchmark? A selectively funded system inflicts real hardship on both those who exit and those who dissent but cannot afford to exit. Parents of comfortably mainstream views are unlikely to give that hardship due weight, because they know it is unlikely the tables will ever be turned. It would be otherwise in an impartial referendum on selective funding—one in which parents could not know in advance whose views on the content of public education were likely to prevail. Most parents attach more importance to the freedom to educate their own children as they think best than they do to the power to influence the education of other people's children. Consequently, parents would reject selective funding in order to ensure that their freedom to educate their own children would not be distorted by financial pressure.[14]

Educational majoritarianism is also objectionable because it causes needless suffering. Political control of subsidized schools, at whatever level, necessarily means that some parents are winners and others are losers.[15] (Indeed, in a heterogeneous society like ours, the losers will often be quite numerous.) By shifting the locus of decisionmaking from school districts to individual families, a voucher system eliminates these losers without making the former winners worse off—at least, not worse off in any way about which they have a legitimate complaint. Under a voucher system, parents in the political majority can still give their children an education consistent with their values. What has changed is that majority parents can no longer use public fiscal leverage to pressure parents in the minority to give their children the kind of education the majority prefers. Should we be concerned about that? Liberal parentalist theory says not, because individual parents are the best educational agents for their own children.[16] A political majority—even one that includes most parents—has far weaker incentives to choose an appropriate education for the children of parents who disagree with the majority's values. When the interests of majority and minority children diverge (as they inevitably will) we would expect the majority (like any self-interested group) to put the interests of its own children first. By empowering individual parents rather than local majorities, vouchers eliminate the occasions for such conflicts of interests, and thus protect the educational best interests of all children.[17]

But even if political majorities are less faithful to the educational interests of some children, aren't they more faithful to the educational interests of society as a whole? On the contrary: Political majorities ordinarily pursue the interests of the various factions that comprise the majority coalition. The public school monopoly on public funding creates powerful incentives for teachers, administrators, suppliers, and other interest groups to use the politics of education for their own ends. Much of the history of public education in the United States consists of the efforts of these well-organized groups to advance and entrench their own interests while purporting to be engaged in public-spirited action on behalf of children and society.[18] As John Chubb and Terry Moe have argued, many of the organizational characteristics and educational practices of public school systems are best explained in just these terms.[19] The interest group winners in educational politics seek to impose hierarchical controls on individual teachers, principals, and other actors in the system while at the same time insulating those controls from future democratic choices that might undo the spoils of victory. To make matters worse, the larger voting public is apathetic (turnout in school board elections is notoriously low) and parents of school-age children are neither well organized nor homogeneous in their educational preferences.

Especially in light of these pathologies, the claim that democratically determined educational choices will be more socially beneficial than the choices of individual parents rings false. Parents have strong incentives to want their children to be responsible citizens who share our common (albeit pluralistic) political culture and values. Undoubtedly there are some outliers who seek to teach their children extremist views (though it is an open question whether they are as numerous or influential as the politically correct ideologues who constitute at least a modest fraction of the public school establishment). But it makes little sense to design a subsidized educational system around zero tolerance for the excesses of a few. The overwhelming majority of parents in our society adhere to one or another reasonable conception of citizenship and social responsibility, expect their children to do the same, and want schools that will teach them accordingly. Moreover, the evidence available directly contradicts any suggestion that vouchers will erode civic education or public spiritedness: Private and religious schools do at least as well as public schools at teaching children basic moral and political values such as toleration, law abidingness, and respect for others.[20] Giving state or local majorities rather than individual parents control over how educational subsidies are spent is no more justifiable in terms of the common good than it is in terms of children's best interests.

A Parentalist Critique of the Principal Objections to Vouchers

So much for the affirmative case for vouchers. Now I take up some of the leading arguments put forward by defenders of the public education monopoly. My focus is on the distinctive contribution that a liberal parentalist analysis can make to the evaluation of these arguments.

One common argument against voucher reform is that we would do better instead to concentrate on reforming school politics and improving public education.[21] The fact that this strategy has been tried continuously over the past fifty years—with little to show for it—justifies a certain skepticism. But the problem is not just the difficulty of transforming school politics. From a parentalist standpoint, schools that are more responsive to local majorities (which ordinarily consist primarily of local parents) would be a great improvement on schools that respond primarily to the demands of bureaucrats, politicians, and teachers' unions. Yet responsive public schools would not solve the problem faced by parents whose educational preferences clash with the majority's preferred version of public education. No amount of spending on public education will ensure that political winners will not exclude or marginalize political losers. More generous accomodation rules—such as a blanket policy that parents may remove their children from any public school courses or classes to which they object, without prejudice to the children's right to all other aspects of free public education—would be a big step in the right direction. For millions of parents, however, secular public education is basically a hostile environment vis-à-vis their basic religious values. Accommodation policies will not help them. Vouchers would.

But what about children whose parents would make foolish educational choices under a voucher system? This objection is unpersuasive for two reasons. First, there is no reason to think mistakes by the worst parental choosers would be any more frequent or serious than the mistakes the worst public schools currently inflict on their captive and largely impoverished clients. Second, insofar as parents lack information about how to choose schools, the solution is to supply them with information, not to disable them from choosing. For example, smaller supplemental vouchers that would pay for independent educational counseling could be made available to parents upon request. More important, the increased competition that vouchers would introduce should greatly increase the supply of information to parents, as voucher schools would strive to distinguish themselves from their rivals in the educational marketplace.

Some opponents of vouchers also argue that public subsidies to private education will simply shift the locus of political struggle from public schools to regulation of private ones.[22] This objection has some force as a prediction about the behavior under vouchers of teachers' unions and other organized interest groups that oppose vouchers for self-interested reasons. Capturing voucher schools by subjecting them to the same sorts of restrictions that handicap public schools is exactly the fallback strategy one would expect from those who have long tried (with some success) to capture public education. But in a voucher system one would expect advocates of deregulation—such as the people who run voucher schools and the parents who choose them—to be a more effective counterbalance to these pressures. Voucher proponents who assume that voucher schools will enjoy as much freedom from regulation as private schools currently do are probably too optimistic. The price of vouchers, over time, may impose a significant degree of unnecessary regulation. It would be surprising, however, if voucher schools were as susceptible to regulatory capture as public ones.

Voucher critics argue that favoring public over private education is necessary to promote citizenship and break down racial and class barriers.[23] But private schools are generally as racially and socioeconomically diverse as public ones.[24] And no wonder: In America, public schools are typically exclusive local institutions that fence out children who do not live within the school districts that operate them. Public schools thus tend to replicate, not break down, patterns of residential segregation by race and class. And although school choice could make it easier for some parents to shield their children from persons of different races or ethnicities, it should also make it easier for parents who value diversity to find viable racially mixed schools.

A related defense of the public school monopoly on free education, offered by James Liebman, is that it puts pressure on parents who are sophisticated consumers of education to keep their children in the public schools, thereby enabling children from less educationally attuned families to benefit from the efforts of these education "connoisseurs."[25] From a parentalist standpoint this argument is wrong in principle, because it pressures parents to make decisions that are not based on the best interests of their own children. But it is also wrong in practice. Insofar as parents still have exit and mobility options, many will use them to escape this sort of conscription. And parents who do not have those options will move away from educational efforts where they capture a small share of the gains to those where their share is larger. Liebman is right in thinking that much of what is right with good schools (public and private) is attributable to the monitoring, volunteering, and involvement of committed parents. But it is neither necessary nor fair to use selective funding to coerce parents into playing this role in public schools. The supply of school-centered parents will increase under vouchers, because the returns to parental involvement will be higher in a more competitive system.

And then there is the establishment clause excuse. In its strong form the argument is that the Establishment Clause of the First Amendment forbids vouchers to be used for tuition at religious schools. About this I need say only that the Supreme Court's cases over the last decade or so pretty clearly imply that an evenhanded voucher scheme would not violate the Establishment Clause.[26] The weaker form of the argument—that even if vouchers for religious schooling are not unconstitutional, they are objectionable because they would compel some taxpayers to support religious schooling with which they disagree[27]—is unpersuasive for a different reason. As long as voucher amounts do not exceed the value of the secular components of religious schooling, taxpayers will be in reality subsidizing K–12 education, not religion.[28] Given the combination of low tuition and relatively high academic achievement that characterizes the average religious school, it seems clear that the public would almost always get its secular money's worth.

Of course a voucher system could turn out to be disappointing in practice. There is some truth to Amy Gutmann's observation that "it would be very difficult to predict the consequences of a thoroughgoing voucher plan versus an improved public school system."[29] But because reasonable people disagree about the costs and benefits of vouchers, the responsible, pragmatic course is to experiment with vouchers so that we can substitute experience for predictions. Opponents of vouchers, however, typically ignore this option; they prefer to leave the controversy over the consequences of vouchers in the realm of speculation. But there simply is no worst-case voucher scenario that would provide a consequentialist justification for refusing to experiment with vouchers.

There is, however, a nonconsequentialist justification—what we might call public school foundationalism. The idea is that public schools are an essential part of our democratic regime because they are "the primary means by which citizens can morally educate future citizens."[30] This conception makes public education central both to the formation of new citizens and to the practice of citizenship by existing ones. Communitarians and civic republicans may find this vision of democratic education liberating.[31] It will not appeal to liberal parentalists or to anyone else for whom democracy—and public education—are instrumental goods, chosen for the sake of their overall contribution to the cause of flourishing individuals and families rather than as ends in themselves. Seen in this perspective, the legal right of parents to opt for private over public schools is not a narrow accommodation of vital public values to stubborn parental prejudices. Rather, it is an application of the general principle that the welfare of children and the interests of society are best served by giving parents the right to direct and control the education of their children. That principle argues strongly for using vouchers to remove the coercive financial pressure on parents to choose public over private schools even if, in their judgment, public schooling is not in the best interests of their children.

Notes

1. For a fuller account, see Stephen G. Gilles, *On Educating Children: A Parentalist Manifesto,* 63 U. Chi. L. Rev. 937 (1996).

2. The first section of this chapter is adapted from Stephen G. Gilles, *Liberal Parentalism and Children's Educational Rights,* 26 Capital L. Rev. 1 (1997) (forthcoming).

3. See John Rawls, *Political Liberalism* (Columbia University Press, 1993), p. 61.

4. See, for example, Amy Gutmann, *Democratic Education* (Princeton University Press, 1987), pp. 69–70; Ira C. Lupu, *The Separation of Powers and the Protection of Children,* 61 U. Chi. L. Rev. 1317 (1994).

5. For example, Amy Gutmann insists that each child must receive a "democratic" education that will instill certain egalitarian values, develop the capacity for critical reasoning, and expose the child to diverse ways of life. See Gutmann, *Democratic Education,* p. 63.

6. See, for example, James G. Dwyer, *Parents' Religion and Children's Welfare: Debunking the Doctrine of Parents' Rights,* 82 Calif. L. Rev. 1371, 1374 (1994) (proposing that "children's rights, rather than parents' rights, be the legal basis for protecting the interests of children"); Barbara Bennett Woodhouse, *A Public Role in the Private Family: The Parental Rights and Responsibilities Act and the Politics of Child Protection and Education,* 57 Ohio St. L. J. 393, 416 (arguing that conservative supporters of parental rights "have always viewed children's rights as inimical to parental authority").

7. For example, children have an inalienable right not to be abused by parents, the state, or third parties.

8. Because it is less influential, I am passing over a third school of thought, which we might call liberal childism, which takes as its goal the maximization of the child's autonomy throughout life—including throughout childhood. See, for example, Bruce A. Ackerman, *Social Justice in the Liberal State,* 139–67 (Yale University Press, 1980);

Patricia White, *Beyond Domination: An Essay in the Political Philosophy of Education* 81–118 (Routledge, 1983). But even a view of this kind does not necessarily entail giving children themselves expansive legal rights. Ackerman's proposals, for example, rely heavily on fragmenting adult authority over children so that no one adult can dominate a child's developing personality.

9. Gutmann, for example, would require private schools as well as public ones to teach "a common democratic morality" (Gutmann, *Democratic Education*, p. 118).

10. See Douglas D. Dewey, "Separating School and State: A Prudential Analysis of Tax-Funded Vouchers," *Policy Analysis,* March 12, 1997 (arguing against vouchers on the grounds that government should neither compel nor fund education).

11. See Joseph L. Bast and David Harmer, "The Libertarian Case for Vouchers and Some Observations on the Anti-Voucher Separationists," *Policy Analysis,* March 12, 1997 (arguing that, given the overwhelming popularity of public funding of education, even opponents of subsidizing education should support vouchers as a second-best solution).

12. 268 U.S. 510, 534–35 (1925) (invalidating on substantive due process grounds an Oregon law requiring all students to attend public schools).

13. See Stephen Arons, *Short Route to Chaos: Conscience, Community, and the Re-Constitution of American Schooling* (University of Massachusetts Press, 1997); Stephen Arons, *Compelling Belief: The Culture of American Schooling* (University of Massachusetts Press, 1983); Stephen Arons, *The Separation of School and State: Pierce Reconsidered,* 46 Harv. Educ. Rev. 76.

14. This is an application of a more general argument against majority control over the content of children's educations. See Gilles, 63 U. Chi. L. Rev. at 967–72.

15. See John E. Coons and Stephen D. Sugarman, *Education by Choice: The Case for Family Control* (University of California Press, 1978), pp. 7–17.

16. Individual parental decisionmakers are preferable even compared to an electorate composed exclusively of parents of school-age children. In any event, parents-only elections are not an option, because the Equal Protection Clause requires that elections for local school boards be open to all local citizens of voting age. See *Kramer v. Union Free School Dist.,* 395 U.S. 621 (1969) (striking down a state statute restricting the school board franchise to parents of children in public schools and owners or lessees of taxable property).

17. Of course even under a voucher plan the problem of disagreement within the family itself remains. There is also no guarantee that every family will find a voucher school to its liking. But if (as I would propose) vouchers could be used to defray the expenses (including parental opportunity costs) of home schooling, even this limitation on parental choice would largely disappear.

18. See generally Paul Peterson, *The Politics of School Reform 1870–1940* (Chicago University Press, 1985); David Tyack, *The One Best System: A History of American Urban Education* (Harvard University Press, 1974).

19. See John E. Chubb and Terry M. Moe, *Politics, Markets, and America's Schools* (Brookings, 1990), pp. 26–68.

20. See, for example, Andrew M. Greeley, *Catholic High Schools and Minority Students* (Transaction, 1982), pp. 54–56; Andrew M. Greeley and Peter H. Rossi, *The Education of Catholic Americans* (Aldine, 1966), pp. 153–55.

21. See, for example, Gutmann, *Democratic Education,* p. 70.

22. See Ronald L. Trowbridge, "Devil's Deal," *National Review* 56 (September 15, 1997).

23. See, for example, Cass Sunstein, *The Partial Constitution* (Harvard University Press, 1993), p. 308.

24. See Michael W. McConnell, *The Selective Funding Problem: Abortions and Religious Schools,* 104 Harv. L. Rev. 989, 1013–14 (1990), and sources cited therein.

25. James Liebman, *Voice, Not Choice,* 101 Yale L.J. 259, 298–302 (1991).

26. The most suggestive decisions are *Agostini v. Felton,* 117 S. Ct. 1997 (1997) and *Witters v. Washington Department of Service for the Blind,* 474 U.S. 481 (1986).

27. See Sunstein, *Partial Constitution,* p. 307.

28. This argument is developed in McConnell, *The Selective Funding Problem,* 104 Harv. L. Rev. at 1017–18.

29. Gutmann, *Democratic Education,* p. 67.

30. See Jerome J. Hanus, "An Argument in Favor of School Vouchers," in Jerome J. Hanus and Peter W. Cookson, eds., *Choosing Schools: Vouchers and American Education* (Washington, D.C.: American University Press, 1996), p. 19 (arguing that opponents of school choice generally appeal to the tradition of "strong democracy" as opposed to "liberal democracy").

SIXTEEN

School Choice and State Constitutional Law

Joseph P. Viteritti

THERE ARE PRESENTLY three major constitutional cases wending their way through the state courts to determine whether parents should be allowed to send their children to religious schools using publicly supported vouchers. Given the present political climate in the nation and the apparent widespread dissatisfaction with public schools, it is difficult to predict how many similar cases will follow. But as school choice moves center stage in the national policy arena, cases like those argued in Wisconsin, Ohio, and Vermont are bound to become more common, and in the process point to a serious constitutional dilemma indigenous to our unique system of federalism.

That these legal battles are being fought before state rather than federal judges is no accident. The venue is part of a legal strategy adopted by opponents of school choice who have a keen understanding of how the United States Supreme Court interprets the First Amendment.[1] A body of case law handed down over the last fifteen years suggests that the High Court is not likely to find anything in the Establishment Clause that prohibits parents from sending their children to sectarian schools with public monies.

Less predictable is how state courts will rule on such programs, for each has promulgated its own standard for the separation of church and state.

409

Opponents of choice such as the American Civil Liberties Union, People for the American Way, and teachers' unions are counting on the fact that some states have stricter standards of separation set forth under their own constitutions than those that have been adopted by the Supreme Court in its interpretation of the First Amendment. They want these state courts to enforce their own guidelines to exclude sectarian institutions from participation in publicly supported choice programs.

Herein lies the constitutional dilemma. Although our system of federalism allows the states to define individual rights more broadly than those in the Constitution, the states cannot impose legal requirements that abridge federally protected liberties. By imposing more rigid rules of separation to exclude religious institutions from government-financed choice programs, state courts may be treading on the First Amendment rights of parents who seek to have their children educated in schools that reflect their own religious values—rights specifically protected under the Free Exercise Clause.

This is the ultimate issue that the federal judiciary will need to resolve as school choice programs become more common, reconciling strict standards of separation imposed by some states with the religious freedom of individuals who desire a sectarian education. It is one thing for the High Court to declare it legally permissible for parents to use government-financed vouchers to send their children to parochial schools; it is quite another for the Court to find it unconstitutional for states to discriminate against religious institutions or parents when implementing school choice programs. In this chapter I argue the latter point.

Judicial Federalism and the First Amendment

American law functions under a system of judicial federalism. The federal and state courts review questions of law under distinct standards set by the federal and state constitutions—fifty-one documents in all. The concept of judicial federalism reached new prominence among legal scholars and political scientists in the middle of the 1980s.[2] Its was a response to the anxieties of civil libertarians who, after more than a decade of experience with the Burger Court, began to express alarm over a noted retreat from the rights-based jurisprudence of the preceding Warren Court. Whether this perceived retreat was as radical as some had understood it to be is somewhat debatable.[3] Less arguable is the fact that the Warren Court had ushered in a revolution in civil rights by using the Fourteenth Amendment to impose new constitutional protection on the states.

Applying the Civil War amendment to incorporate the Bill of Rights had been an incremental and selective process that was played out for nearly a century. On several occasions after the passage of the amendment the High Court had actually rejected the idea of incorporation.[4] A turning point did not occur until 1905, when the court issued the landmark *Lochner* decision.[5] Only seven such decisions incorporating the Bill of Rights had been handed down as of 1949; whereas between 1961 and 1969 the Court used the Equal Protection Clause on ten occasions to impose restrictions on state action in areas such as education, voting rights, public accommodations, and criminal procedure.[6]

It is no wonder that one of the early calls for more aggressive action on the part of the state courts came from a member of the Warren Court majority itself. Reflecting on the jurisprudence of the Burger Court, Associate Justice William Brennan, standing before an assembled group of faculty, students, and alumni at New York University Law School, bemoaned the "contraction of federal rights and remedies on the grounds of federalism" and urged the state courts to interpret the new philosophy as an invitation to "step into the breech."[7]

There was an underlying irony to the whole episode in American legal history that began with the former justice's impassioned plea. Surely there are signs that some state judiciaries have taken the challenge seriously, especially in limited areas of the law such as criminal procedure.[8] But a conspicuous historical fact pertained, underscoring the twisted logic that was unfolding: Originally it had been the blatant disregard for individual rights on the part of some states that had led to assertive intervention by the federal courts under the banner of the Fourteenth Amendment. Now the state courts were being beseeched to rescue freedom from the federal judiciary by insinuating the provisions of their own constitutions into contemporary policy debates.

The issue becomes even more paradoxical when the focus of attention is the First Amendment. What does it mean for a state to have stricter standards of separation between church and state? Does it enhance the religious freedom of individuals? Although the Establishment and Free Exercise Clauses should be read in tandem as instruments to protect individual freedom, the two provisions are often found to be in tension.[9] Elaborating on the definition of the former can carry us over the safe province of protection in the latter, especially when it comes to school choice. Our Constitution and its Bill of Rights were adopted to protect individuals from excessive governmental intrusion on their rights; invoking public authority to constrain individual choice seems to undermine that purpose.

Notwithstanding the significance of the issue and its potential impact on the educational opportunities of children, there is a rather meager professional literature on how the various state constitutions address the subject of religious freedom.[10] Nevertheless, the research evidence is revealing of the problem at hand. It documents the wide variety of standards among the states, some of which directly and deliberately contradict constitutional criteria established by the Supreme Court.

One survey shows that courts in nearly half the states have handed down decisions declaring that they do not consider Supreme Court rulings binding in interpreting their own constitutions.[11] Twelve states have indicated that they have stricter standards of separation.[12] Several have directly stated that they reject the "child benefit theory,"[13] a principle applied by the High Court in making an important distinction between aid directed to families and aid given to institutions in determining the constitutionality of programs. Even though permitted by federal rulings, state courts in a number of jurisdictions have rejected government programs that provide transportation or textbooks to parochial school students.[14]

These prohibitions do not tell the entire story. Another survey reports that forty-two states provide some kind of support to children who attend religious schools.[15] This assistance appears in a variety of forms, including transportation, textbooks, materials, health services, and lunch programs. Not all state judiciaries are antagonistic to federal criteria. Citing instances in New Jersey, New York, and Wisconsin, Alan Tarr has explained that some states have actually revised their constitutions to align their legal standards with evolving interpretations of the First Amendment by the Supreme Court.[16] In a recent examination of fifty state constitutions and case law, Kemerer found that jurisdictions divided almost evenly into three categories: restrictive (seventeen), permissive (fourteen), and uncertain (nineteen) on the subject of school vouchers.[17]

The chaotic condition of state level jurisprudence has all the makings of a severe constitutional crisis: highlighting the widespread inconsistency that prevails among fifty distinct jurisdictions, the powerful role that state judiciaries will play in both interpreting their own constitutions and reconciling them with existing federal standards, and—most troubling of all—the vulnerable position in which the fundamental liberty of religious freedom has been placed under the crunch of American federalism.

The Litigation Front

With prodding from Governor Tommy Thompson, the Wisconsin legislature attracted national attention in 1990 when it enacted a law that provided publicly supported scholarships for poor children in Milwaukee's troubled school district to attend nonsectarian private schools.[18] This law, in its original form, sustained two legal challenges. One suit was brought in state court claiming that the bill was a private law and that it violated a Wisconsin constitutional provision requiring the creation of a uniform system of schools. The Wisconsin Supreme Court upheld its constitutionality, finding that the program was a limited experiment to improve the educational opportunities of disadvantaged children.[19]

Another suit was initiated by the Landmark Legal Foundation in federal court in 1993 challenging the exclusion of parochial schools from the program on the grounds that it violated the Free Exercise Clause of the First Amendment and the Equal Protection Clause of the Fourteenth Amendment. The district court upheld the law, focusing on the fact that tuition payments were made directly to schools rather than students or parents.[20]

In 1995 the Wisconsin legislature amended the law. Under its new provisions, the method of payment was changed so that funds were channeled indirectly to the schools through parents, the program was expanded to include more students, and the restriction against participation by religious schools was lifted. The latter amendment led to another round of litigation. On petition from Governor Thompson, the Wisconsin Supreme Court accepted original jurisdiction over the proceedings, and in August 1995 it issued a preliminary injunction against the expansion of the program. In March 1996 the court deadlocked in a 3–3 vote, with one member removing herself from the case. The case was then remanded back to the Dane County Circuit Court, where Judge Paul B. Higginbotham partially lifted the injunction against the enrollment expansion but, citing provisions in the state constitution, kept in place the prohibition against participation by religious schools.[21] That decision was upheld by an appellate panel,[22] and appealed to the state's highest court.

The Ohio school scholarship program came into existence in 1995 as a mechanism to create new educational opportunities for poor children attending the Cleveland public schools. The school system of that city had been such an abysmal failure that, under the sanction of a federal court order, its operation was taken over by the state. The choice program permitted families to use their scholarships at eligible private schools in

Cleveland or at cooperating public schools in adjacent districts. No public school districts in outlying areas expressed an interest in participating, however.

Unlike in the Milwaukee program, students in Cleveland were permitted to use their scholarships to attend sectarian schools from the outset, which immediately led to litigation. The first step in the legal battle proved victorious for choice advocates when Judge Lisa Sadler of Franklin County issued a trial court decision in July 1996 upholding the legality of the program under both the federal and state constitutions.[23] This decision, however, was overturned by a unanimous appellate court in May, 1997[24] and was appealed to the state Supreme Court.

Vermont has the longest standing school choice program in the nation. Since 1869 the state has had a law that permits students whose towns do not have high schools—there are 91 in all—to use state vouchers to attend public or private schools in other districts. Over the years many students have used these vouchers to attend religious schools. Some have actually attended private schools in nearby Massachusetts and New Hampshire and as far away as Connecticut, New York, and Pennsylvania. In 1996 the Vermont Board of Education refused to reimburse the town of Chittenden for tuition expenses incurred by seventeen students attending a Catholic school. The state education commissioner had ruled that to do so would run afoul of the federal and state constitutions. His decision has been upheld by a trial court,[25] and is currently being appealed before the state supreme court.

An examination of the case law in these three jurisdictions serves to illustrate the widely divergent constitutional traditions that exist among the states regarding education,[26] underscoring discord about the proper relationship between government and religious schools.

Wisconsin

Although the plaintiffs in the Milwaukee case sought to strike down the participation of sectarian schools on both state and federal constitutional grounds, Judge Higginbotham studiously avoided the First Amendment issue as being dispositive in this case. His decision and order regarding the religious aspect of the program rested on provisions within the Wisconsin Constitution forbidding that "any person be compelled to attend, erect or support any place of worship, or to maintain a ministry, without consent, . . . nor shall any money be drawn from the treasury for the benefit of religious societies, or religious or theological seminaries."[27]

In writing his opinion Judge Higginbotham concluded that the Wisconsin constitution "provides an independent and more prohibitive basis for review than federal jurisprudence related to the Establishment Clause."[28] Although conceding that the choice program, in providing unparalleled opportunities for poor children, made "sound public policy,"[29] he was more concerned that in the end the program might coincidentally aid parochial schools. Judge Higginbotham's ruling was upheld 2–1 by an appellate panel that also emphasized more restrictive standards of separation within the Wisconsin Constitution. Whether the decision is ultimately allowed to stand depends on how Wisconsin's highest court interprets both the state constitution and an existing body of case law, much of which is inconsistent.

Plaintiffs in the case cite a 1962 ruling in which the Wisconsin Supreme Court struck down a state statute requiring school districts to provide bus transportation to students attending parochial schools, noting that the First Amendment "lends itself to more flexibility of interpretation"[30] than the Wisconsin constitution. They also cited a 1972 decision in which Wisconsin's highest court invalidated a contract between the state and a Catholic university in which the school provided instruction at a state dental college.[31] In the latter case, however, the court decided on the basis of both federal and state constitutional prohibitions. Reflecting what it then believed to be more restrictive standards of separation apparent on the Supreme Court, the state court began to treat the two standards as being more harmonious.

In 1974 the same Wisconsin court upheld a law in which school districts contracted for special education services with private and parochial schools.[32] Recognizing the secular purpose of the act—the provision of educational services for handicapped children—the court again reasoned that it was in concert with federal judicial standards. At this point in time the Supreme Court seemed to be adopting a more permissive attitude toward the separation of church and state. In a subsequent decision the Wisconsin court declared, "We interpret [the Wisconsin Constitution] in light of United States Supreme Court cases interpreting the Establishment Clause."[33]

In 1996 Wisconsin's highest court again returned to a line of reasoning that distinguished its own jurisprudence from that of the federal judiciary when it held "the Wisconsin Constitution is not constrained by the boundaries of protection the United States Supreme Court has set for the federal provision."[34] But in this case the court was not seeking to develop a more prohibitive standard of separation; instead it was emphasizing its desire to afford more extensive protection of religious liberty than the federal judiciary, which is entirely appropriate under our system of judicial federalism.

Here, in a strong show of sympathy for religious liberty broadly defined, the court lifted penalties imposed on Amish defendants who had failed to display legally required traffic emblems on their horse-drawn buggies because it violated their religious customs.

Insofar as state constitutional law is concerned, the final outcome of the Milwaukee school choice case will be determined when it is returned to the Wisconsin Supreme Court. When the case was originally heard by that panel in March of 1996, three judges found the program constitutional in all respects, and three found that it violated the religion and uniformity clauses of the state constitution. Since then one judge who ruled against the program has retired; another judge has been added to the court who appears to be more accommodationist on the issue of school choice. Although the change has heartened choice proponents, the outcome is far from assured given the erratic approach to religious jurisprudence exhibited by the court over time.

Ohio

Behind the strong decision by Judge Lisa Sadler upholding the legality of the Cleveland program on both state and federal grounds is a more affirmative constitutional tradition in Ohio regarding religious freedom and the permissible association between church and state in education. Similar to Wisconsin, the Ohio Constitution requires that "no person shall be compelled to attend, erect, or support any place of worship, . . . against his consent."[35] But the same provision continues to read: "Religion, morality, and knowledge, however, being essential to good government, it shall be the duty of the General Assembly to pass suitable laws, to protect every religious denomination in the peaceable enjoyment of its own mode of worship, and to encourage schools and the means of instruction.[36]

The principles embedded in the Ohio Constitution are directly derived from the Northwest Ordinance,[37] which incorporated the land mass from which the Ohio Territory was carved. The authors of that original document had proceeded on the assumption that religious association and religious training had a significant role to play in the development of civic virtue and the societal values that were needed to foster democratic government. At the time of its writing, most education was carried out under the supervision of the clergy.

Although the Ohio courts have not supported the notion of providing direct aid to religious schools, they have adopted a strong posture of neutrality toward religious institutions, a commitment to parents' rights in determining the most appropriate education for their children, and an inclination to harmonize their constitutional standards with the more accommodationist attitude recently evident on the Supreme Court. In 1968 an Ohio trial court found that the First Amendment "requires the state to be neutral in its relations with groups of religious believers and non-believers; it does not require the state to be their adversary."[38] In 1976 the Ohio Supreme Court recognized a "natural law" precept in its own constitution undergirding the fundamental right of parents "to direct the upbringing and education of their children in a manner in which they deem advisable."[39] The latter is one of several key decisions that affirmed the philosophical accord between Ohio law and the First Amendment jurisprudence of the Supreme Court.[40]

Notwithstanding a solid constitutional tradition of accommodation that one would expect to be supportive of school choice in Ohio, Judge Sadler's decision was reversed by a unanimous appellate court on both federal and state constitutional grounds. The decision was a remarkable exercise in judicial reasoning that actually commented on the merits of school choice as a policy issue. Noting the "well documented failure" of the Cleveland public schools, the panel observed that giving children the option to attend private schools could hardly be seen as an opportunity equivalent to staying in public school, even when enriched programs were provided for the latter.[41] That, of course, was the point of the choice program: to give poor children an opportunity for a decent education that they ordinarily would not enjoy. But this opportunity, according to the court, would provide students with an impermissible incentive to attend religious schools.

Once again, in analyzing legal issues the Ohio court attempted to harmonize the religion clauses from its state constitution with the First Amendment rulings of the Supreme Court. Its reading of the Establishment Clause, however, proved to be much more restrictive than the approach taken by the Rehnquist Court, leaving serious doubt that the decision would be sustained upon appeal.

Vermont

Two key factors define church-state jurisprudence in Vermont: an unusually generous definition of permissible cooperation within its own constitution and the disposition of its courts to defer to federal standards when reviewing issues of separation. Whenever these two factors are in tension, it is the latter that usually prevails.

Up until 1961, whether tuitioning towns reimbursed students to attend public, private, or parochial schools was not really an issue of debate as long as the school chosen was an accredited institution. That year the Vermont Supreme Court, following guidelines that were then becoming apparent on the United States Supreme Court, ruled that the inclusion of sectarian schools violated the First Amendment of the Constitution.[42]

Notwithstanding a long tradition of aid to parents who chose to send their children to religious schools, the court conceded after reviewing its own state constitutional history, "In the domain of religious liberty, the resolute history of the First Amendment is more demanding. Following the pattern established below, we search the question from the federal aspect."[43] This standard of separation continued to govern the tuitioning program in the state until 1994, when Vermont's highest court issued a new ruling designed to reflect more permissive federal standards.

The recent ruling, allowing the state to reimburse parents for tuition at an Episcopalian school, deliberately and resolutely revisits the issues outlined in the 1961 (Swart) decision claiming, "This holding was based on the First Amendment jurisprudence as it then stood. [J]urisprudence has evolved greatly since 1961. . . . Thus, we must examine . . . issues anew in light of more recent teachings."[44]

The 1994 guidelines were not only compatible with a developing federal jurisprudence; they were more consistent with the principles laid down in Vermont's own constitution—which is worth quoting at length because of the document's open embrace of organized religion and its potential role in education:

> Laws for the encouragement of virtue and the prevention of vice and immorality ought to be constantly kept in force, and duly executed; and a competent number of schools ought to be maintained in each town unless the general assembly permits other provisions for the convenient instruction of youth. All religious societies, or bodies of people that may be united or incorporated for the advancement of religion and learning, or for other pious and charitable purposes, shall be encouraged or protected in the enjoyment of the privileges, immunities, and estates, which they in justice ought to enjoy, under such regulations as the general assembly of this state shall direct.[45]

If not for the receptivity of the Vermont courts to federal constitutional standards, these words might give cause for concern among even more timid separationists. But since 1994 the most compelling story in Vermont concerns the extraordinary lengths that public officials have gone in order to exclude religious institutions from participation in the tuitioning program. That year the state commissioner of education issued an opinion, approved by the state attorney general, that it was impermissible under the state tuitioning law to channel reimbursements to parents rather than schools and that payment of tuition directly to a sectarian school violates both the federal and state constitutions.[46]

This was the first time in the 126-year history of the tuitioning statute that a ruling had been issued by a public authority—administrative or judicial—indicating that it mattered whether a tuition reimbursement was channeled to the parents or the school. By deciding to direct payments to schools rather than parents, however, state authorities effectively weakened the prospects that the program would pass constitutional scrutiny in the federal courts.

It was on the basis of the state commissioner's opinion that the Vermont Education Department refused to reimburse the Chittenden School Board for tuition payments to a Catholic high school, thus provoking a suit by aggrieved parents. As anticipated, the trial court focused on the direct payment factor in rejecting the plan on both federal and state constitutional grounds.[47] This case may ultimately provide the United States Supreme Court with an opportunity to clarify the procedural question regarding the method of payment—an issue illustrated in this case as a matter of principle versus form, exploited by opponents of school choice to undermine a long-standing policy. It is hoped that the Supreme Court will see through this ploy and recognize that check delivery is not the crucial factor in determining the constitutionality of the program; what matters is the fact that funds were channelled to parochial schools as a result of free choices made by parents.

The Blaine Amendment

Although the recent school choice litigation is instructive regarding the diversity of constitutional standards among the states and the rather inconsistent policies that prevail within particular jurisdictions over time, these cases do not give a full picture of the legal obstacles that portend under our system of federalism. Notwithstanding the legal uncertainty that overshadows school choice programs in Wisconsin, Ohio, and Vermont, the constraints imposed under other state constitutions are even more restrictive. Many have "Blaine Amendment" provisions that mark a tradition of strict separation beyond the requirements imposed by the Supreme Court in its interpretation of the First Amendment.

The Blaine Amendment has a curious and disturbing history. It dates back to 1875, when Congressman James Blaine of Maine proposed an amendment to the Constitution that would prohibit the states from allocating funds to parochial schools.[48] As he then explained in an open letter to the *New York Times,* Congressman Blaine believed he was correcting a "constitutional defect," because the First Amendment functioned only to prevent Congress from establishing a religion, and the "states were left free to do as they pleased."[49]

Blaine's proposal reflected a nativist sentiment that was sweeping the country during the latter part of the nineteenth century. Its proponents sought to use the public school curriculum as a tool to acculturate the hoards of immigrants who were arriving in American cities and to indoctrinate them with the teachings of mainstream Protestantism. The animosity of educators toward religious minorities provoked a strong political reaction. Many Catholics and Jews were offended by the public school curriculum, which required their children to read and recite from the King James version of the Bible. Catholics had begun to assemble in large enough clusters within urban centers to demand public support for their own school system,[50] which further fed an ugly anti-Catholic sentiment led by Protestant political leaders.[51]

Although the Blaine Amendment fell four votes short of the two-thirds majority needed to pass in Congress, it would have a lasting impact. The Republican Party embraced public acrimony toward the growing "Catholic menace" by adopting a party platform to eradicate "Rum, Romanism and Rebellion."[52] Many states would fill the legal void left by the four-vote deficit in Congress by adopting Blaine-like provisions either in their own constitutions or through legislation.[53] By 1876 fourteen states had enacted laws prohibiting the use of public school funds for religious schools; by 1890 twenty-nine had done the same.[54]

In 1894 New York became the first state to add a Blaine Amendment to its constitution prohibiting direct or indirect state aid to parochial schools. Five years later Congress passed a law requiring North Dakota, South Dakota, Montana, and Washington to adopt the language of the Blaine Amendment in drafting their own constitutions in order to obtain admission to the union. Congress permitted New Mexico to attain statehood on the condition that it adopt a strong constitutional provision against state aid to religious schools.

These measures have had a continuing influence on state-based jurisprudence. Although New York amended its constitution in 1938 to allow the state to provide free transportation to parochial school students and its courts have permitted school districts to make textbooks available,[55] opponents of school choice still point to the Blaine Amendment as a constraint on tuition relief. Since 1949 the Washington Supreme Court has handed down a number of decisions in open defiance of federal legal standards—at one time proclaiming: "Although the decisions of the United States Supreme Court are entitled to the highest considerations . . . , we must, in light of the clear provisions of our state constitution and our decisions thereunder, respectfully disagree."[56]

Although neither Massachusetts nor New Hampshire has ever had a school choice law adopted, the highest courts in both states have issued advisory opinions to their respective legislatures holding that providing tuition relief to parochial school parents violates their state constitutions.[57] These judicial proclamations have, for all practical purposes, foreclosed the possibility of serious legislative action in the two New England states.

Evolving Federal Jurisprudence

It is one of the great ironies of American constitutional law: The Blaine Amendment, which was conceived in a spirit of religious bigotry, ardent anti-Catholicism, and an obnoxious form of government-sponsored Protestantism within public schools, has become an emblem of religious freedom among strict separationists in some states. This constitutional paradox is at least in part attributable to the inconsistent, confusing, and tortured way in which the Supreme Court itself has interpreted the First Amendment over time.

Through imaginative, albeit ill-founded interpretation, the Court has intermittently transformed the Establishment Clause from its originally intended purpose of protecting against the creation of a state-supported church that intermingles civil and ecclesiastic authority into a legal doctrine that treats any interaction between religious organizations and government as legally suspect. Such unyielding intolerance actually serves to undermine the fundamental religious rights that the First Amendment was meant to sustain, conferring a mandate within public policy that confuses freedom of religion with freedom from religion.[58]

Fortunately, the High Court has become more balanced in its approach to the First Amendment over the last decade. Nevertheless, as the recent appellate decision in Ohio has demonstrated, there is enough to draw upon from the previous body of federal case law so that First Amendment reasoning can be used to impede and delay[59] constitutionally legitimate programs that offer school choice to children whose parents might not otherwise be able to afford it. And, as the Wisconsin trial court decision suggests, there are fifty other constitutional documents to draw from for those choice opponents who are disinclined to fight their legal battles on federal grounds.

A Permeable Wall of Separation

Most strict separationists rest their constitutional arguments on a body of federal case law that began with the *Everson* decision of 1947, in which Justice Black invoked the famous Jeffersonian metaphor (originated by Roger Williams) erecting a "high wall of separation" between church and state. All the imagery aside, the oft-quoted opinion actually upheld transportation aid made available to parochial school students in New Jersey, with the majority finding that "New Jersey cannot hamper its citizens in the free exercise of their own religion."[60] *Everson* actually incorporated the Free Exercise Clause protection of the First Amendment for application to the states.

It was not until 1971, when the Supreme Court promulgated the "*Lemon* standard" proscribing any government action that had no secular purpose, had a "primary effect" of advancing religion, or fostered "excessive entanglement" between church and state. Although in this decision the Court invalidated a Pennsylvania law that provided direct aid to religious schools and a Rhode Island law that provided salary supplements to parochial school teachers, Chief Justice Burger declared for the majority, "Our prior holdings do not call for a total separation of church and state. . . . Some relationship . . . is inevitable."[61] Just a year earlier the Court had upheld the practice of granting tax exemptions to religious institutions.[62]

In 1973 the Court handed down the *Nyquist* decision invalidating a complex New York statute that gave maintenance and repair grants to private schools and offered tuition allotments and tax relief to private and parochial school parents.[63] In addition to the direct aid feature, the Court now seemed to focus on the fact that financial aid benefited only private and parochial school parents. What followed was a ten-year period of confused legal reasoning and contradictory decisions that provided little guidance on the proper relationship between government and nonpublic schools.

Accommodating Religion

The Supreme Court began to develop a more coherent set of standards on financial aid in 1983 when it upheld a Minnesota law that granted a tax deduction for tuition, textbook, and transportation expenses incurred by parents whose children attended either public, private, or parochial schools. Although the Court in this case recognized factually that most of the tuition benefits would find their way to Catholic schools, it emphasized that "aid to parochial schools is [made] available only as a result of decisions of individual parents."[64] Writing for the majority, Justice Rehnquist suggested a relaxation of the primary effect prong of the *Lemon* test, which he declared to be no more than a "helpful signpost" rather than a hard and fast rule in reviewing Establishment Clause challenges.[65]

Two years later Chief Justice Rehnquist responded directly to the *Everson* edict when he opined, "There is simply no historical foundation for the proposition that the Framers intended to build the 'wall of separation' that was constitutionalized in *Everson*."[66] Once again addressing the *Lemon* test, he noted that the *Lemon* standard merely repeated the historical error and promotes a body of case law that "has no basis in the history of the amendment it seeks to interpret."[67]

What followed was a series of decisions that would establish a legal framework for reviewing questions regarding the permissible use of public funds for children who attend religious schools. In 1986 the Supreme Court ruled unanimously that the First Amendment was not offended when a blind student used a public scholarship to attend a Bible school. Once again the Court, this time in the words of Justice Marshall, approvingly reinforced the concept that any benefit derived by a religious school is "only the result of the genuinely independent private choices of aid recipients."[68]

In a concurring opinion Justice Powell outlined three principles that would guide the Court in future decisions on matters of state aid: The program is neutral regarding religion, funds are equally available to students who attend public and private schools, and any aid going to religious schools is a result of private choices made by individuals.[69]

In 1991 the Supreme Court ruled that public schools must permit religious clubs to meet on campus under the same terms as other student organizations. To do otherwise, it declared, would "demonstrate hostility not neutrality towards religion."[70] In 1993 the Supreme Court reversed a Ninth Circuit decision to uphold the right of a student in a Catholic school to receive the services provided under the Americans with Disabilities Act.[71]

In 1995 the High Court found that the University of Virginia violated the constitutional rights of students when it refused to allow them to use student activity fees for the publication of a newspaper with a Christian message. The university, a public institution, claimed that it was inappropriate to use public funds to support organizational activities that promote a particular belief. The Court disagreed. Finding the payment neutral, it distinguished between "government speech endorsing religion which the Establishment Clause forbids, and private speech endorsing religion, which the Free Speech and Free Exercise Clauses protect."[72] Rendering a concurring opinion on the requirements of the Establishment Clause, Justice Thomas noted, "The Clause does not compel the exclusion of religious groups from government benefit programs that are generally available to a broad class of participants."[73] Most recently, in 1997 the Supreme Court acknowledged a philosophical change of heart when it overturned a twelve-year precedent that had prevented public school teachers from providing federally supported remedial instruction to students in parochial school buildings.[74]

Conclusion

Decisions by the Supreme Court have cast great doubt on the prospect that it would look favorably on programs that give direct aid to schools with a religious orientation.[75] However, a jurisprudence has emerged on the Court that suggests that providing aid to students and parents who might be inclined to choose sectarian institutions is indeed permissible. Moreover, to specifically exclude religious schools from a choice program that includes other private institutions raises significant constitutional questions regarding the religious rights of parents that are protected by the Free Exercise Clause.

Certainly one could not argue that under present constitutional standards states are under any legal obligation to provide either private or parochial school options at government expense. However, in situations such as those in Wisconsin, Ohio, and Vermont in which states have adopted choice programs that permit the involvement of private institutions, the specific preclusion of religious institutions from participation represents a form of religious discrimination that is not permissible under the First Amendment. Although states might look toward their own constitutions to define individual liberties more broadly than those protected in the Bill of Rights, they cannot use these documents to abridge federally protected rights.

The Rehnquist Court has been particularly vigilant in protecting the states from undue interference by the federal government in affairs that rightly belong under their jurisdiction.[76] However, the Court has not been reluctant to intervene in situations where the states have undertaken action that compromises entitlements protected either by the Constitution or by federal law.[77] Excluding religious schools from participation in choice programs constitutes such impermissible action. The practice should be struck down when the first of these cases comes before the Supreme Court.

Notes

1. "Congress shall make no law respecting an establishment of religion, or prohibiting the free exercise thereof." U.S. Const., Amend. I.

2. See, for example, Robert F. Williams, *Equality Guarantees in State Constitutional Law,* 63, Texas Law Review 1141–93 (1985); Stewart G. Pollock, *State Constitutions as Separate Sources of Fundamental Rights,* 35 Rutgers Law Review 707–22 (1983); Earl M. Maltz, *The Political Dynamic of the "New Judicial Federalism,"* Emerging Issues in State Constitutional Law 233–23 (1989).

3. See Vincent Blasi, ed., *The Burger Court: The Counter-Revolution That Wasn't* (Yale University Press, 1983).

4. See *Slaughter House Cases,* 83 U.S. 36 (16 Wall.) (1872); *Twining v. New Jersey,* 29 U.S. 14 (1908); *Gitlow v. New York,* 268 U.S. 652 (1925).

5. *Lochner v. New York,* 198 U.S. 45 (1905).

6. William C. Louthan, *The United States Supreme Court: Lawmaking in the Third Branch of Government* (Prentice Hall, 1991), pp. 205–06.

7. William J. Brennan, Jr., *The Bill of Rights and the States: The Revival of State Constitutions as Guardians of Individual Rights,* NYU Law Review 548 (1986). See also William J. Brennan, Jr., *State Constitutions and the Protection of Individual Rights,* Harvard Law Review 489–504 (1977).

8. See Shirley S. Abramson, *Criminal Law and State Constitutions: The Emergence of State Constitutional Law,* 63 Texas Law Review 1141–93 (1985); Donald E. Batterson, *A Trend Ephemeral? Eternal? Neither?: A Durational Look at the New Judicial Federalism,* 42 Emory Law Journal 209–52 (1993).

9. See Ronald F. Thieman, *Religion in Public Life: A Dilemma for Democracy* (Georgetown University Press, 1996); Jesse H. Choper, *Securing Religious Liberty: Principles for Judicial Interpretation of the Religion Clauses* (University of Chicago Press, 1995); Frederick Mark Gedicks, *The Rhetoric of Church and State: A Critical Analysis of Religion Clause Jurisprudence* (Duke University Press, 1995).

10. See generally Joseph P. Viteritti, *Choosing Equality: Religious Freedom and Educational Opportunity under Constitutional Federalism,* 15 Yale Law & Policy Review 113–92 (1996).

11. Note *Beyond the Establishment Clause: Enforcing Separation of Church and State through State Constitutional Provisions,* 71 Virginia Law Review 634 (1985).

12. *Beyond the Establishment Clause,* 641.

13. *Beyond the Establishment Clause,* 636.

14. G. Alan Tarr, *Church and State in the States,* 64 Washington Law Review 98–99 (1989).

15. Joseph E. Bryson and Samuel H. Houston, *The Supreme Court and Public Funds For Religious Schools: The Burger Years, 1969–1986* (Jefferson, N.C.: McFarland, 1990), p. 54.

16. Tarr, *Church and State,* pp. 96–97.

17. Frank R. Kemerer, *State Constitutions and School Vouchers,* Education Law Reporter, October 2, 1997.

18. See Daniel McGroarty, *Break These Chains: The Battle for School Choice* (Rocklin, Calif.: Prima Publishing, 1996); Paul E. Peterson and Chad Noyes, "School Choice in Milwaukee," in Diane Ravitch and Joseph P. Viteritti, eds., *New Schools for a New Century: The Redesign of Urban Education* (Yale University Press, 1997).

19. *Davis* v. *Glover,* 480 N.W.2d 463 (Wis 1992).

20. *Miller* v. *Benson,* 878 F. Supp. 1209, 1216 (E.D. Wis 1995).

21. *Jackson* v. *Benson,* slip. op., nos. 95 C.V. 1889 (Jan. 15, 1997).

22. *Jackson* v. *Benson,* 1997 W.L. 476290 (Wis. Ct. App. Aug. 22, 1997).

23. *Gatton* v. *Goff,* case no. 96CVH-01-193 (Franklin County C.C.P. 1996).

24. *Gatton* v. *Goff,* nos. 96APEO8-982 and 96APEO8-991 (Ohio 1997).

25. *Chittenden Town School District* v. *Vermont Department of Education,* no. S0478-96 Rc.C. 46–47.

26. See generally David Tyack, Thomas James, and Aron Benavot, *Law and the Shaping of Public Education, 1785–1954* (University of Wisconsin Press, 1987).

27. Wis. Const., Art. I, sec. 18.

28. *Jackson* v. *Benson,* 17.

29. *Jackson* v. *Benson,* 3.

30. *State ex rel.*Reynolds v. *Nusbaum,* 115 N.W.2d 761, 769–70 (Wis. 1962).

31. *State ex rel.* Warren v. *Nusbaum,* 198 N.W.2d 650 (1972).

32. *State ex rel.* Warren v. *Nusbaum,* 219 N.W.2d 577 (1974).

33. *King* v. *Village of Waunakee,* 517 N.W.2d 671, 683 (Wis. 1994).. See also *Freedom from Religion Found., Inc.* v. *Thompson,* 476 N.W.2d 318, 320–21 (Wis. Ct. App. 1991).

34. *State* v. *Miller,* 549 N.W.2d 235, 238–39 (1996).

35. Ohio Const., Art. I, sec. 7.

36. Ohio Const.

37. That document reads, "Religion morality and knowledge being necessary to good government . . . schools and the means of education shall ever be encouraged."

38. *Honohan* v. *Holt,* 244 N.E.2d 537, 541 (Franklin County C.C.P. 1968).

39. *State* v. *Whisner,* 351 N.E.2d 750, 769–70 (1976).

40. See *Protestants and Other Americans United for the Separation of Church and State* v. *Essex,* 275 N.E.2d 603 (1971); *In re Landis,* 448 N.E.2d 603 (1971); *South Ridge Baptist Church* v. *Industrial Commission of Ohio,* 676 F. Supp. 799, 808 (S.D. Ohio 1987).

41. *Gatton* v. *Goff,* no. 96APE08-991 (Ohio Ct. App. May 1, 1997) 1576.

42. *Swart* v. *South Burlington Town School District,* 167 A.2d 514 (1961).

43. *Swart* v. *South Burlington Town School District,* 518.

44. *Campbell* v. *Manchester Board of School Directors,* 641 A.2d 352, 357 (1994).

45. Vt. Const., Chapt. II, sec. 68.

46. 16 VSA, secs 822–28.

47. *Chittenden Town School District* v. *Vermont Department of Education,* no. S0478-96 Rc.C. 2.

48. See generally Joseph P. Viteritti, *Blaine's Wake: School Choice, the First Amendment and State Constitutional Law* 21 Harvard Journal of Law & Public Policy (1998).

49. F. William O'Brien, *The States and "No Establishment": Proposed Amendments to the Constitution Since 1789,* 4 Washburn Law Journal 183–210 (1965).

50. See Diane Ravitch, *The Great School Wars: New York City, 1805–1973* (Basic Books, 1974) pp. 3–76.

51. See Stephen K. Green, *The Blaine Amendment Reconsidered,* 36 American Journal of Legal History 38–69 (1992).

52. Marie Carolyn Klinkhamer, *The Blaine Amendment of 1875: Private Motives for Public Action,* Catholic History Review 42 (1955), p. 15.

53. See Viteritti, *Choosing Equality,* 146–47.

54. See Green, *The Blaine Amendment Reconsidered,* 43.

55. *Board of Education* v. *Allen,* 20 N.Y.2d 109, affirmed 392 U.S. 236 (1968).

56. *Visser* v. *Nooksack Valley School District* no. 506, 207 P.2d 198, 205 (Wash. 1949). See also *Weiss* v. *Bruno,* 509 P.2d 973 (Wash. 1973); *Witters* v. *State Commission for the Blind,* 771 P.2d 1119 (Wash. 1989).

57. *Opinion of the Justices to the Senate,* 514 NE2d 353, 356 (Mass 1987); *Opinion of the Justices (Choice in Education),* 616 A.2d 478, 480 (N.H. 1992) (citing N.H. Const., Pt. I, art. 6).

58. See Joseph P. Viteritti, *The Last Freedom: Religion, the Constitution, and the Schools,* Commentary 102 (November 1996), pp. 21–25.

59. For a review of the federal case law, see Viteritti, *Choosing Equality,* 127–42.

60. *Everson* v. *Board of Education,* 330 U.S. 1, 16 (1947).

61. *Lemon* v. *Kurzman,* 403 U.S. 602, 614 (1971).

62. *Walz* v. *Tax Commission,* 397 U.S. 664 (1970).

63. *Committee for Public Education and Religious Liberty* v. *Nyquist,* 413 U.S. 756 (1973).

64. *Meuller* v. *Allen,* 463 U.S. 387, 399 (1983).

65. *Meuller* v. *Allen,* 393.

66. *Wallace* v. *Jaffree,* 472 U.S. 38, 106 (1985).

67. *Wallace.* v. *Jaffree,* 112.

68. *Witters* v. *Department of Social Services,* 474 U.S. 481, 487 (1986).

69. *Witters* v. *Department of Social Services,* 490–92.

70. *Board of Education* v. *Mergens,* 496 U.S. 226, 248 (1990).

71. *Zobrest* v. *Catalina Foothills School District,* 509 U.S. 1 (1993).

72. *Rosenberger* v. *Rectors of the University of Virginia,* 115 S.Ct. 2510, 2522 (1995).

73. *Rosenberger* v. *Rectors of the University of Virginia,* 2532.

74. *Agostini* v. *Felton,* 117 S.Ct. 1997 (1997).

75. See, for example, *Kiryas Joel Village School District* v. *Grumet,* 512 U.S. 687 (1994).

76. See, for example, *Seminole Tribe of Florida* v. *Florida,* 116 S.Ct. 114 (1996); *United States* v. *Lopez,* 514 US 549 (1995); *New York* v. *United States, 505 U.S. 144 (1992).* But see also *U.S. Term Limits, Inc.* v. *Thornton,* 514 U.S. 779 (1995).

77. See *Romer* v. *Evans,* 116 S.Ct. 1620 (1996); *Garcia* v. *San Antonio Metropolitan Transit Authority,* 469 U.S. 528 (1985).

Contributors

David L. Armor
George Mason University

John E. Brandl
University of Minnesota

Louann A. Bierlein
Office of the Governor, Louisiana

John E. Chubb
Edison Project

Jiangtao Du
Harvard University

Chester E. Finn Jr.
Hudson Institute

Stephen G. Gilles
Quinnipiac College School of Law

R. Kenneth Godwin
University of North Texas

Jay P. Greene
University of Texas, Austin

Bryan C. Hassel
Public Impact

Frederick M. Hess
University of Virginia

William G. Howell
Stanford University

Caroline M. Hoxby
Harvard University

Frank R. Kemmerer
University of North Texas

Sally B. Kilgore
*Modern Red Schoolhouse
Institute*

Brunno V. Manno
Hudson Institute

Valerie J. Martinez
Texas Christian University

Brett M. Peiser
*South Boston Harbor Academy
Charter School*

Paul E. Peterson
Harvard University

Gregg Vanourek
Hudson Institute

Joseph P. Viteritti
New York University

David J. Weinschrott
*United Way of Central
Indiana*

Index

431